Planters, Paupers, and Pioneers

ALSO BY LUCILLE H. CAMPEY

An Unstoppable Force:
The Scottish Exodus to Canada

"A Very Fine Class of Immigrants":
Prince Edward Island's Scottish Pioneers, 1770–1850

"Fast Sailing and Copper-Bottomed":
Aberdeen Sailing Ships and the Emigrant Scots
They Carried to Canada, 1774–1855

The Silver Chief:
Lord Selkirk and the Scottish Pioneers of
Belfast, Baldoon, and Red River

After the Hector:
The Scottish Pioneers of Nova Scotia and Cape Breton, 1773–1852

The Scottish Pioneers of Upper Canada, 1784–1855:
Glengarry and Beyond

Les Écossais:
The Scottish Pioneers of Lower Canada, 1763–1855

With Axe and Bible:
The Scottish Pioneers of New Brunswick, 1784–1874

THE ENGLISH IN CANADA

Planters, Paupers, and Pioneers

English Settlers in Atlantic Canada

Lucille H. Campey

A NATURAL HERITAGE BOOK
A MEMBER OF THE DUNDURN GROUP
TORONTO

Published by Natural Heritage Books
A Member of The Dundurn Group

Editor: Jane Gibson
Copy Editor: Allison Hirst
Design: Jennifer Scott
Printer: Transcontinental

Library and Archives Canada Cataloguing in Publication

Campey, Lucille H.
    Planters, paupers, and pioneers : English settlers in Atlantic Canada / by Lucille H. Campey.

Includes bibliographical references and index.
Issued also in electronic format.
ISBN 978-1-55488-748-4

1. English--Atlantic Provinces--History. 2. Colonists--Atlantic Provinces--History. 3. United Empire loyalists--Atlantic Provinces--History. 4. Atlantic Provinces--Emigration and immigration--History. 5. England--Emigration and immigration-- History. 6. Ships--Atlantic Provinces--Passenger lists. 7. Atlantic Provinces--Genealogy. I. Title.

FC2050.B7C34 2010   971.5004'21   C2010-902312-9

1   2   3   4   5   14   13   12   11   10

We acknowledge the support of the **Canada Council for the Arts** and the **Ontario Arts Council** for our publishing program. We also acknowledge the financial support of the **Government of Canada** through the **Canada Book Fund** and **The Association for the Export of Canadian Books**, and the **Government of Ontario** through the **Ontario Book Publishers Tax Credit program**, and the **Ontario Media Development Corporation**.

Care has been taken to trace the ownership of copyright material used in this book. The author and the publisher welcome any information enabling them to rectify any references or credits in subsequent editions.

J. Kirk Howard, President

Printed and bound in Canada.
www.dundurn.com

Front cover image: Pownal Wharf, Charlottetown, Prince Edward Island, in 1849, watercolour by George Hubbard. The red ship's hull is the remains of the *Castalia*, built in 1835 by James Ellis Peake at his Charlottetown shipyard. Following her demise in a storm in 1838, Peake converted the hull into an office and rigging loft. It was affectionately known as "Peake's Ark." Peake's house is the brick building to the left of the "ark." It still stands today. *Courtesy of the Prince Edward Island Museum and Heritage Foundation.*

Back cover image: Settler's cabin between Halifax and Windsor as seen from a train in June 1867, a watercolour-over-pencil by Juliana Horatia Ewing. *Courtesy of Yorkshire Libraries and Information, Wakefield, Ewing Gatty Collection.*

Dundurn Press	Gazelle Book Services Limited	Dundurn Press
3 Church Street, Suite 500	White Cross Mills	2250 Military Road
Toronto, Ontario, Canada	High Town, Lancaster, England	Tonawanda, NY
M5E 1M2	LA1 4XS	U.S.A. 14150

CONTENTS

LIST OF MAPS[*]

* All maps are © Geoff Campey, 2010

LIST OF TABLES

ACKNOWLEDGEMENTS

I am indebted to a great many people. I would like to begin by thanking the many archivists in England and Canada who have helped me. In particular, I wish to thank Angela Broome at The Royal Institution of Cornwall in Truro, Kim Cooper at the Centre for Cornish Studies in Redruth, Renée Jackaman at the Devon Record Office in Exeter, Sally Morgan at the Dorset History Centre in Dorchester, Vicky Grindrod at the West Yorkshire Archive Service in Leeds, Angela Plumb, Sue Barnsley, and Heather Marshall at the Suffolk Record Office in Ipswich, and Bill Wexler and Emma Sealy at the Suffolk Record Office in Lowestoft. Special thanks are owed to Ruth Hobbins, Janice Uthing, Margaret Daley, Pauline Cass, Brenda Muller, and Margaret Parry at the Liverpool Record Office for their unstinting help. In Canada, I would like to thank Melanie Tucker at the Provincial Archives of Newfoundland and Labrador, Gail Judge at the Nova Scotia Archives, Heather Lyons at the New Brunswick Archives, and Pam Wheatley at the Prince Edward Island Archives. As always there were many people at Library and Archives Canada, too numerous to mention, who assisted me in many ways.

I am grateful to the many people who assisted me in obtaining illustrations. In particular I wish to thank Lord Dartmouth for his help in obtaining a portrait of the second Earl. I thank Munroe Scott of Peterborough, Ontario, for his permission to print the Duke of Cumberland Regiment picture. Thanks are due also to Kate Holliday, manager of the Yorkshire Libraries in Wakefield (Yorkshire), who helped me to locate and obtain the Juliana Ewing paintings. David Watkins, services and operations manager of the Poole Museum (Dorset), gave me invaluable help in locating portraits of Benjamin Lester and Robert Slade, while Caroline Stone, curator of The Rooms Provincial Art Gallery in St. John's, directed me to important visual material in Halifax and Dorchester (Dorset). Sandi Hartling, Interim Registrar of the Confederation Centre Art Gallery in Charlottetown, and Linda Berko, curator of the P.E.I. Museum and Heritage Foundation, were instrumental in my being able to locate and obtain the exquisite paintings of Robert Harris and George Hubbard.

I am greatly indebted to the editor, Jane Gibson, and the copy editor, Allison Hirst, for their painstaking work in correcting and polishing the manuscript. I also thank my dear friend Jean Lucas for her helpful guidance and advice.

But my husband, Geoff, deserves the largest accolade. We are a team, and without him the book would never have been written. He produced the tables, maps, and appendices, located the illustrations, helped with the research, and was a guiding beacon in all aspects of the book's production. This book is dedicated to him, with all my love.

PREFACE

*P*LANTERS, *P*AUPERS, AND *P*IONEERS, the first of three books on the English in Canada, deals with emigration from England to Nova Scotia, New Brunswick, Prince Edward Island, and Newfoundland. In writing about the English, I have transferred my focus from the high-profile Scots, who formed the basis of my previous books on emigration, to the inconspicuous English. They represent a completely different challenge and their emigration story is very different.

A popular misconception is that Canada was settled primarily by the Scots and Irish. Although the English elite have caught the attention of commentators, the English as an immigrant group have been largely ignored. This has happened despite the fact that the English were the dominant immigrant group. Along with the French, the English were regarded as one of Canada's two "founding peoples," but they were not seen as a recognizable ethnic group. As immigrants they were assimilated into a country which had adopted their language and values. Showing a curious disinterest in their national identity, the English were happy to fade into the background. Failing to register as a culturally distinctive immigrant group, they escaped the notice of contemporary observers and later historians. This book aims to redress this past neglect by concentrating on the important role played by the English in the settlement of Atlantic Canada.

Planters, Paupers, and Pioneers studies English immigration to Atlantic Canada over two centuries, beginning with the major movements of the eighteenth century. The New England Planters, along with the others of English ancestry who came as displaced people from the United States, are one strand of the story, while the English who arrived directly from England are another. Both groups played their part in the settlement of Atlantic Canada. Both retained a sense of their Englishness, although their attributes and values were very different. While most emigration was self-financed, a significant proportion of the people covered in this study were very poor. The English tendency of exporting paupers to Canada helped give Newfoundland its Devon and Dorset fishermen, Prince Edward Island its Suffolk farm workers, and Nova Scotia and New Brunswick their many Liverpool and Birmingham immigrants who arrived as mere children.

Philip Buckner's various publications gave me an excellent grounding in the subject, while the provincial studies of Bruce Elliott relating to Prince Edward Island and New Brunswick, Graham Hancock relating to Newfoundland, and Bernard Bailyn relating to Nova Scotia's early Yorkshire influx, were the essential building blocks of my work. However, apart from these studies, little literature exists on the English in Atlantic Canada. No comprehensive study has been carried out thus far.

In seeking to develop the broader picture I have relied heavily on the wide-ranging primary sources to be found in English County Record Offices, the Canadian national and provincial archives, and in the Special Collections at English universities, especially the reports of Anglican and Methodist missionaries. However, one limitation is the incompleteness of the customs and shipping data, which has meant that accurate figures on the numbers who came from England cannot be given. The task of quantifying English immigration statistics was made even more difficult in Newfoundland by the fact that settlement had long been discouraged in order to safeguard the interests of the West Country merchants who controlled its economy.

English emigration to Atlantic Canada was driven partly by major economic changes taking place in England and partly by the lure of opportunities and benefits that emigrants hoped to obtain in their chosen destinations. However, each province had a different set of advantages and the emigrant streams from England worked to a different timescale. New Brunswick's timber trade, Prince Edward Island's shipbuilding industry, Newfoundland's cod fishery, and Nova Scotia's more diversified economy created distinctive regional patterns and directed concentrations of English settlers to many different areas.

Religion was a constant theme, but only in the sense that the Established Church of England had to play second fiddle to the newer nonconformist religions that had far greater appeal to settlers.

And some factors worked against settlement. The unsuccessful attempts by the ruling classes to establish feudal landholding regimes in Prince Edward Island and Nova Scotia retarded settlement. The early take-up of much of Nova Scotia's good agricultural land by Planters and Loyalists meant that it attracted relatively few English emigrants after the 1820s. As transport systems developed, the Maritime provinces faced increasing competition from Upper Canada's much better land, and few emigrants came to Atlantic Canada after the mid-nineteenth century.

The English were characterized by their energy, enterprise, and determination. Their rugged independence meant that they fitted seamlessly into an egalitarian pioneer society. Their story deserves to be told and their lasting contribution recognized.

ABBREVIATIONS

AR	*Acadian Recorder*
BA	*Berwick Advertiser*
BCL	Birmingham Central Library
BM	*Bristol Mercury*
BRO	Berwick-upon-Tweed Record Office
DCB	*Dictionary of Canadian Biography*
DGC	*Dumfries and Galloway Courier*
DRO	Devon Record Office
DHC	Dorset History Centre
EC	*Eastern Chronicle*
HA	*Hull Advertiser*
HCA	Hull City Archives
LAC	Library and Archives Canada
LCA	Liverpool City Archives
LMS	*London Missionary Society Papers*
MHC	Mildred Howard collection, Public Archives of Newfoundland and Labrador
MMS	*Methodist Missionary Society Papers*
NAB	National Archives of Britain, Kew

NBC	*New Brunswick Courier*
NC	*Newcastle Courant*
NSARM	Nova Scotia Archives and Record Management
PANB	Provincial Archives of New Brunswick
PANL	Provincial Archives of Newfoundland and Labrador
PAPEI	Public Archives and Records Office of Prince Edward Island
RHL	Rhodes House Library, Oxford University
RIC	Royal Institution of Cornwall
SOAS	School of Oriental and African Studies, University of London
SORO	Somerset Record Office
SROI	Suffolk Record Office (Ipswich)
SROL	Suffolk Record Office (Lowestoft)
STRO	Staffordshire County Record Office
TEFP	*Trewman's Exeter Flying Post*
UHA	University of Hull Archives
UNBA	University of New Brunswick Archives
WRO	Warwickshire Record Office
WYAS	West Yorkshire Archive Service
YCWA	*York Chronicle and Weekly Advertiser*

CHAPTER 1

Leaving England

In the English farmer will be observed the dialect of his country, the honest John Bull bluntness of his style and the other characteristics that mark his character. His house or cottage is distinguished by cleanliness and neatness, his agricultural implements and utensils are always in order and where an English farmer is industrious and persevering he is sure to do well.[1]

THIS RESTRAINED COMPLIMENT from John MacGregor was rare praise indeed, since few early observers of people and places in the Maritimes took much notice of English settlers. Adding the barbed comment that the Englishman "does not reconcile himself as well as Scottish settlers to the privations and extreme difficulties of pioneer life,"[2] he hardly gave them a ringing endorsement! But at least he mentioned an English farmer. Studies of immigration to Canada (initially British North America) have neglected the English.[3] The popular perception is that Canada was settled mainly by the Scots and Irish, when in fact the opposite is true. Although they formed only around a quarter of the total British influx to

Canada before Confederation,[4] the English actually dominated the much larger emigrant stream that arrived from Britain between 1867 and 1915. The Scots came in the largest numbers initially, with the Irish quickly overtaking them, but the English were actually the dominant ones overall.[5] And yet, while copious emigration studies have been undertaken on the Scots and Irish, very little has been written about the English.

Part of the reason for this neglect is the invisibility of the English when they reached Canada. They were defined, together with the French, as forming one of its two "founding peoples." Thus the English were not regarded as an ethnic group, and if any categorization did register, it was their association with Canada's elite, since the English were extremely well-represented in business and in the upper echelons of government. A further complication is that they themselves drew little distinction between being English and being British. The English regarded the Union Jack, the monarchy, and parliamentary institutions as symbols of their English identity. In this confusion it becomes difficult to define Englishness, but, nevertheless, it can be stated with total certainty that the English were and remain a distinctive ethnic group. It is perverse in the extreme that the largest country in the British Isles, which contributed the most people to the emigrant stream from Britain to Canada, should have been so completely ignored.[6] This study, the first of three to be carried out on English emigration to Canada, assesses their colonizing endeavours and impact in the Atlantic region during the period from the late seventeenth century to the early twentieth century.

The English influx to Atlantic Canada grew appreciably in scale from the late eighteenth century. England was by then the wealthiest and most industrialized country on Earth, having long-established cities, towns, and villages, most of the land having been cleared long before the time of the Norman Conquest in 1066. Underpinning them was a highly developed society and economy that offered the most advanced way of life on the planet. Understandably, many early arrivals were shocked by their first glimpse of the crudely built log houses and vast wildernesses of the Maritimes. In 1775, as his ship approached Malpeque Bay, on the Island of St. John (later Prince Edward Island), Thomas Curtis, a south of England labourer, thought he had seen "a cow house, or a place for cattle." Later on, he was informed "that it was a dwelling house and, when on shore, I found none much better."[7] After learning that local people generally survived the winter on salt fish and potatoes, his heart sank. An anonymous English observer echoed Curtis's view in 1808 when he stated that Charlottetown had fewer than 150 houses, which were "small and wretchedly built," although "some of the streets were well laid out."[8]

A view of Charlottetown, Prince Edward Island, painted in 1843 by Fanny Bayfield. Despite the handful of large and prestigious buildings that can be seen, Charlottetown remained principally a wooden town with very wide streets, designed to offset the spread of fires.

Of course, the English were not alone in forming negative first impressions. An immigrant guide of 1808, extolling the advantages of Prince Edward Island, warned British people not to be deceived by overly optimistic reports. When immigrants arrived they found "woods to be cut down," hordes of mosquitoes, unfinished roads, "a limited society," and "cold weather, the ground being covered with snow nearly four months in the year."[9] Scottish Highlanders also reacted badly to their first sight of North America, but they were concerned by the vast forests, coming as they often did from nearly treeless areas. But as former inhabitants of Britain's poorest region they appeared to have less difficulty in accepting rough-and-ready conditions.

The large group of settlers who came to the Maritimes from the North and East Riding of Yorkshire in the 1770s balked initially at the scale of the task they had taken on, but most remained and became outstanding pioneer farmers.[10] MacGregor greatly approved of these "industrious and careful settlers from Yorkshire," comparing them favourably with settlers from Dumfriesshire and Perthshire in Scotland.[11] As they came from thinly populated and fairly remote regions in northern Britain, such people would have been better able than most to cope with the isolation, privations, and drudgery of pioneer life.

However, according to Walter Johnstone, a Presbyterian minister from Dumfriesshire who visited Prince Edward Island in the 1820s, "the English are the most unsuitable of all settlers…. Such of them as bring property with them generally keep up their old mode of living till they are as poor as their neighbours and then they are destitute in the extreme."[12] Perhaps he was a little biased, believing as he did that "no settlers are prized more" than those from Dumfriesshire. In any case, his comments could equally well have applied to Scottish Lowlanders or people from any other part of the British Isles who had unrealistic expectations of pioneer life. Meanwhile, Edward Walsh, who had visited Prince Edward Island in 1803, blamed what he saw as its decline on the Scots:

> By far the greater number of farmers on the Island are Scotch Highlanders, ignorant, indolent and selfish in the extreme, who have no idea of agriculture and who are content to clear away some wood in a slovenly manner, in order to breed cattle, from which to breed cattle, from which they derive their sole sustenance.[13]

The large number of Yorkshire emigrants who settled in 1774–75 in Nova Scotia and what later became New Brunswick were unusual in having their sea crossings well-documented. Because they left at a time of rising alarm over the large number of British people being lost to North America,

Courtesy of Yorkshire Libraries and Information, Wakefield, Ewing Gatty Collection.

Settler's cabin between Halifax and Windsor as seen from a train in June 1867, a watercolour-over-pencil by Juliana Horatia Ewing. She wrote, "They begin by setting fire to the under-wood, which clears the way to the felling of trees. The result is that a cleared place like this is covered with charred stumps of pines and many of the pines lie full length, being I suppose too much burnt to be worth removal." (Mcdonald, *Illustrated News*, 34–35.)

details of who they were and why they emigrated were recorded by customs officials. This is one of the rare instances when English emigration has been well-documented. Unlike the Scots, who were associated with infamous clearances, and the Irish, who were associated with great famines, the English slipped away without either, and in most cases virtually unnoticed. Writing in 1806, John Stewart wondered why so much alarm was being expressed over the loss of Scottish Highlanders to Canada while "at the same time not a word is said" of emigration from England, "which is of so much more real consequence."[14] But he was a lone voice.

When they emigrated, the English left very few newspaper records or personal letters behind. Their exodus also escaped the notice of most contemporary commentators and later English historians. Their departure was treated with less disquiet by people in authority than was the case with the Scots. Nobody seemed to care about the diminution in England's workforce and armed services. And after they arrived at their chosen destinations, the religious ministers who served them seemed unusually disinterested in their cultural and social needs. Anglican missionaries, appointed by the London-based Society for the Propagation of the Gospel, did not see it as their job to offer a cultural lifeline in the way that Roman Catholic priests did for the Irish or Presbyterian missionaries did for the Scots. They rarely mentioned individual English settlements in their twice-yearly reports. Although Methodist missionaries had closer links with ordinary settlers, they hardly ever described their communities, unlike Presbyterian clergymen, who wrote lengthy accounts of Scottish pioneering activities. Thus, the English were overlooked as they left and widely ignored after they arrived.

And yet, by 1865, by which time Canada had acquired well over a million people from Britain, the majority of the immigrants were coming from England.[15] However, relatively few of the English actually settled in Atlantic Canada, with most preferring to go to the United States, Upper and Lower Canada, and the Prairies.[16]

Of great importance to this study is what happened a century earlier, when Atlantic Canada acquired thousands of people with English ancestry from the United States. The driving force behind this influx was Britain's defence interests. Facing ongoing hostilities with France, Britain was concerned that the French-speaking Acadians living in Nova Scotia might side with France in any future conflicts. It therefore took the unprecedented and brutal step of expelling some thirteen thousand Acadians in two separate deportations carried out in 1755 and 1758.[17] And to assist the process of colonization even further, the hunting and fishing territories of the Native peoples were also seized.[18]

This ethnic cleansing paved the way for the arrival of eight thousand New England Planters,[19] all of whom could trace their ancestral roots back to England. Given generous incentives by the British government to relocate to the Maritimes, and being enticed by its good agricultural land, they arrived between 1759 and 1762, primarily from Massachusetts, Connecticut, and Rhode Island. The second group, consisting of thirty-five thousand Loyalists, came in 1784–85 from the United States, many

Courtesy of Library and Archives Canada, Acc. No. 1972-26-768, C-073709.

Reading the order of expulsion to the Acadians gathered in the parish church of Grand Pré in the Annapolis Valley of Nova Scotia, 1775. Watercolour by C.W. Jefferys (1869–1951).

originating from New York and New Jersey. Having suffered defeat in the American War of Independence and fearing a further loss of territory to the United States, the British government had financed their removal costs and placed them along both sides of the strategically important Bay of Fundy.[20] These Loyalists, many of English descent, swelled the population of the Nova Scotia peninsula and gave the newly created province of New Brunswick an instant population. Planters and Loyalists, together with their descendents, dominated the population of Nova Scotia and New Brunswick for many decades, but, with the rapidly growing influx directly from Britain after 1815, the British component of the population eventually became even larger, although the exact numbers are unknown. Eventually two types of English came to be recognized in the region. There were the American-born, having distant English ancestry, and there were those whose ancestors, or they themselves, had emigrated directly from England.

Planters and Loyalists brought their Yankee ways with them and were, first and foremost, Americans. They were fiercely independently minded, built American-style houses, and favoured the nonconformist religions that were popular in the United States. Their family links were with the United States and not with England. Yet, when asked to state their ethnic origins in 1871, they defined themselves as English, however distant that connection was.[21] As a result, some 29 percent of the population in both Nova Scotia and New Brunswick were categorized as English. The customs and shipping data, although incomplete, reveal that both provinces attracted relatively few English immigrants during the first half of the nineteenth century, with Scottish arrivals being more significant in Nova Scotia and Irish arrivals dominating much of the influx to New Brunswick. Thus, the substantial English presence, revealed by the census, owes more to its eighteenth-century antecedents than to the later arrival of emigrants directly from England.

Meanwhile, Prince Edward Island, which had no Planters and very few Loyalists, had to acquire its English directly from England, giving its population a relatively low English component of only 20 percent by 1881. On the other hand, Newfoundland, which relied almost entirely on West Country fishermen to bolster its early immigrant population, ended up as Canada's most English province. The 1991 census records that a staggering 82 percent of the population claimed to have some English ancestry, although most of the influx occurred long before Newfoundland had officially recorded immigration statistics.[22]

The emigrants who came from England to settle in Atlantic Canada were driven primarily by a desire for economic self-betterment. Some were fleeing dreadful poverty, but most had positive motives for leaving, with many seeking the ultimate prize of owning land and the independence that went with it. Paradoxically, emigration increased with the rapid rise in England's industrial output. Because machines increasingly replaced people, thousands of agricultural labourers working on the land and tradesmen in traditional jobs like handloom weaving had been displaced from their jobs. An oversupply of labour led to pitiful wage rates and chronic unemployment levels. The upheaval caused by the introduction of large commercial farms on Yorkshire estates during the eighteenth century fuelled the exodus from this one region. Rather than endure higher rents and an uncertain future, the Yorkshire tenantry immigrated to Nova Scotia. They were the largest single group to leave,

Map 1. Reference Map of England.

but, generally-speaking, most settlers came as families, usually in small numbers, and were drawn from many parts of England and from every social class. Most could afford to emigrate unaided, and they considered the opportunities available in various destinations very critically before deciding where they would finally settle.

Although each of the four Atlantic provinces has its own individual story, their emigration sagas have some common threads. In each case a significant component of the English influx had been driven by long-established trade links with the southwest of England. This one region supplied each of them with more immigrants than any other part of England and it did so over the longest period. The timber trade propelled the stream of emigrants from the West Country to Prince Edward Island, Nova Scotia, and New Brunswick, while the fishing trade did the same for Newfoundland. People from Devon and Cornwall hopped on the ships that were regularly crossing the Atlantic to collect their timber cargoes, while fishermen, drawn mainly from Devon, Dorset, Hampshire, and Somerset, who had been brought to Newfoundland on short-term contracts, occasionally opted to become permanent settlers. People leaving from Devon and Cornwall tended to be agricultural labourers, farmers, and tradesmen, mostly of modest means, although in some cases they included well-off farmers, but the English males recruited to work in the Newfoundland cod fishery were universally poor. Those who took temporary employment in Newfoundland during the summer often had to rely on poor relief paid by their parishes to see them through their winters in England.

Without Atlantic Canada's timber trade with England, the influx of English settlers could not have happened. The doubling of the already high duties on Baltic timber in 1811 had the effect of pricing it out of the market and making North American timber the cheaper alternative. As the trade soared, regular and affordable sea crossings came within the reach of the average emigrant as ships set sail from the major English ports to collect their cargoes. Although the industry was regularly plunged into boom and bust, according to fluctuations of business cycles in Britain, it offered diverse employment opportunities and was a vital component of a settler's livelihood. And while a substantial part of the influx came from the West Country it was not the sole supplier of emigrants by any means. The ports of Liverpool, London, Hull, Great Yarmouth, Newcastle, Whitehaven, Workington, and Maryport also had their emigrant departures, normally linked with collections of timber from the Maritimes (see Map 1). John Kerr, a Northumberland immigrant who settled in 1843 on land he obtained from the New Brunswick and Nova Scotia Land Company in Stanley (York County), was probably fairly typical. He informed his parents that "the land is good and free from stone; it will grow any kind of grain once the plough [is] in it" but that "the trees is [*sic*] standing as thick as they can grow and you can't see far before you."[23] The forests were said to be so dense that even before beginning the task of chopping down trees to create farms, settlers had first to "cut their way in."[24]

Another common factor in all four Atlantic provinces was the importance placed by English settlers on their religion. In his 1832 emigration pamphlet, the land agent John Lewellin advised people to seek others who shared their "feelings, manners, usages and sentiments,

Courtesy of Library and Archives Canada, C-000370.

Timber booms on the Saint John River, New Brunswick. Woodcut printed in *The Illustrated London News*, April 7, 1866, 232.

morals and religion." Doing so, he claimed, would "stifle many a sigh in present difficulties and hush many a regret."[25]

Religion was an important support mechanism for immigrants struggling to cope with a new and challenging environment. The Methodist and Baptist preachers, who trudged huge distances speaking of God's love and salvation, had the greatest appeal. The Baptist preacher Henry Alline worked among the New England Planters in Nova Scotia; the Yorkshire-born William Black brought his brand of Methodism to the entire region; while Laurence Coughlan, an Anglican minister who converted to Methodism, attracted an enthusiastic following in the Conception Bay area of Newfoundland.

Despite being the official religion, the Church of England attracted relatively few followers. Anglican clergymen were remote figures who adhered to rigid hierarchical structures and seemed not to appreciate the hunger among their congregations for uplifting messages and a kindly smile. As J.F.W. Johnston observed in his travels through the Maritimes, "The Church of England has less hold on the people than either Presbyterians, Baptists or Roman Catholics." He blamed this on the fact that, while other religions had to raise most of their funds from their congregations, Anglican missionaries could rely on funds supplied from Britain by the Society for the Propagation of the Gospel. This made them "independent of the people on pecuniary matters and they have not cultivated them as other sects have."[26]

The bitter winters were another common feature. The Methodist minister Joshua Marsden wrote, in 1816:

> [T]hose who are accustomed only to the cold of England cannot conceive the intense severity of winters in Nova Scotia: the snow is often from four to six feet deep; the ice upon the rivers is two feet thick; the cold penetrates the warmest rooms, the warmest clothes, and will render torpid the warmest constitutions; it often freezes to death those who lose their way in the woods, or get bewildered in the thick and blinding fury of a snow drift.[27]

Courtesy of Library and Archives Canada, Acc. No. 1939-161, C-009336.

The Right Reverend John Inglis, the third Anglican bishop of Nova Scotia and son of Charles Inglis, the first bishop. Lithograph by William Charles Ross, engraved by M. Gauci. Bishop John worked hard to extend the influence of the Church of England, but his hostile and high-handed approach toward other Protestant religions made him out of step with his time.

And New Brunswick was even colder in his opinion. Newspaper reports in Newfoundland speak of similar conditions. It was an insurmountable deterrent for some. Having emigrated to Prince Edward Island from Barnstaple in 1832, William Holmes and his wife, Betsy Richards, decided very soon after arriving that they "did not like the climate and moved on to Boston."[27]

A striking theme in this study is the relatively large number of English immigrants who came from extremely poor backgrounds. In addition to the desperately poor fishermen who went to live in Newfoundland during the late eighteenth and early nineteenth centuries, there were the many hundreds of destitute children, from English cities like Liverpool and Birmingham, who were sent to the Maritimes a century later. They were the so-called "home children," whose relocation had been arranged by an assortment of English do-gooders who believed that such children needed to be saved from the corrupting influences of their families and guardians and given a fresh start in life. In addition, there were those people who were assisted to immigrate to Atlantic Canada by their parishes.[29] Assistance was justified on the grounds that it offered them an escape from their poverty and it reduced the burden on the ratepayers who were having to contribute to their maintenance. However, only a minority ever received financial help, and those who did originated mainly from East Anglia, this being one of the regions that experienced disturbances during the Swing riots of 1830–31.[30] Impoverished labourers agitating for better wages and the removal of the new threshing machines that threatened their livelihoods failed to win these changes and were dealt with severely. Just after these disturbances a large group from Suffolk immigrated to Prince Edward Island, although shortly thereafter people from this county switched their allegiance to Upper Canada.

After the 1830s, when Upper Canada acquired its internal routes and became more accessible, it became the prime destination of most British immigrants. The Maritime provinces could not match its better land and job prospects and each lost their already-established settlers to it. People bypassed Nova Scotia, since most of its good land had already been snapped up by Planters, early Yorkshire settlers, and Loyalists, and they were deterred by Prince Edward Island's semi-feudal land system, since it denied them the freeholds they sought.

This was the stark reality that the Colonial Office sought to address in 1832 when it advised that "Prince Edward Island, Newfoundland, Nova Scotia and Cape Breton … do not contain the means either of affording employment at wages to a considerable number of emigrants or of settling them upon land."[31] New Brunswick's better land opportunities, especially those being marketed at the time by the New Brunswick and Nova Scotia Land Company, made it still a viable destination, but, because of the loss of most of the province's customs data, the number of immigrant arrivals will never be known with any accuracy. Meanwhile, this preference for Upper Canada suited the British government. English Protestants streaming into Upper Canada offered a welcome counterbalance to the very large French-speaking, Roman Catholic population in Lower Canada. Preserving its hold on British America always remained a top priority.

William Cobbett, the radical journalist and champion of the English agricultural labourer, had strong views on emigration.[32] He was opposed to it. To him, Prince Edward Island was "a rascally heap of sand, rock and swamp ... in the horrible Gulf of St. Lawrence ... a lump of worthlessness ... [that] bears nothing but potatoes," and he was equally scathing about the other provinces.[33] Having served as a soldier in the British Army in New Brunswick for a few years, he had first-hand knowledge of the region, but being a fiery opponent of emigration, his purple prose must be taken with a pinch of salt. However, his words probably reflect the received wisdom of the day. Vessels lined up almost daily at large ports like London and Liverpool to take people to Quebec, but few were heading for Maritime ports.[34]

Nevertheless, as is so often the case, most ordinary people made up their own minds. Many English, particularly those living in the West Country, streamed into Prince Edward Island during the 1830s and 1840s, hoping to benefit from its burgeoning shipbuilding industry.[35] Meanwhile, Nova Scotia's mining industry attracted a growing number of English coal miners during the second half of the nineteenth century and still more arrived later with the province's growing industrialization.[36] The views of people already settled carried far more weight than official advice or outspoken commentators, and this, more than anything, drove the later influx to the Maritimes.

The British government's land policies, such as they were, promoted everything under the sun except effective colonization. Land speculators were thriving, but ordinary colonists found it extremely difficult to cope with the many obstacles that were placed in their way. They had low priority. Since the late eighteenth century the government had been granting huge quantities of wilderness land as rewards to favoured individuals. Most recipients sold their land on to speculators, who amassed huge holdings but did nothing to further colonization. Settlers had the residue, which was often inferior, and what holdings they could obtain were relatively small and scattered over huge distances. It was a bureaucratic muddle that favoured the rich and privileged while hindering the growth of compact settlements. Conditions were especially bad in Prince Edward Island, where settlers were actually prevented from purchasing land. The land on the island had been divided and sold off by lottery in 1767 to various claimants, irrespective of their willingness to promote settlements.[37] They simply waited for their land to increase in value, and, in the meantime, sought people willing to take up leaseholds.

Courtesy of Library and Archives Canada, Acc. No. 1989-519-1, C-083499.

Late eighteenth-century portrait of Walter Patterson, who became Prince Edward Island's first governor in 1769. His corrupt and incompetent handling of land transactions following the 1767 lottery made him a controversial figure, and, after seventeen years as governor, he was forced to leave office. In 1798, Patterson died in poverty at his lodgings in London.

When Lord Seymour of Ragley took possession of Lot 13 in Prince Edward Island, Charles Morris, the surveyor, selected "1,000 acres of the best land" for him and allocated the remainder to his future tenants. This was all going to be very beneficial to his lordship, since the rents collected from tenants would more than pay for the quit rents — land fees that were payable to the Crown.[38] Lord Seymour grabbed most of the economic benefit for himself, denying his settlers the prospect of owning land. This aspect of Old World thinking caused considerable resentment in Prince Edward Island, and many settlers left the province.

The situation in Newfoundland had been even worse. There the West Country merchants had an iron grip on the island's economy and did what they could to stop colonizers, fearing that they would interfere with the smooth functioning of the fishery. They wanted Newfoundland to be a British off-shore fishery with no other function than to make them wealthy and benefit the West Country economy. However, the young lads and men who took up temporary employment in the fishery had other ideas. Once they appreciated the province's benefits, some voted with their feet, thus setting in train a small but regular supply of immigrants who contributed greatly to its development.

The city of St. John's, Newfoundland, in 1892, lithograph by an unknown artist. The cityscape reveals a metropolis focused around a busy harbour. Water Street and the Military Road, running parallel to the waterfront, were the earliest streets; they once linked two forts.

A recurring theme in emigrant letters and official reports is the sheer hard work involved in becoming a pioneer farmer. An advertisement in the *Berwick Advertiser* in 1843, aimed at "persons desirous of obtaining cleared or uncleared farms" in Prince Edward Island, stated that no one need apply who could not "command £100 upwards to commence cultivations."[39] Settlers with capital could buy already-established farms in settled areas, but they were a fortunate few. Most people were like William Grieve, a shepherd from Whittingham in Northumberland, who planned his transformation to pioneer farming in the Harvey settlement in New Brunswick very carefully. The writer J.F.W. Johnston was clearly awestruck by the man's resilience and staying power:

Courtesy of Library and Archives Canada, Acc. No. R9266-1657, Peter Winkworth Collection of Canadiana.

He landed at Fredericton in 1837 with a family of ten and only 7 [shillings] and 6 [pence] in his pocket. He did not come out to Harvey along with the other settlers but, having received his grant of land, he hired himself as a farm-servant to Colonel Shore at Fredericton at £30 a year; and such of his children as could do anything he hired out also. Supporting the rest of his family out of his earnings, he saved what he could and whenever he had a pound or two to spare he got an acre or two of his land cleared. In this way, he did good to the other settlers, by bringing some money among them and giving a little employment. At last, four years ago — that was after seven years' service — he came out and settled on his land himself, building a good house for his family right away — that is without the previous erection of a log house, as is usually the case, and a very good house he appeared to have. He now owns seven hundred acres of land in different lots and had clearings of twenty acres on each of three or four of these farm lots intended for his several sons, who appear to be as industrious as himself.[40]

There were many William Grieves in this emigration saga. Agricultural workers, farmers, tradesmen, craftsmen, miners, and fishermen came with little spare money, but they had an overwhelming desire to succeed. To do so they had to show enormous courage and resilience. They built their communities on the west side of Nova Scotia, on the east side of Newfoundland, and in many parts of southern New Brunswick and Prince Edward Island. The first large group came from Yorkshire, and following them were people who left from across the length and breadth of England. This is their story.

CHAPTER 2

Laying the Foundations: Yorkshire Emigration

Remember the rock from whence ye was hewn.[1]

CHARLES DIXON RECORDED his pioneering experiences for the benefit of his children. "It was for your sakes we crossed the ocean so that you would out-strip us in purity of heart and holiness of life."[2] This was seemingly an unconventional motive for emigrating, but Dixon was a devout Methodist who wished to escape the social injustice and "troubles … befalling my native country." A bricklayer's son from Kirk Leavington in the North Riding of Yorkshire, he was a man of strong convictions and a natural leader. He rose to become one of Nova Scotia's leading figures, and, following the separation of New Brunswick from Nova Scotia in 1784, served in New Brunswick's first House of Assembly. Yet he could never have imagined this outcome when he first learned about the advantages of the New World.

Dixon had established a profitable paper factory for himself at Hutton Rudby, and his relocation to Nova Scotia seems unexpected. However, he was dissatisfied and restless and, learning about the favourable accounts of Nova Scotia being circulated by agents of Lieutenant Governor

Michael Francklin, he considered emigrating. But, lacking sufficient funds, he remained where he was. When "a gentleman" called to see him out of the blue and offered "to pay [his] stock and interest in Hutton Mills," he immediately persuaded his wife and family to move with him to Nova Scotia. They were among the group of sixty-two emigrants (seventeen families) from the North Riding who set sail from Liverpool in the *Duke of York* in 1772:[3]

> We had a rough passage, none of us having been to sea before, much seasickness prevailed. After six weeks and four days we arrived at Halifax ... and were received with much joy by the gentlemen in general, but were much discouraged by others, and the account given us of Cumberland[4] was enough to make the stoutest heart give way.[5]

Fort Cumberland, near Sackville (later New Brunswick), was their destination, but upon their arrival in Halifax, Dixon and the others "heard all kinds of negative reports" about it — "enough to sway many peoples' opinions." When he actually reached Fort Cumberland, Dixon realized that the discontent felt by the local New Englanders "was mainly due to indolence and lack of knowledge." The enormous potential of the land was immediately obvious to the Yorkshire group, and those with sufficient funds acquired land and livestock and some even helped friends and relatives to do the same. Fourteen Yorkshire settlers acquired over eight thousand acres in the Sackville area alone.[6] Dixon set an example by purchasing a 2,500-acre farm from Daniel Hawkins for £260. Thomas Bowser, from Acklam near Birdsall,[7] leased a 750-acre farm in the same area for four pounds, ten shillings per annum,[8] while the thirteen-year-old George Bulmer, an apprentice mason, eventually purchased one thousand acres and obtained a grant for a further three hundred.[9]

Meanwhile, James Metcalf from Hawnby in the North Riding, who had also sailed in the *Duke of York*, bought 207 acres along the Maccan River farther to the south and shared with two others in the purchase of an additional forty-five acres. Writing to his fiancée, Ann Gill, in Huby, to the south of Easingwold, he described "a little fly called a mosquito that is troublesome in summertime and bites like a midge," but added that was "the only thing I wish to say against the country."[10] He hoped that she would come immediately and advised her not to be fearful of the ocean crossing and not to listen to adverse comments about Nova Scotia:

> If you come be not discouraged by anything in the country for it is good; if you come you will sail up to Fort Cumberland and when you are there write … to me at Maccan River … and I will come for you…. I will be as good as my word … the passage is paid at Liverpool before you go on board but, if you should not be able to pay, make friends to some that come and I will pay … may ye Lord bless you and conduct you safely hither.[11]

James's letter took two years to reach her, but when it did, Ann reacted immediately. She left for Nova Scotia, and upon her arrival in Fort Cumberland (now known by its original name of Fort Beauséjour) dispatched a message to James, who rushed to meet her. They were married the following day in the stockade of Fort Cumberland, and, after producing a large family, both lie buried on the banks of the Maccan River.[12]

The Yorkshire influx to Nova Scotia had been encouraged and directed by no less a dignitary than the lieutenant governor. The Poole-born Michael Francklin became one of Halifax's leading merchants after amassing a fortune during the Seven Years' War (1756–63) by supplying troops to the British and privateering. He was the ultimate wheeler-dealer who exploited his political office to the full, but his enormous appetite for land speculation was his ruination, since it left him heavily in debt. Having acquired thousands of acres in Nova Scotia, he failed to attract New England settlers as he had hoped, thus leaving himself with no revenue and a sizable bill in quit rents to pay to the Crown.[13] His solution was to seek settlers from overseas, concentrating his efforts in the North and East Ridings of Yorkshire, where he knew there was considerable discontent over enclosures and rent rises.

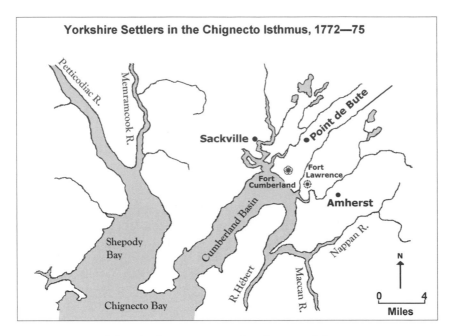

Map 2. Yorkshire Settler Locations in the Chignecto Isthmus, 1772–75.

Francklin offered one-hundred-acre lots at "Francklin Manor" — a choice tract in the Chignecto Isthmus that offered prime sites along the rivers that empty into the Cumberland Basin, especially the Hébert, Maccan, and Nappan (see Map 2). "None but Protestants will be admitted … and none need apply but husbandmen or artificers, and such as are possessed of at least £50 in money, that they may be able to carry on their improvements."[14] Each family that could satisfy these criteria was to receive "at least ten acres of cleared land for the immediate culture of grain, or providing winter fodder for not less than 20 head of horned cattle," and for this the settler would pay "a yearly quit rent of one penny per acre for the first five years, sixpence per acre for the next five years and, after that period, one shilling per acre for ever…. The climate is healthy and temperate, and the lands are surrounded by settlements already made; the rivers abound with fish, the woods with game, and good timber fit for building."[15] And there was icing on this cake: "There are no game-laws, taxes on lands, or tithes in this province." Francklin knew that emigration offered a welcome release from the feudal constraints and payments of the Old World.

Michael Francklin, lieutenant governor and sometime temporary governor of Nova Scotia between 1766 and 1776, oil portrait by J.S. Copley, *circa* 1762.

   Seeking settlers for the land he had previously hoped to populate with New Englanders, Francklin left for England in 1769 to personally direct a recruitment campaign in Yorkshire. He concentrated his efforts in the farming areas of the North and East Ridings, where the great upheaval being experienced by the creation of large consolidated holdings from former scattered strips in the common fields made farmers and agricultural workers particularly receptive to his offer. Through his family and business contacts he had inside knowledge of tenant grievances on the Duke of Rutland's estate. Here, it was simply a matter of directing resentful tenants toward Nova Scotia. Francklin placed his agents in Rillington, Skelton, Thirsk, Hovingham, Sowerby, Whitby, and Burniston — all towns in the North and East Riding of Yorkshire. The agents located potential settlers and arranged for their sea crossings from the nearby ports of Hull, Scarborough, Stockton-on-Tees (Durham), and Newcastle-upon-Tyne (see Map 3).[16] By 1775, when the American Revolution halted the exodus, eight vessels had carried around nine hundred emigrants from the north of England to Nova Scotia.[17]

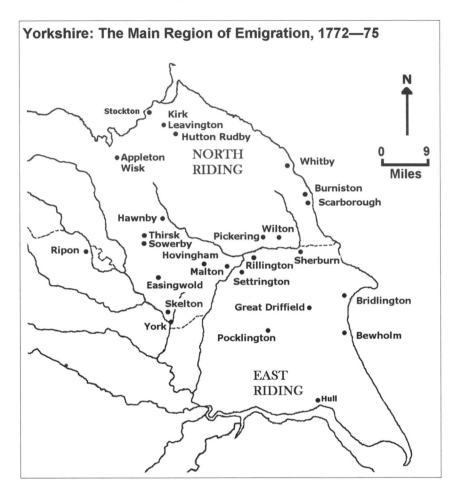

Map 3. Yorkshire: The Main Region of Emigration, 1772–75.

Francklin's campaigning efforts attracted "a fine quality of substantial, knowledgeable men to whom the land was remarkable for not needing manure and the terms unbelievably tempting."[18] The Reverend John Eagleson, an Anglican missionary sent by the Society for the Propagation of the Gospel in London, observed in 1773 how "the country is fast settling, many English farmers annually coming over and settling among us; whose favourable accounts of the country to their friends seem to induce still more to emigrate hither." His hope that "in a short time, this district will be settled with a sober, industrious and religious set of people"[19] was borne out, although not without controversy and setbacks, and few would support his religion.

As the exodus grew, emigrants had to withstand criticism from Britain's ruling classes, who feared that emigration would seriously deplete the country's workforce and armed services. A correspondent writing in the *York Chronicle* in 1773 thought "it a matter of astonishment to every rational being in this Island, that the Government should permit such numerous emigration from the mother country."[20] And in his view, Michael Francklin's involvement made a bad situation even worse:

> It may be said that Government has just granted a large portion of land, in a neighbouring forest, for the purpose of population and agriculture. But how have they granted it? Not in the judicious manner in which settlers receive it in the American provinces…. The very land should have been parcelled out in small lots. Instead of this, one great man has the whole, and he naturally will make the most of it.[21]

The government's anti-emigration stance required it to lament the loss of people, and yet it needed loyal British emigrants for its North American colonies. It would have to face up to this quandary eventually, but in 1773 the government's principal aim was to contain the exodus that appeared to be spiralling out of control. Although parliamentary action to curb emigration was resisted, the government instructed customs officials at every port to record the numbers emigrating, thus providing passenger lists for the period from 1773 to 1775, showing who left on each ship and their reasons for leaving.[22] Overall, the results reveal that farmers and craftsmen and tradesmen were particularly well-represented among the Yorkshire emigrants, while there were relatively few labourers and unskilled workers.

The disruption and higher rents caused by the creation of enclosed farms in Yorkshire was given as the principal motive for emigrating. As Mathew Walker, who sailed from Scarborough in 1774, explained, "all the small farms [had been] taken into large ones in his parish" and he "could not get bread."[23] Michael Pinkney, who travelled at the same time, said that he had been "turned off his farm, it being taken into a larger one."[24] In fact, Yorkshire had the largest acreage enclosed of any county in England, most of which took place from the late 1760s to the 1770s in the North and East Ridings. Men like Walker and Pinkney were in the front line. They faced higher rents, and eviction if they could not afford to pay them.

Lord Dartmouth, secretary of state for the American colonies and owner of estates in the West Riding of Yorkshire, had first-hand knowledge of enclosures. The distress being caused by rent rises on his estates was made very clear to him by William Lister, one of his tenants: If his Lordship "could see the tears running from his eyes I'm sure it would melt your heart."[25] Claiming that Edward Elmsall, Lord Dartmouth's farm manager, was singling out tenants whom he disliked to raise their rents and evict them if they could not pay, he thought the situation to be very unjust and that his Lordship should know that his neighbour Robert Dixon had "now gone to America." But Lister knew his place: "Nay my dear, dear Landlord ... I had rather go to my bare and bended knees [than cause any provocation]."[26]

However, contrary to William Lister's account, Elmsall was well aware of the discontent on Lord Dartmouth's estate and advised against further rent rises and brutal evictions. He deplored the extent to which "old tenants" were being removed by Thomas Gasgoine's agent in Shropshire, stating that "the tenants have made much noise in this country," and conveying his hope that similar action in West Yorkshire would "be disagreeable to your Lordship."[27] But although the pain was as great, few people emigrated from the West Riding since, in this more industrialized region, people had more employment alternatives and wages were generally regarded as good.[28]

Around the time that Lord Dartmouth was raising rents on his Yorkshire estates, he was also speculating on land in Nova Scotia and east Florida. Conveniently, his cousin Francis Legge happened to be governor of Nova Scotia and could offer sound advice:

> Many of the nobility are soliciting for grants of land
> within this province [Nova Scotia] ... and considering

William Legge, second
Earl of Dartmouth
(1731–1801). Portrait
by Pompeo Batoni, *circa*
1753–56.

*Courtesy of the Hood Museum of Art,
Dartmouth College, Hanover NH.
Purchased through gifts from Jane and W.
David Dance, Class of 1940; Jonathan
Cohen, Class of 1960, Tuck 1961;
Frederick B. Whittemore, Class of 1953,
Tuck 1954; Barbara Dau Southwell, Class
of 1978; and David Southwell, Tuck 1988;
Parnassus Foundation/Jane and Raphael
Bernstein; and an anonymous donor.*

your numerous family, it may be of some advantage
hereafter to some of your younger sons if they could
obtain grants ... if your Lordship could procure for four
or five of your sons twenty thousand acres each, I shall
take care to have them located in such places as they
must of course in time become valuable, in the doing of
which I shall be assisted by the Surveyor General.[29]

Benefiting financially from one's political position carried little or no
stigma at the time. People in high office, with large ambitions, felt they
were entitled to grab the choicest land and did so. And yet, seemingly
unmindful that colonizers would have to be found for his and his sons'
newly acquired lands, Lord Dartmouth railed against the rising level of
emigration from Yorkshire:

> The increase of the inhabitants in the province of Nova
> Scotia by emigration from this Kingdom may be of local
> advantage to this colony but is a circumstance of very
> alarming consequence and consideration in respect to
> the interests and security of Great Britain ... it is an evil
> that must soon require some remedy.[30]

Nevertheless, despite the government-inspired pressure on people not to emigrate, the exodus from Yorkshire continued. The numbers peaked during the three-month period from March to May 1774 when the ships *Two Friends*, *Albion*, *Thomas and William*, *Prince George*, *Mary*, and *Providence* carried around seven hundred Yorkshire emigrants to Nova Scotia. John Bulmer, who sailed with his wife and family in the *Two Friends*, said that he had left "on account of their rents being raised" by Beilby Thompson, MP; Christopher Harper from Rillington, who sailed in the same ship, made the same complaint about his landlord, William Weddell, MP.[31] Both landlords contributed unwittingly to the peopling of Nova Scotia, with substantial numbers leaving from Thompson's estate just south of York and Weddell's estate near Ripon (see Map 3). Both groups were among the 103 passengers who sailed in the *Two Friends* from Hull. It had clearly been a very difficult crossing. An unnamed young woman said it gave her "great pleasure to see land after being nine weeks at sea, and the ill-treatment that we met with. I assure you that our usage was as bad as though we had been transports, not being permitted to go on deck when the weather permitted, but as the captain pleased."[32]

Those who sailed in the *Albion* included the former tenants of the Duke of Rutland, Lord Cavendish and Thomas Duncombe, and they, too, complained of increased rents. In fact, "rents being raised" was the repeated refrain of people who were asked why they were leaving England. Some men, like Thomas Lumley from Rillington and William Chapman from Hawnby, both farmers, and William Trueman, a miller from Bilsdale (near Thirsk), were probably sufficiently affluent to have afforded higher rents, but preferred emigration to lowered living standards. Nathaniel Smith, a farmer from Appleton-by-Wisk who came with his entire household, including servants, certainly had considerable means. Complaining that "Hull and York have lightened our purses," he had to finance lodgings for his large contingent at the exorbitant rate of a guinea a day while awaiting the *Albion's* departure from Hull. Captain James Watt added to their woes when he said "to our comfort, if I may use the expression, he shall think himself well off if one third of us survive our journey."[33] Enduring seasickness, an outbreak of smallpox, and dreadful storms, the ship's 188 passengers finally reached Halifax: "When we came nigh the shores we thought it prudent to take a pilot up the Bay as our captain was altogether a stranger to the place." They anchored two miles from shore, with the governor's schooner blocking "our people from landing" for fear of spreading the infection.[34]

In the same month that the *Albion* had sailed, the *York Chronicle* claimed that three ships carrying emigrants from Sutherland in Scotland to North America had suffered serious fatalities: "One was wrecked on Shetland, and most of the people perished; another is thought to be totally lost, no account being received of her arrival; and the third arrived after a dismal passage of three months with the loss of 70 people."[35] However, anti-emigration campaigners sometimes resorted to rumours and scare stories, and the reporting of such faraway incidents in a Yorkshire newspaper, whether true or not, was clearly intended to focus attention on the perils of an ocean crossing. But Yorkshire people were impervious to such tactics.

Agents working for Michael Francklin in the East Riding had clearly been deluged with requests for places on ships.[36] Samuel Pattindon, captain of the *Thomas and William*, reported that the ship would be leaving late in order to give people time to raise the necessary funds, but the delay gave scaremongers the time they needed to sow doubt and confusion:

> [A]s persons who … intend to remove their habitations
> to this land of liberty, not being judges of a proper
> ship to accommodate them for such a passage, have
> been intimidated by threatening advertisements, and
> in doubt how to proceed — The owner of the above-
> named ship [*Thomas and William*] begs of such persons

as intend to take their passage to Nova Scotia this season, that they will make inquiry at Scarborough of any interested persons, who are conversant in maritime affairs, and hopes they will go on board of such ship, as they shall be advised is properly fitted, and sufficient for the performance of the voyage.[37]

The *Prince George*,[38] which was also due to sail from Scarborough at this same time, suffered equally bad press:

> Some evil-disposed person or persons have maliciously reported that the ship, *Prince George*, advertised for taking passengers from Scarborough to Nova Scotia, is totally unfit to perform the voyage, and that therefore the persons going therein must do so at the hazard of their lives and fortunes. The owner of the said ship takes this method of informing the public in general, and particularly all such persons who have engaged to go in his said vessel, that the said report is without the least foundation, and merely intended to draw all such passengers from him, for the emolument of some other owner, the above-named ship being in not only good condition, but as well calculated for the above purpose as any other vessel advertised for such voyage.[39]

The *Thomas and William* and *Prince George* were hardly the best of ships, both being rated by Lloyd's of London as "E1" (seaworthy but only second class). The real issue though was not the quality of the ships but the extent of overcrowding. As a correspondent to the *York Chronicle* noted, "few of them had considered the consequences attending so large a number of people being, for at least two months, crowded together four in a bed and the beds one upon another three deep with not so much room between each to admit even the smallest person to sit up on end."[40] Many people had wanted to leave from Scarborough and shipowners had met the demand. They offered affordable fares, but to maximize profits they had packed passengers like sardines into the holds of their ships.

The actual number of passengers carried in the *Thomas and William* and *Prince George* is difficult to assess. The confusion may have been deliberate, since the suffering endured in overcrowded ships often generated adverse publicity for shipowners. A list of 193 people who had sailed from Scarborough in April 1774 was provided to British customs officials, but the ship carrying them was not recorded.[41] Presumably this was done on purpose to conceal the fact that 193 people had actually sailed in the three-hundred-ton *Thomas and William*,[42] when the captain claimed the smaller total of 105 passengers on reaching Halifax.[43] Meanwhile, the crossing of the 150-ton *Prince George* was mysteriously left out altogether from the British customs register. On arrival in Halifax, the captain claimed that she had carried 143 people, but according to John Robinson, one of the passengers who kept a meticulous account of his journey to Nova Scotia, there were 170 people onboard.[44] Robinson's figure is probably the more reliable. If that number did sail, the overcrowding must have been unbearable. Apart from slave-trade regulations, there were no enforceable legal limits at the time restricting passenger numbers in ships. Later, with the passing of the Passenger Act of 1803, a formula was introduced allowing only one person for every two tons burthen.[45] Applying this ruling to the *Prince George*, she should have had a maximum of seventy-five passengers, when in fact she carried 170.[46]

The *Thomas and William*'s passengers were reported to be "all well" on arrival after a five-week crossing, with their number increasing by two — "two women being safely delivered in the passage."[47] But a more negative spin was given to the *Prince George*'s arrival. Yorkshire people were told that all of her passengers had returned to England "and many more would have gladly returned, but could not pay for their freight, the country not being in any respect equal to the favourable idea they had formed of it."[48] This was utter nonsense, but it did illustrate the serious concerns being felt over the growing loss of people, some of whom were surprisingly affluent. One large family, probably the Harrisons from Rillington, were reported to have taken £2,200 with them.[49] Fares alone in the *Thomas and William* for two adults and nine children would have cost between twenty-five and thirty-three pounds, and the Harrison family probably spent far more besides on lodging costs.[50] Having come laden with many household possessions, they were almost certainly among the forty men, women, and children who stayed at an inn in York en route to Scarborough to board ship.[51] And people like Ralph Stibbins, a forty-year-old merchant with three children, and Robert Wilson, a forty-nine-year-old farmer with a wife and seven children, who sailed in the same ship as the Harrisons, were probably also men of substance. John Robinson, a farmer from Bewholm in Holderness who had sailed in the *Prince George*, said that if he found Nova Scotia to be "as favourable as represented" he would "make a purchase there and return to take his family over."[52] He and his friend, Thomas Rispin from Fangfoss, had the time and resources to explore the entire Francklin Manor and write a detailed account of their findings for the benefit of people back in Yorkshire.

As the zeal to emigrate spread north, the *Providence* set sail for Halifax in April 1774 from Newcastle-upon-Tyne, and the *Mary* did the same from Stockton-on-Tees. While the thirty-four people who sailed in the *Mary* were all from County Durham,[53] some of the seventy-three people in the *Providence*,[54] like John and Mary Richardson, George and Margaret Foster, Mary, George, and John Oxley, and Christopher Flintoff, certainly came from Yorkshire.[55] Most of the *Mary*'s passengers sought "better employment," but Thomas Lancaster, a linen-draper's apprentice, had come "to dispose of goods" and presumably return, while the shopkeeper Thomas Miller stated that he had "goods to sell and [would] return."[56] Strangely, the *Providence*'s crossing was not recorded in the British customs register but her passengers were included in a list sent by Governor Legge to Lord Dartmouth.[57]

Rising alarm in Britain over the loss of so many people energized anti-emigration campaigners, who used negative feedback from Nova Scotia, whether accurate or not, to discourage even more people from leaving. This account printed in the *York Chronicle* by an anonymous "North American correspondent" was fairly typical:

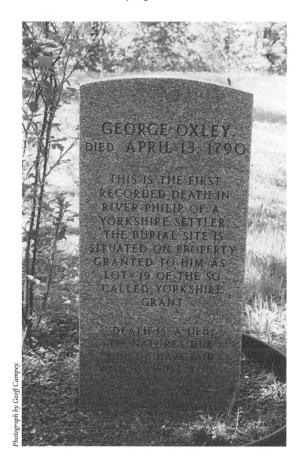

Photograph by Geoff Campey.

GEORGE OXLEY
DIED APRIL 13, 1790

THIS IS THE FIRST
RECORDED DEATH IN
RIVER PHILIP OF A
YORKSHIRE SETTLER.
THE BURIAL SITE IS
SITUATED ON PROPERTY
GRANTED TO HIM AS
LOT # 19 OF THE SO
CALLED YORKSHIRE
GRANT

DEATH IS A DEBT
TIS NATURE'S DUE
WHICH I HAVE PAID
AND SO MUST YOU

Tombstone of George Oxley, passenger on the *Providence*, at the United Church cemetery, River Philip, Cumberland County, Nova Scotia. His death in 1790 was the first to be recorded in River Philip.

I am sorry to hear ... that a great many farmers are quitting the northern parts of Yorkshire for America; I fear that most of them will change for the worse. They little know what they must suffer from change of soil and climate, and the toil they must endure before they can make bread to eat; and if, by their industry, they at the last attain to live free from want, they must never expect to grow rich, for they must settle so far inland, that the produce of their land will bear a very low price, and in all the back settlements cash is very little known among them…. Those who are gone to Nova Scotia will have five or six months winter.[58]

Politically, emigration was bad news in Britain. Lord Dartmouth described it as "an evil" that needed to be stopped and Governor Legge, appreciating its negative undertones, gave a very cautious report of immigrant arrivals: "Those that are able are purchasing lands of the former settlers, others [are] hiring themselves out to service, and others, wishing themselves at home again, will soon quit the Province."[59] In a later report in 1774, Legge doubted that any more Yorkshire people would come to Nova Scotia "as they seem not to be well pleased with the country, the best lands are already granted, the rest being wilderness land; those people have returned home who were dissatisfied or were not able to purchase of the former inhabitants."[60] But Legge was wrong. More people emigrated in 1775.

The last ship to leave was the *Jenny*, which sailed from Hull in April 1775 with eighty Yorkshire passengers. They included households that came with their servants, such as the families of William Black, a linen draper, and William Johnson and William Robinson, both farmers. Christopher Harper, from Barthorpe-Bottoms near Malton, who came with his wife and seven children, had travelled alone the previous year in the *Two Friends* to visit Fort Cumberland, where he purchased a 143-acre farm "with a good house upon it, elegantly furnished with barns and other conveniences besides woodland at a distance and 20 cows with other cattle etc. for which we were told he gave £550."[61]

The shipping agents for the *Jenny* crossing included the same Christopher Harper and John Robinson, another affluent farmer, who, from his extensive travelling, could describe the region's excellent agricultural potential.[62] The *Jenny* was a superior vessel, being classed as "A1," and unlike the others was almost new. She was reported to be "a remarkably fine and lofty ship," suggesting that the steerage space was more spacious than normal.[63] Quite clearly, the more affluent folk deliberated longest and were the last to leave, doing so just before the outbreak of the American Revolution brought a halt to emigration.

Most new arrivals were shocked by the scale of the wilderness that greeted them. As their ship neared Halifax Harbour, John Robertson and Thomas Rispin thought the coastline "appeared very discouraging and disagreeable — nothing but barren rocks and hills presented themselves....

This unfavourable appearance greatly dampened the spirits of most of the passengers and several of them began to wish themselves in Old England before they had set foot in Nova Scotia." And, on the way from Halifax to Sackville they "passed through nothing but dreary wastes or forests of rocks and wood."[64] Robertson and Rispin blamed this "unfavourable appearance" on the place being "populated so thinly" and the failure of its New Englander settlers to adopt good farming practices.

However, the immense potential of the land soon became apparent, and the two men concluded that their economic future and that of the others lay in improving it. It was theirs for the taking: "A man may have as much land as he pleases; the first year he pays nothing; for the next 5 years a penny an acre; the next 5 years 3 [pence]; for 5 years after that 6 [pence]; and then 1 shilling an acre forever to him and his heirs."[65]

Charles Dixon had recognized the importance of land drainage and, when he arrived in 1772, set to work almost immediately, building dykes and reclaiming more of the salt marshes at his farm in Sackville. By 1787 he had built dykes around 104 acres of his own marshland in Sackville, while Thomas Bowser had done the same for his forty acres. However, some settlers went through a longer and more traumatic period of adjustment.[66]

The Harrisons, from Rillington in the East Riding, had stocked their large farm with cattle and seemed to be doing well, but they hated their place along the River Hébert. John's eldest son, Luke, wrote home to his cousin, complaining bitterly about the mosquitoes and climate:

> We have all gotten safe to Nova Scotia but do not like it all and a great many besides us, and [we] are coming back to England, all that can get back. We do not like the country nor never shall. The mosquitoes are a terrible plague.... You may think that mosquitoes cannot hurt a deal, but if you do you are mistaken, for they will swell one['s] legs and hands [so] that some is blind and lame for some days.... One is tormented all the summer by mosquitoes and almost freeze to death in the winter.[67]

However, the Harrisons did not leave, and twenty-nine years later Luke was extolling the merits of Nova Scotia to the same cousin back in Yorkshire:

> I cannot help but praise up Nova Scotia for growing the greatest crops of potatoes and the best, which answer well to eat with the fish, as we have plenty…. Dear cousin you gave me an invitation of coming to purchase a place in my native country but I had rather ten to one to stay where I am…. People that come from England like the country very well and those that are advanced in years live to a great age.[68]

At first the Trueman family, from Bilsdale in the North Riding, disliked their place at Pointe de Bute, but after finding their bearings they flourished, and at least five successive generations of Truemans would live there.[69]

The memorial stone archway at Pointe de Bute Cemetery, New Brunswick, dedicated to the early Yorkshire settlers. A bronze tablet commemorates the building in 1788 of the province's first Methodist church.

Nathaniel Smith, the prosperous farmer from Appelton-by-Wisk, enjoyed a smooth transition to his new life in Fort Cumberland, but he knew some discontented people who felt they had been misled by Charles Dixon's overly optimistic accounts of the region. He thought that a few of them might return to Yorkshire, but that if they did, they would not "bring a bad report" of the land: "One gallon of cream will yield as much butter as two in Old England upon the best of lands [that] I was ever concerned with."[70] Although the land was good, he wrote, "let none come here and expect to sit down at ease free from troubles, trials and disappointments … but according to human reason most of the English settled in Fort Lawrence[71] and Cumberland have a hopeful prospect." Nathaniel certainly expected to prosper quickly: "Any industrious man capable of purchasing two cows may do well … but the man of money is the man for Nova Scotia. Some have already made purchases of excellent houses and fine lands … and in a little time will be as compact and elegant as the most gentlemanly house in England."[72]

Nathaniel might have been referring to John Weldon, from the North Riding village of Crathorne near Kirk Leavington. One of Michael Francklin's 1772 recruits, he had wasted no time in equipping himself with cattle for his farm along the Petitcodiac River off Shepody Bay, to the west of where the main group had settled (see Map 2). In three years' time he had twenty-two oxen, twenty-six cows, six horses, thirty-two sheep, and eighteen swine, and had acquired sufficient capital to change his status from tenant to landowner. Joshua Gildart, from nearby Carlton in Coverdale, who brought three servants with him, also prospered. He, too, rented 150 acres from Francklin on the Petitcodiac and within a year of his arrival had acquired even more livestock than Weldon. He later purchased five hundred acres farther up the Petitcodiac at Moncton, and spent three hundred pounds in improving his various landholdings.[73] Obtaining a further 753 acres along the Petitcodiac, near its juncture with a river he called the Coverdale to commemorate his native origins (it was also known as Little River), Gildart demonstrated the Yorkshire flair for rapidly acquiring real estate.

At the other end of the social spectrum were farm workers like Jonathan Barlow, who struggled just to survive:

Tombstones of the early Yorkshire settlers at Five Points Baptist Cemetery, Coverdale, near Salisbury, New Brunswick.

Photograph by Geoff Campey.

I found everything very dear in Cumberland, and was glad to lay among the hay. So I fell to work for eighteen pence per day and victuals found some days. On June 3rd I hired to Samuel Rogers of Westcock [near Sackville] for £1, 15 s. per month; stayed with him most of the summer. I found the mosquitoes very troublesome, but the land was very good. Therefore I bought 150 acres of land, but having no house or habitation.[74]

And servants also faced difficult times:

I went to a place of service for three weeks, and had I been a poor beggar I could not have been worse used; and indeed the inhabitants in general seem to be poor miserable beings, which was very mortifying to me, who had been used to good living at home. It is a desolate, depressed, and almost uninhabited country, their food is chiefly fish, which is not very delicate, but cheap. If anyone should inquire about my situation here, pray describe the country as I have done, every word that I have wrote being truth. I am going to leave this place soon, and when I am settled shall let you hear further from me.[75]

Nathaniel Smith thought that "many of the poorer sort seem very discontented … as none is able to employ them," partly because the wealthier farmers generally brought their own servants and farm labourers with them. "Some I believe will return … others would return but have not therewith to pay their passage; those I greatly pity."[76]

According to Major General Eyre Massey, the commanding general in Halifax, some did return in 1776, and were helped to do so with government funds. They "seemed heartily sick of their jaunt," having received "no encouragement in America." Giving "some their passage to England," he hoped that they would serve as a lesson to deter "the Old Country from losing so many of her subjects,"[77] although the many hundreds who remained would prove him wrong.

The Yorkshire settlers scattered far and wide, choosing their locations according to land and job availability.[78] In this respect they were very different from the Scottish Highlanders who came to the region at this time and relocated themselves as entire communities on land granted by the government. Highlanders sought to preserve their culture and traditions and so progressed in groups rather than singly. However, as Governor Legge explained to Lord Dartmouth, the Yorkshire immigrants "do not come with the expectation of lands [being] granted to them." They did not wish to settle as one community, but as individuals. "Some come to purchase [land], others perhaps to become tenants and some to labour."[79] Having rented substantial farms in Yorkshire that had been handed down from father to son, they were accustomed to renting, and took their time before making the transition from renter to owner. And when they bought farms from their New England predecessors they became widely dispersed in the Chignecto Isthmus, including the area to the west, along the Petitcodiac and Memramcook rivers, off the Shepody Bay, and the region to the south along the River Philip. Several families went even farther afield, settling in Annapolis and nearby townships in the southwest of the province.[80]

Yorkshire settlers had to cope with the privations, drudgery, and isolation of pioneer life, and endured testing conditions that seem almost incomprehensible today. Yorkshire men had to turn wildernesses into cleared farms, while the women would have had to become completely self-sufficient in meeting the domestic needs of their families. To do so they would have had to remember old skills and learn new ones. They clearly rose to the challenge. As John Robertson and Thomas Rispin observed:

> [T]he women are very industrious house-wives and spin the flax, the growth of their own farms, and weave both their linen and woollen cloth; they also bleach their linen and dye the yarn themselves. Though they will not descend to work out of doors, either in time of hay or harvest yet, they are exceedingly diligent in every domestic employment. The candles ... soap and starch which are used in their families are of their own manufacturing.[81]

Methodism played its part in helping settlers like Charles Dixon find a moral dimension to their new life. They had wanted to escape from what they saw as England's corruption and over-worldliness, and sought a refuge for themselves and their families in a British-held wilderness. Their Methodist religion provided a vital support mechanism by drawing people together regularly for worship, and it was also an important link with their English past. Methodist fervour was sustained by a great many of the immigrants, but by far the most outstanding example was William Black, who arrived in the *Jenny* in 1775 as a boy of fourteen with the rest of his family. Thirteen years later he had become the spiritual leader of the entire Nova Scotia Methodist community and thereafter became one of the most important Methodist leaders in North America.[82]

Having completed his tour, John Robinson concluded that he would have a far better life in Nova Scotia than in England, and so returned to Yorkshire to bring back his family: "A large sum of money would not induce me to stay any longer[in England]."[83] A new world with no masters

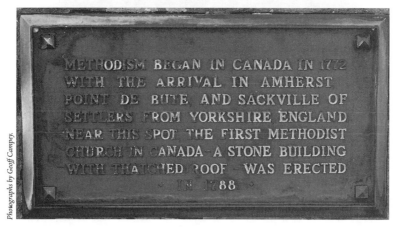

Plaques at Pointe de Bute Cemetery, New Brunswick, commemorating the Reverend William Black, pioneer Methodist preacher, and the introduction by him of Methodism in Canada.

and servants had opened up, and soon the paucity of a population, which had held back the province's development, would find a solution. Oddly enough, the outcome of the American War of Independence, which began in 1775 and ended in 1783, worked to its advantage. Having lost the war, the British government relocated large numbers of Loyalists, many of whom were English or of English descent, from the United States to Nova Scotia, thus beginning a new chapter in the province's development.

CHAPTER 3

The Loyalists Who Followed

You will expect to hear how it fared with me and the rest of the English in the time of the siege.[1]

NATHANIEL SMITH AND the other Yorkshire people living near Fort Cumberland were suffering more than most during the American War of Independence (1775–83), having been subjected to regular attacks by American privateers (legalized pirates) and to an actual siege by a small group of rebels. Understandably, as their houses and barns came under attack, many left the area, including the families of Nathaniel and John Smith who moved to Cornwallis (Kings County) and Newport (near Windsor) respectively, and Christopher Harper and family who relocated just a short distance to Sackville.[2]

Faced with marauding privateers and a population dominated by New Englanders, whose loyalty to Britain was questionable, Governor Legge tried to take preventive action. Although the risk of an all-out invasion by an American army seemed slight, Legge felt that the Atlantic region required a localized defence capability. So, shortly after the outbreak of the American Revolution in 1775, he called for a provincial militia and a tax to support it, but such was the outcry from local inhabitants that the legislation had to be dropped. Two hundred and forty-six people in Cumberland County, a group that included fifty-five Yorkshiremen, signed a petition stating that they did not wish to enlist for military service. Having just arrived a year or so earlier, the Yorkshire settlers said they needed to establish their farms. They stated that the raising of a militia would deplete the area of its men and compound an already serious labour shortage, thus jeopardizing their livelihoods. When a regiment of British soldiers arrived at Halifax, the need for a homegrown militia subsided, but the continuing discontent of American sympathizers ensured that turmoil would persist.

In the summer of the following year, a small band of rebels formed under Jonathan Eddy, a long-term resident of the Chignecto Isthmus. Having failed to persuade George Washington, the American commander-in-chief, to mount an invasion of Nova Scotia, he recruited a private army himself, finding his men chiefly from Machias (now in Maine) and Maugerville (now in New Brunswick).[3] In all, Eddy gathered around 180 men, only a minority of whom were residents of the Cumberland area. His group made their way toward the British outpost at Fort Cumberland in November, where, joined by a few local residents, they mounted an attack. But the siege was quickly suppressed by British reinforcements who had rushed to the fort. Two hundred marines and Royal Fencible Americans swiftly overcame Eddy's men and then scoured the countryside in search of rebels, torching the houses and barns of anyone whose loyalties were felt to be suspect.[4] Some rebels escaped behind American lines, leaving behind wives and families to be abused and sworn at until they could be exchanged for Loyalist prisoners three years later.[5]

Hit-and-run attacks by American privateers were widespread in the Atlantic region from 1776 to 1782. Defenceless coastal communities were plundered and vessels at sea had their provisions and valuables looted. Guerrilla raids brought commerce to a halt and caused severe food shortages, especially in Newfoundland and the Island of St. John (Prince Edward Island). Back in England, the Poole merchant Benjamin Lester learned through his Newfoundland agent that cargoes of seal skins and seal oil were ready to be loaded in his vessels anchored at Trinity

Photograph by Geoff Campey.

Plaque at Fort Beauséjour, erected in 1927. Built by the French in 1751, the fort was captured by the British in 1755 and renamed Fort Cumberland. The plaque commemorates the loyalty of the Yorkshire people who supported the British side.

Bay but that privateers were lurking. They had already seized the ship of someone known to him and boarded two of his other ships. Fleeing with a salt cargo and much of the ships' rigging and guns and ammunition, the privateers gave Lester one crumb of comfort in that "they did not injure the ships."[6]

In these troubled times an evangelist by the name of Henry Alline emerged and made his mark in the region. Of New England extraction, he had come to Falmouth, Nova Scotia, as a child with his family during the Planter migration of the 1760s. Having been weighed down for many years by "a load of guilt and darkness, praying and crying continually for mercy,"[7] Alline suddenly found himself, at the age of twenty-six, being called by God. He would go on to lead a popular religious revival known as the "Great Awakening" of Nova Scotia. Its beginnings can be traced back to March 26, 1775, a day when Alline, having read the 38th Psalm in the Bible, felt as if "redeeming love broke into my soul … with such power, that my whole soul seemed to be melted down with love."[8] After a year of intense agonizing he decided to go forth and preach about God's redeeming love. He confined his preaching circuit to the Annapolis Valley until after 1779, when he gradually extended his reach to Nova Scotia's south shore, the Island of St. John, and parts of the territory that would become New Brunswick. He attracted large crowds and usually preached outdoors, since most church buildings were closed to him.

Alline's rejection of tradition and embracing of an individual's inner feelings made him particularly appealing to New World settlers. He spoke of a loving God before whom all people were equal. It was essentially an egalitarian message that transcended the harshness and tribulations of everyday life. And his conviction that all people were capable of salvation in the next world brought enormous comfort to countless people who were caught up in the chaos and economic uncertainty of the war years. Organizing two churches in the Minas Basin region, one in Annapolis County and others in Liverpool and Maugerville — all areas where traditional churches were weak or absent — he roused nonconformist Nova Scotia to its core. But the so-called "New-Light" churches that he founded in Nova Scotia and New Brunswick did not remain true to his teachings, reverting, after his death in 1784, to Baptist churches that adopted more sober and conservative ways.[9]

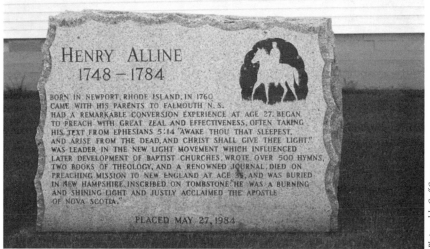

Memorial stone to Henry Alline, United Baptist Church, Falmouth.

Following Britain's defeat in the American Revolutionary War, officially recognized by the Treaty of Paris in 1783, around forty thousand people who had taken the British side (known collectively as Loyalists) fled from what became the independent country of the United States and sought sanctuary in the British-held northern colonies. The Loyalist influx had an explosive impact on the Atlantic region's population.

Receiving land grants and financial help under the British Loyalist Assistance program, about thirty-five thousand refugees moved to Nova

Scotia, while another five thousand went to the old province of Quebec.[10] When New Brunswick was divided from the peninsula as a separate colony in 1784, around fifteen thousand Loyalists would find themselves in it, and around nineteen thousand would be in Nova Scotia. Taken together, these Loyalists doubled the population of peninsular Nova Scotia and swelled the population count to the north of the Bay of Fundy by fivefold.[11] Only about six hundred Loyalists were allocated land in Prince Edward Island, but, because of great difficulty in obtaining grants, many left.[12] This was the case despite attempts by the island's proprietors and government to attract Loyalists. It was a similar situation in Cape Breton, created as a separate colony in 1785. Having acquired about four hundred Loyalists initially, it probably only had around two hundred by 1786.

About half of the thirty-five thousand Loyalists who came to the Maritime region were civilian refugees. The other half were disbanded British soldiers and provincial soldiers[13] who had served in regiments raised in North America, including the New Jersey Volunteers, King's American Regiment, Queen's Rangers, Loyal American Regiment, Royal North Carolina Regiment, King's Carolina Rangers, and the Loyal Nova Scotia Volunteers. Men from the provincial corps were known as the "Provincials" to distinguish them from civilian refugees, although the difference was not always clear since many civilians had also served during the war, in regiments.[14] Most civilians went to Nova Scotia while the Provincials were mainly sent to New Brunswick. In addition to being provided with free land, Loyalists could also claim provisions and other help from the government. Former soldiers were granted land according to their rank, with the usual amount ranging from one thousand acres for officers to one hundred acres for privates. Civilians normally received one hundred acres for each head of family and fifty additional acres for every person belonging to the family.

The origins of those who made their way to Nova Scotia and New Brunswick were roughly similar, with the majority coming from New York and New Jersey. Just over 60 percent of New Brunswick Loyalists originated from these two colonies, but they represented only a slim majority in Nova Scotia. New Brunswick had a higher proportion of Loyalists from Connecticut (13 percent), but Nova Scotia had more southerners (about 25 percent), who came principally from North and South Carolina.[15] A full 10 percent of Nova Scotia Loyalists were Blacks who fared badly in spite of the varied skills that they brought with them.[16]

Loyalists began to pour into the Maritimes throughout the summer and fall of 1783, but their first year was marked by hardship and uncertainty. As winter approached, many lacked proper shelters and, because of difficulties in transporting provisions to them, they suffered severe food shortages. Civilian refugees in Halifax were said to be living in deplorable conditions, while, according to the Anglican clergyman Jacob Bailey, there were 1,500 distressed people in the Annapolis Valley who were "fatigued with a long stormy passage, sickly and destitute of shelter from the advances of winter. Several hundred are starved in our Church and larger numbers are still unprovided for."[17]

Men from the 38th and 40th Regiments were accommodated in huts during their first winter, the Duke of Cumberland's Regiment in tents in the woods outside Halifax, while men from the 60th Regiment were accommodated in a ship off Falmouth until severe weather forced them to come ashore.[18] They were all British regulars who had been disbanded in the province, and were entitled to the same land and provisions as exiled Americans.

Loyalists were widely dispersed in the southwestern peninsula of Nova Scotia,[19] but in New Brunswick they were mainly concentrated along the St. John River valley and its tributaries (see Map 4).[20] By 1785, Halifax, Nova Scotia's capital, had acquired about 1,200 Loyalists. Another two thousand were settled in the Annapolis Valley, especially in Annapolis, Clements, Granville, Wilmot, and Aylesford, and another thousand were scattered about the fertile Minas Basin, especially at Parrsboro in Kings County (now Cumberland County). Around 1,300 went to Digby, while Shelburne (formerly Port Roseway) suddenly gained ten thousand Loyalists, making it the fourth largest town in North America, after Philadelphia, New York, and Boston. There were further Loyalist population clusters to the southeast of Truro in Hants County[21] and on the east side of the province, especially at Pictou,[22] Merigomish, Guysborough (formerly New Manchester) on Chedabucto Bay, and Country Harbour. Men from the Duke of Cumberland's Regiment

Courtesy of Library and Archives Canada, Acc. No. 1937-427.

Uniform of the 60th Regiment of Foot Guards, 1756–95, watercolour by Frederick M. Milner (1889–1939).

settled at Guysborough, while men from the disbanded South Carolina Regiment, King's Carolina Rangers, and North Carolina Volunteers were allocated land at Country Harbour, but a good many drifted away from the area.[23] After the American war ended, the Antigonish area acquired disbanded soldiers from the Nova Scotia Volunteers,[24] who founded a settlement at Town Point (renamed Dorchester) and gradually moved upriver to the present site of Antigonish.[25]

Most of the Loyalists who settled in New Brunswick were directed to the fertile land to be found along the St. John River valley. Military Loyalists were allocated land above Fredericton, and some along the Nashwaak River,[26] while civilians were sent mainly to the lower St. John.[27] However, this separation was never fully realized, since many

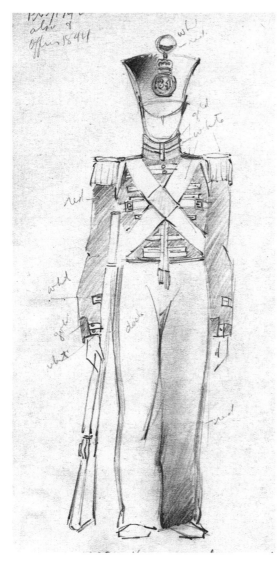

The uniform of the Cumberland Regiment of Foot (34th) in 1844. Detail is taken from a pencil drawing by Lloyd Scott (1911–68).

Courtesy of Library and Archives Canada, Acc. No. 1973-8-814. From Miss Lulu Dodds, Lakeview Manor, Beaverton, Ontario, through Munroe Scott, Manotick, Ontario. Reproduced by permission of Munroe Scott, Peterborough, Ontario.

ex-soldiers rejected their allocations and moved downriver to join the civilian refugees in the lower St. John Valley.[28] Meanwhile, another large group of displaced Loyalists from the Penobscot region of Maine[29] settled mainly in St. Andrews and along the St. Croix River (Charlotte County) in the Passamaquoddy Bay area, at the southwestern corner of New Brunswick.[30] They were joined by men from the Argyll Highlanders (74th), who were given lots on both sides of the Digdeguash River, and the Royal Fencible Americans, who were allocated land in the parish of St. George on Passamaquoddy Bay.[31]

With its excellent harbour at the mouth of the St. John River and an extensive fertile valley as its hinterland, it was inevitable that the future city of Saint John would experience a rapid rise in its fortunes. The neighbouring towns of Parr and Carleton were incorporated as the City of Saint John in 1785, and three years later the city was said to have "near 2,000 houses." According to Edward Winslow, a prominent Loyalist leader, it was "one of the best cities in the New World."[32] And unlike Shelburne, which quickly went into a downward spiral, Saint John prospered and became the largest urban centre in New Brunswick.[33]

Shelburne's rapid demise seems difficult to comprehend. Jacob Bailey thought its harbour in 1786 was "not being exceeded by any one in America," having three thousand houses and thirteen thousand people. He observed the "greatly improved lands" and the "great number

Photograph by Geoff Campey.

Memorial Stone to the United Empire Loyalists at the gate of the Old Burial Ground in St. Anne's (later Fredericton). Being the highest point on the St. John River that was navigable for large vessels, Fredericton was chosen as the capital of the province in 1785. It was named after Prince Frederick, the third son of King George III.

of shipping belonging to the merchants, nearly equalling that of Halifax ... several of which are employed in the whale fishery, a still greater number in the West Indies and the rest in the cod fishery along the banks."[34] Sawmills had been erected and large quantities of cut timber were being exported to the West Indies. Shelburne appeared to be on its way to becoming a major commercial centre, and yet 120 men and their families took one look at the place and left for Prince Edward Island soon after their arrival. Claiming that they had been enticed by offers of good land on the island by an agent of Governor Patterson, they relocated themselves in the summer of 1784. After much delay in securing their grants, they settled at Bedeque Harbour.[35] But why did they leave Shelburne?

It seems that Shelburne had acquired the wrong balance of people. They were mainly New Yorkers, too many of whom were carpenters, tailors, and other types of craftsmen, and too few were farm workers and fishermen. People suited to a city life lacked the hardiness and practical skills needed to tame a wilderness. Moreover, Shelburne's land was not particularly good: possibly the 120 families who left for Prince Edward Island in search of greener pastures were its potential farming community.

As a result Shelburne was short of people to clear its hinterland and create the farms that were necessary to support the town's economy. It had acquired a few merchants, but they were self-focused men who neglected to organize the town's overall economic framework. Also, those farmers it did have were naively optimistic about the future and built fine houses before securing the income stream that would pay for them.[36]

Lord Selkirk noticed how Loyalists in Prince Edward Island were inclined to fall into debt. John Laird, who settled at Lot 50 along the Vernon River, was typical. "He could not deny himself luxuries" and thus bought expensive goods on credit. It took him six to seven years before he paid off his debts, "and in that time he built a comfortable house, acquired cattle and sheep and cleared about 50 acres."[37] However, Shelburne Loyalists could not take such a long-term view. They had to limit their losses and leave. Money had been squandered on grandiose, ill-conceived schemes and too little had been invested in providing a workforce that could catch fish, build ships, grow crops, and cut timber.

Shelburne's isolated location on the Atlantic side of the peninsula was another disadvantage. It was eclipsed by the rapid growth of Saint John and was only a minor player in the timber trade, since the industry's prime focus was much farther to the east along the Northumberland Strait. Although Shelburne had been well placed to take advantage of the lucrative West Indies trade, it was badly hurt economically by American traders who flouted the Navigation Acts that were intended to exclude them. The mushrooming growth in timber exports to Britain, which occurred from 1815, would benefit Pictou, Charlottetown, and later the Miramichi, but it would completely bypass Shelburne. Lieutenant Colin Campbell of the Argyll Highlanders Regiment (74th) wanted to live in a town but rejected Shelburne on hearing "some unfavourable accounts" about it, settling instead in nearby St. Andrews, which he was told "has a good harbour and is well situated for the fishing and lumbering business."[38] Campbell made up his mind about Shelburne by August 1783 — only months after it had been opened up to settlers. Many more Loyalists would have done the same.

With the ending of provisions and portable pensions in 1787, Shelburne emptied quickly. It had fewer than three thousand inhabitants by the following year. To add to its economic woes it suffered from severe droughts and fires, a smallpox epidemic, and its black Loyalists, the principal source of cheap labour, were leaving for Sierra Leone.[39]

When the Reverend Munro visited in 1795 he found that Shelburne had only 150 families and that there were fewer that two thousand people in the vicinity. By the time the Methodist minister, William Black, visited in 1804, its population had shrunk to one-tenth of its original size.[40] The Reverend W. Bennett, an Anglican missionary appointed by the Society for the Propagation of the Gospel to Liverpool (Nova Scotia), observed its "small settlements along the sea coast ... many of the houses much demolished and without inhabitants, having been under a necessity of removing through the poverty of the Country." It had "a neat English Church and a small Baptist Meeting House" and a dwelling house used by Methodists for their services. "The society of Whites and Blacks" numbered between fifty and sixty, living in circumstances that "in general are low," with "most of their living" being derived from fishing.[41]

Joshua Marsden, a Methodist preacher, found Shelburne "almost deserted" in 1815, a description confirmed by the Reverend Gavin Lang, a Presbyterian missionary, when he saw it nearly fifteen years later:

> The harbour of Shelburne is well known in America as being one of the most beautiful and secure…. When viewed in the distance Shelburne looks somewhat considerable, but alas, on closer inspection, desolation and decay manifest themselves all around. Shelburne has fallen, I am afraid, never more to rise, for the few who remain neither possess wealth nor influence, and are in our mind strongly contrasted with the active and highly polished sons of Caledonia.[42]

Loyalists drawing lots for their lands in 1784, watercolour by C.W. Jefferys.

Courtesy of Government of Ontario Art Collection, Archives of Ontario, Toronto.

The fortunate Sons of Caledonia had settled on the east side of the province, which by this time was benefiting from the growing timber trade with Britain. Like Shelburne, Digby was almost entirely Loyalist, although smaller in size. And, like Shelburne, it had a naturally good harbour but had mediocre land, and it, too, ended up in a spiral of economic decline. Its badly organized and demoralized settlers suffered terribly from the confusion and delay they experienced over their land allocations. The Connecticut-born Amos Botsford, agent for the New York Refugee Association, had the task of organizing their grants, but he was an autocratic and divisive character who left in 1784, having made a bad situation considerably worse.[43] With the delayed arrival of provisions in the following year, tempers frayed, and the disturbances that broke out had to be quelled by troops sent from Halifax. It would take some fifteen years before the settlers finally resolved their land ownership rights.[44]

Despite this turmoil, Digby had impressed Jacob Bailey when he visited in 1786. It was "a very handsome town ... the situation of it is [an] exceedingly well chosen site both for the fisheries and every other trade adopted to the Province." With the arrival of Loyalists the town grew sixfold to a population of 2,500 and "the country about it [was] clearing fast of the woods.[45] Some three hundred families were to be accommodated around St. Mary's Bay and the Sissibou River, but more than one-third never reached their lands, and by 1795 only sixty-eight families remained.[46] By 1802 a consortium had been formed to market Digby properties to the outside world.[47] Digby's Loyalist residents were selling up and moving on:

> [A]s it is probable that the peace which has lately taken place, may occasion many military and other transient persons to look for settlements in these provinces and some such may incline towards Digby ... several gentlemen of that place [Digby] have associated for the purpose of removing ... such difficulties as are most likely to oppose themselves to new settlers ... they have selected and secured a number of commodious house lots ... a proportion of these adjoining the water are

adapted to trading persons — others are calculated
for mechanics — and a few more for such as are only
concerned in having an agreeable spot for a house, and
room for a garden. The first applicant will have the first
choice, and so on with other applicants in succession,
until the whole are sold at the prices fixed.[48]

The Loyalists who streamed into the Maritimes created an instant
population, but their relocation was far from straightforward. They had
come as refugees and occupied land, principally in the Bay of Fundy
region to satisfy the British government's defence concerns, this being
an area of prime military importance. However, although ex-soldiers
could act as guardians of territory and take up arms quickly if need
be, their training and experience did not necessarily prepare them for
the rigours of pioneer life. Also, a location chosen for its military value
did not always provide top-quality land. Beyond this was the seething
discontent felt over the government's failure to administer land grants
satisfactorily. The problem was compounded in Nova Scotia by the
fact that most of the best agricultural land had already been granted
to New Englanders. Another problem was the shortage of women. A
substantial number of Loyalists were young, single men who had served
in the disbanded Loyalist regiments or as regulars in the British Army.
Men from the Duke of Cumberland's regiment went as far as asking the
government for help in getting wives, as there were few eligible women
in the district in which they lived. There were only ten married women
in the regiment. Solving this severe gender imbalance was a pressing
concern in many parts of the Maritimes.[49]

Loyalist grievances and complaints fed a festering resentment
toward Britain and growing dissatisfaction over land allocations.[50]
These factors, plus an ongoing desire for a better situation, stimulated
a constant movement of Loyalists both within and from the Maritime
provinces. In fact, the most remarkable feature about the Loyalist influx
was the speed and extent of the exodus that followed it.[51] Within a year
of their arrival, even while provisions were being supplied, nearly two
thousand Loyalists are believed to have left Nova Scotia, almost half from

Shelburne, although other districts, like Antigonish and Pictou in the eastern side of the province, actually saw their populations grow.[52]

These were defeated and demoralized refugees who had come down in the world with a jolt. Some, having left relative comfort back in the United States, faced the daunting and strenuous task of hacking out a farm from the wilderness. They were more fortunate than most settlers in being entitled to free land, food, and clothing allowances, as well as farming and building supplies. Yet, this, too, had its downside. Resentful and antagonistic neighbours, jealous of their provisioning and other advantages, often made their lives a misery. Greatly disillusioned, thousands of Loyalists simply gave up. Some went to other areas of the Maritimes or other parts of British America, a few returned to Britain, but most of those who left went back to the United States, where they normally received a cordial welcome.[53]

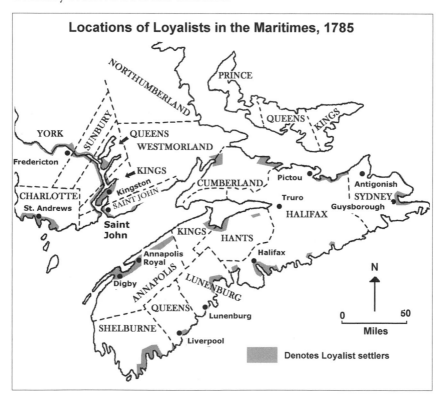

Map 4. Based on Wynne, "A Region of Scattered Settlements," 322.

However, despite early disappointments and setbacks, many Loyalists remained and benefited from the region's improving economic growth. In due course, the 1871 census would go on to reveal a striking predominance of people of English ancestry in the Loyalist strongholds of the Bay of Fundy region. The English were concentrated in western Nova Scotia, the St. John River valley, and Charlotte County in New Brunswick, mirroring exactly the principal areas chosen to accommodate Loyalists (see Map 4). Although their number cannot be quantified, it appears that the English represented a high proportion of the Loyalist intake in these areas. However, while many had English roots, most Loyalists had been born in the United States. The Chignecto Isthmus also acquired large English concentrations, but this stemmed from the large intake of Yorkshire immigrants just before the outbreak of the American Rebellion.

The Society for the Propagation of the Gospel was always anxious to send Anglican missionaries to areas of the New World where Church of England congregations might be formed. In fact, Anglican churches had been built in Nova Scotia long before the Loyalist influx reached Nova Scotia. St. Paul's Church had been founded in Halifax in 1749, while churches at Lunenburg, Annapolis, and Windsor followed soon after. Lunenburg is particularly interesting since its congregation was composed of former Lutherans, who were indisputably German. Yet Lunenburg County became strongly Anglican, its German population having adopted the Church of England from the time of their arrival in the town of Lunenburg in the early 1750s.[54]

Thus, support for the Church of England in itself is not a reliable indicator of the predominance of English settlers. In fact, the Church of England was fairly accommodating in accepting non-Anglicans, being driven strongly by the desire to exert its influence within communities generally. Oozing respectability and conservative values, Anglican missionaries sought to dissuade people from supporting the emotional evangelism that was sweeping the area, but they were no match for the charismatic preachers who spoke the language of ordinary people.

The Anglican bishop Charles Inglis, who arrived in Halifax in 1787 as the first North American bishop of the Church of England, hoped that loyalty to Britain would translate into support for Anglicanism, but he was sadly disappointed. He soon discovered that there were more non-Anglicans than Anglicans among the Loyalists. He also discovered even less support for Anglicanism amongst the pre-Loyalist communities. There was a small but powerful Anglican presence in Halifax, but beyond this, Nova Scotians had shown only patchy support for the Anglican faith. Over 60 percent of its population was made up of New England Congregationalists who later joined Baptist churches. Apart from the Chignecto Isthmus, where Methodism prevailed, there was little church presence anywhere in New Brunswick before 1784. Consequently, while the Church of England was an important denomination, it did not attract sufficient support from Loyalist immigrants to achieve numerical superiority throughout the region.[55]

Undaunted, the Church of England persisted in its efforts to promote the Anglican religion in Loyalist areas. Principally through funding received in the form of government grants, new churches suddenly sprouted in 1783 at Cornwallis, Horton (Wolfville), and Parrsboro in Kings County, Digby, and Shelburne. Shortly after, the town of Halifax, Cumberland County, Sydney in Cape Breton,[56] and the town of Guysborough acquired their Anglican churches[57] (see Map 4). New Brunswick's Loyalist churches were slightly later. Maugerville's church appeared in 1784, and it was followed soon after by churches at Fredericton, Saint John, St. Andrews, and Kingston.[58] However, according to the Reverend Samuel Cooke, the Anglican missionary who visited St. Andrews in 1785, there were a good many Scottish Loyalists among the St. Andrews congregation. "The majority of settlers profess themselves to be Kirk of Scotland,"[59] but in spite of this, fully accepted his ministry.

Loyalists identified principally with the colony in the United States from which they had come rather than the part of England from which they or their forbears may have originated. As a result English Loyalists did not, as a rule, attract followers from England. In any case, most of the British immigration to Atlantic Canada that occurred immediately after the Revolution was dominated by Scots who mainly settled in eastern Nova Scotia, Cape Breton, and Prince Edward Island. With the end of the Napoleonic Wars in 1815, when emigration soared ahead, the English and Irish gradually overtook the Scots numerically, settling in all three

Maritime provinces, although Prince Edward Island and New Brunswick attracted most of the English during the first half of the nineteenth century.

Around 150 English immigrants arrived in Nova Scotia in 1784, but they were Loyalists who, having returned to England the year before and not finding it to their liking, sought a better situation. They were immediately followed by English merchants and fortune seekers, and later by convicts who arrived in a ship from Liverpool. Needless to say, the governor of Nova Scotia put a stop to any further shipments of English convicts![60] Relatively few English followed them. Skilled miners came from England to work in Nova Scotia's coal mines but most of the growth in its English population was generated by its existing communities. Yet, in a sense Nova Scotia already was English. With its large Planter and Loyalist intake, Nova Scotia had a majority of native Americans with mainly English roots, some traceable over several generations.

British settlement in Nova Scotia was driven far more by power politics and war than by the province's farming or timber trade potential. The struggles between Britain and France determined that colonization proceeded initially along its militarily strategic coastal areas. People of English descent were in the vanguard of this population movement as it gathered strength in the middle of the eighteenth century.

CHAPTER 4

Nova Scotia's English Settlers: Two Types of English

There is a continual passing and returning of people from the western shore of this province [Nova Scotia] to New England, from whence these people originally emigrated and still have property and family connections, — but I think the balance of population retained, is in favour of this province.[1]

LIEUTENANT GOVERNOR JOHN Wentworth was relieved to note that the Nova Scotia of 1806 still retained a sizable portion of the New England population that had been acquired forty-five years earlier when around eight thousand Planters came to the province. As the descendents of English immigrants who had settled in New England, they were Americans of English ancestry, although in most cases their Englishness was very distant.

When two Yorkshire farmers, John Robinson and Thomas Rispin, first met Nova Scotia's New Englanders they deplored their farming methods: "Nothing can be said in favour of the inhabitants as to their management in farming. They neither discover judgment or industry."

To Robinson and Rispin they were "lazy, indolent people."[2] There was no sense of a shared English kinship here! This is hardly surprising since, although they spoke the same language, the New England and Yorkshire settlers had little in common. They had different backgrounds, values, religions, mannerisms, work ethics, and traditions. Although they and their descendents would both use the label of "English" to describe their ethnic origins, they were effectively two types of English. Those like Robinson and Rispin who came to the province directly from Yorkshire and other parts of England were recent English, while those who came in the large-scale migrations from the United States were Americans with distant English roots.

Immigrants began arriving directly from England, from the mid-eighteenth century, but their number was dwarfed by the large influx from Scotland that followed. The ongoing wars between Britain and France from the 1790s to 1815 had been obvious disincentives to emigration, although a significant number left the Highlands and Islands of Scotland for various parts of British North America during this time, despite the obvious risks.[3] The economic depression that followed the end of the Napoleonic Wars in 1815 stimulated a great rise in emigration from Britain, but, because of gaps and ambiguities in shipping and customs records, it is impossible to state precisely how many British people permanently established themselves in Nova Scotia.[4] The recorded data reveals that at least 39,243 British immigrants arrived between 1815 and 1838, of whom only 2,120 (5 percent) were English, the majority being either Scottish or Irish in origin.[5] However, the actual number of British arrivals may have been a great deal higher.[6]

Customs records show that nine hundred English immigrants arrived at Halifax between 1817 and 1819, although few ship crossings were recorded for this period.[7] The surviving shipping data reveals that the majority embarked from Plymouth in Devon, indicating that southwest England supplied a goodly share of the immigrants (see Appendix II). A total of ninety-four people arrived from the Cumberland ports of Workington and Whitehaven in 1819 and 1822 respectively, but no further emigrant departures were recorded in later years from either port.[8] There were regular passenger arrivals from Liverpool between the mid-1820s and mid-1830s, and some from London and Jersey, but the numbers were generally small. Notable examples were the seventy-nine people who arrived at Pictou from Liverpool in the *Penelope* in 1828, the fifty people who arrived at Halifax from London in the *Minstrel* in 1831, the 102 from Liverpool who came in the *Mary Ann, Jean Hastie*, and *Lady Dunmore* in 1832, and the sixty-seven people who sailed from Jersey in 1833, 1834, and 1836.[9] But at this stage English immigrants were very much in a minority.

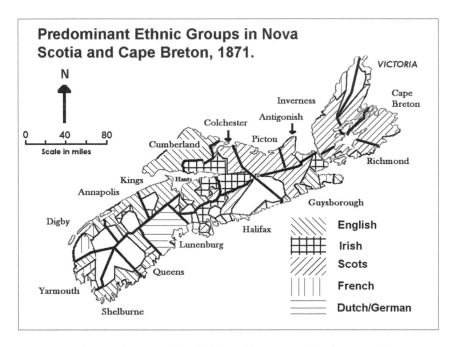

Map 5. Based on Andrew H. Clark, "Old World Origins and Religious Adherence in Nova Scotia," *Geographical Review*, Vol. 1 (1960), 320.

With the growing economic opportunities that stemmed from the province's mining industry the proportion of English immigrants rose between 1839 and 1851. Instead of being a poor third, the English moved into second place, representing 22 percent of the total, but once again they were a mere fraction of the Scots, who accounted for 61 percent of the influx.[10] By 1871 the English represented 29 percent of the population, just five percentage points below the Scots. And they were the dominant ethnic group in Kings, Annapolis, Yarmouth, Shelburne, and Queens counties on the west and Cumberland County on the east (see Map 5). With its large influx of settlers from Yorkshire during the eighteenth century, Cumberland's later classification as an English county was inevitable, but the dramatic improvement in the English ranking in the western counties has a different explanation. This was a mainly American population, with distant English roots, that later classified itself as English.

Looking back to the time when it first became a British possession, Nova Scotia looked set to become a very English colony. Having acquired Acadia (renamed Nova Scotia) from France in 1713, Britain launched a large-scale immigration program thirty-six years later, after establishing Halifax as the capital. The government took the unprecedented step of actually sanctioning public funds to finance the relocation costs of over 2,500 people: such was their desire to place British settlers in Halifax in order to counterbalance the French-speaking Acadian population. The immigrants, recruited in London, included ex-soldiers and sailors, some of whom were of Irish descent, and tradesmen who worked in wide-ranging occupations.[11] They were brought out by Governor Edward Cornwallis in 1749 to build the new capital, but the extremely tough conditions prompted many to leave.[12] Around 1,500 or so of the hardiest remained and founded the town, as was intended, but they were soon joined by large numbers of merchants and other settlers from New England who had correctly anticipated Halifax's potential as a future economic hub. Although there was much conflict between the immigrants from England and New England initially, both groups eventually came to live in harmony, as they shared common economic and political aspirations.

The Society for the Propagation of the Gospel had immediately sent an Anglican minister, together with funding to build St. Paul's Anglican Church, one of the first Protestant places of worship in British North America. A school and hospital were hastily constructed and a site was chosen for the marketplace. By 1765 the Reverend John Breyton could report that the "Church of England is in a flourishing state. St. Paul's is furnished in a most elegant manner and harmony prevails."[13] The

Photograph by Geoff Campey.

St. Paul's Church, Halifax, erected in 1750. Its architectural plans were based on the design of St. Peter's Church, Vere Street, in London, which was created by James Gibbs, a pupil of Sir Christopher Wren. With the arrival of Charles Inglis in 1787 as the first Anglican bishop of Nova Scotia, St. Paul's was made a cathedral and continued as such until 1865.

church's congregation of 1,300 symbolized the town's strong English presence, despite growing rivalry from the Congregationalists, of New England origin, who had also built their own church by this time.

Halifax attracted many Loyalists and, after the Napoleonic Wars ended, immigrants from Britain. Notable were the West Country arrivals who came in a short-lived influx from 1817 to 1819. Devon ancestry would be claimed later by a number of Halifax residents, including Francis Paulin, whose ancestors came from Jacobstone; Florence Edwards, whose father had been a carpenter in Barnstable; Thomas Maynard, who was descended from "a gentleman born at Tavistock"; and John Bond, whose father was born near Torquay.[14] When John MacGregor visited Halifax in 1828, he concluded that "the style of living, the hours of entertainment and the fashions are the same as in England as were their 'amusements' — such as picnics, amateur theatricals, riding, shooting and fishing."[15] But eleven years earlier Lord Dalhousie had thought that Halifax was still "in its infancy." He was shocked to find a town of around ten thousand people in which "there is not a bookseller's shop." He immediately authorized funds for a library at the military garrison, having previously "suggested to the officers the great comfort and advantages"[16] that might result from it.

Shortly after establishing Halifax's population in 1749, the British government had sought a second source of settlers.[17] Up to 2,700 so-called "Foreign Protestants," chiefly Germans, Swiss, and French Huguenots, were recruited from Europe between 1750 and 1752 and they, too, received a free passage, land, and a year's subsistence. However, because of difficulties in obtaining suitable sites, most remained in Halifax, but around 1,450 (mainly German immigrants) were moved to a location fifty miles west of Halifax, where they founded the town of Lunenburg. Despite an early riot sparked off by grievances over land allotments and later raids by Native people who were being encouraged by the French authorities at Louisburg to cause trouble, the settlers flourished.[18]

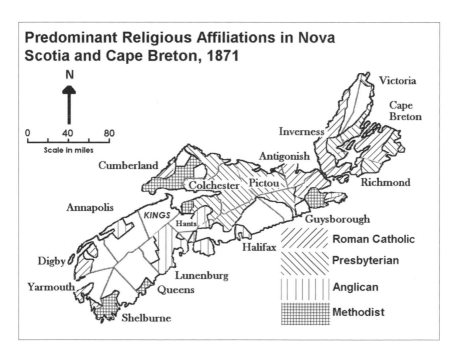

Map 6. Based on Clark, "Old World Origins and Religious Adherence," 327.

Since they immediately transferred their religious affiliation from Lutheranism to Anglicanism, the new Lunenburg arrivals gave the Church of England's mission in Nova Scotia a terrific boost (see Map 6). By 1845 the Anglican minister, sent by the Society for the Propagation of the Gospel to Lunenburg County, could take pride in the four Anglican churches, capable of holding 1,900 people, and ten outlying preaching stations.[19] When Lord Dalhousie visited in 1817, he noticed that people still spoke their native language: "All here is German, scarcely do they speak English intelligibly. Agriculture is their only pursuit, they are not wealthy, but live very frugally and are all comfortable … there never has yet been a pauper maintained by the parish." However, he was less approving of nearby Mahone Bay, with its "miserable farms, all in patches, raising potatoes and hay for the Halifax market."[20] Here, too, a committed Anglican minister would deal with the religious needs of its mainly German population, travelling to the various preaching stations which were sometimes twenty miles distant, including the one at Mahone Bay, to the north of Lunenburg town, and the one at New Dublin (now Dublin Shore), just south of it.[21]

Meanwhile, back in 1755, Britain's continuing hostilities with France were causing it to revise its military strategy in Nova Scotia. Acadians were now regarded as potential accomplices of the French, and the British solution to this threat was immediate and brutal. The entire Acadian population was deported in 1755, and a third group of land-hungry New Englanders was brought in to take their place.[22] The expulsion certainly undermined French power and fighting ability in the region, but the policy was exceedingly inhumane for the people who were displaced. Civilized behaviour was thrown aside, and this terrible, barbaric act would continue to haunt the British for many years.

Launching a generously funded emigration scheme, the government recruited eight thousand New Englanders who mainly originated from Massachusetts, Connecticut, and Rhode Island — areas where good agricultural land was in short supply. Arriving between 1759 and 1762, they came in large family groups and sometimes as entire communities, with farmers settling mainly on the former Acadian lands in the Annapolis Valley, and fishermen along the southwestern coastline.[23]

The province's fertile acreages also attracted the attention of high-ranking officials and politicians. After all, they had the easiest access to the choicest land. John Perceval (second Earl of Egmont), first Lord of the Admiralty and a prominent politician, helped himself to several thousand acres in Nova Scotia and East Florida. He hoped to establish a mansion house, park, and castle on his twenty-two-thousand-acre estate at Egmont Harbour, just east of Halifax, but his silly notions of creating a fiefdom in Nova Scotia bore little relevance to the needs of the province or its prospective settlers.[24]

Lord Dartmouth, secretary of state for the Colonies from 1772, grabbed forty thousand acres of land in the same area for himself, although he at least intended to find tenants to work his land:

> I daresay that your lordship is acquainted with the method practised by proprietors of great territories in the northern district of North America; they lay out their tracts in several hundred lots, ensure some of them are in a favourable place for themselves and then let every 3rd or 4th lot by lease to tenants at a certain rent per annum.[25]

Ten other prominent people, who included Halifax merchants, a former governor, and a naval commander, claimed tracts of land near to Lord Egmont's property in Nova Scotia, although few made any serious attempt to recruit settlers or provide funds for commercial development.

Being creatures of the New World, New Englanders refused to have anything to do with European-style leaseholds and insisted on having freeholds. While these aspirations were met, many were disappointed both with the quality of the land they received and the Nova Scotia government's unwillingness to tolerate a strong local democracy. They became dissatisfied and possibly half of the new arrivals left within a few years of the termination of subsidies. Few had brought much capital with them, and, as a consequence, new communities progressed very slowly. With the great Loyalist influx of the mid-1780s, thousands more Americans came to the province. Many had English ancestry and were drawn mainly from New York and New Jersey. But, unlike the Planters before them who simply took over Acadian farms, they often had the backbreaking task of clearing vast wildernesses, and, feeling dispirited, many left. Like the New Englanders, they, too, insisted on having freeholds.

Cornwallis and Horton (later Wolfville) acquired their settlers from Connecticut in 1760 and became two of the most populated townships in the Annapolis Valley[26] (see Map 7). Large numbers of Loyalists later came to the area, as did a few Yorkshire families who had previously settled in Cumberland County. Having been caught in the line of fire during the American Rebellion, men like Nathaniel Smith and his family had left

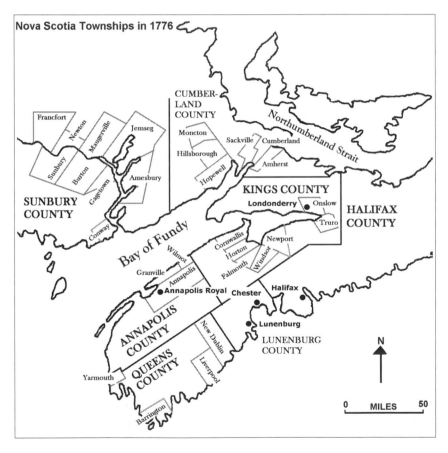

Map 7. Based on Margaret Conrad, *They Planted Well: New England Planters in Maritime Canada* (Fredericton, NB: Acadiensis Press, 1988), 8.

their farms in Fort Cumberland in 1778, hoping for better conditions in Cornwallis. Smith sold his property and stock, for which he obtained five hundred pounds, but he felt as if he had "[fallen] into the hands of worse plunderers than those that break [into] houses and rob shops."[27] In 1775 he had owned more than 1,500 acres of land in Cumberland, but four years later, after falling victim to the swindlers, he was only able to rent land in Cornwallis, and a small amount at that.

By Nathaniel's time the area was "pretty thickly settled in many places where there [are] rivers, marshes and intervales, and in many places along the shores by the Minas Basin and the Bay of Fundy."[28] The Cornwallis that Lord Dalhousie observed thirty years later had a small Anglican congregation, this being a region where Baptists were in the ascendancy, and the Established Church of England "was scarcely entitled to a name."[29] He was appalled by the people "living poorly or chiefly upon rum ... they are idle, insolent and quarrelsome. All in debt ... they are strongly tinctured with Yankee manners, ideas and principles — canting and preaching constantly, they have no thought of religion or morality. The state of agriculture is wretched." However, Lord Dartmouth had to admit that, however poor they were, they could each afford to have a "horse and gig or shay at the church service of the Established Church and that of the Anabaptists; we counted 70 of these buggies hung up to the rails or trees nearby."[30]

Meanwhile, his lordship found Parrsboro, on the opposite side of the Minas Basin, more to his liking. He greatly approved of James Ratchford, who had the entire township under his thumb: "Keeping a shop for every sort of supply the whole population is individually indebted to him. Selling his goods at enormous profit, he makes money of those that pay their accounts and, of those that do not, he takes mortgages on their lands, and takes that in payment."[31] Lord Dalhousie believed that ordinary people needed to be controlled by someone in authority, irrespective of how much they were exploited, placing him somewhat at odds with the egalitarian ideals of the New World!

The New Englanders, and Loyalists who poured into the rest of the Annapolis Valley, founded new communities at Annapolis, Granville, and Wilmot, townships with some of the finest land in the region[32]

Courtesy of Library and Archives Canada, C-005958.

George Ramsay, ninth
Earl of Dalhousie. He was
lieutenant governor of Nova
Scotia from 1816 to 1820,
and afterward governor
general of Canada until 1828.

(see Map 7). When he passed through Wilmot nearly six decades later, Lord Dalhousie was enraged by the defiant manner of the local people: "They stood and stared at us, as we passed, with the utmost American impudence." He greatly disapproved of their freehold grants, since it made every man think that he "is laird here" and "fostered a dangerous levelling mentality."[33] He was shocked to find that a member of the Assembly dressed like a common labourer in his own home. Where was his coat and waistcoat? But dress codes and social etiquette were not high on his host's list of priorities. As is apparent, Lord Dalhousie never came close to understanding the harsh realities of pioneer life.

Annapolis Royal had an unusually high proportion of Anglicans by 1871, as well as a substantial Methodist congregation, possibly signifying a stronger than average English presence. The first Anglican church had been founded in 1764 and nearly thirty years later a second church had been built at Wilmot. On a tour of the province in 1791, Bishop Charles Inglis had preached "in the new church, which was the first time that divine services had been performed in it."[34] Having previously enjoyed the blueberries at nearby Aylesford (later in Kings County)[35] Bishop Inglis was in high spirits, but his mood changed when he met the "infirm" local minister, who stumbled through prayers at the inaugural service:

> Hitherto Mr. Wiswell officiated in the School House or in a private home on the mountain … and to my very great surprise he had neither gown or surplice…. I told him I would have read the prayers myself rather than let him officiate without his clerical habit … his excuse was that he had but one gown and it was at Aylesford in St. Mary's Church.[36]

Meanwhile, the Methodists of Annapolis Royal had built themselves a chapel by 1894 capable of accommodating four hundred people, and

Photograph by Geoff Campey.

Holy Trinity Anglican Church at Middleton (previously Wilmot). It was established in 1789.

another at Granville that could house one hundred. This despite the fact that the congregations often went without a minister for up to six months at a time.[37]

New England fishermen and their families settled along the south shore at Yarmouth, Barrington, and Liverpool in the early 1760s (see Map 7), but with the arrival of around five hundred Loyalist families just over twenty years later, the instant town of Shelburne sprang up and the new county divisions of Yarmouth, Shelburne, and Queens suddenly appeared (see Map 5). Although Shelburne's growth had been dramatic, its demise was equally spectacular, as Lord Dalhousie observed thirty years later:

> Bringing with them very large property in money they [Loyalists] built fine houses, neglected the more immediate objects of new settlers, the clearing of land for food, or the establishment of fisheries, for which the situation of the settlement was admirably adapted, and having very soon wasted and squandered their funds were obliged to fly back to America leaving large grants of land untouched to this day, but laying still as the property of these individuals. Now, Shelburne is the picture of despair and wretchedness.... The large homes rotten and tumbling into the once fine and broad streets, the inhabitants crawling about idle and careworn in appearance and stuck in poverty and dejected in spirit.[38]

A Methodist missionary ruefully noted how "the population of the town has exceedingly decreased, so it does not contain one tenth of the inhabitants who settled in the year [17]83."[39] "The neat Methodist Chapel, capable of holding 400 people," was a very sad reminder of better times.[40] However, Yarmouth fared much better, having attracted Massachusetts settlers from 1761, Acadians six years later, and large numbers of Loyalists.[41] The Cheshire-born Loyalist Joseph Bond certainly did well here. Having first gone to Shelburne, he swiftly moved on to the town of Yarmouth, where he practised as a physician for twenty years. When he died, he left a homestead of sixty acres, various properties in Yarmouth, including a wharf, and three thousand acres of land.[42]

The New England advance continued into Falmouth and Newport in 1761, when Rhode Islanders founded communities there. And Windsor's first Anglican church materialized by 1764, soon after its New Englanders arrived.[43] Loyalists went on to found King's College at Windsor in 1789, the oldest degree-granting institution in the Atlantic region. An exclusively Anglican college, it was visited in 1801 by Bishop John Inglis, who welcomed the consignment of books that had just arrived: "It will be a respectable beginning for our library ... unquestionably it [the College] will be the best and most reputable seminary of learning in North America."[44] But when Lord Dalhousie came in 1817 the college had a leaky roof and only fourteen students. "The state of the building is ruinous; extremely exposed by its situation, every wind blows through it. The passage doors are torn off, the rooms of the students are open and neglected."[45] Given the appeal of the other dissenting religions in Hants County and in the region generally, the college had little chance of attracting sufficient pupils to be viable[46] (see Map 6). Lord Dalhousie pressed for it to be made non-denominational, which happened in 1829, and after that its future was secured.[47]

Liverpool, founded in 1760 as a fishing port, benefited from the piratical activities of its privateer ships during the American Revolution and the War of 1812, and went on to become a major seaport, second only to Halifax. But its rise was checked with the growth in the timber trade, which gave Pictou an unrivalled advantage. Methodism had become well-established in the town of Liverpool by 1804, although the minister struggled to cope financially, since the congregation was poor and he had not received his full allowance for several years.[48] Writing in 1818, a Methodist minister found the Liverpool inhabitants to be "in general very respectable and very friendly ... it is a Maritime town and their trade is chiefly in lumber and fish."[49] This assessment was corroborated by Lord Dartmouth:

> Liverpool is in all respects a most striking contrast to
> Shelburne. The houses large and clean and handsome,

many new ones building, the streets broad, gay and
bustling in work, the people wealthy and confessing
themselves to be so. Their concerns are mercantile and in
the Labrador fisheries. They do trade to the West Indies
but on a small scale; they were fortunate in privateering
speculations during the war with America and keenly
bent on that pursuit against the States.[50]

Anglicans established their first congregation by 1820, this being
the only part of Queens County where the Church of England attracted
significant support.

Immigration to the province had reduced to a trickle during the mid-
1760s but increased dramatically between 1772 and 1775, when around
nine hundred people from Yorkshire and nearby parts of northern

Holy Trinity Anglican
Church, Liverpool, built in
1821.

Photograph by Geoff Campey.

England took up residence on both sides of the isthmus connecting Nova Scotia with New Brunswick. A combination of high rent increases in Yorkshire and the desire to benefit from Nova Scotia's agricultural potential were the main driving forces, although many were Methodists seeking a safe haven in which to practise their faith. Having been enticed to the Chignecto Isthmus by the availability of rich marshland, they joined New Englanders who had already established themselves at Amherst, Cumberland, and Sackville[51] (see Map 7). The Yorkshire settlers effectively doubled the population of the isthmus and, by bringing their

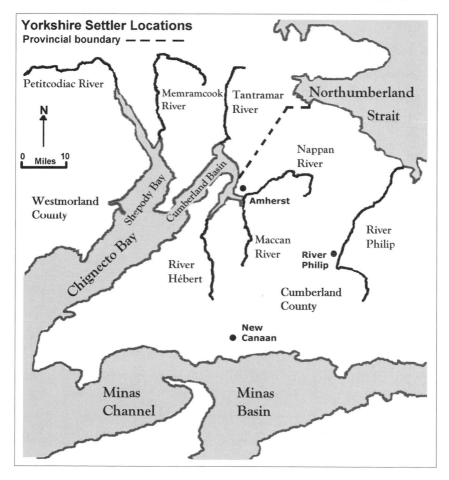

Map 8. Yorkshire Settler Locations in Cumberland County, Nova Scotia, and Westmorland County, New Brunswick.

advanced farming techniques with them, greatly enhanced the economic development of the area.[52]

When he visited Cumberland County in 1829, Thomas Haliburton observed the rivers "emptying into the Bay of Chignecto, upon which there are extensive tracts of alluvial land, and flourishing settlements. On the Maccan and Nappan rivers are to be found many substantial farmers, composed of Yorkshire men and their descendants." Many more were situated along the River Hébert, "up which the tide flows thirteen miles, enriching it with 1,800 acres of excellent marsh land."[53] Yorkshire settlers were also to be found along the River Philip, farther to the east (see Map 8). Eleven years earlier, when our roving reporter Lord Dalhousie had arrived on the scene, he described their farms in glowing terms: "The large fields, extensive crops and gardens about their houses show them strangers in this country and more industrious than others of their class."[54] He had seen their New Canaan settlement, established in 1798, indicating that further contingents of Yorkshire people had followed the initial groups of the early 1770s. Undoubtedly, the Yorkshire farmers were in a class of their own and, according to his lordship, were "more rich and comfortable" than people in the rest of the province.

However, success had come at a price. Having recently lost his father, John Harrision wrote to a cousin he had had not seen for thirty-six years, to try to reconnect with his long-lost Yorkshire past. He recalled how he and his family had first brought an untamed wilderness into cultivation:

> I settled here on this River [Maccan] about 23 years ago [1787] upon lands that had never been cultivated, all a wilderness. We cut down the wood of the land and burnt it off, and sowed it with wheat and rye, so that we made out a very good living. Here we make our own sugar, our own soap and candles and likewise our own clothing. We spin and weave our own linen and wool and make the biggest part of it into garments within our own family. This I suppose you will think strange but it is merely for want of settlers and more mechanics of different branches.[55]

But he was so very lonely: "Dear cousin, I could wish to see you once more to talk with you face to face." Having left as a fourteen-year-old, he hardly knew his cousin, but he inquired whether they could now begin to correspond "every year or at every opportunity." John was also deeply troubled by the shortage of people in the Maccan River area: "If there are any young men have any notion of coming to this country, of an industrious turn of mind, there is no doubt of making out very well for himself, for if he does not like this part he can soon earn money to carry him out again for wages are very high here." Also, his two grown-up sons each needed "a good industrious wife." Likewise, thinking beyond his needs, he wrote, "Pray send out a shipload of young women, for there is great call for them that can card and spin. The wages is from five to six shillings a week." Like his brother Luke, who "oftimes visits Rillington"[56] in his dreams, John would never forget his Yorkshire origins.

The naming of New Canaan, with its biblical connotations, suggested a people who hoped to find their "promised land" in Nova Scotia. Having strong Christian beliefs, they had been drawn specifically to Methodism because it "was of that strenuous type which must give expression to its faith in hearty song and lively preaching."[57] Even during the *Jenny*'s sea crossing in 1775, the eighty passengers were called by the captain "to come to his cabin, morning and evening" to pray together.[58] Many of the Yorkshire families who came to Nova Scotia had been influenced by John Wesley's teachings and sought to live according to the Christian disciplines that he had enunciated. Their great spiritual leader, William Black, only a boy of fourteen when he emigrated in 1775, would devote his life to the Methodist cause.

Like Henry Alline, who was twelve years older, Black had suffered from a sense of profound guilt over his perceived wickedness. But he experienced a dramatic conversion one day in 1779 "when his guilt was removed" and "a sweet peace and gladness were diffused" through his soul.[59] Feeling himself to be saved, the nineteen-year-old Black went on to become a preacher, concentrating initially on the Yorkshire settlers on the isthmus. Embarking on a single-minded mission "to save souls," he travelled far and wide, bringing the message of redemption to many hundreds of people across Atlantic Canada. Known affectionately as

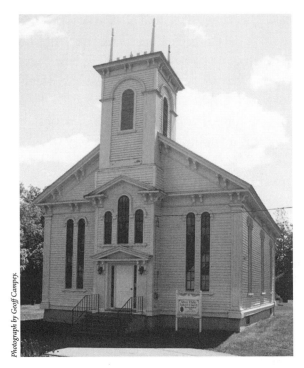

Photograph by Geoff Campey.

United Church, River Philip (Cumberland County), built in 1862. It replaced the original log-built Methodist meeting place that had been constructed in 1827.

Courtesy of Library and Archives Canada, e010764804.

The Reverend William Black, Methodist minister.

Bishop Black, he was often referred to, long before his death in 1834, as the father of Methodism in Nova Scotia and New Brunswick.[60]

Although he was more anxious to save souls than build organizations, Black secured the appointment of further preachers, thus establishing Methodism firmly in many parts of the province. With the help of the British Methodist Missionary Society[61] a structure was in place by 1804 that had Black based in Halifax but taking charge of Liverpool and Shelburne, William Bennett taking services in Cumberland from his base in Annapolis, John Mann presiding over Horton (where he lived), and his brother John doing the same at Windsor.[62] By 1817 there were sufficient Methodists in Ramsheg (near Wallace) in Cumberland County to attract a minister there, where a congregation of 120, spread over an area of around fifty miles, would have been an enormous challenge.[63] By 1871 Cumberland County was almost entirely Methodist, having the largest concentration in the province[64] (see Map 6). Meanwhile, the Church of England commanded some support at Amherst, which had its first Anglican church built by 1822.[65]

With the opening up of Guysborough on the east side of the province to Loyalists, the county acquired an instant population in the mid-1780s, but its settlers struggled to survive. Lord Dalhousie found "utmost poverty in every hut" when he visited in 1817. The people subsisted as best they could "by fishing and their small potato gardens."[66] An Anglican church had been built as early as 1787, and by 1845 the county had five other churches and ten outlying preaching stations. One of the stations was at Marie Joseph, where that year "a body of 50 men marched joyfully into the woods to procure materials" for a chapel, and "a singular harmony of religious sentiment appears to prevail."[67] Methodism also enjoyed support in and around Guysborough itself, with the first mission having been established in 1838 (see Map 6).

Lord Dalhousie's tour of the province occurred just as British immigrants were streaming into the Maritimes. With the growing timber trade, ships sailed regularly from the major British ports to Pictou, Saint John, and Charlottetown, and when the ships docked they often arrived with a fresh batch of immigrants in their holds. However, when Upper Canada, with its more favourable climate, fertile soil, and

Courtesy of Library and Archives Canada PA 020712.

The Old English Church at Guysborough, 1910.

job opportunities, became more accessible once inland routes were established in the mid-1820s, the Maritimes experienced a steady decline in immigrant numbers. The majority of those who did arrive came from Scotland, not England, but the province's ability to attract immigrants improved somewhat when the coal-mining industry began to develop, although the numbers were relatively small.

The English-owned and managed General Mining Association, which controlled operations at the Albion mines near New Glasgow (Pictou County) and the Sydney mines in Cape Breton, sought its skilled workforce initially from Britain. The *Acadian Recorder* had first alerted its readers to the arrival of English miners and labourers in 1827 when the *Margaret* came to Pictou from Liverpool "with 85 miners and all the necessary engines and machinery to work the mines at this place."[68] Miners from the north of England played an important role in laying the foundations of Nova Scotia's coal-mining industry, as shown by the larger than average number of English passenger arrivals between 1827 and 1832, in 1838, and again between 1842 and 1847.[69] However, English settlers were only ever going to be a small fraction of the total immigrant population in the coal-producing regions, which was heavily dominated by Scots.[70]

Lord Dalhousie had been astonished to learn of the thickness of the Albion coal seam: "They have bored 47 feet and did not get through the pure seam." By comparison, "the thickest seam in England ... is 30 feet of solid coal."[71] Oddly enough, the province's lucrative coal mines were first owned by a firm of London jewellers. In 1826–27, Rundell, Bridge and Rundell acquired the rights to virtually all of the province's mineral resources in settlement of the Duke of York's debts.[72] Taking its acquisition very seriously, the London jewellers formed the General Mining Association and invested large amounts of capital in state-of-the-art machinery.[73] Although initially many of its workers were recruited from Britain, most of the later workforce were locally based. Coal was extracted through the use of steam-driven mining equipment,[74] and by 1830 the province's first railway line was in place to take coal from the pits to Pictou Harbour, where it was shipped onward, primarily to the United States.[75] While Cape Breton's coal mines had been worked much earlier, their productivity had initially been very low.[76] But with the General Mining Association's involvement, coal production and the numbers employed rose sharply beginning in 1830.[77] By 1846 the company had invested some three hundred thousand pounds in Pictou's and Cape Breton's coal mines.[78]

Thomas Neville, from Lichfield in Warwickshire, had sailed on the *Thomas Battersby* to Pictou in 1828 with his wife, Frances Bridgen, as part of a larger group that had been recruited in England by the General Mining Association. Working initially at the Albion Mines as an engineer fitter until 1841, he later found work at the Sydney mines in Cape Breton, being paid six shillings per day, "and having his travel expenses paid."[79] With the money accumulated from working in the mines, he then went on to buy a farm at Denmark, near Tatamagouche in Colchester County, in 1849.[80]

The 1840s were difficult years for family and friends still living in the Midlands. Joseph Bridgen, Neville's brother-in-law who lived in Coventry, described the "very great distress in this town and everywhere; there is no work to be had of any kind."[81] The large number

of ribbon-makers who were concentrated in Coventry suddenly found
that their jobs were being taken over by machines: "Three parts of the
hands are out of employ[ment] and everything seems to be getting
worse. I am sorry to say that my father has not had scarcely a day's
work this summer ... my brothers were all out of work last winter."[82]
This calamitous situation would stimulate further emigration, although
it was directed principally to the United States and Upper and Lower
Canada, but not to the Maritimes.

Meanwhile, Thomas's brother Simon had immigrated to Quebec in
1840, where, as a skilled tradesman, he easily found work in stencilling,
plastering, and brick setting. But he wondered whether he should join
Thomas in Nova Scotia: "Please send me word as I can do well in almost
any place, and send me word how far you are from Saint John, New
Brunswick and the name of your landing place, as a gentleman wanted
to hire me to go to there; but I did not know what sort of place it was."[83]
However, Thomas was clearly thinking about doing the reverse. Asking
Simon about conditions in Quebec, he was told that "engineers get from
6 to 7 [shillings,] 6[pence] per day; and as you wanted to know the price
of land, you can buy 100 acres of good land and a house on it for £30 and
there is 20 acres cleared of it.... If you think of coming please to send me
word and I will look out for a comfortable [place] for you."[84] Yet, despite
these tempting advantages, Thomas remained in Nova Scotia.

Peter Barrett was another English recruit. The son of a Cornish farm
labourer from St. Mellion, he had found work in 1865 in the Cramlington
Colliery in Northumberland, unwittingly arriving as a blackleg "to fill
the places of native miners" during a strike. Emigrating a year later, he
sought employment at the Albion Mines, but initially was turned away.[85]
The local Wesleyan Methodist minister, the Reverend Chapman, came
immediately to his aid. He took him to the "mission house," where he
lived for a few days, and helped him to secure a job at the mines. Peter
was clearly shocked by the "old dilapidated log houses" that were used
to accommodate local workers and their families. He disapproved of the
"herding together of the sexes" and the use of the same room for sleeping
and cooking.[86] "There were to be seen one to three beds in the room
where cooking had to be done." However, to his relief, he learned that

Miners' dwellings, Sydney, Cape Breton, photograph *circa* 1890.

General Mining Association employees of his status were to be housed in "nice cottage rows."[87]

Two years later Peter became "deputy under boss," a position he held for two years, after which time he went gold prospecting in the United States and, after visiting Ontario, returned to the Albion Mines.[88] While in Ontario he wondered "why tenant farmers in England don't leave their high rented farms with their cursed game laws and other grievances shackled upon them? Why don't they go out by the thousands to that free and prosperous country of Canada and become their own landlords?"[89] Moving to Stellarton, he took up employment with the Acadia Coal Company at the Drummond colliery "and, by dint of hard work and economy was able to save several hundred dollars."[90] Marrying Hortense Langille, daughter of John Langille, a farmer and miller from River John, Pictou, in 1873, Peter Barrett was fast becoming a man of substance. That same year a tragic explosion occurred at the colliery, causing seventy deaths, some of whom were Cornishmen.[91]

Peter and Hortense then moved to Springhill Mines (Cumberland County) and boarded briefly in temporary accommodation "until a company house was ready for us." In the meantime, Peter's entrepreneurial talents had led him into property speculation and moneylending. Having bought land "at between £100 to £200 per acre," he sold it "as small building plots at £800 to £900 per acre." He claimed that he "accumulated property fast and there were not wanting those who envied my prosperity."[92] Possibly it was envy that triggered off his swift downfall. He became embroiled in a legal battle that resulted in the loss of all his property and a spell in prison. Claiming that he had been defrauded, Peter felt bitter that he had ended up "a pauper (thanks to Nova Scotians)." After working hard for twenty-seven years and "having been nearly 12 years in North America,"[93] he and his family returned to Cornwall with no money except what Peter had borrowed from his brother-in-law to finance their crossing.

Few men would have experienced Peter Barrett's rapid rise and downfall. Most English immigrants were like the Yorkshire-born Adam Bousfield, who found work at the mines in Stellarton and later moved on to the Sydney mines as job opportunities presented themselves.[94] Thomas Dixon, born in Exeter, ended up in South Harbour, Cape Breton, after becoming shipwrecked near the entrance of Cape North Harbour in 1834. After marrying Martha Fitzgerald, a local girl, he turned his hand to fishing, and together they "left many descendents [sic]."[95] In fact, Cape Breton had a fair sprinkling of English inhabitants who struggled to make a living as fishermen. A plaintive request was sent in 1819 to the London Missionary Society[96] by householders living at Ship Harbour, near Port Hawkesbury, who claimed they were "destitute of every means of religion." Their community, "spread over 30 miles," was increasing, "amounting to 1,000 souls."[97] Described as "extremely poor" fishermen living along the coast, they could not support a minister themselves, and hoped that the London Missionary Society would be able to provide financial help.[98]

The London Missionary Society also provided funding in 1815 for the Reverend John Mitchell, who was based at River John (Pictou County) but served the people in nearby Tatamagouche, as well. Intriguingly, he described the inhabitants as being "almost entirely French, but [they] always call themselves Protestant," possibly indicating that many had Channel Island ancestry. The Reverend Mitchell had a gruelling life: "The place where I preach in Tatamagouche every fortnight is 13 miles from my house on River John ... [each year] I travel upwards of 600 miles on very bad roads."[99]

By 1823 there were sufficient Anglicans in the town of Pictou for it to have its first Anglican church, which was completed in 1827 with funds provided by the Society for the Propagation of the Gospel and by Samuel Cunard, the local shipbuilder. But it was not until 1851 that the first Anglican church was built at Albion Mines.[100] The Reverend Joseph Forsythe had "much difficulty" in dealing with newly arrived immigrants from Britain: "They have not been accustomed to religious or even moral habits." As far as he was concerned they were "worthless demoralisers" who were "sunk in poverty."[101]

The Reverend William Elder, the Anglican missionary based at Sydney Mines a decade earlier, reported that there were forty-six families (about three hundred people), living at or near the mines, who supported the Church of England.[102] However, his successor, the Reverend Robert Arnold, found that few of the new arrivals "professed themselves to be of the Church of England" and felt that "the paucity of the clergy was a barrier to conversion."[103] He presumably agreed with the Reverend Forsythe!

Meanwhile, the Reverend William Young Porter, based at St. George's Anglican Church in Sydney, had a more positive outlook but had to endure a staggering work schedule, as he travelled far and wide in Cape Breton County.[104] His preaching commitments brought him to Sydney Mines, Baddeck, Northwest Arm, Coxheath, Glace Bay, Bridgeport, Cow Bay, Main-a-Dieu, Louisburg, Gabarus, Catalone, Mira, and the Forks of Sydney River. His claim that "members of other denominations seldom attended services" suggests that he mainly attracted people with English ancestry, who were clearly scattered along these coastal communities.[105] The fisheries and coal mines were probably their principal sources of employment.[106]

Apart from mining industries, the province had little to attract immigrants, since most of the good farming land had long been settled by the earlier arrivals. About 174 immigrants arrived from Britain in 1850 and only about half that number the year before. The United Kingdom Commissioners of Land and Emigration concluded that "it did not seem that the people of Nova Scotia wanted any emigration."[107] The reality was worse than that, since not only was the province failing to attract immigrants, but much of its population was draining away to Upper Canada and the United States. The issue of prime concern to the province's administrators was how to direct the outflow to Upper Canada rather than have people lost to the United States. Rising to the challenge, the Canada Company[108] issued advertisements urging people "who may contemplate leaving Nova Scotia" to go to Upper Canada

> rather than that they should proceed to the United States.... In Upper Canada they will find a most healthy climate, the soil very fertile, and abundance of excellent land to be obtained on easy terms from the Government and Canada Company. The great success which has attended settlers in Upper Canada, is abundantly evidenced by the prosperous condition of the farmers throughout the Country, and also shown by the success of many natives of New Brunswick and Nova Scotia who have settled in many townships of the country.[109]

Anxious to attract further immigrants, the provincial government organized an assisted emigration scheme in 1857 for some 350 Germans who arrived at Halifax in the *Golconda*: "During the afternoon crowds of these strangers could be seen on the streets.... There are many fine athletic fellows among them who bid fair to make good settlers."[110] The group, which included many tradesmen, had been recruited to work either in the Acadian Charcoal Iron Company's iron mines at Nictaux Falls (Annapolis County), "which are now in active operation," and at the smelter in Londonderry (Colchester County). But the initiative prompted an irate response from a Halifax resident, who criticized the government for being overly concerned about the needs of industry while neglecting the agricultural development of the province, since large areas of the interior still remained unsettled.[111]

Around seventy immigrants, mostly single miners, labourers, and domestic servants, arrived at Halifax from Liverpool in 1862,[112] while more couples and families came in 1864, when seventy-eight English immigrants landed[113] (see Table 1). Two years later nearly seven hundred

Table 1
Passenger Lists for Crossings from Liverpool to Halifax, 1862 and 1864

1. *British Queen*, **Aylward master, April 1, 1862**
[NSARM RG1 Vol. 272 Doc. 142]

Name	Age	Occupation/Other
Barrett, Henry	adult	Labourer
Condon, Mary	adult	Spinster
Fitzgerald, Mary	adult	Spinster
Foxe, Cathe	adult	Spinster
Griffiths, Margaret	adult	Spinster
Hodgson, Robert P.	adult	Farmer
Holmes, Robert	adult	Labourer; plus 1 m. adult.
Hornsby, John	adult	Labourer
Jones, Chas	adult	Labourer
Lyons, Bridget	adult	Spinster
Mason, Mrs.	n/k	n/k
Matthews, John	adult	Labourer
Moyahan, Cathe	adult	Spinster
Price, Josh	adult	Labourer
Sahegan, Mary	adult	Spinster
Smith, Edward	adult	Farmer plus 1 f. adult/1 f. child 1–14

2. *Morning Star*, **McKenzie master, April 1, 1862**
[NSARM RG1 Vol. 272 Doc. 141]

Name	Occupation	Total in Family	Adults M	F	Children M	F	Infants
Richard Peeling	Farmer	8	1	1	3	2	1
Mr. Edwards	Miner	1	1				
Mr. Thomas	Miner	1	1				
Mr. Lather	Miner	5	1	1		2	1
Mr. Lester	Miner	1	1				
Michael Calden	Miner	1	1				
John Henry	Miner	1	1				
Thos. White	Miner	1	1				
	Total	19	8	2	3	4	2

Name	Occupation	Total in Family	Adults		Children		Infants
			M	F	M	F	
(Cabin)							
Richard David		4	1	1		1	1
John Bett		2	1	1			
Mr. Hooper		1	1				
John Harris		1	1				
Mrs. Edwards		3		1	1	1	
	Total	11	4	3	1	2	1

3. *Frank Flint*, Fabeg master, May 28, 1862
[NSARM RG1 Vol. 272 Doc. 144]

Surname	Occupation/Other
Anderson, H.	Labourer
Davies, David	Farmer
Dockerall, Ed	Labourer
Entwhistle, John	Labourer
Griffiths, L.	Labourer
Harker, T.L.	Labourer
Hughes, Thomas	Labourer
Jones, Charles	Labourer
Jones, David	Labourer
Jordan, James	Labourer
Maghee, Samuel	n/k
Moore, Stephen	Labourer
Mullen, Alice	Spinster
Power, Bridget	Spinster
Riley, John	Labourer
Salter, William	Labourer
Smith, Taylor	Labourer
Sullivan, Michl	Labourer
Thomas, John	Labourer
Thomas, Nath	Labourer
Vaughan, William	Labourer
Williams, William	Labourer
Young, David	Labourer, plus one adult

4. The *Euroclydon*, arrived May 1864
[NSARM *Journals of the House of Assembly*, 1865, Appendix 24, 5]

Name	Age	Country	Occupation
Charles Thomson	45	England	Labourer
John Fox	24	England	same
Walter Loughran	22	Ireland	same
James Wilson	19	Ireland	same
Adam Beusefield	23	Ireland	same
William Evans	40	England	Farmer
Ann Evans	35	England	Wife of W.E.
Thomas Evans	18	England	Labourer
James Evans	16	England	same
William Evans	11	England	Child
Ann Evans	9	England	same
John Leviday	40	England	Labourer
Frederick Paulbridge	29	England	same
Samuel McLeary	23	Ireland	same
William Brownler	21	Ireland	same
Thomas Kelly	25	Ireland	same
Michael Rooney	21	Ireland	same
Mary Keating	20	Ireland	Spinster
Thomas Apsley	11	England	Child
Johanna Gleary	20	Ireland	Spinster
Frederick Lonan	25	England	Labourer
Josh. Can	30	Ireland	same
Robert Bowes	25	Ireland	same
Comer Conty	20	Ireland	same
Anna Nepath	22	Ireland	Spinster
Sabrina Muldre	20	Ireland	same
Thomas Burke	20	Ireland	Labourer
Bridget Burke	22	Ireland	Spinster
John Conna	19	Ireland	Labourer
Wm. H. Arndell	27	England	same
Edward Elliott	31	England	same
Wm. H. Antha	20	England	same
John Whitford	26	England	same
C. Shadden	21	England	same
Samuel Phillips	30	England	same
Robert Shadden	21	England	same

Name	Age	Country	Occupation
John Gilbert	33	England	same
Joseph Barlow	26	England	same
Catherine Brien	40	Ireland	Married Woman
Fanny Brien	11	Ireland	Children
Jane Brien	7	Ireland	of
Ann Brien	5	Ireland	Catherine
John Brien	3	Ireland	Brien

5. The *Indian Queen*, arrived June 1864
[NSARM *Journals of the House of Assembly*, 1865, Appendix 24, 6]

Name	Age	Country	Occupation
Charles Wills	20	Ireland	Surgeon
David Die	22	Ireland	Labourer
Patrick Ockly	38	England	Labourer
Catherine Wheely	26	England	Spinster
Patrick Magher	n/k	England	Labourer
Johanna Magher	11	England	Child
James Spencer	25	England	Labourer
John Lemas	35	England	same
Ellen Landrikin	21	Ireland	Spinster
Margaret O'Shaughnasey	20	Ireland	Spinster
Bridget Burns	30	Ireland	Married woman
Honora Burns	6	Ireland	her child
Jonah Ezra	29	England	Labourer
Ann Ezra	28	England	his wife
Mary Ann Ezra	3	England	Child
David Ezra	18	England	Labourer
Mary Thomas	30	England	Married woman
Rachel Thomas	11	England	her children
William Thomas	9	England	same
Mary Thomas	3	England	same
Elizabeth Thomas (infant)	n/k	England	same
James Davis	24	England	Labourer
Sarah Davis	22	England	his wife
Sophia Davis	infant	England	his child
Julia Martin	19	Ireland	Spinster
Mary O'Leary	22	Ireland	Spinster

Name	Age	Country	Occupation
Timothy Hagan	20	Ireland	Labourer
John Rickards	37	England	Farmer
Ann Rickards	31	England	his wife
Catherine Burke	11	England	Child
R.D. Watts	20	England	Labourer
Edward Lynch	24	England	same
Charles Hinden	25	England	same

assisted English immigrants arrived at Halifax from Liverpool expecting to find work in the mines and the Pictou Railway.[114] The 260 or so Cornish miners included in the group headed chiefly for the gold-mining districts,[115] while the other miners went to the coal mines at Cape Breton, Pictou, and New Glasgow.[116] However, a sudden downturn in the province's coal trade with the United States depressed employment prospects, and, feeling disappointed, most of the newly arrived coal miners either moved to the United States or returned home. But some of the Cornish men did well from contracts "for work in sinking shafts in the gold districts."[117]

Nova Scotia attracted mainly assisted immigrants in the 1870s, including seventy-one "home children" who arrived in 1873 under the care of Colonel John Laurie, acting on behalf of Louisa Birt, founder of the Liverpool Sheltering Homes.[118] Some "221 men, 35 women and 45 minors under 17 years of age" were "forwarded to the coal districts in the counties of Pictou and Cape Breton" that same year, many having had their passages paid by the Nova Scotia government.[119] Following them in 1875 were 165 Cornishmen who found employment at the Londonderry iron mines. Cheap imports from Australia had decimated the Cornish tin industry, leaving "many able-bodied miners seeking in vain for employment."[120] Attracted by the prospect of well-paid mining jobs in Nova Scotia, they obtained some government assistance. Also arriving that same year were fifty adults and 123 of Louisa Birt's "home children," who would be sent to different parts of the province.[121]

Most British immigrants arriving in the province during the early twentieth century were labourers and tradesmen who hoped to find work in the province's growing industrial sector. Some, like the fourteen families from Leeds who emigrated in 1906, were desperately poor, having to rely on their parishes to finance their relocation costs.[122] Being tradesmen, most of the heads of households had transportable skills that would enable them to make an easy transition into the province's urban and industrial life.[123] But although there was a substantial increase in English immigration to the province between 1911 and 1921, very few settled permanently, since by then its industries were in decline and ambitious men and women were moving west to other parts of Canada or the United States.

The English of Nova Scotia had recent or distant connections with England, depending on whether they or their descendents had come directly from Britain or from the United States. The descendents of the New Englanders and Loyalists defined themselves later by their far-off English ancestry, and this fact alone accounts for the large English concentrations on the west side of the province (see Map 5). Digby and Yarmouth, with their significant Acadian populations, and Lunenburg, which was largely German, broke the otherwise uninterrupted pattern of distant Englishness to be found in the western counties. Yorkshire immigrants transferred their distinctive culture to their new communities in Cumberland County, the only county to have actual English immigrants as the dominant ethnic group. The province's other English settlers would have left no trace of their Englishness behind, since they had little or no lasting affinity with any particular part of England. The province's industrial sector attracted most of the English who came after the mid-1820s, placing them on the east side of the mainland and Cape Breton, but their numbers were relatively small.

English settlers were even more widely scattered in New Brunswick, having been attracted to it after 1815 by its hugely important timber trade. The trade in masts for the British navy, the most valuable commodity, had begun in the late eighteenth century, but this rapidly changed into a more general trade as the demand for North American timber increased. Timber exports doubled between 1785 and 1800, and by the turn of the century more than half of the province's exports to Britain derived from timber. The timber trade provided the ships that carried the English to the province and it gave them much-needed employment when they arrived. But the vast and unbroken forests had to be cleared before settlement could begin.

CHAPTER 5

Scattered Far and Wide
in New Brunswick

*They have with the axe chopped out a home for themselves
and their rising progeny, and feel that they are lords of the
soil they till.*[1]

THIS, THE ENGLISH settlement in Queens County, founded in 1819, was a shining example of pioneer success, and much was made of it in promotional literature. The province had acquired its first immigrants from New England sixty years earlier, and they had been followed by a large group from Yorkshire. But it was not until 1784, when New Brunswick became a separate province, that the first major influx of immigrants began. Loyalists came in their thousands from the United States, a great many having English ancestry. They formed the initial core of New Brunswick's immigrant society, most being concentrated along the St. John River valley[2] and in the southwest at Passamaquoddy Bay. The large influx from Britain after 1815 included English immigrants who became widely scattered in the southern half of the province. And where regional origins have been uncovered, they reveal strong links with the north and southwest of England.

However, despite its promising beginning, New Brunswick struggled to retain its settlers. Having become dissatisfied, many Loyalists had left and returned to the United States or moved to other parts of British America. Later immigrants sailed to its ports to avoid American immigration taxes and thus obtain a cheaper route to the United States. As a consequence, the province appeared ill-suited to immigrants, at least initially. By 1806 New Brunswick's population was only thirty-five thousand, nearly half that of Nova Scotia and Upper Canada, and just a fraction of Lower Canada's population, which was almost seven times greater.[3]

Although it had plenty of good agricultural land, New Brunswick had been the slowest of the Maritime provinces to attract immigrants directly from Britain. Far from gaining immigrants, it actually lost many of its established settlers to other parts of North America. The unpopularity of the governor, Thomas Carleton, and the off-putting behaviour of the elite families who controlled the province were both said to be deterrents to immigration.[4] The province's climate also seemed to militate against its agricultural development. During his 1827 tour of British North America, Lieutenant-Colonel Cockburn commented on "the greatest inconvenience arising from the length of the winters," since large quantities of fodder were required for farm animals and early frosts were a serious problem.[5] Another serious impediment to colonization was the British government's decision to restrict the granting of land to settlers in order to protect areas that could otherwise supply timber masts to the Royal Navy or might be offered as rewards to officials and dignitaries.[6] Settlements eventually materialized from a chaotic mishmash of part-land grants and part-land sales and from settlers circumventing the law by seizing possession of land through squatting.[7]

It actually took the severe economic depression that followed the end of the Napoleonic Wars in 1815 to kick-start New Brunswick's flow of British immigrants. Large numbers started to arrive in 1817, although their numbers cannot be quantified owing to the lack of official data. The odd reference to particular groups, such as the seven thousand (mainly Irish) immigrants who arrived in 1819, suggest that the province's ports must have been deluged with people.[8] Most were very poor, and New Brunswick residents soon grew weary of having to subsidize them. The people of St. Andrews complained the loudest, having more cases of distress to deal with than any other part of the province. The townspeople were having to support the feeble and infirm who remained in the area, while looking on askance as the able-bodied and independent-minded took the first opportunity they could of going off to the United States.[9] Nevertheless, despite the loss of many new arrivals to the United States, the growing flood of immigrants led to a doubling of the population between 1806 and 1824 (to just under seventy-five thousand), and by 1840 it had doubled again to just over 156,000.[10]

The timber trade drove New Brunswick's economic development. It built the towns of Saint John, Chatham, St. Andrews, and Fredericton, created employment for countless men, and encouraged the investment of capital in the province. It had mushroomed after 1805 with the imposition of tariffs on Baltic timber, and by 1826 wood products accounted for 75 percent of the province's export revenues.[11] As Peter Fisher noted in his *History of New Brunswick*, published in 1825, "the woods furnish a sort of simple manufactory for the inhabitants, from which, after attending to their farms in the summer, they can draw returns during the winter for those supplies which are necessary for the comfort of their families."[12] For the very poor, it provided the means to earn money to purchase land, although there were plenty of lumbermen who never became farmers. But, since fluctuations in Britain's economy caused huge variations in the demand for timber, the province had to cope with periods of economic stagnation. Nevertheless, the trade propelled the province's economic development during the first half of the nineteenth century and in doing so attracted a growing influx of immigrants who were, by the 1840s, nearly all Irish.[13]

It is impossible to determine precisely how many British immigrants settled in New Brunswick.[14] The available evidence indicates that the influx before 1817 was dominated by Scots,[15] and after that time by the Irish, who far outnumbered all other immigrant groups. The influx averaged about seven thousand immigrants a year between 1834 and 1847, although most were in transit to the United States.[16] Thus only a minority of the immigrants who arrived each year actually remained in New Brunswick. By 1851 the Irish-born accounted for a staggering 71 percent

Courtesy of Canada, Department of Interior/Library and Archives Canada, C-010360.

Axemen felling trees in New Brunswick. In the early nineteenth century, horses and oxen were used to haul sawn timber to the nearest river. Before the arrival of power saws, lumber production was tediously slow and labour-intensive.

of total immigration, with the Scottish-born representing 12 percent and the English-born 10 percent.[17] However, if ancestry rather than country of birth is considered, the picture changes dramatically. When the descendents of the numerous English Loyalists who arrived during the late eighteenth century are taken into account, the English component of the population rises significantly. According to the 1871 census, the first to record Loyalist numbers along with immigrants directly from England, the English represented 29 percent of the population — only six percentage points behind the Irish, who represented 35 percent of the total.[18]

Unfortunately, English immigrant totals are only available for 1833–34, but, based on this tiny sample, it can be argued that few English people immigrated to New Brunswick in the first half of the nineteenth century. Only around 450 English immigrants arrived in those two years, this being a time when England was gripped by a deep economic recession and when much higher than average immigration

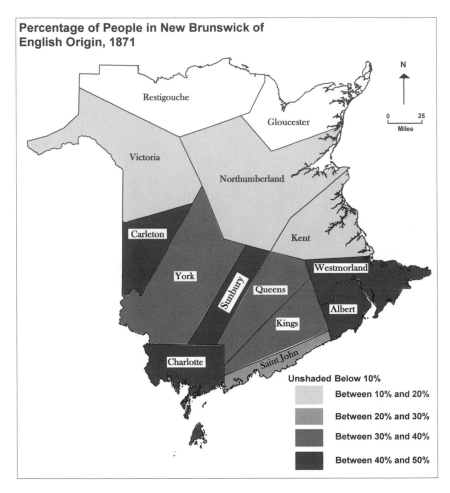

Map 9. Based on data from the 1871 Census of New Brunswick.

levels would have been expected. The inescapable conclusion is that
the province only acquired a few hundred English immigrants, at most,
each year. Thus, the relatively strong showing of English ethnicity in the
population figures owes much more to the province's Loyalist past than
to emigration directly from England. The eighteenth century influx of
Yorkshire settlers to the Chignecto Isthmus made the English a dominant
ethnic group in Westmorland and Albert[19] counties, but elsewhere their
numeric strength was only in the Loyalist parishes of the St. John River
valley and in Charlotte County.

Table 2

Passenger Lists for Crossings from English Ports to Saint John, 1833–34, 1838

[Source: *Passengers to New Brunswick: The Custom House Records* — *1833, 34, 37, 38*, New Brunswick Genealogical Society, n.d.]

Please note: This list is restricted to ship crossings with a minimum of ten passengers.

1. *Alchymist* (barque) from Falmouth, Godfrey Wills, master, March 21, 1833, arrived April 25.

No.	Names	Age	Occupation
1	Stephens, Jane	35	wife of a farmer
2	Stephens, Mary	12	child
3	Stephens, Abraham	15	child
4	Stephens, Catharine	8	child
5	Stephens, Frances	6	child
6	Stephens, Jane	4	child
7	Stephens, Charles	16 mo	child
8	Brown, Maria	33	lady
9	Jenkins, William	42	taylor
10	Jenkins, Bridget	40	wife
11	Jenkins, Philippa	14	child
12	Jenkins, William	12	child
13	Buzza, Ann	48	wife of a farmer
14	Buzza, Elizabeth	18	child
15	Buzza, George	14	child
16	Buzza, Edmund	12	child
17	Buzza, Samuel	10	child
18	Buzza, Bartholomew	8	child
19	Buzza, Joseph	2	child
20	Lewis, Joseph	27	chord winder
21	Jenkins, George	50	chord winder
22	Jenkins, John	25	bookbinder
23	James, Jane	34	wife of a farmer
24	James, Thomas	20	child
25	James, Ann	9	child
26	James, Caroline	7	child
27	Jenkins, Hope	5	child

Alchymist cont'd

No.	Names	Age	Occupation
28	Jenkins, Jane	3	child
29	Jenkins, William	9 mo.	child
30	Bowden, William	32	gentleman
31	Hayne, John	55	labourer
32	Elliot, Thomas	20	chord winder
33	Tippit/Tippet, Catherine	15	child
34	Hawswell, Tresa	35	spinster

2. *Lord Goderich* (ship, 367 tons) from London, John Hopper, master, April 6, 1833, arrived May 29.

No.	Names	Age	Occupation
1	James, George	36	merchant
2	James, Mary	36	wife
3	James, George	11	child
4	James, Thomas	5	child
5	James, Mary Jr.	8	child
6	James, Elizabeth	14	child
7	James, James	inf.	infant child
8	Kindred, Henry	36	carpenter
9	Kindred, Susan	35	wife
10	Kindred, Mary Ann	1	child
11	Kindred, Henry	4 mo	child
12	Carter, Timothy	29	labourer
13	Carter, Mary	27	wife
14	Carter, Mary	3 mo.	child
15	Downey, John	30	labourer
16	Downey, Anne	8	wife
17	Downey, Patrick	inf.	child
18	Downey, Margaret	2	child
19	Downey, Elen	1	child
20	Lantry, John	26	labourer
21	Lantry, Mary	24	wife
22	Lantry, Mary	inf.	child
23	Mahony, John	30	labourer
24	Mahony, Elen	28	wife
25	Mahony, Elen Jr.	inf.	child

Lord Goderich cont'd

No.	Names	Age	Occupation
26	Mahony, Margaret	2	child
27	Speedy, John	27	labourer
28	Speedy, Mary	24	wife
29	Mahony, Mary	18 mo.	child

3. *Amynta* (ship, 214 tons) from Plymouth, E. Moon, master, April 3, 1833, arrived June.

No.	Names	Age	Occupation
1	Westlake, Samuel	24	farmer
2	Westlake, John	29	farmer
3	Bloggett, Charles	14	gentleman, age possibly 74
4	Oliver, John	23	tinsman
5	Richards, James	19	tinsman
6	Orchard, Thos	19	farmer
7	O'Neil, Eleanor	42	no occupation
8	O'Neal, Eleanor	20	child of the above
9	O'Neal, Parmelia	16	same
10	O'Neal, Thos	14	same
11	O'Neal, Abraham	7	same
12	O'Neal, Isaac	7	same
13	O'Neal, David	2	same
14	Seight, Wm	28	gentleman
15	Bond, Mary	20	spinster
16	Longmead, Mary	28	same

4. *Augusta* of Saint John (417 tons) from Liverpool, William Petrie, master, April 4, 1833, arrived June.

No.	Names	Age	Occupation
1	Buxton, T.	30	merchant
2	McIntyre	30	clergyman
3	Goff, D.	20	surgeon
4	Wilmot, R.D.	25	merchant
5	Gilbert, Willm	30	labourer
6	Gilbert, Rachel	30	same

Augusta cont'd

No.	Names	Age	Occupation
7	Michi, Willm	25	same
8	Williams, John	22	same
9	Roberts, John	20	labourer
10	Crawford, Peter	25	same

6. *Margaret* from London, William Frances Nunn, master, April 15, 1833, arrived June.

No.	Names	Age	Occupation
1	Gibbs, John Cornelius	35	owner's representative
2	Everitt, Job	50	labourer
3	Fensham, John	25	same
4	Fleckney, Joseph	26	same
5	Lacy, Richard	18	same
6	Lacy, Abel	20	same
7	Everitt, Eve	28	Everitt's wife
8	Everitt, Mary	5	child
9	Everitt, John	3	same
10	Everitt, George	5m	same
11	Gibson, Thomas	16	clerk
12	Scott, William Absalom	35	mason
13	Scott, Ellen	35	wife
14	Scott, Nicholas T.	7	child
15	Scott, William	5	child
16	Scott, James	3	child
17	Scott, John	18 mo	child
18	Wright, Thomas	21	shoemaker
19	Gee, Thos.	19	same
20	Walker, John	17	same
21	Barron, Edward	28	tailor
22	Nunn, Mary	28	master's wife

7. *Percival* from Plymouth, April 6, 1833, arrived June.

No.	Names	Age	Occupation
1	Nash, Edward	28	gentleman
2	Nash, C.	24	wife
3	Nash, John	2	child
4	Nash, Wm.	1	child
5	Hampton, C.	21	gentleman
6	Gee, Soloman	31	labourer
7	Gee, Mary	29	wife
8	Gee, Soloman	7	child
9	Gee, Mary	4	child
10	Gee, Robert	2	child
11	Rowe, Mary	21	spinster

8. *Branches* (ship, 452 tons) from London, George Forsyth, master, May 2, 1833, arrived July.

No.	Names	Age	Occupation
1	Power, Robert	38	gentleman
2	Power, Maria	34	his wife
3	Power, Maria Jr.	9	child
4	Power, Louisa	7	child
5	Power, Thomas	6	child
6	Power, Jane	5	child
7	Power, John	3	child
8	Thorne, Jane	28	servant
9	Thorne, Sarah	24	servant
10	Carey, Thomas	18	servant
11	Wallace, Sarah	22	servant
12	Davies, John	37	carpenter
13	Oliver, John	25	mariner

9. *Legatus* of Saint John from London, Wm. Ord, master, April 1833, arrived July.

No.	Names	Age	Occupation
1	Robert, C.S.	32	gentleman
2	Robert, Louisa	22	wife

Legatus cont'd

No.	Names	Age	Occupation		
3	Robert, Chas. Wm.	3	child		
4	Cranfield, John	26	gentleman		
5	Dyer, Mary	24	spinster		
6	Hunt, Margaret	40	widow		
7	Hunt, Jno	16	child		
8	Hunt, S.	15	child		
9	Hunt, E.	13	child		
10	Teesdale, I.	50	pensioner)	Did	
11	Teesdale, Ma	44	wife)		
12	Teesdale, H.	17	child)	not	
13	Teesdale, Jno. A.	15	child)		
14	Teesdale, T.	12	child)	embark	
15	Teesdale, W.	8	child)		

10. *Mercator* **(ship) from Sunderland, Robert Mackie, master, April 18, 1834, arrived July.**

No.	Names	Age	Occupation
1	Mass, Thomas	57	labourer
2	Mass, Ann	67	wife
3	Nisbit, Thomas	25	pitman
4	Nisbit, Jane	27	wife
5	Nisbit, Thomas	4	child
6	Mass, Anthony	28	pitman
7	Mass, Mary Ann	25	wife
8	Mass, Mary	6	child
9	Mass, Ann	4	child
10	Mass, Dorothy	2	child
11	Bell, Thomas	25	pitman
12	Bell, Isabella	25	wife

11. *Pacific* (ship, 348 tons) from Liverpool, Nicholas Johnston, master, May/June 1833, arrived July.

No.	Names	Age	Occupation
1	Thompson, George	15	gentleman
2	Thompson, John	13	
3	Thompson, Helen	11	
4	Thompson, Jessie	9	
5	Thompson, David	5	
6	Thompson, Andrew	6 mo.	
7	Thompson, John Sr.	50	gentleman
8	Thompson, Jessie	32	
9	Bell, Agnes	55	
10	Cowden, Agnes	19	
11	Christian, John	23	
12	Marchbank, David	60	farmer
13	Newton, Mary	60	
14	Smith, William	24	
15	Marchbank, Ann	22	
16	Marchbank, Margaret	20	
17	McAllister, Mary	10	
18	Johnston, John	33	farmer
19	Johnston, Isabella	33	
20	Johnston, Francis	10	
21	Johnston, Jessie	7	
22	Johnston, Robert	4	
23	Johnston, Thomas	inf.	

12. *Caledonia* of Saint John (497 tons) from Liverpool, David McLay, master, July 1, 1833, arrived August.

No.	Names	Age	Occupation
1	Parry, John	35	blacksmith
2	Parry, Jane	7	none
3	Parry, Charles	5	none
4	Parry, Daniel	3	none
5	Parry, Hannah	6 mo	none
6	Parry, Ann	35	none
7	Miller, Margaret	35	none

Caledonia cont'd

No.	Names	Age	Occupation
8	Miller, James	9	none
9	Miller, Mary Ann	7	none
10	Miller, Sarah Elizabeth	20 mo	none

13. *Alchymist* (barque) from Falmouth, Godfrey Wills, master, July 24, 1833, arrived September 1833.

No.	Names	Age	Occupation	Parish
1	Martin, George	26	blacksmith	Cubay
2	Scobera, John	29	shoemaker	Falmouth
3	Scobera, Acaden?	30	wife	same
4	Scobera, Mary	5	child	same
5	Scobera, John	3	child	same
6	Scobera, Joseph	17 mo.	child	same
7	Lewis, Mary	28	wife	Falmouth
8	Lewis, Mary Jane	2	child	same
9	Rendall, Thomas	32	printer	Truro
10	Rendall, Mary Ann	31	wife	same
11	Rendall, Julia	19 mo.	child	same
12	Rendall, Hannah	3 mo.	child	same
13	Gapes, James	40	farmer	Mylor
14	Gapes, Grace	39	wife	same
15	Gapes, George	11	child	same
16	Gapes, Elizabeth	7	child	same
17	Gapes, Agnes	9	child	same
18	Gapes, Grace	4	child	same
19	Gapes, Thomas	18 mo.	child	same
20	Sarah, William	30	miner?	Perran
21	Sarah, Mary Ann	28	wife	same
22	Sarah, Elizabeth	2	child	same
23	Sarah, William	4 mo.	child	same
24	Tong, Andrew	16	Taylor	Flushing

14. *Sarah* (Barque) from Bristol, Joseph Hamm, master, August 14, 1833, arrived September.

No.	Names	Age	Occupation
1	Ruel, Edward	48	officer of marines
2	Ruel, Mary	42	lady
3	Ruel, John	16	their family
4	Ruel, James	15	their family, plus four children below 14 years and three below 7 years
5	Harris, Mrs.	56	lady
6	Thomas, Mrs.	35	lady
7	Lillyman, Mr.	40	draper
8	Lillyman, Mrs.	35	lady plus three children below seven years of age.
9	Nichols, Mr.	30	shoemaker
10	Nichols, Mrs.	30	his wife

15. *New Brunswick* of Saint John (414 tons) from Liverpool, Thomas Green, master, April 7, 1834, arrived June.

No.	Names	Age	Occupation
1	Mansel, James	45	farmer
2	Jenning, Francis	34	same
3	Marshall, Robert	26	same
4	Bainbridge, William	24	same
5	Fryere, William	24	same
6	Bradley, John	23	same
7	Bradley, Francis	21	same
8	Bradley, Thomas	19	same
9	Medcalf, George	19	same
10	Jennings, Sarah	30	same
11	Marchall, May	22	same
12	Marshall, Mary		child
13	Marshall, Thomas		child
14	Marshall, William		child
15	Jennings, Sarah		child
16	Jennings, John		child

16. *Breakwater* (brig, 180 tons) from Plymouth, R. Rowland, master, April 12, 1834, arrived July.

No.	Names	Age	Occupation
1	Filmer, William	20	gentleman
2	Cummins, Margaret	23	spinster
3	Sleep, Mary	33	widow
4	Sleep, Mary	4	her child
5	Sleep, Lavinia	2	her child
6	Goldsmith, G.	25	gentleman
7	Goldsmith, Jno.	19	gentleman
8	Spillett, Wm.	44	farmer
9	Spillett, Thomas	26	farmer
10	Barrington, Jno.	26	labourer
11	Bowden, Saml.	30	labourer
12	Demcaster, Thos.	40	labourer

17. *Rebecca* of Saint John (barque, 251 tons) from Liverpool, Edward Pickles, master, April 1838, arrived July 4.

No.	Names	Age	Occupation
1	Lyle, Andrew	30	master mariner
2	Maxwell, Thomas	34	master mariner
3	Maxwell, Mary (Mrs.)	32	wife
4	Maxwell, Elizabeth	8	child
5	Maxwell, Margaret	4	child
6	Maxwell, Mary	4	child
7	Maxwell, Thomas	3	child
8	Maxwell, Alexander	10 mo.	infant
9	Ritch, Andrew	38	mariner
10	Ritch, Jennet	32	wife
11	Ritch, Ann	4	child
12	Ritch, Peter	10 mo.	infant
13	Houston, Jessee	20	family—poss. Houston, Jannet
14	Jenner, Patrick	26	labourer
15	Vincent, John	26	boot/shoemaker—this family for Nova Scotia
16	Vincent, Mary Ann	21	family
17	Vincent, Elizabeth	50	family

Rebecca **cont'd**

No.	Names	Age	Occupation
18	Vincent, Thomas	5	family—child
19	Vincent, Mary Jane	10 mo.	Family — infant
20	Addy, Bessy	14	family
21	Dyus, Bessie	23	farmer's wife — this family for Nova Scotia
22	Dyus, Margaret	8	family — child
23	Dyus, Jane	6	family — child
24	Dyus, Sarah Ann	4	family — child
25	Dyus, Maria	2	family — child
26	Lonergan, Edmond	30	labourer
27	Naugle, Ann	25	soldier's wife — 65th Regiment
28	Moran, Patrick	35	farmer
29	Moran, Nancy	35	family
30	Moran, Margaret	18	family
31	Moran, Margaret	6	family — child
32	Moran, Dennis	4½	family — child
33	Moran, Patrick	2½	family — child
34	Dalton, Thomas	35	farmer

Little is known about their regional origins. Surviving passenger lists for 1833–34 reveal that most immigrants in those years sailed either from the West Country ports of Falmouth and Plymouth or from Liverpool and London[20] (see Table 2). A total of 140 people arrived at Saint John in eleven crossings from five West Country ports,[21] two hundred came from Liverpool, and just over seventy from London. They were mainly tradesmen, labourers, and farmers travelling with their families, and two were Cornish tin miners. Undoubtedly, immigrants from Devon and Cornwall were particularly well-represented and the relatively high number from Liverpool probably points to a significant number of arrivals from the north of England.

Judging from the shipping advertisements for crossings appearing in the *Newcastle Courant* from 1819 to the mid-1820s, the northeast of England must have lost people to the province during this very brief period (see Appendix III). The *Bittern*, due to sail from Sunderland, was said to be ideal for "persons desirous of emigrating," while "families desirous of settling in North America" were invited to contact Messrs. S. Dodd & Co., "who will have a vessel to sail direct to Chaleur Bay, New Brunswick."[22] West Country newspaper advertisements reveal that regular crossings to Saint John and St. Andrews were readily available from this region, particularly during the 1830s. The *Bristol Mercury* reported how the *Unity*, with its three-pound fares, was geared to English labourers, who were "in demand in New Brunswick,"[23] while it extolled the virtues of vessels like the *Pilot*, which offered "a height between decks of seven feet" to passengers.[24] Odd references to immigrants like Devon-born John Sheppard, born in 1780, who immigrated to Saint John County "when a youth"; Edward Stentiford from Ashburton in Devon, who emigrated around 1830 and later settled in St. Andrews, where he "was engaged in the carriage trade"; and Sarah Bradford from Exeter, who married Richard Isaac in 1832 and immigrated that same year to Saint John, confirm a long-standing West Country connection, although its extent cannot be quantified.[25]

The largest and longest sustained influx was focused on the Chignecto Isthmus. It began in 1761 when twenty-five Rhode Island families arrived in Sackville[26] (see Map 7). They were followed two years later by families from Massachusetts and other New England states who settled in Cumberland Township (later Westmorland Parish).[27] Charles Morris, the chief surveyor, had predicted then that the region "when fully peopled and all the marshes improved would be the granary of Nova Scotia." He would be proved right.[28] But progress was slow at first, as the lack of consumer markets and the steady movement of troops from Fort Cumberland to Halifax had a devastating effect on the local economy. Faced with this gloomy situation, fifty New Englanders had left Sackville by 1774 and were only too happy to dispose of their lands to the incoming Yorkshire settlers, who would flourish as pioneers.[29]

Having first colonized Sackville and Westmorland parishes, Yorkshire settlers sought new places for their communities to grow by extending their reach along the Memramcook River in Dorchester, the Petitcodiac River in Moncton, Coverdale, and Hillsborough,[30] and the Shepody River in Hopewell[31] and Harvey (see Maps 8 and 10). They were joined, starting in 1783, by Loyalists like Robert Colpitts, who settled in Coverdale, John Palmer, who went to Dorchester, and Jeremiah Brownell, who settled in Westmorland.[32] Secondary migration from Sackville and Westmorland continued along the Petitcodiac River into Salisbury and from there along the Coverdale and Pollet rivers, reaching Elgin Parish by about 1810.[33] Meanwhile, Shediac's intake of Loyalists and follow-on English settlers was sparked off by the arrival in 1785 of London fish merchant William Hanington, who had obtained a large grant of land on the west side of the harbour.[34] And Botsford, to the east of it, having attracted its settlers from Sackville and Westmorland initially,[35] acquired a number of families directly from England in 1820–21, who founded a settlement at Murray's Corner, lying between Shemogue and Cape Jourimain, along the Northumberland Strait.[36]

While long-established Yorkshire settlers were extending their territory in the isthmus, a fresh batch of Yorkshire immigrants arrived in 1817, some 159 having sailed in the *Trafalgar* to Saint John[37] and another 196 in the *Valiant* to Charlottetown.[38] Those who had sailed in the *Trafalgar* were lucky to have escaped with their lives when their ship became grounded at Brier Island on its approach through the Bay of Fundy.[39] Hitting rocks in a thick fog, Captain Welburn had his navigational skills tested to the full. Fortunately he managed to save the passengers and crew, but not the ship:

> I had been running up all day; it being thick [with fog]
> I could not see anything; at seven p.m. I hove the ship
> to, with her head to the westward, thinking we were well
> over to the westward, sounding in 40 fathoms; the tide
> running very strong, and before we could see the land,
> we heard the surf against the rocks; got sail upon the
> ship but being so close the strong tide set us upon the
> rocks; it being high water when we got on, run out a
> kedge to heave her off, but all to no use. At low water the
> ship was dry all round, amongst the rugged rocks, which
> went through her in different parts; the ship having as

much water in the inside as there was on the outside
at high water. The passengers were all safe landed that
were brought out, and got all their baggage on shore.[40]

Both groups sought suitable farming locations on either side of the
Northumberland Strait. While some of the *Valiant*'s passengers, including
John Rennison, John Millner, John Towse, and Thomas Fawcett, opted
for the isthmus, most remained in Prince Edward Island, establishing
their communities near Charlottetown and along the south shore of
the island.[41] After being rescued, those of the *Trafalgar*'s passengers
who did not travel on to Quebec mainly settled in Westmorland and
Albert counties, among them being the families of Thomas Beal and
David Cook, who settled in Sackville, and William Lowther, who went
to Westmorland. Some, like the Short, Harrison, and Burgess families,
who had originated from Bewholme in the East Riding of Yorkshire
(Nunkeeling Parish), headed instead for the new Yorkshire communities
being formed at New Jerusalem in Queens County. And some, like
Robert Stailing, went even farther afield, opting for Annapolis Royal in
Nova Scotia (see Table 3).

Michael Cunningham, the Congregationalist minister sent by the
London Missionary Society to Dorchester sometime before 1804, wrote
disapprovingly of "the Romanists who have greatly multiplied" and "the
late emigrations from Scotland," but failed to mention the many Yorkshire
settlers who also lived in the area. As a Congregationalist minister, his only
hope was to enlist the forty or so families — several of whom were "free
negroes" — who seemed willing to contribute fifty pounds toward the
upkeep of a minister. Judging from his request to the London Missionary
Society for a minister "with a knowledge of Gaelic and moderately
Calvinistic," he was clearly targeting Highland Presbyterians, not English
settlers.[43] But he was in unpromising territory, since most of the English
inhabitants, being of Yorkshire stock, were Methodists.

Having built a church at Pointe de Bute (Westmorland) by 1788,
Methodists erected another one at Sackville two years later, these being
among the earliest Methodist churches ever to be built in Canada.[44]
The preaching circuit, extending from the Petitcodiac River region in

Table 3

**Partial Passenger List for the *Trafalgar*,
Crossing from Hull to the Bay of Fundy in 1817
[NAB CO384/1, 127–33]**

Please note: "f" denotes "with family."

Francis Best	William Wilkinson (f)
Thomas Whyte (f)	William Lowther (f)
John Diggit	William Kidney
Robert Harrison	William Jackson
John Foulding	Robert Stiling [Stailing] (f)
William Burgess (f)	John Harrison (f)
George Tennison	William Atkin
William Saunderson	John Johnston
John Watson	John Bartchard
William Scott	David Cook
William Hare	Thomas Osgodly
Isaac Johnston	Thomas Cliff
Stephen Jefferson	John Short (f)
George Gowland	Mr. Yaving
John Jeffry	Mrs. Cross
George Kirkey	Joseph Cross
Jno. Lear	John Hill
Samuel Walker	Sarah Lowell
James Milburn	John Smith
Stephen Madd	Thomas Fraser
William Simpson	Richard Consitt
Thomas Beal (f)	Mary Dunn
Richard Marginson (f)	Jonathan Milliner
Thomas Hotham	Thomas Millner (f)
Thomas Drissel (f)	Thomas Walgate
Mary Johnston	Edward Wright

---

the west to Bay Verte and Cape Tormentine in Botsford on the east, was an arduous challenge, particularly the sections than ran through the Tantramar marshes. A guide "armed with a pole" had to walk ahead "and find safe footing amidst the bogs, pools and streams."[45] Sackville went on to experience "revivals of great power" in 1823, 1836, 1839, and 1841, resulting in larger congregations and the construction of "a mission house, tolerably well furnished, with four acres of land attached to it, with a barn, outhouses and other things necessary for the comfort and accommodation of the occupants."[46] Organ music was introduced in 1854, "when the old practice of giving out the hymns, two lines at a time, was of necessity abandoned."[47] By 1871 significant Methodist communities were still to be found at Westmorland, Botsford, Sackville, and Dorchester, no doubt reflecting the relatively high number of Yorkshire settlers and their descendents in these areas.[48]

Ever mindful of its missions abroad, the Church of England had a minister in place at Fort Cumberland by 1755, even before the New Englanders arrived. Those attending the Reverend Thomas Wood's first service were mainly soldiers, but by 1769 the Anglican congregation in Westmorland was large enough to warrant its own church — the "old St. Mark's Church," built in 1794 at Mount Whatley. By 1818, Sackville had its first Anglican church as well as a minister, the Reverend Christopher Milner, who extended his pastoral duties to cover Dorchester, Shediac, Moncton, and Hopewell. Shediac's Anglicans were sufficiently numerous to have a church of their own by 1830, and, fifteen years later, five preaching stations were in place at the Bend (of the Petitcodiac River), on the Dorchester Road, on the Memeracook River, and at Cogagne and Bouctouche in Kent County. The Reverend Jarvis, the resident minister, noted how his congregations fluctuated greatly, "those engaged in lumbering being migratory."[49] However, the Church of England's support was swiftly lost to the much more popular Methodist and Baptist faiths, and by 1871 less that 1 percent of Westmorland and Albert County's population were Anglicans.[50]

The fertile belt along the St. John Valley had accommodated much of the Loyalist influx to the province, many being of English descent. In 1803, the city of Saint John, at the mouth of the great river, seemed to the Methodist minister William Bennett to be little more than "a small English town."[51] But by 1840 it had twenty thousand residents, outstripping Halifax as the largest and most important city on the Atlantic seaboard.

Courtesy of Library and Archives Canada, Acc. No. R9266-1655, Peter Winkworth Collection of Canadiana.

View of the city of Saint John, New Brunswick, from Sandpoint, Carleton.
Lithograph with watercolour on paper by George Neilson Smith (1789–1854),
engraved by John H. Bufford.

Saint John dominated the business life of the river valley, its tributaries, and the Bay of Fundy counties in both New Brunswick and Nova Scotia.[52] Saint John County attracted 30 percent of the English-born immigrants who arrived in the province in 1851, many of them being tradesmen and labourers who would have been seeking city jobs.[53] The "professional men, merchants, tradesmen, mechanics and labourers" who attended the city's Anglican church no doubt included such arrivals, but the nearby Portland church had only "poor emigrants" in its congregation, who depended "on their daily labour" for survival.[54]

The rich intervale lands along the Lower St. John River below Fredericton had the largest number of Loyalist clusters in the valley, with the English predominating most in Sunbury County, where they represented 42 percent of the population by 1871. Having acquired a small number of Massachusetts families in 1763,[55] Maugerville (Sunbury County) went on to attract a much larger group of Loyalists, and they became concentrated

Map 10.

along Little River and around French Lake.[56] English immigrants began arriving in Blissville Parish from 1819, settling in one-hundred-acre lots along the Saint John to Fredericton Road (Colonel Ludlow's Road), running parallel with the nearby Oromocto River[57] (see Map 10). By 1823 the area had attracted the attention of the London Missionary Society, in particular Sheffield, where "the dissenting church and congregation" were fearful of losing the lot of land "that had been reserved for the support of a minister of the Presbyterian or Congregationalist profession."[58] In fact, The Church of the Seceders at Sheffield was the oldest Protestant house of worship in the entire province.[59] The Church of England had some success, as well, building the province's first Anglican church in 1784 at Maugerville.[60]

The Loyalists in Gagetown, farther downriver in Queens County, had followed the much smaller group of settlers from New England, Britain, and Nova Scotia who had starting to arrive in 1765[61] (see Map 10). The county had one of the province's most important immigrant settlements, this being at Goshen (Johnston Parish), founded in 1819 by eleven English families, some of whom had originated from Yorkshire.[62] There were also one or two householders of West Country origin, such as John Crealock from Littleham Parish in Devon, and the Somerset-born William Gamblin, who had probably sailed from Plymouth.[63]

The so-called "English settlement," located near the boundary with Kings County,[64] attracted followers, and clearly prospered. A Saint John newspaper offered this glowing account in 1832:

> We feel pleasure in having to report so favourably on this thriving little colony [English settlement]. It is eight years since the inhabitants began to clear the forest; and, short as is the period, the settlement at this time affords a surplus of produce adequate to the support of double its population. It has thirty families, thirty farms, each of which has from twenty-five to thirty-five acres under cultivation, about 300 head of horned cattle, and a proportionate number of horses, sheep, pigs, poultry, etc. It is within our knowledge that they were burdened with a number of small children at the time of their going on their allotments of land; add to which, they were destitute of almost every resource, and nothing but a steady perseverance and industrious course could, in so short a time, have placed them in circumstances comparatively independent.[65]

The Yorkshire-born John and Henry Applyby [*sic*] were two of the Loyalists who ventured into nearby New Jerusalem (Hampstead Parish), which was also the destination of some of the Yorkshire immigrants who had sailed in the *Trafalgar* in 1817.[66] Intriguingly, a "New Yorkshire" sprouted a short distance from Gagetown in 1826, reinforcing the already strong Yorkshire presence in the area.[67] Gagetown acquired its first Anglican church in 1797, while Waterborough, another Loyalist stronghold that was settled around Grand Lake, had its first church by 1820, serving Youngs Cove and Whites Point.[68]

Although the English were widely scattered in Kings County, most were concentrated along the extensive river frontages in the Kennebecasis Valley as a result of the large-scale Loyalist influx of the 1780s (see Map 10). Becoming a prosperous farming district, the county was said to have acquired "the air of a civilized old settled region" by 1840.[69] When J.F.W. Johnston visited ten years later, he noted how "good soils had rewarded those who found courage enough to clear them of trees and stones and the beautiful landscape gave to a stranger's eye a double value to homes established, despite the obstacles in this portion of Kings county." Moreover, he was assured by local inhabitants that "an industrious emigrant without capital will thrive even in this more stony part of their district."[70] And Abraham Gesner had observed how the English and Irish immigrants in Springfield Parish who arrived in the 1830s "without any means of subsistence" had to live "in shanties among the trees and survive on the most humble fare…. By their industry they afterwards paid for their lots, cleared away the forest, made farms and now drive their wagons to the market at Saint John loaded with the surplus produce of their fields."[71]

With its "rich lands and excellent communication," Sussex Parish (Kings County) became one of the most prosperous farming areas in New Brunswick, although by the time the Reverend Christopher Atkinson visited it in 1844 its agricultural output appeared to be declining.[72] He found it to be "in a wilderness state or is again growing up with bushes, and in some instances has fallen into neglect, owing to the erection of saw mills which have called away the attention of the farmer from the more profitable and certain pursuits of agriculture."[73] Yet, like so many other contemporary commentators, he failed to appreciate the dual nature of the local economy. Farming was important, but the province's wide rivers and interconnecting tributaries were tailor-made for the timber trade, which became the mainstay of the local economy. Early arrivals engaged in timber production both for its own sake and as a means of clearing land for settlement.

By 1871, around 30 percent of Kings County's population was Anglican, the largest showing for the Church of England in the province. This result is probably attributable both to its large intake of English Loyalists and to a sizable immigrant flow directly from England.[74] Kingston's Anglican church was first to appear, having been built in 1788, followed by a church at Sussex, the minister of which presided over the preaching station in the English settlement.[75] The Hampton and Upton church appeared next in 1819,[76] Westfield and Greenwich in 1822,[77] while Springfield and Norton parishes had their churches by 1842.[78]

Like the St. John Valley, Charlotte County in the southwest of the province had acquired a great many Loyalists, but their eventual progress as settlers owed far more to the timber trade than to farming.[79] Predating the Loyalist influx had been thirty-eight Lancashire men, all recruited as indentured servants, who arrived in 1770 at Campobello from Liverpool (see Map 10). Captain William Owen, a retired Welsh naval officer, had brought them to settle on his recently purchased lands, in what he hoped would become New Warrington.[80] Most returned to England, but some remained, joined by New Englanders and later immigrants.[81] Although New Warrington failed as a settlement, the English Bar and English Island place names that did survive in the West Isles suggest that some of the original settlers, or their descendents, ventured to these neighbouring islands. Grand Manan, just to the south, had its first Anglican church by 1832, and a resident minister who complained that "in the summer almost all the males are engaged in hurrying over their little farm work and fishing, and I cannot get a congregation together except on a Sunday in fine winter weather!"[82] By 1871, Campobello, West Isles, and Grand Manan accounted for one-third of the county's English residents.

As forest clearance progressed in Charlotte County, communities formed around the Passamaquoddy Bay and along the lower St. Croix River. Thin lines of settlement also followed the St. Andrews to St. John River Road and the middle stretches of the Magaguadavic River going northward. Population densities were particularly high in the three adjoining parishes of St. Andrews, St. David, and St. Stephen on the west side of the county, but even here agriculture remained secondary to lumbering.[83] The Loyalist town of St. Andrews, with its port in the

Courtesy of Canada, Department of Mines and Resources/Library and Archives Canada, PA-020698.

Photograph of the
Episcopal church at
Grand Harbour, Grand
Manan Island, date
unknown.

Passamaquoddy Bay, was second only to Saint John in population and
economic importance. But as the Anglican minister, Reverend Samuel
Cooke, discovered when he visited in 1785, St. Andrews was largely
Scottish. Yet, "although the majority of settlers profess themselves to be
Kirk of Scotland," they fully accepted his Anglican ministry.[84] Visiting in
1832, Thomas Baillie found St. Andrews to be flourishing, having 2,200
inhabitants, a church, Scotch kirk, and a Catholic chapel.[85]

By 1871 most of the county's English inhabitants were located in
the parishes of St. Stephen, St. David, and St. George. Because the St.
Croix River offered excellent waterpower sites, the western end of the
county became a particularly important sawmilling district, with the
highest concentration of mills being in St. Stephen.[86] The Reverend
Atkinson observed how the men in this area "go into the woods for the

purpose of lumbering, without which many would not be able to raise their numerous families."[87] Before doing so they would purchase food, clothing, equipment, and supplies from local storekeepers on credit, and would later offer their cut timber as repayment.[88] By 1830 the sawmills to the west of St. Andrews were producing around 20 percent of the province's annual lumber output.[89] Twenty years later Charlotte County had 1,600 men working at ninety-seven sawmills, of which thirty-seven were in St. Stephen, each employing about forty men.[90] Milltown (Parish of St. Stephen), together with the town of St. Stephen, had sufficient Methodists by 1804 to warrant a minister supported by the Methodist Missionary Society, a more reliable indicator of the presence of English settlers than were the well-supported Anglican churches at St. George, St. David, and St. Stephen.[91]

From the mid-1820s, as the focus of the timber trade gradually shifted from the Passamaquoddy region northeastward to the Northumberland Strait, the counties of Kent, Gloucester, and Northumberland came to be exploited for their huge timber reserves.[92] Joseph Bouchette found their thickly forested areas to be "the thinnest settled and the worst cultivated in the whole province. There is scarcely any collection of houses worthy of the name of a town in any of them."[93] There was a wealth of wood but only marginal amounts of farmland, and so settlements had spread as long, slender fingers along the coastline and riverbanks.

Although no Loyalists were actually placed in Kent County by the government, it soon attracted a stream of already-established English settlers from the Chignecto Isthmus, as well as immigrants who came directly from England. A notable arrival in 1787 was the Loyalist Solomon Powell from Poughkeepsie, New York, who, having first gone to the St. John Valley, re-established himself along the Richibucto River, becoming one of its earliest permanent settlers. Going into partnership with William Pagan, he founded a prosperous shipbuilding firm and trading centre.[94] By 1848 the firm that he founded had a large steam sawmill employing about one hundred men. With a population of three thousand, Richibucto could now boast of five inns, fifteen stores on both sides of the river, a jail and court house, and could support an Anglican church, a Roman Catholic church, and a "Scotch Kirk and a Methodist place of worship."[95]

Powell's efforts in establishing the Richibucto's lucrative timber trade must have been the spur that prompted Englishmen like Robert Belyea, Tucker Hard, Abraham Downey, Richard and Thomas MacDonald, and Henry Mills to petition for two-hundred-acre lots in the Richibucto area in 1798. Further petitions followed a year later from Peter Luke and Joseph Richard and in 1800 from Robert Taylor and Donald McLean and the Peters, Ricker, and Fairweather families. The land being sought in these and later petitions was situated along the Richibucto River (plus a coastal stretch from its mouth to Bouctouche), the Kouchibouguasis River (plus a coastal stretch from its mouth to Point Esquimicack), and the Cocagne River in the southeastern end of the county.[96] This land granting pattern almost certainly led to the later clustering of English residents in Richibucto, Weldford, and Wellington parishes, visible in the 1871 census.

The rapid growth in Richibucto's timber production that began in 1818–19 coincided with the sudden arrival of English immigrants from Cumberland and Westmorland. With the growing introduction of power looms in England, handloom weavers in the English and Scottish Borders had been experiencing redundancy and low wages since 1815, and in these adverse conditions many emigrated.[97] A group of just over five hundred people, mostly from the north of England, sailed from the Scottish port of Dumfries in 1819, many heading for Kent County, although some also went farther north to the Miramichi.[98] Despite the modest means of most, the *Dumfries and Galloway Courier* claimed that "no less than £18,000 will be carried out" by the emigrants.[99] Three years later the same newspaper condemned the loss of so many unemployed handloom weavers from the Carlisle area (Cumberland) to New Brunswick.[100]

No doubt the brief flurry of advertisements for ship crossings to New Brunswick in the Newcastle and Hull newspapers at this time reflected interest from people in the northeast of England who wanted to benefit from the region's growing timber trade.[101] And such was Richibucto's pulling power that it soon attracted additional English settlers from both Prince Edward Island and Nova Scotia, which by this time were experiencing a relative decline in their timber production.[102] In fact, by 1828–29 Richibucto would be producing almost as much timber as the southwest Miramichi, the region which came ultimately to dominate the trade.[103]

The 1851 census for Weldford Parish (Kent County) reveals that its population included an appreciable number of English farmers, lumberers, and labourers who had come either from England or via Prince Edward Island. The majority originated from the northern counties, especially Cumberland, Westmorland, and Northumberland, but a sizable number also came from Kent, in the south of the country.[104] Despite this influx, twenty years later the English would only account for 13 percent of the county's population, being greatly outnumbered by the Acadians, Scots, and Irish. Nevertheless, the Society for the Propagation of the Gospel still managed to establish an Anglican church and minister at Richibucto (covering Weldford) by 1836. Ten years later the Reverend A.A. de Wolf would note that the people were "agricultural, mercantile and professional. Nearly all attend [church]."[105]

Some English immigrants ventured farther north to the Miramichi in Northumberland County, but they were more the exception than the rule. John Emmerson, who had emigrated from Newcastle-upon-Tyne to Prince Edward Island with his parents when a child, ended up settling along the Northwest Miramichi River, probably North Esk. He and his wife, Maria Tozer, had twelve children, but by 1855 the family had moved to Minnesota.[106] Sometime in the early 1800s John Sewell emigrated from Cumberland to Alnwick (Northumberland County), where he established a large trading, lumbering, and fishing business.[107] Although such examples were fairly uncommon, the Church of England had seen fit to build churches at Chatham and Newcastle by 1821. Nineteen years later the Reverend Samuel Bacon was attending to the "labourers and mechanics connected with the mills and shipyards and timber trade." He was particularly pleased to have the few merchants and professional men in his congregation, "who belong to other religious denominations."[108]

Meanwhile, the Loyalist progression along the upper St. John Valley had created early settlements in York and Carleton counties, with Fredericton, the capital city, having just over 20 percent of York County's English residents by 1871 (see Map 9).[109] However, Fredericton did not seem like a provincial capital to Juliana Horatia Ewing, an officer's wife from Ecclesfield near Sheffield who lived there in 1867. It was simply "a dear lovely place" with "pretty wooden houses." Struck by the fact

Courtesy of Yorkshire Libraries and Information, Wakefield, Ewing Gatty Collection.

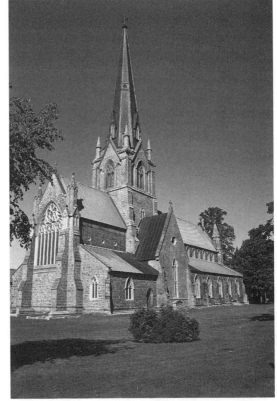

Above: "Our Street" in Fredericton (Waterloo Row). This view was painted by Juliana Horatia Ewing in 1867. The building on the right, at the far end of the street, is "Reka Dom," the rented house used by the Ewings in Fredericton. Juliana's husband, Rex, is on the left, walking toward their home.

Left: Photograph of Christ Church Anglican Cathedral in Fredericton. The cathedral was founded in 1845, with the first bishop being the Reverend John Medley.

Photograph by Geoff Campey.

that most of the streets were still unnamed, she likened them to "shady lanes."[110] She clearly equated Fredericton with a small English town but, compared with the griminess of her home town in industrial Yorkshire, it must have seemed a paradise.

Fredericton also had an Anglican King's College by 1829, but it was more broadly based than its counterpart in Windsor, Nova Scotia, since it allowed non-Anglican students to attend: "Hewn from the rough stone of the country it was long regarded as the province's finest building."[111]

The English concentrations apparent by 1871 in the parishes of Canterbury and St. Mary's (York County) are probably traceable to the influx of settlers from the various disbanded Loyalist regiments in the mid-1780s, as was the sizable Anglican congregation that formed at nearby Prince William and Dumfries. That said, "the numerous souls under the care of the Church of England" by 1857 included many Irish and Scots.[112] Juliana Ewing witnessed the great dedication of Anglican ministers for herself: "I have driven 19 or 20 miles with one of these parsons to visit one sick person. The Anglican Church of All Saints Magaguadavic (Prince William Parish) ... was built with the hard labour of the parson and his parishioners. The day the roof was put on they all flung their hats into the air and shouted."[113]

While parishes situated along the upper river valley acquired many of their settlers by the late eighteenth century, the more remote regions of York County had to await the formation of the English-owned New Brunswick and Nova Scotia Land Company[114] before colonization could proceed.[115]

Purchasing 589,000 acres of Crown land, a tract that stretched north from the St. John River and west along the Nashwaak River and the portage road to the Southwest Miramichi River, the company sought colonizers from Britain. In fact, it was one of two land companies that became operational in 1834, the other being the British American Land Company, which strove to convert the wilderness of the Eastern Townships in Lower Canada into a settled landscape.[116] Both were modelled on the Canada Company, established eight years earlier, which promoted settlement schemes over its two million acres in Upper Canada. And yet, although their holdings were closer to Britain, both companies faced stiff competition from the Canada Company because of the superior quality of its land. This advantage enabled the Canada Company to attract many more British immigrants than its two rivals.[117] Thus, while the New Brunswick and Nova Scotia Land Company's promotional literature enthused over its "vast tracts of fertile forest lands watered by numerous rivers," the reality was very different.[118] Much of its land was relatively poor, and the company struggled long and hard to attract settlers.[119]

The flourishing English settlement[120] created at Stanley (Douglas Parish), primarily by immigrants from Northumberland and to a lesser extent the Scottish Borders, brought credit to the company.[121] Even so, the settlement at Stanley had a difficult beginning. Oddly, its first settlers were thirty-five orphaned and destitute boys from Christ's Hospital in London.[122]

Placed under the care of the Children's Friend Society, the so-called "Blue Boys," named after the blue coats they wore,[123] attracted considerable attention when they reached Saint John. But they were totally unsuitable for the job at hand.[124] Despite considerable public alarm in the province over the proposed relocation of London's street urchins to the province,[125] the New Brunswick legislature co-operated with the company scheme, viewing the children as a welcome source of cheap labour. Nonetheless, the boys were treated wretchedly. John Harvey, very astute for his age, devised a plan to expose the company's despicable behaviour and the Children's Friend Society's connivance in its venture. He wrote a letter to his mother and had her read it aloud in the Marlybone Magistrates Court in London. An obliging *Times* reporter, who was in the court at the time, made sure that it was published:

> When I arrived at Saint John I sailed up to Fredericton
> in a steam boat and then we come up to Stanley and
> then we had to sleep in a barn amongst horses and lay in
> amongst straw and then we was put out to the woods in
> the camp by ourselves and the meat was only fit for hogs;
> and dear mother we was sent out to work and we could
> not walk because we was all ragged like a beggar and

starved with cold. And then we last winter was took out
further to the woods and Mister Forss had us chopping
down his trees and all the boys mostly left him.[126]

Harvey went on to work in a tavern, having "very heavy work to do"
and being "bad situated for clothes," but the tough days ended and by
1851 he had become a farmer/lumberer with a wife and three children of
his own. Other boys included John Thomas, who married and became
a farmer/lumberer and was a noted gardener, and Richard Bellamy, who
became a land surveyor and member of the Legislative Council.[127]

Next to arrive were 110 settlers from Berwick-upon-Tweed
(Northumberland) and the Scottish Borders, who set sail for Saint John
in the summer of 1836 in the *D'Arcy* of Sunderland, "a fine new brig"
chartered by the land company "for the conveyance of agricultural
labourers, etc. to settle on their lands."

The arrivals greatly impressed a reporter from the *British Colonist*,
who described them as "regular practical farmers of good character
and highly respectable appearance ... and bring along with them the
unsophisticated and gentle manners of 'Merry England' with the beautiful
associations of Border ballad and Border chivalry."[128] However, they were
actually poor agricultural labourers who, having suffered low wages and
poor job prospects in Northumberland, hoped for a better future.[129] Most
came with little or no capital, their passage money being advanced to
them, and they had to rent land from the company, although later they
could buy their own land. An unnamed young man quickly assessed the
situation and wrote home, stating that "no man need be afraid to come
on to the company's land as they pay ready money for all their work;
whereas in other parts of the country everything is done by barter."[130]

Yet all was not well initially. Having been promised "considerable
advantages" by the company, they "found that there were neither houses
nor crops ready for our reception as promised," and to make matters
worse, the company had reneged on its commitment to provide them
with employment.[131] Being "in danger of starving for want of food" by
1838, eighteen family heads petitioned the British House of Commons
for help[132] (see Table 4). The company had little choice but to concede

Table 4

The "English" Emigrants Residing at Stanley, 1838
[NAB CO 188/61 147–8, 288–9; 1851 Census; Elliott, "Emigrant Recruitment
by the New Brunswick Land Company," (Spring 2005): 37]

Name	Occupation (1851 Census)	Ethnic origin
George Humble	farmer/lumberer	English
William Humble	farmer/lumberer	English
Walter Dixon	*	English
Andrew Gray	farmer	English
Robert Waugh	surveyor	Scottish
William Pringle	*	English
John Douglass	farmer	Scottish
Thomas Winter	*	English
Thomas Allan	*	English
James Allan	tailor	English
William Currie	farmer/lumberer	English
David Turnbull	farmer	Scottish
Thomas Jaffrey	*	Scottish
James Duncan	*	Scottish
Matthew Johnson	farmer/lumberer	Scottish
John Kerr	*	English
Joseph Young	*	not shown
Thomas Young	*	not shown

* Denotes not in 1851 Census.

---

the "advantages" that it had initially promised, and more. The Stanley immigrants were to be given more time to pay for their sea crossings, free transport from Saint John to Stanley, provisioning payments for their first fourteen days, compensation for past deficiencies, and employment to tide them over until their crops were ready. Also, each settler was to have a fifty-year lease for every one hundred acres, and pay one shilling per acre.[133]

Clearing town plots at Stanley. The New Brunswick and Nova Scotia Land Company established the town of Stanley on the Nashwaak River in 1834. The lithograph, dated October 1834, is by W.P. Kay, printed by Day & Haghe, London, England, and published by George Ackerman & Co., London, England.

But when the Berwick settlers wrote home to their friends in Wooler and Ford in Northumberland, they put quite a different gloss on these happenings:

> Their lands were not prepared for crops nor their houses built on their arrival, this instead of being a disappointment we consider rather a fortunate circumstance as everyone has been allowed to choose his own farm from the best lands round Stanley and to have his house built to answer his own taste and to suit the prospects of his family. Everyone of us is well pleased with the land he has chosen and the house built for his accommodation; indeed we have all been kindly treated by everyone belonging to the company…. There are many thousand acres of land around Stanley of good quality fit to produce excellent crops of wheat, barley, oats, potatoes, turnips etc … the land only wants to be cleared and cultivated to produce crops equal to any in England.[134]

They even wrote approvingly of the company's generous treatment, stating that fifteen families had been advanced £2,968 in 1837.[135] Needless to say, the company's promotional literature incorporated such plaudits, with a later booklet providing extracts of John Kerr's letter to his parents in Coldstream near Berwick: "The land is good and free from stone; it will grow any kind of grain once the plough was in it.... If anyone was intending to come to America, Stanley is as good a part as [Upper] Canada and you get the land cheaper than Canada … people must work hard but you have a chance of a return in the end for your labour and that is more than you will have in the old country, for you will never have a chance of having any land of your own there."[136]

Despite being mainly English, most of the Stanley people were Presbyterians, although no regular religious services were held at Stanley until 1845. Stanley residents had to wait another twenty-three years before their first Presbyterian church was built, while a Methodist church followed shortly after, in 1874.[137] Later inhabitants recalled how isolated the first settlers were. There was "no conveyance except by boat in summer," and in the winter transport depended "on the river ice." People often swept the snow from the ice to provide "a threshing floor to thresh their wheat." Sometimes it had been necessary to grind the wheat "by hand between stones or eat it boiled whole, there being no mill nearer than the mouth of the Keswick."[138] But they were hardy people, and judging from the Stanley settlers' request in 1871 for fifteen thousand acres near the Miramichi River, they were going from strength to strength, seeking territory far beyond the company's control.[139]

The Harvey settlement, founded a year after the one at Stanley, also attracted families from Northumberland (especially the Wooler area) as well as some from the Scottish Borders. In all, 137 people (twenty-three families and several single men) sailed in 1837 from Berwick to Saint John in the *Cornelius* of Sunderland.[140] A settler list, produced by the company in 1837, giving family member names and ages, reveals that, as was the case with the Stanley settlers, the men were mostly labourers (see Table 5). Some were tradesmen, but there were no farmers in the group.[141] The *Berwick Advertiser* was happy to report their safe arrival and two births during the crossing.[142] Intending to obtain company land,

Table 5

Harvey Families Who Ask for Land on the New St. Andrews Road
[PANB RG637 #26d: Records of the Surveyor General, 1837]

Name	Age	Station	Occupation
David Cesford	34		labourer
Margaret Cesford	34		his wife
Wm Taite	50		nk
Barbara Cesford	9		
Margaret Cesford	6		
John Cesford	3		
Infant	4 mo.		
Robert Wilson	34	husband	labourer
Mary Wilson	34	wife	
Betsy Wilson	18	daughter	
Thomas Wilson	16	son	
Mary Wilson	10	daughter	
Margaret Wilson	8	daughter	
Robert Wilson	6	son	
Alexander Wilson	3	son	
Jane Wilson	3 mo.	daughter	
John Thompson	35	husband	teacher
Isabella Thompson	29	wife	
John Thompson	16½	nephew	
John Thompson	5	son	
Betsy Thompson	3	daughter	
Margaret Thompson	1½	daughter	
Thomas Herbert	37	husband	miller
Isabell Herbert	26	wife	
Eleanor Embleton	20	sister	
Elisabeth Embleton	18	sister	
Robert Embleton	16	brother	labourer
Margaret Herbert	12	daughter	
Isabella Herbert	10	daughter	
Robert Herbert	8	son	
Mary Herbert	3	daughter	

Name	Age	Station	Occupation
Christina Herbert	1	daughter	
John Cockburn		husband	labourer
Betsy Cockburn?		wife	
James Cockburn	22	son	taylor
George Cockburn	20	son	labourer
Isabell Cockburn	18	daughter	
Betsy Cockburn	16	daughter	
William Cockburn	14	son	
Charlotte Cockburn	12	daughter	
Andrew Cockburn	10	son	
Thomas Cockburn	7	son	
Ralph Cockburn	3	son	
Alexander Hay	46	husband	bl smith
Jane Hay		wife	
William Hay	21	son	bl smith
Andrew Hay	20	son	bl smith
Alexander Hay	18	son	
Mary Hay	14	daughter	
John Hay	12	son	
Jane Hay	6	daughter	
Isabell Hay	4	daughter	
Eleanor Hay	1	daughter	
Thomas Piercy	48	husband	labourer
Mary Piercy	47	wife	
Betsy Piercy	20	daughter	
Mary Piercy	18	daughter	
Isabell Piercy	16	daughter	
Walter Piercy	10	son	
John Gregg	45	husband	labourer
Mary Gregg	43	wife	
Jane Gregg	21	daughter	labourer
James Gregg	20	son	labourer
Andrew Gregg	18	son	painter
Esther Gregg	17		

Name	Age	Station	Occupation
Agnes Gregg	16		
Thomas Kay	42	husband	mason
Isabell Kay	43	wife	
Jane Kay	7	daughter	
Mary Ann	3	daughter	
Andrew Montgomery	50	husband	labourer
Nancy Montgomery	50	wife	
Andrew Montgomery	22	son	labourer
David Montgomery	20	son	labourer
William Montgomery	17	son	
Jane Montgomery	15	daughter	
Margaret Montgomery	11	daughter	
James Montgomery	9	son	
Thomas Thomson	34	brother	labourer
James Thomson	24	brother	labourer
James Mowet	28	husband	labourer
Catherine Mowet	30	wife	
Agnes Mowet	3 mo.		
Thomas Mowet	30	husband	miller
Betsy Mowet	30	wife	
James Cowe	32	husband	labourer
Isabell Cowe	31	wife	
Mother in Law	50		
Eleanor Cowe	7	daughter	
Mary Cowe	4	daughter	
David Cowe	1½	son	
John Scott	39	brother	carpenter
Scott	41	sister	perhaps
John Wightman	45	husband	labourer
Mary Wightman	44	wife	
Eleanor Wightman	14	daughter	

Name	Age	Station	Occupation
Isabell Wightman	11	daughter	
John Wightman	8	son	
Elisabeth Wightman	6	daughter	
William Grieve	47	husband	shop
Elean Grieve	47	wife	
John Grieve	15	son	
Patrick Grieve	13	son	
William Grieve	11	son	
George Grieve	9	son	
Alison Grieve	8	daughter	
Henry Grieve	6	son	
Margaret Grieve	3	daughter	
Matthew Piercy	22	husband	labourer
Agnes Piercy	21	wife	
James Cockburn	22		taylor
William Messer	36	husband	labourer
Elean Messer	35	wife	
Elisabeth Messer	10	daughter	
Walter Messer	5	son	
William Messer	3	son	
Thomas Messer	9 mo.		
William Bell	26	husband	labourer
Jane Bell	26	wife	
Thomas Brown	37	single man	labourer
James Nesbit		widower	labourer
George Nesbit	21	husband	labourer
Elspeth Nesbit	18	daughter	
James Nesbit	15	son	
John Nesbit	43	husband	
Susan Nesbit	21	daughter	
Thomas Nesbit	19	son	
Anne Nesbit	17	daughter	

Name	Age	Station	Occupation
John Nesbit	15	son	
Elisabeth Nesbit	12	daughter	
James Nesbit	10	son	
Jane Nesbit	7	daughter	
Robert Nesbit	5	son	
Ann Nesbit	42	wife	
William Embleton	27	husband	carpenter
Jane Embleton	26	wife	
George Embleton	2½	son	
James Embleton	1	son	
John Carmichael	31	husband	labourer
Margaret Carmichael	31	wife	
James Carmichael	3	son	
Samuel Carmichael	2	son	
Robert Carmichael	4 mo.		
Mary Hume	19	sister	
Jane Hume	6 mo.		
William Robson	25	single	labourer
Andrew Montgomery	22	single	labourer
James Craigs	23	single	labourer

they rejected the site offered and instead opted to settle along the road then being constructed between Fredericton and St. Andrews [143] Yet, as was the case with Stanley, things did not go according to plan, although this time the provincial government, and not the land company, had to pick up the pieces.

"A competent person" was employed to manage "the labours of the settlers and to instruct in the process of clearing and preparing the land for cultivation and in the erection of log houses."[145] But work only began in August, and, although they had constructed twenty-one log houses by the time winter arrived, inadequate progress had been made for them to be self-sufficient. Spending their first winter in Fredericton, where they were accommodated in a "new hospital" and provided with provisions, the cost of maintaining them began to rocket. By February 1838 the authorities had spent around seven hundred pounds on the settlers, of which around two hundred was claimed back as settler earnings for working on the roads, but around five hundred pounds remained "unpaid."[145] However, the situation improved dramatically, and by the end of that year twenty-three families "had cut down about 200 acres and had at least 160 acres fit for crops in the ensuing Spring." Officials had "much pleasure reporting most favourably of their conduct and deem[ed] them a most valuable acquisition to the country and especially to the road on which they [were] located."[146] The news got better, since by 1843 some 292 acres had been planted with crops.[147] And the superlatives continued, as officials appointed to oversee the scheme stated that "for industry, sobriety and perseverance no men can surpass them while they only want an opportunity to introduce the most approved systems of agriculture as now pursued in England."[148] The Reverend Atkinson was also impressed by what he saw when he visited Harvey: "A few years ago they suffered severe hardships and privations but at present they are in comfortable dwellings and making great clearings in the woods."[149]

Favourable reports sent back to Northumberland led Thomas Craigs to chance his luck in Harvey in 1841. A handloom weaver and an ardent Presbyterian from Lanton (Northumberland), he emigrated with his sons and, although it was against his religious principles, raffled off his possessions to raise the money for the voyage, sailing in the *Glengarry* of Saint John which departed from Liverpool.

Thomas wrote to the minister at Wooler, where he had himself been a church elder, describing the crossing:

> The ship we sailed on was large, and employed in the timber trade, having many sailors for her crew. At first, these spoke very unguardedly, but I believe that I have seldom had a better opportunity of doing good; for being much in their company, I failed not to let drop such words of advice as might be of use to their immortal souls. So favourable seemed the impression at

length made that we parted with great reluctance at the
end of the voyage — by which time our conversations
had become very different from what they were at
first; and when taking leave, I said, I hoped we should
all meet in Heaven. One of them came with us several
miles, helping us to bear part of our goods to another
ship, which was to take us up the river.[150]

Wasting no time, the seventy-year-old Thomas Craigs walked five
miles to the nearest church the day after his arrival in Harvey.[151] "There
is here as yet no regular preacher to preach the Word and, having been
called upon, I made some remarks from the 7th, 8th and 9th verses of the
89th Psalm."[152] Thomas must have been a considerable asset to Harvey.
Three of his sons stayed in Harvey while other children dispersed to
other parts of Canada, one daughter ending up in Australia. Continuing
favourable reports back from Harvey probably stimulated the trickle
of departures in 1842.[153] By the following year, Harvey had forty-five
families and was held up as a prime example of what could be achieved
by competent and industrious settlers:

> The great success which has followed the labours of these
> industrious and valuable settlers is an unquestionable
> proof of what may yet be done on our millions of
> Wilderness Lands. The returns show that from land
> where not a tree had been felled in July 1837 there
> have been taken during the past autumn 260 tons hay
> and straw and 15,000 bushels of grain, potatoes and
> turnips It is desirable that the accompanying return
> may be circulated among the settlers' friends and
> countrymen in the north of England as well as in other
> parts of the UK so that the capabilities of our new land
> soil may appear and that it may also be known that at
> least 5 million acres are yet undisposed of most of it
> better quality land than at Harvey, whereon the sober
> and industrious emigrant may create a home under

the protection of British laws and in the enjoyment of
British institutions.[154]

The settlers themselves were happy to concur: "The climate of New
Brunswick agrees well with the constitution of Englishmen; the air is
salubrious and the water as pure and wholesome as any in the world....
Six years experience have [sic] convinced us that notwithstanding the
early privations into which new settlers are exposed diligence and
perseverance must ensure success."[155]

Farther up the St. John Valley, Carleton County[156] had been acquiring
its initial settlers from disbanded Loyalist regiments and later immigrants
who arrived from Britain. Having built its first Anglican church by
1791, Woodstock Parish had a strong Loyalist nucleus and a sizable
Church of England congregation, but by 1837 its inhabitants were in an
"almost unprecedented and unparalleled state of distress," driven to the
alternative of "either digging their potatoes planted for seed or starving,
although here the population was probably largely Protestant Irish."[157] Just
over 40 percent of its population by 1871 was English, with the largest
concentrations being at Woodstock, Brighton, and Wakefield (see Map 10).

As large numbers of British immigrants came and left immediately
for the United States throughout the 1840s, administrators agonized
over solutions to halt the drift.[158] By the 1850s the influx had practically
stopped. A bleak report in 1852 to the British Parliament recorded only
2,165 immigrant arrivals — a decrease of 1,305 compared with the
previous year.[159] The slighter better results reported for 1853, when 3,762
people arrived, was attributed to "the English and Scotch," who took up
jobs working on the railway or as agricultural labourers.[160] Nonetheless,
this number was still only a small fraction of the total British outflow,
which favoured Upper Canada and the United States. Faced with this
alarming situation, the House of Assembly appointed James Brown as an
emigration agent in 1861.[161] Undertaking a promotional tour of Britain
to sell the province's merits, Brown made much of his penniless arrival
in New Brunswick, his ability to buy a farm seven years later, and his
subsequent rise to prosperity and public acclaim. It was a dream come
true for his audiences, yet few people responded.[162]

Brown spent most of his time lecturing in Scotland and Ireland, and only conducted a partial tour of England, taking in Grantham and Bennington (both Lincolnshire), Newark (Nottinghamshire), Doncaster and York (both Yorkshire), and Durham.[163] He was careful to promote the success of the Harvey settlement, realizing that it provided an outstanding example of how farm labourers who "began with nothing" could, in just six years, accumulate "property in cleared land, farm produce, cattle, sheep, swine, etc. to the value of £4,289."[164] However, Brown's influence was minimal. The province's timber trade was its key attraction initially, but as time went on immigrants sought the richer opportunities to be had farther west.

The timber trade was also the bedrock of the Prince Edward Island economy, but unlike Nova Scotia and New Brunswick, most of its inhabitants could trace their roots back to people who had actually emigrated directly from England. Planters never came and few Loyalists actually remained. The English were successful pioneers and came to dominate the island's economic and political life, but they encountered immense hurdles along the way.

CHAPTER 6

With Ships to Launch:
The Prince Edward Island English

> *The ships got under way and were cheered by not less than*
> *5,000 persons, who lined the quay and bridge [of Bideford,*
> *Devon]. Many of those persons who have thus expatriated*
> *themselves are respectable farmers and families who carry*
> *with them very considerable property.... And such is the*
> *prevailing rage for emigration that a female, who had*
> *given birth to a child but three days before, would not be*
> *persuaded by the most urgent entreaties of her friends to*
> *remain behind until another season.[1]*

THE RAGE TO emigrate during the 1830s caused the greatest excitement in Devon and Cornwall, but even here the exodus to the island only happened in fits and starts. Having sold the island's land to wealthy proprietors in a lottery held in 1767, the British government saddled its inhabitants with a semi-feudal landlord regime that retarded its early development. Following the lottery, its townships fell under the control of private landowners, who had to pay annual quit rents and recruit settlers for their holdings. But because there were no effective sanctions, few proprietors met these obligations. The only group to arrive in any appreciable numbers during the 1770s were Gaelic-speaking Scottish Highlanders, who were a far cry from the government's preferred English-speaking, Church of England stereotype.[2] The conflicting interests of proprietors and local government officials blocked land reform, thus leaving island inhabitants vulnerable to the uncertainties and economic disadvantages inherent in leasehold tenure for the best part of a hundred years.[3] Settlers faced a murky world of land dealers and absentee landlords, who effectively held power but yet felt no sense of responsibility for the economic well-being of the island. Little wonder that, initially, few English people wanted to immigrate to the island.

Predictably, the island's population grew slowly. By the late 1770s it had only 1,300 inhabitants of European origin, with forty-nine of the sixty-seven townships having no settlers at all.[4] Some thirty years after the lottery, the island could claim only 4,400 inhabitants, and by the end of the century, twenty-three townships still remained completely uninhabited.[5] However, with the large British exodus that followed the end of the Napoleonic Wars in 1815, the island's population increased more rapidly, and by 1827 reached just over twenty-three thousand.[6] The census counted around forty-seven thousand people in 1841, with more than half of them living in Queens County.[7] And while Scots dominated the British influx during the late eighteenth and nineteenth centuries, they were overtaken by the English and Irish, who came in much larger numbers between 1820 and 1850. By 1881 the English were an important element of the population in Queens County and much of Prince County.

The 1881 census reveals that English numbers were greatest in Queens County — especially in the Charlottetown area (Lots 32 and Lot 33), where people of English ancestry accounted for around 50 percent of the total population (see Map 11). Given that they were also the second largest ethnic group in New London (Lot 20), the Rustico Bay area (Lots 23 and 24), Bedeque (Lots 25 and 26), Tryon (Lot 28), and Lot 31, to the west of Charlottetown, the English presence in this one county was substantial.[8] It was a similar picture in Prince County, but although people of English ancestry had a strong presence here, they never

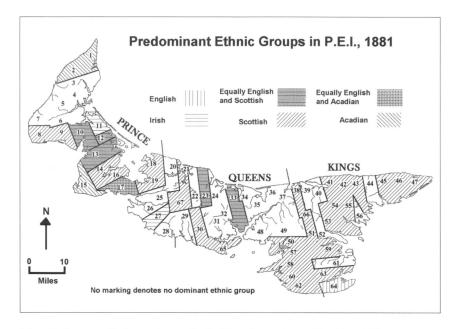

Map 11. Source of information is Clark, *Three Centuries and the Island*, 90.

actually dominated any one township. They were second numerically to the Acadians[9] in St. Eleanors (Lot 17), yet outnumbered the Scots and Irish, and shared first place with the Scots in West Devon (Lot 10), Bideford (Lot 12), and Port Hill (Lot 13). While Kings County had a scattering of English settlers in several townships, Murray Harbour (Lot 64) was the only area where they predominated, but a sizable proportion of those claiming English ancestry here were probably the descendents of Channel Islanders.[10]

Although several Scottish proprietors recruited settlers for the lands they had acquired by lottery, their English counterparts failed to do the same, apart from Robert Clark, a London merchant, who tried but had little to show for his efforts.[11] The island had to wait until the ending of the Napoleonic Wars in 1815, when the British economy went into a sharp decline, before acquiring a significant number of English colonizers. The first large group arrived from Yorkshire between 1817 and 1819, but there were few followers. Emigrants from Devon also came at this time, beginning what would become a major influx that lasted

into the 1830s and 1840s. Suffolk lost an appreciable number of people
to the island, and a scattering also came from other parts of England
— especially Cornwall, Norfolk, Somerset, Wiltshire, Gloucestershire,
Lincolnshire, Lancashire, and Cumberland.[12] However, the island faced
stiff competition from the United States and Upper Canada, which
offered far better land and job opportunities, and its appeal progressively
waned. By the mid-nineteenth century very few immigrants had arrived
from anywhere in Britain.

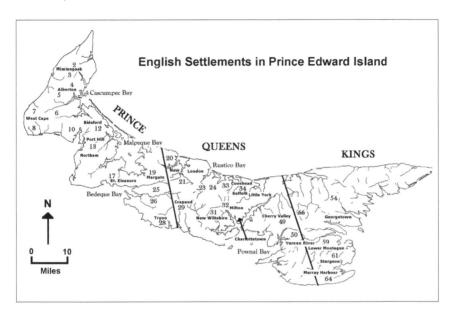

Map 12. The Lot numbers shown on the map had English communities.

English colonization began in 1774 when Robert Clark brought one
hundred settlers,[13] recruited mainly from London, to the north shore of
the island. There they founded New London (Lot 21), known initially as
Elizabethtown, named after the ship *Elizabeth*, in which they had sailed
(see Map 12).[14] Most of them came as indentured servants to work for
Clark in the lumbering enterprise that he would establish.[15] The most
notable arrivals were Benjamin and Elizabeth Chappell, a married couple
from London.[16] Benjamin, a wheelwright and Methodist lay preacher,
kept a diary of the group's harrowing experiences and contributed

greatly to public life on the island, becoming a member of the island's assembly in 1779, soon after his indenture expired.[17]

According to Governor Walter Patterson, Clark "really thought himself a second Penn ... who hoped to make New London a place for the recovering of sinners."[18] Being a Quaker, Robert Clark probably wanted to provide a religious haven for people like himself, and this aspect of the venture may have appealed to Chappell, who was said to be a very pious man. While Clark's New London settlement struggled from crisis to crisis, Clark could at least take comfort in the knowledge that he had established Prince Edward Island's first Methodist stronghold. However, when the Reverend William Black of Nova Scotia came to preach in 1783 at Chappell's invitation, he claimed to have met people who "in general appeared stupid and senseless as stones, altogether ignorant of the nature of true religion and of that faith which worketh by love."[19]

Having completed his initial preparations, Clark had returned to London, leaving his colonists to fend for themselves, without sufficient food or shelter.[20] Benjamin Chappell recorded how the group came close to starving during the winter of 1775. On February 24 they reached the point where they had "no flour, no rum, no meat flesh and no bread in the stores," and a month later illness had struck through "want of provisions." Feelings ran high as the people organized "a party to supprize Charleytown," but even more trouble lay in store in April, when the first shots were fired in the American War of Independence.[21] Although the island itself was never involved in any conflicts, the war severely impeded its trade and economic life. To add to these concerns, the settlers lost most of the supplies that were due to arrive from London later that year. Having run aground in November on the great sandbar near Princetown, about a mile from the shore, the Elizabeth became wrecked, leaving her twenty passengers to fend for themselves until they were reached by rescuers from Malpeque Bay.[22] They endured exposure and near-starvation because of inadequate provisions at New London. It was a miserable beginning for the two groups of settlers.

Thomas Curtis, a labourer from Hampshire and one of the 1775 arrivals, had anticipated a land of plenty, but his "first view" of New London shattered his illusions. He wrote that there was "a little row of log houses and one large house ... in all about sixteen" and that "where the agent lived might have had two stories." To put it mildly, he wrote, "[I] was much surprised to see what a place it was — it being so very different from the idea I had formed of it; I then began to repent of my voyage and wish myself in Old London again.... I soon came to the determination of leaving this place as soon as possible." Curtis felt that Clark had misled him, having described a place "well stocked with timber," where easy profits could be made — so much so that Curtis had been convinced that "any man could live much more comfortable there than in England.... Nay don't think if any one would have given me £500 I should have been satisfied to have stayed in [Old] London."[23]

The reality was very different.

Curtis left the island in 1776, but worked a few months in the Newfoundland fisheries before returning home: "I can't convey the Joy I Felt when I got on my native Country the 2nd of February, 1777."[24]

Meanwhile, Robert Clark's financial problems were multiplying. According to John Cambridge, his New London agent and fellow Quaker, Clark, along with Robert Campbell (the co-owner of Lot 21), had advanced up to fifteen thousand pounds of credit in promoting the settlement by the end of 1774, but had little to show for their investment. In 1792, by which time Clark moved to the island, he was said to be in financial ruin.[25] Following his death in 1794, which was preceded by several lawsuits over debts, his estate was sold, and by 1800 the houses of New London were reported to have been torn down or moved.

However, John Stewart, who visited New London in 1806, reported that although the settlement had experienced "unfortunate circumstances," it was "still going on."[26] The arrival in 1831 of Thomas Billing, a Plymouth merchant, along with twenty-eight settlers,[27] reveals that the New London settlement continued to attract English settlers. But by 1851, however, the town was described as having "principally Lowland Scotch" inhabitants.[28] Perhaps reflecting some loyalty to Clark's original dream, at least three of the settlers who arrived in the 1770s — John and Thomas Adams from Derbyshire and James Townsend from Park Corner, Berkshire — remained at Lots 20 or 21, and ended their days there.[29]

English settlers were among the Loyalist arrivals of 1784, but their number is uncertain and they scattered to many parts of the island.[30] Following Britain's defeat in the American War of Independence, six hundred Loyalists were apparently moved at government expense from the United States, but this number is far greater than the two hundred reported by Governor Walter Patterson.[31] The discrepancy can be explained, at least in part, by Loyalist dissatisfaction over land-granting procedures, which prompted many to leave. Whatever their number, Loyalists mainly took up residence on the isthmus between Malpeque Bay and Bedeque in Prince County (Lots 16, 17, 19, 25, and 26). Smaller groups were to be found in Queens County at Lots 32, 35, and 65, in the middle of the island, and at Lots 49 and 50, along the upper reaches of Orwell Bay.[32]

When W.H. Crosskill visited these areas in 1906, he discovered "the many well-known families of ... thrifty and prosperous citizens of such fine farming districts as Bedeque, Pownal (Lot 49), Vernon River (Lots 49 and 50), etc. who are descendents of those who, in 1783, preferred George of England to his namesake, Washington."[33]

S.S. Hill, who visited Bedeque (Lot 26) much earlier, in 1839, also found that it was "chiefly occupied by the descendants of Loyalists."[34] St. Eleanors (Lot 17), the major hamlet on the isthmus, acquired a substantial English population by 1881 that probably had its roots in the Loyalist influx to the area. The Church of England congregation, which had 576 members in 1854, was then building its third church, and could support a resident Anglican priest, who regularly travelled to five scattered preaching stations.[35] Unlike St. Eleanors, which had a thriving Anglican congregation by 1881, the other Loyalist areas like Bedeque and Vernon River were strongly Methodist.[36]

The 174 people from the Isle of Wight who arrived in 1791 at Cascumpec, on the northwest end of the island, left no trace, and may have moved on to another part of the Maritimes[37] (see Map 12). Sailing from Cowes in the *Minerva*, they were accompanied by Captain Alexander Fletcher "of the Island," who belonged to an influential group led by Walter Patterson, the former governor. The group, which included John Hill and John Cambridge, both West Country merchants, was highly critical of Governor Edmund Fanning's dismal record in running the island's economy.[38] The

Photograph by Geoff Campey.

St. John's Anglican Church at St. Eleanors.

group hoped to entice settlers, and possibly Fletcher had gone to the Isle of Wight with this purpose in mind. While large numbers of Gaelic-speaking, Catholic Highlanders arrived in 1790–91, there is no evidence that an Isle of Wight contingent actually settled at this time. A small trickle of arrivals did come from the Isle of Wight, but not until 1807.[39]

Despite the hazards of crossing the Atlantic during the Napoleonic War years (1803 to 1815), the island acquired more British settlers in 1806 when eighty Channel Islanders from Guernsey arrived at Charlottetown in the *Neptune*.[40] They headed for John Cambridge's land at Murray Harbour (Lot 64) in Kings County (see Map 12). The name of Guernsey Cove near Murray Harbour is a lasting testimony to their presence. Like the original New London settlers, they were mostly Methodists.[41] Cambridge, who had worked as Robert Clark's agent, was by this time one of the island's most successful merchants and greatest landowners.[42] He had written a pamphlet, *circa* 1798, advocating emigration, and later claimed that he and other proprietors had brought many people to the island, although, apart from the Channel Islanders, little evidence survives of Cambridge's other recruits.[43]

Overcoming the many perils and privations of pioneer life, the Channel Islanders created the "very pleasant, thriving and comfortable settlement" at Murray Harbour that Walter Johnstone observed in 1820–21.[44] However, Richard Cotton could remember a time before this when the Guernsey people had great difficulty in acquiring food. When they did procure their wheat and other goods "they had to carry it on their backs through the woods to their needy families or drag it on the snow and ice on a small hand-sledge."[45] Murray Harbour's population[46] was augmented in 1839 with the arrival of "some good farmers" who "had lately come" (from England), resulting in "a great improvement in the system of cultivating the land."[47] John Lawson found Lot 64 to be "a flourishing settlement" when he visited it in 1851.[48]

All the while, John Cambridge and his sons had been benefiting from the island's timber trade, which expanded rapidly after 1811, when tariffs on Baltic timber were doubled, pricing it out of the market.[49] In 1807, Prince Edward Island had exported only one thousand loads of timber to Britain, but by 1819 it exported over seventeen thousand.[50] Cambridge already had a large sawmill in place along the Murray River in 1808, and beginning in 1811 he financed the building of large ships to carry his ever-increasing timber cargoes from Murray Harbour to Bristol.[51] His ships returned to the island with merchandise and occasionally with some passengers[52] (see Appendix IV). The timber trade gave Cambridge his fortune and gave emigrants, with access to Bristol, affordable transport to the island as well as winter employment opportunities once they had settled.[53]

The greater availability of transatlantic crossings, made possible by the timber trade and bleak economic conditions in England just after the Napoleonic Wars ended, brought a sudden influx of Yorkshire settlers to the island. Some of the names of the 196 people who sailed in 1817 from Hull in the *Valiant* were later recalled by two of the passengers (see Table 6).[54] More Yorkshire settlers came the following year, but their number is uncertain, while 101 people arrived in 1819, sailing on the *Dixon* from Hull.[55] Benjamin Chappell observed that the 1817 Yorkshire people "appear very cautious; they don't settle as yet but a Mr. Fishpond is here from Bedeque endeavouring to get them to go there."[56] Mr. Fishpond

Table 6

Partial Passenger List for the *Valiant* Crossing from Hull to Charlottetown, in 1817.
[**Murray, *The "Valiant" Connection*, 6–7**]

The list is based on names provided by two passengers — Reverend Matthew Smith and Mrs. William Court, who were both children at the time of crossing. Those from Reverend Smith only are marked by an *, while those only mentioned by Mrs. Court are marked by @. The remainder are common to both.

Name	[Status]	Settled
William Baker	and family	Tryon
Richard Hudson	Preacher	Tryon
Christopher Smith	and family	Crapaud
Joseph Trowsdale	and family	Crapaud
George Wiggington	and family	Crapaud
Thomas Carr	single	Crapaud
John Pearson	single	Crapaud
Robert Hawks	and family	Albert County, NB
Isaac Smith		Charlottetown
Henry Smith		Charlottetown
William Lund	and family	Lot 48
Thomas Fawcett	and family	Covehead
Mr. Sigsworth		St. Peter's Road
Thomas Hardy		Little York
George Hardy	and family	Little York
Vincent Bell	and family	Tracadie
John Hutchison	and family	Tracadie
@Robert Dodd	and family	Cherry Valley
@Anna Moore	single	
@T. Mason	single	
@William Mason	single	Little York
@Mr. Fox	single	
@William Weldon	single	cabin passenger
@Matthew Burdett		cabin passenger
@Christopher Cross		cabin passenger
*William Hodgson	and family	Crapaud
*John Rennison		Albert County, NB
*John Millner		Sackville, NB
*John Towse		Sackville, NB

Name	[Status]	Settled
*Robert Lund		Lot 48
*Thomas Best	and family	Little York
*Robert Vesey	and family	Little York
*George West	and family	Little York
*Richard Cross		Charlottetown
*William Stead	and family	Covehead

would have received little encouragement. Although they were tight-lipped, the Yorkshire settlers appreciated their options. Vincent Bell, one of the *Valiant* passengers, had visited the island in 1816 and concluded that it "suited north of England folk with agricultural leanings."[57] His recommendation no doubt encouraged others to follow. John MacGregor later claimed that the Yorkshire settlers had not intended to remain but, "being delighted with the appearance of the colony," applied to the agent of Sir James Montgomery, Lord Advocate of Scotland,[58] to give them leases of one hundred acres fronting on the road from Charlottetown to Stanhope.[59] Their lack of funds to buy land and/or inability to obtain freeholds had clearly forced them to rent. According to MacGregor, they had each cleared fifteen to twenty acres of land by 1826, "and under excellent cultivation ... the neatness and cleanliness of everything about them reminded me of England."[60] Little York, the name of the community thus formed at Lot 34, would proclaim their Old World origins.[61] Much later, A.B. Warburton would refer with good reason to the "industrious and careful settlers from Yorkshire."[62]

Abraham Gill, one of the original Little York settlers, had originated from Devon rather than Yorkshire. His journal, written from the moment he arrived in 1819 at the age of twenty-three, records the challenges of pioneer life. Although late in the season, he immediately planted potatoes "among the windfalls and stumps." He added, "There were not many cattle about at that time so I made a rough fence and the plants grew well. I put the potatoes in a pit for the winter."[63] Having obtained his land and survived the first winter, Gill began to earn a living "by the sweat of his brow," working for various farmers, who gave him board and lodgings that were "very different from what [he] was accustomed to." Building a log house in the second winter, by which time he had cleared about two acres, he went on to marry Elizabeth Tanner the following year. Then, in 1824, he helped build Little York's first Methodist Chapel, "a task which to him was a labour of love."[64]

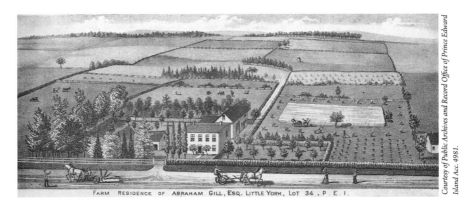

FARM RESIDENCE OF ABRAHAM GILL, ESQ. LITTLE YORK, LOT 34 , P . E . I .

Courtesy of Public Archives and Record Office of Prince Edward Island Acc. 4981.

Meacham's Atlas, 1880, 45a: Farm residence of Abraham Gill, Esq., at Little York, Lot 34.

Ruby (West) Hudson, a descendent of one of the Yorkshire settlers, was told of the care taken by Little York's first settlers "to make their new land as much like their homeland as possible." When cleared, their farms were measured off into square fields surrounded by hedges "which were mainly of thorn trees." Ruby's grandfather, who "always wore a white shirt and was never known to do any manual labouring other than gardening," was clearly enjoying an affluent lifestyle. "With the white shirt he wore a black tie, a black or iron-grey suit and knee-length leather boots. All his attire had to be spotless."[65] This was a far cry from the mean existence that Abraham Gill had endured four decades earlier.

While a good many of the Yorkshire emigrants settled at Little York, a sizable number also went to Crapaud (Lot 29), where they rented land from Lady Westmoreland.[66] A few remained in Charlottetown, while others settled at Covehead (Lot 34) and Tryon (Lot 28), and some may have moved on to New Brunswick[67] (see Map 12). Christopher Smith, who originated from the parish of Harum (Helmsley, in the North Riding), laid the foundations of Methodism in Crapaud. Matthew, one of his sons, became a Methodist preacher, but, after a disagreement with his congregation, he joined the Baptist church and moved to New Brunswick. Although Lady Westmoreland did her best to further the interests of the Church of England, providing money for an Anglican church that was built in 1841, Methodism reigned supreme at Crapaud.[68]

Christopher Cross, a wealthy businessman from Wetwang near Great Driffield in the East Riding of Yorkshire, found Charlottetown to his liking, but for him it was probably just a convenient overseas base from which to avoid his creditors back home. Visiting Yorkshire regularly, he kept a close control over his business interests there.[69] After his return trip to Charlottetown in 1843, when he sailed from Bideford in the *Civility* as a cabin passenger, he left behind an irate Yorkshire publican. According to William Spence, Cross still owed "a sum of money, advanced by his father to Cross, when he was last in England."[70] But Cross was miles away in Charlottetown, taking pleasure in morning snowfalls, cheap and plentiful food provisions, and the Yorkshire newspapers that his brother Thomas sent to him.[71]

In addition to attracting Yorkshire emigrants, the island also received settlers from other northern counties, although their numbers were much smaller. In 1820–21 two groups, totalling twenty-eight emigrants who would have originated from Northumberland and Durham, sailed from Newcastle-upon-Tyne in the *Caldicott Castle*.[72] Between 1820 and 1822 just over one hundred people came to Charlottetown from the Cumberland port of Whitehaven, but they probably included former weavers from Dumfriesshire and other parts of the southwest Scottish Borders, who were leaving in large numbers at this time.[73] The port of Liverpool frequently sent ships to the island, although most carried only a few people. The ninety-three people who sailed in the *Pitt* from Liverpool in 1821 would have originated primarily from Lancashire and Cheshire, and possibly West Yorkshire, but given Liverpool's huge pulling power as a major port, other county origins, such as Derbyshire, cannot be ruled out.[74] Cemetery transcriptions and death notices reveal that these northerners scattered to many parts of the island.[75]

The Yorkshire influx diminished by the early 1820s when Upper Canada's better, fertile land became more accessible after new roads and waterways were built to provide inland routes from the St. Lawrence ports. To make matters worse, the island's economic prospects were being severely damaged by the catastrophic economic downturn experienced in Britain at this time. The slump meant falling timber sales and lower prices, and because timber exports were the bedrock of the economy, islanders faced a grim future.[76] According to Fade Goff, agent for the London merchants George and Alexander Birnie, "the lumber trade is destroyed." Newly arrived settlers "are making hard struggles to subsist, and many of them are doing all in their power to get forward with their farm; their industry and superior management must at some future day serve the Island … when a change of times for the better happens."[77] However, eight months later the situation was even worse. "Our Gaol is filled with debtors and with felons in irons," he wrote, and business had become "a source of extreme misery to me."[78]

By 1825 the British economy was growing again and the island enjoyed greater prosperity, although the cycle of boom and bust would repeat itself many times over.[79] Despite this upturn, most English settlers rejected the Maritime provinces and headed off instead to the United States or Upper Canada. There was, however, one group who remained loyal. Devon people continued to arrive, especially during the 1830s and 1840s, when conditions for agricultural workers were dire. Recognizing the island's great shipbuilding potential, West Country merchants bankrolled numerous enterprises, thus offering important employment opportunities to settlers during the winter months. And because they had extensive landholdings, they also provided the land on which immigrants could settle. John Cambridge had told his sons that "the most effectual way of getting my debts remitted" was by "building a ship annually and loading her with timber," and selling both in Britain.[80] This is precisely what these merchants did. They reaped the combined profit of the timber and shipbuilding trades. Easily accessible transport links and good job opportunities encouraged large numbers of Devon settlers to come to the island long after its rejection by most other English emigrants. They founded their communities first on the west side of the island in Prince County and later colonized large parts of Queens County.

John Cambridge had been first to found a shipyard, doing so in 1811, and John Hill soon followed, focusing his efforts on Lots 3 and 4 to the north of Cascumpec Bay on the west of the island.[81] In 1830, when he was residing in Exmouth, Hill sought workmen for his Cascumpec lumber business, claiming that he had eighty thousand acres to lease or sell, and adding that "those who are industrious cannot fail of doing well."[82] Thomas Pope, a Plymouth shipbuilder and timber merchant, had sent his sons to the island in 1817 to establish a shipyard at Charlottetown, and another shipbuilding enterprise soon followed at Bedeque. James Peake, also from Plymouth, arrived in 1823 to found his shipyard in Charlottetown, and so it went on. West Country merchants were regularly sending shipwrights, carpenters, and skilled workmen from Bristol and Bideford to their island shipyards to build vessels; and from the 1830s, ships arrived at Charlottetown from these same ports with crews in their holds to navigate their newly built ships back to Britain.[83] Around thirty-four vessels a year came off the production line in the 1820s, and by the 1860s, when production peaked, an average of ninety ships a year were being launched.[84]

Of all the shipbuilders, Thomas Burnard, Bideford's leading merchant and shipowner, was to have the most profound impact on the

Photograph by Geoff Campey.

James Ellis Peake's brick house on Water Street, Charlottetown. The house was close to his stores and wharves and had a view of the harbour, where his ships would leave and enter.

island. When he recruited a small group from North Devon to establish a shipyard at the western end of the island, he provided the catalyst for the large-scale emigration from Devon, and to a lesser extent from Cornwall, that occurred during the 1830s and 1840s. It had a low-key beginning. In 1818 Thomas had sent his nephew Thomas Burnard Chanter to the island, together with William Ellis, a shipwright, and his two apprentices, Edward Williams and John England, in the *Peter and Sarah* to found a shipyard at what would become New Bideford (Lot 12). The 342-ton *Mars* duly appeared in 1819. It was the first of many ships to be built by Ellis over the following eight years.[85]

Thomas Burnard's venture proved to be a godsend to the long-established Scottish and English families who were living on scattered farms at the adjoining Lot 13. Reputed to be one of the best townships on the island, having fertile land and a superb natural harbour, Lot 13 had previously accommodated a substantial Acadian community.[86] When they vacated their houses, barns, and 750 acres of cleared land in 1765,[87] the ready-made site soon attracted colonists like the Dorset-born George Hardy, one of the rescuers of the ill-fated New London-bound group that had arrived on the *Elizabeth* in 1775. He lived there from as early as 1769, although he moved to Lot 6 when the ownership changed and rents rose.[88] But by 1793, when Lot 13 was in the possession of Lord Seymour of Ragley, its tenant farmers were many and included James Smith, Alexander Brown, Roderick Gillies, Donald Forbes, Donald Ramsay, Malcolm Ramsay, Daniel Murphy, William Hunter, George Penman, and Dugald Campbell.[89] Their landlord, Lord Seymour, had provided a basic infrastructure, including outbuildings, roads, and mills, within which settlements could develop, while Thomas Burnard's shipbuilding venture, at Lot 12, brought a second injection of capital to the area. An important spinoff for Seymour's tenants was the opportunity they now had of selling their labour and lumber in exchange for imported goods.[90]

Yet Lord Seymour's tenants were appalled by the semi-feudal conditions that were attached to their leases. According to Seymour's agent, they threatened to seek a new landlord in 1793 "who would insist on none but the payment of their rent" unless he became "as liberal as other proprietors," which he presumably did, since they remained.[91] Lot 13 had more than forty families in 1824, but with its major North Devon shipbuilding connections many more would join this and other communities on the island. Between 1830 and 1844, when economic conditions in Devon were particularly dire, around 1,500 people sailed to the island from West Country ports, with the majority leaving from Bideford.[92]

The Port Hill and Northam place names that emerged in Lot 13 commemorate Devon and reflect the prevalence of Devon settlers[93] (see Map 12). An Anglican preacher from St. Eleanors who visited Lots 12 and 13 in 1825 reported that he usually attracted around eighty people,[94] but it would be another sixteen years before Port Hill would have its first Anglican church — the so-called "Old Shipbuilders' Church."[95] The influx to New Bideford (Lot 12) and Port Hill (Lot 13), which began from 1830, occurred at roughly the time when James Yeo, a humble carter from Kilkhampton in North Cornwall, was making his mark on the area.[96] After Thomas Burnard died in 1823, bequeathing his shipyard, together with the leases on various landholdings, to his nephew, Thomas

James Yeo Sr. (1788–1868), portrait by Robert Harris (1849–1919).

Burnard Chanter, Yeo moved in for the kill. Chanter, having no interest in running the business, sold everything to William Ellis, who was then outfoxed by Yeo.

Yeo had all of the gifts necessary for success in a pioneer society. He was ruthless, lawless, had a phenomenal memory, and was a wizard with figures. Beginning in 1818 as a mere employee of Thomas Burnard Chanter, he assumed responsibility for collecting debt payments owed to the business after Burnard's death, even though they belonged to Ellis. An honest master craftsman, Ellis was no match for a wheeler-dealer like Yeo,[97] who soon accumulated sufficient capital to become a storekeeper, lumber dealer, and shipowner. By the 1830s Yeo was on his way to becoming the island's principal shipbuilder, with Ellis being a mere employee of his firm.[98] His 283-ton *British Lady*, built in 1836, would regularly ply between Charlottetown and Bideford, carrying lumber one way and passengers and goods the other. In 1843 the ship arrived with crewmen to sail three new vessels back to Bideford, and the process was repeated in 1846 when the "masters and outfits" for five more new vessels arrived at Port Hill.[99] Yeo had arrived.

Establishing his headquarters on the east coast of Lot 13, Yeo went on to acquire large quantities of land and was elected to the island's assembly in 1839. He came to be regarded as the richest man on the island and it was claimed that his payroll and credit advances to his employees alone far exceeded the whole revenue of the government.[100] He was the top man in the powerful clique of mainly English shipbuilders and merchants who came to control the economic and political life of the island.

A good many of the seventy-four people who sailed in 1830 from Bideford in the *Collina* were thought by the *Royal Gazette*'s correspondent to be "in good circumstances"; the men were "farmers, labourers and mechanics" who originated chiefly from Devon and Cornwall, the latter reflecting Yeo's pulling power in attracting his fellow countrymen.[101] There were a further seventy who came that year in the *New Bideford* from Plymouth and another 197 who sailed two years later from Bideford in the *Calypso*.[102] Among the passengers in the *Collina* crossing of 1830 were Humphrey Dyment, his wife, Mary Ashton, and their children, from Barnstaple in Devon.[103] Humphrey found work at Yeo's Port Hill shipyard,

James Yeo's son, James Jr., built this magnificent house in the mid-nineteenth century. It has since been restored and is open to the public.

while the family settled initially on Lord Seymour's land at Lot 13, but moved to Northam in 1855, founding the Dyment homestead. Yeo, who was agent for Lord Seymour's holdings in Lot 13, described Humphrey Dyment and another tenant, William Birch, as "good respectable tenants" and a William Dyment, presumably a relative of Humphrey's, as "a new tenant" who had "very good land."[104] Feeling bullish about his position, Yeo informed Lord Seymour that his tenants were "glad to hear I was appointed the agent," since he would follow a long-standing practice of taking a tenant's produce as payment for rent or goods: "In no part of the Island have they the same privilege as they have in this place."[105]

Yeo was building ships on a large scale from 1840, and in doing so played a vital role in the island's economic development. His success had been a magnet for the ever-increasing influx from the West Country. Even the affluent Henry Shearman had opted for the better life that he believed the island offered. He had read in John MacGregor's *Maritime Colonies of British America*, published in 1828, that Prince Edward Island was "a very desirable colony for an emigrant to settle in" and that it had "land sufficient to engross the labour of from 10,000 to 20,000 persons in the cultivation of it."[106] Writing to the Colonial Office in 1835, he asked about the availability and cost of obtaining "untilled land." He apparently received an encouraging reply, since he and his family sailed in the *Castalia* from Plymouth to Charlottetown as cabin passengers the following year.[107] Establishing themselves at Keston Farm along the Hillsborough River (near Charlottetown), the family's social circle soon included Lady Westmoreland, who visited regularly. A major worry in 1840 was the wild animals that were damaging the garden. But although he gave his sister "a pretty long catalogue of grievances sufficient to deter any reasonable person from seeking to emigrate," he admitted that "after all, I dare say we shall some day laugh at all the annoyances."[108]

At the other end of the social spectrum were Thomas Hammond, his wife, Dorothy Goss, and their family — ordinary folk from Barnstaple who immigrated to the island in 1840. Joining them two years later was Dorothy's father, also from Barnstaple.[109] Small family groups such as this made up the contingents that regularly sailed from Bideford. Around one hundred people left in 1841, while in the following year the same number sailed in Yeo's *British Lady* from the vicinity of Kilkhampton, Yeo's native village.[110] A further three hundred arrived from Bideford and Falmouth that same year, while another 150 came from Bideford in 1843.[111] Most were labourers, craftsmen, and small farmers from North Devon and North Cornwall.[112] Yeo's ships, especially the *British Lady*, carried West Country emigrants to the island until at least 1847, but, with the coming of a railway to Bideford in 1855, giving people easier access to Bristol, Plymouth, and later Liverpool, Bideford's role as an emigrant departure port ended.[113]

Becoming a major economic hub, Lot 13 attracted many of the early Devon and Cornwall settlers, but it soon filled up. They became widely dispersed as Francis Metherall, the island's first Bible Christian missionary, would soon discover.[114] Established in 1815, mostly in Devon and Cornwall, as a separatist Methodist group, the Bible Christian Mission was bound to have widespread appeal. Metherall, a native of North Devon, came with his Guernsey wife and children in 1832 to seek supporters but, oddly, they settled in Kings County, well away from the West Country settlers, who were primarily concentrated in Prince and Queens counties. Metherall had seized the opportunity extended to him by the Vernon River (Lot 50) inhabitants, a settlement that included many Loyalists and their descendents. Accepting a preaching appointment, he made Vernon River his home and in time extended his missionary work to Lower Montague (Lot 59), Georgetown (Lot 54), and Sturgeon (Lot 61).[115]

Soon after his arrival in Vernon River, Metherall was joined by Philip James, who came from Appledore (Devon). Between them, the two missionaries presided over thirty-six preaching places that extended from Sturgeon and Murray Harbour in the east to West Cape and Cascumpec (Lots 5 and 6) in the west. Metherall took care of the area to the east of Hillsborough River and James dealt with the rest. Metherall's impact is reflected in the substantial Bible Christian congregation that formed at Vernon River, but there was little support for it elsewhere in Kings County, apart from Murray Harbour (Lot 64), which had a long-standing affiliation with Methodism. Predictably, the Bible Christian movement did well in Prince County, especially at West Cape (Lots 7 and 8) and West Devon (Lot 10), but it was far less successful in Bideford (Lot 12) and Northam and Port Hill (Lot 13), where Wesleyan Methodism and Anglicanism attracted relatively large numbers.[116] Apparently, the Bible Christian church, built at Bethel (Lot 8) in 1873–74, had a "bible on the Communion Table [that] was brought from England."[117] Although Wesleyan Methodism was strong in Kensington and Margate (Lot 19), there were few Bible Christians. This was the case despite its sizable intake from Devon and Cornwall.[118] Falling in an area occupied by Loyalists and their descendants, local people were possibly less receptive to the teachings of this new religious sect.

Large Bible Christian congregations were also to be found in Queens County, particularly along the Winsloe and Union roads (Lot 33) running north from Charlottetown.[119] Again, this was an area with a striking Devon and Cornwall presence.[120] The Charlottetown preaching circuit extended to the Hunter River area (Lot 23) and to the west where people like Isaac Oxenham were based.[121] He and his family had arrived in 1832 with "a shipload of Devonians."[122] Purchasing land at Lot 23, he became "most successful," leaving behind comfortably off children in various parts of

Photograph by Geoff Campey.

St. James Anglican Church, Port Hill, consecrated in 1843.

the island and in the United States. Other Devon families who came with the Oxenhams included the Rattenburys, who also settled at Lot 23.[123]

A religious revival, which began in the Vernon River district in 1842, augmented the Bible Christian membership across the island, but total numbers were never very significant.[124] Replacing Metherall in 1856 was Cephas Barker from Chatham (Kent). Although he promoted "aggressive evangelism" for nine years, his influence on the Bible Christian cause was slight.[125] An obscure and little-known religion, it could not compete with the dominant Roman Catholic and Presbyterian faiths. Edward Pigeon,[126] a nonconformist preacher sent by the London Missionary Society and based in St. Peters, remarked ruefully that "a man who could preach in the Gaelic tongue would be a great blessing to these parts."[127] The Reverend William Stewart, an Anglican minister who presided over Cherry Valley (Lots 49 and 50), made that leap, boasting how he had "cultivated with success the Gaelic language which is much spoken in Prince Edward Island."[128] But he, too, had an uphill struggle to win converts, despite being bolstered by the immense resources of the Church of England.[129] Wesleyan Methodism fared little better, accounting for only 7 percent of the island's population in 1855. Its missionaries were based in Charlottetown, Bedeque (Lot 17), Murray Harbour (Lot 64), and later Pownal (Lot 49), all areas with long-established communities (see Map 12). Perhaps this made them more conservative and more resistant to the unorthodox brand of Methodism being offered by the Bible Christian incomers.[130]

The influx from East Anglia began during the 1830s, the time when large numbers from the West Country had been making their way to the island. Along with the rest of southern rural England, East Anglia was experiencing desperate rural poverty, prompting large-scale emigration. While Upper and Lower Canada acquired most of the impoverished southerners, many Suffolk and some Norfolk people opted initially for the island. Some 540 emigrants sailed from Great Yarmouth, East Anglia's principal port, between 1829 and 1834, with the first arrivals being merely twelve people, including William Butcher and his family, from South Elmham St. James in Suffolk. William was clearly pleased with what he saw, since he returned home a year later to collect his grandparents and take them back to Charlottetown, where they all settled.[131] Possibly he had gone as a scout on behalf of his wider community, since many more Suffolk people emigrated over the next five years. Although they were widely scattered, they became concentrated in the Charlottetown area (Lot 33). The Suffolk place name in the adjacent Lot 34 is a lasting testimony to their presence. Roger Harper, arriving in 1830 and settling on Suffolk Road, and Samuel Aldridge from Laxfield, settling in Suffolk a year later, are probably two of the original founders of the Suffolk community in this Lot.[132]

Although most of the people who came during this short-lived influx were self-financed, the arrivals also included poor farm labourers who had been given the money to emigrate by their parishes. Enduring low wages and dismal employment prospects, they were the poorest of the poor. William Dowse, governor of the Stradbroke Workhouse in the Blything Poor Law Union[133] of North Suffolk, explained how, with the coming of greater mechanization, rural unemployment had been soaring, placing an increasingly heavy burden on ratepayers: "The principal part of the corn being thrashed with machine has caused the labourers to be unemployed — also a great deal of the draining of land is done by machinery when the labourer is standing still and paid by the parish — which cause so much money to be paid for unemployed labour."[134] The enactment of the Poor Law of 1834 enabled English parishes, which were struggling with the problem of chronic unemployment and rising poor rates, to raise funds for assisted emigration to British colonies.[135] These one-off payments gave the poor a chance of a better life, and, because they were no longer placing an ongoing demand on public resources, ratepayers had a sharp reduction in their poor rates.[136]

But some people argued that emigration was an inhumane solution. The poor were being dispatched to a faraway land simply to lessen the poor rates burden of the rich, who wanted rid of them.[137] An 1833 booklet, aimed at "the working and labouring classes of Suffolk and Norfolk," offered "a complete exposure of emigration — showing the hardships and insults the working and labouring classes have to undergo before reaching their destination and of the scandalous tricks practised upon them by certain interested individuals."[138] There was also hostility to the harshness of the New Poor Law regime, which denied wage subsidies to the able-bodied, forcing them to choose between the miseries of a workhouse or seek nonexistent jobs.[139] Faced with this dilemma, many people left the area, finding employment in factories in the industrialized regions of the north. Others clamoured for aid to emigrate. This route offered a welcome escape from a cycle of despair and poverty, and held out the hope of a better life.

After the modest intake of 1829, the island acquired 210 settlers from Suffolk and Norfolk in the following year, many with sufficient capital to buy farms.[140] The group may have also included Samuel Holland, from Halesworth Parish, who had been given seven pounds, five shillings for his passage money to the island or Upper Canada, "whichever place he preferred to go."[141] Abba Short, a twenty-seven-year-old woman, came that same year from Huntingfield Parish, but she and her two young sons died soon after their arrival. Both Huntingfield and Halesworth parishes were in the Blything Poor Law Union, a Suffolk district in which one-third of the male population was unemployed.[142] Most of the island's intake from Suffolk was, in fact, drawn from the Poor Law

Unions of Blything, Plomesgate, Hoxne, and Wangford, all situated in the northeast of the county where unemployment was rife. People from the Blything parishes of Benacre, Kelsale, Uggleshall, and Covehithe seemed particularly keen to accept help, although most of those assisted to emigrate in later years went to Upper Canada.[143]

Included among the 160 settlers who arrived in 1831 in the *Baltic* and *Minerva* were the families of John Birt, John Cook, William Smith, Charles Gibbs, and Samuel Mayhew, all from Benhall Parish (Plomesgate Union). The five families who went "by their own will" received nineteen pounds, ten shillings for clothing, thirty-five pounds, ten shillings as spending money ("to be received at Yarmouth"), seventeen pounds, two shillings, and sevenpence for provisions, and fifty-four pounds for their passages.[144] The total bill, amounting to £126, eight shillings, represented an average cost of twenty-five pounds per family, which approximated the annual cost of maintaining a family in the Plomesgate workhouse.[145] The Cook, Birt, and Smith families even managed to obtain an allowance of one gallon of gin per family for the crossing. Other 1831 arrivals included people from parishes in the Poor Law Unions of Hoxne and Wangford.[146]

Another 149 settlers arrived in the *Baltic* and *Preston* in 1832,[147] twenty-four came in the *Baltic* in 1833, while only nine arrived in 1834, all assisted to emigrate by their parish of South Elmham St. James (Wangford Union).[148] While Suffolk was characterized by some parish-assisted emigration, it should be remembered that there were plenty of men, like William Peacock, who arrived in 1832, with sufficient capital to purchase property. He visited various Suffolk people on the island, each of whom had bought between two hundred and three hundred acres of land, and he himself had similar expectations until he changed his mind and settled instead near York (later Toronto).[149] These comfortably off farmers were far more pernickety about their choice of location than the distressed agricultural labourers, who primarily sought an escape from grinding poverty. Attracted by the greater freedoms and land opportunities of the New World, they looked for the location that provided the best economic return on their capital investment — so, for them, emigration involved far more "pull" than "push."

The influx from East Anglia ended in 1834. With its better opportunities Upper Canada beckoned. William Cattermole, the Canada Company's agent, rammed home its many advantages in the *Suffolk Chronicle* and other East Anglian newspapers. With the availability of parish-assisted emigration schemes, even the very poor had access to Upper Canada, since the added cost of the internal route westward to reach destinations there was included in their allotted payments. From the mid-1830s, London shipowners regularly advertised crossings from London to Quebec in East Anglian newspapers, but not to Charlottetown or other Maritime ports.

Cattermole's persistent hard sell of Upper Canada's perceived virtues undoubtedly weakened the island's ability to attract people from Suffolk and Norfolk.[150] He found people like the disgruntled William Peacock, who, having glimpsed the island briefly in 1832, moved on to Upper Canada, blaming the island's colder climate and less attractive land and job opportunities for his decision. Peacock's letter soon found its way into a Canada Company brochure along with a letter published in an Ipswich newspaper claiming that "Upper Canada has most decidedly the advantage over Lower Canada, Prince Edward's and places adjacent."[151] Such was Cattermole's high profile that the poor even approached him for help. Interceding on behalf of Mr. E. Miles of Halesworth Parish, who needed fifty pounds to emigrate with his family, Cattermole hoped the Poor Law Guardians would "see the propriety of acceding to his desire to emigrate to a part of the world [Upper Canada] in which any industrious man need not have fear of obtaining an independent livelihood."[152]

Although Cattermole and the Canada Company's campaigning would have attracted interest, the letters written by friends and family already settled in Upper Canada carried even more weight. Having moved to Marion, near Palmyra in western Upper Canada, Susan Woolnough told her father living in Beccles in Suffolk how "my brothers would do better here with two days worked in a week than it is possible for them to do in England."[153] Two years later she reported that "there are a great many English settled in this province and I see by the last paper that upwards of 7,000 emigrants has [sic] arrived at Quebec, chiefly from England this season and many more at the quarantine station in the St. Lawrence."[154]

That same year, John Freeman, already ensconced at Goderich, informed William Dove, of Saxmundham in Suffolk, that "if you were to offer me the sum of one thousand pounds to live again in England, it would not the least tempt me…. If I clear ten or twelve acres every year, I shall soon have a good large farm."[155] The island's ability to attract emigrants was severely damaged by such reports.

Wiltshire also lost a small number of people to the island during the 1830s, but despite its association with desperate rural poverty the arrivals appeared to have paid their own emigration costs.[156] They founded New Wiltshire (Lot 31), having been recruited by a compatriot — the Devizes-born William Douse, who arrived a decade earlier. He encouraged them to take up leaseholds on Lot 31, which formed part of the sixth Earl of Selkirk's immense estate (see Map 12). As the estate's land agent, Douse issued the leases and collected the rents.[157] Being elected to the island's assembly in 1834, he became a prominent politician, and twenty-one years later actually acquired the fourteen thousand acres that constituted New Wiltshire.

Judging from a letter written by "one of the New Wiltshire farmers" in 1839, the community flourished, taking pride in "the improvements made by the industrious settlers who so boldly located there." But David Haystead, who had arrived penniless from a Norfolk workhouse, having been assisted to emigrate by his parish, was dissatisfied. The anonymous letter-writer thought that Haystead, who had become "prosperous far beyond any former period of his life," left New Wiltshire "as one discontented in prosperity."[158] But Haystead was also disappointed with the United States, where he had relocated, and returned to the island a year later. Understandably, William Douse offered his letter of contrition to the *Royal Gazette*:

> Although [I am] in purse much poorer, I am returned something wiser than I was when I left you. I have indeed paid rather dearly for my increase of wisdom; but dear as it cost me, I will not be so ungenerous as to withhold the benefit of it from others amongst whom I mean to settle again, and who, as I was, are discontented in prosperity….

> All I saw and heard whilst there [United States]
> tended to convince me that it is certainly not a country
> yielding the advantages to a poor man, which I had been
> led to believe; and I honestly declare that, in returning
> to this Island I have done so under the conviction that
> it is the best country I have seen for the industrious
> agriculturalist.[159]

This positive endorsement of the island appears too good to be true. Upper Canada and the United States were the preferred destinations of most Wiltshire people, and personal recommendations such as this could have swung opinion in the island's favour. Manufactured or not, the publicity must have helped Douse to recruit the thirty-seven people from Devizes, and places nearby, who came to settle in Lot 31 in 1842.[160] They almost certainly included Mary Ann Willis (wife of John), from Potterne near Devizes, who died at Lot 31, and may also have included John Harrell, from Bulkington near Devizes, and James Offer from Wiltshire.[161] According to James Waylen, a contemporary writer, Douse had in fact "established two flourishing settlements called North and South Wiltshire; the site of the chief town whereof bearing the name of New Devizes has just been marked out [in 1859] and enrolled in the government documents."[162] The North and South Wiltshire names survived, but if there ever was a New Devizes, it did not. In any case, judging from death notices and cemetery transcriptions, most of the people who ended their days in North and South Wiltshire (Lot 31) had originated from Devon and Cornwall, with Wiltshire people being far better represented in Lot 33.

As was the case with Wiltshire, Kent's poor were always directed to Upper and Lower Canada, and those who could pay their own way generally went to the United States. However, the island did acquire thirty-two self-financed Kent people in 1829 who mainly settled near Charlottetown (Lot 33).[163] Included in the group was Alfred Horne, who originated from Canterbury.[164] Emigrants from the counties of Somerset, Surrey, Gloucestershire, and Lancashire also tended to congregate near Charlottetown, although they arrived singly or in tiny groups. And the initial pulling power of New London (Lot 21) may have been responsible for the steady trickle of London emigrants who arrived during the late eighteenth and early nineteenth centuries, although most of them eventually settled in Lot 33.

When Sidney Smith visited the island in 1850 he found it to be a "place of pure English society and manners, highly eligible to the capitalist or to persons in the middle ranks of life, while its temperate climate might also allure the labouring man." No doubt his impression of an English aura had been formed as a result of travelling in and around

Courtesy of Confederation Centre Art Gallery, Charlottetown, P.E.I. Gift of the Robert Harris Trust, 1965, CAG H-401.

St. Paul's Anglican Church, Charlottetown, built in 1836. It was replaced on the same site by the present stone church, constructed in 1896. Painting by Robert Harris (1849–1919).

Charlottetown. A member of the Legislature, he went a stage further and claimed that "the state of society ... perhaps as good as in any colony, was due to the "good many English families [who] have, within the last 10 years, settled on the Island, bringing property with them and having by their superior means and number obtained some little influence in the place; they have improved the character of society in it."[165]

This was a time of rising prosperity. Sydney Smith observed how "life seems easy to all classes, wages moderate, provisions and clothing cheap." He credited the island's well-being to "the moderate price of labour and land and of the low price of all the necessaries of life."[166] James Cross, from Babcary Parish in Somerset, having accompanied the Prince of Wales on his tour of North America in 1860, "was very much taken up with it." Writing to his cousin, who lived in Bungay (Lot 23),[167] he told her how he had "such an excellent account of it from one of the officers who is living with the governor; I had some thought to going out to that part and to recommend others to go. I know it would be no use without a few hundreds of pounds so as to buy land and I thought of recommending my brothers George and Tom who has not been very successful in Australia."[168]

The island even managed to attract the Buckinghamshire grandee John Grubb, but he was a very special case. Arriving in 1841 with a family, housekeeper, and eight servants, he built a large house for himself and settled down to a gentleman's life on the island. Having invested in a failed London theatre, he had faced financial ruin. Selling his manor in Horsenden that year, he immediately moved to the island. He probably emigrated to escape his creditors. Grubb's barbed comment to the Duke of Buckinghamshire that Charlottetown society was "by no means despicable" suggests that "push" rather than "pull" had motivated his departure.[169] Grubb died five years later, having been a member of the Legislative Assembly during his brief time on the island.[170]

Grubb's friends in Princes Risborough (Buckinghamshire) hoped that he would smooth the way for people they knew who wished to emigrate. Mrs. I. Shard wrote for advice "on the possibility of a young man being usefully and advantageously employed in your Island ... to any gentleman who was purchasing or had land he would be a valuable assistant as a steady manager and his services might ... be rewarded as to enable him to realize a sufficiency to maintain a family."[171]

Grubb replied:

> He can never succeed here unless he comes out with a capital of £400 or £500 so as to purchase a farm partly cleared with a small house or hut, barn, stable and cow-house thereon, two horses, a little stock and farming implements.... Many come out with the laudable intention of making their own way in the Bush. I am unacquainted with a single instance where the emigrant has not totally failed and to drown care, disappointment and mortification almost invariably ended in perpetual intoxication.[172]

Grubb's perspective was far removed from the world of an agricultural labourer, who could aspire to a weekly wage of eight shillings, fivepence in the south of England or eleven shillings, sixpence in the north — if he was fortunate enough to find work.[173] The emigrants who arrived with large amounts of capital clearly had an easier time, but, contrary to Grubb's claim, most emigrants of modest means did prosper, albeit in some cases slowly and after enduring initial privations and hardships. But Grubb's picture of the despairing emigrant is a salient reminder that some immigrants simply could not cope with the rigours and challenges of pioneer life. S.S. Hill described how "the sight of a tall forest, encircling sometimes a single farm and the stumps of the trees up to the doors of the ill-constructed dwellings of many of the settlers ... quite disheartens" all but the most determined of settlers, and that "in some cases the English farmer goes alone; and lands perhaps where the settlers are from a different part of the United Kingdom and probably speak a different dialect ... and although he is not an alien in their eyes, they to him are as strangers."[174] Success required enormous reserves of courage, resilience, and determination.

The island's shipbuilding industry peaked in the 1860s, but collapsed dramatically a decade later with the arrival of steamships. This was when the Scots and Irish began to leave in droves, but the English remained. While they had accounted for only around 21 percent of the overall British influx to the island by 1881, they increased their proportion of the population later on. Unlike the Scots and Irish, who left in great numbers beginning in the late nineteenth century, most of the English appeared to have remained on the island. As a consequence, the English and Scottish elements of the population were roughly equal, at around 30 percent, by the mid-twentieth century, with the Irish and Acadians making up the difference.[175]

Generally, people of English origin had settled in those areas of the island where agriculture was most intensive and where shipbuilding operations were the best-developed. This, plus the fact that they were more inclined to own land and businesses, probably explains the English tendency to stay. And yet, although the English enjoyed high prominence in economic terms, they were largely invisible as an ethnic group. The Scots, Irish, and Acadians defined themselves by their differences from the English, but no one ever defined what was meant by "Englishness." They could not even be identified by their religion, since Anglicanism had only a minority following and many of its supporters would have included Americans, Irish, and Lowland Scots. In most parts of the island the strength of Methodism, and in some cases the Baptist faith, was a far better barometer of an English presence than was Anglicanism.[176]

Newfoundland's intake of English settlers was influenced solely by its fishing trade, which was financed and organized by merchants from the west of England. The fishery alone created the patterns of settlement that spread throughout the nineteenth century and it alone determined who would come to live in Newfoundland. Initially Britain had been extremely reluctant to recognize that it had a future as a permanently settled colony, preferring to think of it as a mere fishing base.

CHAPTER 7

Newfoundland's
West Country Settlers

The fishery alone created the patterns of settlement and determined who would come to Newfoundland, where in Britain they would come from and where in Newfoundland they would settle.[1]

ᴇᴀʀʟʏ ɪᴍᴍɪɢʀᴀᴛɪᴏɴ ᴛᴏ Newfoundland had not been planned. Although Britain had obtained exclusive sovereignty over Newfoundland by 1713, it did little to encourage permanent settlement, preferring to exploit the island solely as a fishing base. With settlers would come government and unwelcome regulations, which might interfere with the smooth running of a venture that was designed solely as a wealth creator for Britain.[2] But, because some of the Englishmen who had been employed to work in the fishery as seasonal labour opted to remain, emigration from Britain did occur, though it was slow and gradual.

The Newfoundland fishery was mainly financed and controlled by West Country merchants, who recruited their workforce almost entirely from Devon, Dorset, Somerset, and Hampshire. It lined their pockets and, as a welcome spinoff, provided huge job opportunities in the West

Country, not just for fishermen and mariners, but also for the thousands of craftsmen and tradesmen who grew or made every commodity that would be needed for the trade:

> Fortified by religion at home and rum in Newfoundland, generations of men sailed off to the fishery. To the poor it provided a living and for the lucky, a chance to rise; the spirited country boy found a chance of adventure and the ne'er-do-well found a refuge. Though weavers, cobblers, farmers or blacksmiths might never set foot on a ship, the fishery gave them their employment. But those who gained most, upon whom all the rest depended, were the West Country fishing merchants.[3]

Also, apart from its economic benefits, the fishery was seen as a useful training ground for the British Navy, providing as it did "an immense nursery for seamen."[4]

The fishermen who made the transition to settler were hardly typical immigrants. They had not made a decisive break with their past in order to seek a fresh start in the New World. For them emigration was not the outcome of some long-deliberated plan. It was more of an afterthought. Far from being pulled by Newfoundland's perceived opportunities, they had plenty of disincentives to overcome. Because women were in very short supply, the opportunity for men to marry and raise families was restricted. The island's agricultural potential was poor, the climate was harsh, and jobs were poorly paid and mainly limited to the fishery. Yet, some Englishmen did remain, and by so doing, slowly helped to increase Newfoundland's resident population.

Predictably, West Country merchants had resisted the very existence of the Newfoundland Company. Founded by English businessmen in 1610 to promote colonization, the company's leading lights included John Guy, the first governor of the colony, who led forty Bristol colonists to Cupid's Cove (later Cupids) on the southwest end of Conception Bay. Eleven years later Sir George Calvert (Lord Baltimore) brought settlers to Ferryland on the Avalon Peninsula, south of St. John's. And Ferryland

Courtesy of Library and Archives Canada, PA-124337.

Summer fishing station at Newfoundland. Photograph by G.F. Briggs, date unknown.

was also the destination of Sir David Kirke's one hundred colonists who came in 1639. But, encountering enormous difficulties, the settlers floundered, requiring ongoing financial support from the company just to survive. Although this venture failed, European settlement did become firmly established soon afterward. This happened, not from any grand colonization scheme, but as a result of decisions taken by individual Englishmen, associated with the fishery to remain in Newfoundland. A census of 1657 reveals their presence. Of the British population living on the island, some 80 percent originated from the West Country, with the descendents of the Newfoundland Company colonists constituting only a tiny minority.

Confining themselves mainly to the east coast, between Salvage in the north and Trepassey in the south, the English settled separately from the French inhabitants, who occupied the southern coastal region[5] (see Map 13). However, following Britain's victory over France in wars fought during the late 1690s and early eighteenth century, French settlers were required to leave their Newfoundland homes.[6] Under the Treaty of Utrecht (1713), which resolved a number of European conflicts, France was forced to relinquish all sovereign rights in Newfoundland, in return for maintaining its fishing rights on what would become

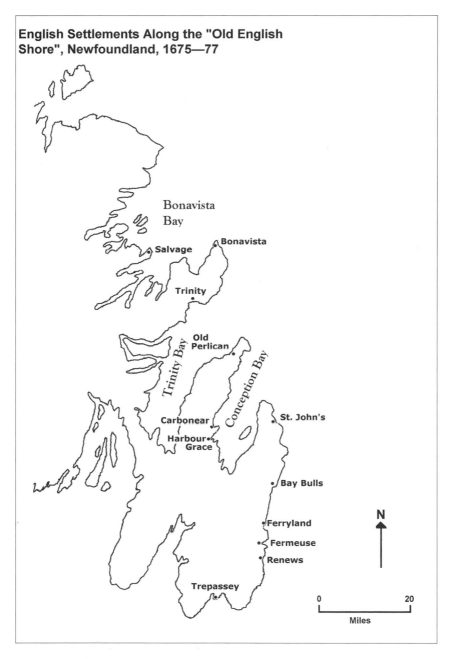

Map 13. Based on Graham Handcock, "English Migration to Newfoundland," in Mannion, ed., *Peopling of Newfoundland*, 17.

known as the "French Shore." The agreement required France to relocate Newfoundland's French inhabitants to Île Royale (later Cape Breton) and to desist from maintaining any fortifications. However, Irish fishermen soon came to the south coast to replace the departed French settlers. By 1742 they outnumbered English residents in the harbours between Placentia and St. John's, especially at Ferryland, thus reinforcing the transition to a permanently settled population.[7]

The fishermen stopped coming in 1775 as the American Rebellion unravelled and American privateers caused mayhem in Newfoundland. Its residents experienced near-famine conditions, and, to add to their woes, local men were being dragooned into the British Army and Royal Navy. John Tilley of Winterbourne Monkton (Dorset) had anticipated "the pressgang" but was wrong in predicting that "this disturbance about the Americans" would quickly end. It went on for a decade.[8] Nevertheless, despite these harrowing events, the American war marked a helpful turning point for the island, since it shamed the British government into ending the West Country trade monopoly when the war ended. For the first time in its history the needs of Newfoundland's residents were taken seriously. Agricultural schemes were encouraged and many trades were established in the commercial centres. People were allowed to import goods from the United States and a major expansion occurred in the fishery's resident-based workforce.

Although the migratory English workforce continued to provide most of the labour for the fishery when peace returned, the island's economy had been given an enormous boost. But progress was slow. In 1787, when William Dyott had sought refuge at Cape Broyle Harbour during a bad storm, he observed "very few inhabitants who remain here all the year." Those who lived there permanently were described as "principally Irish of the lowest class," and he added that "the country is quite a desert — nothing but rocks, spruce and fir. I did not see an animal of any sort."[9]

By the end of the eighteenth century, when the fur trade and seal hunting had been established as winter pursuits, the island could offer even greater incentives for year-round habitation. A steady trickle of West Country fishermen came and settled over the years, but the migration ceased by the late nineteenth century when the labour demands of the fishery could be supplied from the local population.[10]

Owing its settlement origins to the fishery, Newfoundland acquired a class structure based on male occupations. At the top were the merchants, who supplied the capital and kept stores; next came the fishing-boat owners — the so-called planters — who obtained equipment and supplies on credit from merchants and hired a crew from fishermen registered with a firm;[11] and at the bottom were the servants who did the actual work of fishing and curing. Some planters who worked in the trade, such as Abra Targett from Wincanton (Somerset), prospered, leaving around eight hundred pounds to his family when he died in 1821.[12] Others, like John Hagley of Cullompton (Devon), who had worked as a seaman in the 1700s for John Smith and John Miller (both Poole merchants), and later for William Reed, a planter, would have had far less to show for their efforts. Returning to Hemyock in Devon after residing in Newfoundland for a few years, Hagley worked "as a weaver or comber [of textile fibres] by the piece" and then joined the army. After being discharged as disabled sometime before 1770, he became "a pensioner of Chelsea College," where "he lives on his pension and what he can earn [from odd jobs]." And, because he could not support his family, he was a recipient of poor relief from his parish.[13]

However, for men with proven skills, wage rates could be comparatively high. In 1769, a Newfoundland merchant from Bridgwater (Somerset) "agreed with a cooper [that he would] stay the winter and serve the summer" in the stores of a Bristol merchant, for whom he acted as agent: "His name is Stooks, a sober young man of an honest family, whose father comes out annually and keeps on his trade of cooper, hulling fish and [he] is well known. You will think the wages perhaps high, £30 for the year, but the general wages for the coopers [who are] very English ... is from £3 to 55s p.a."[14] Such rates of pay were beyond the wildest dreams of the lowly fishermen, particularly the young and unskilled, who were paid a pittance.

Augustus Jeans, a servant in the Newfoundland fishery, was told by a friend back home in Wincanton (Somerset) that his father "was hanged for horse stealing." He then relayed this information, together with the news that his mother "broke her heart," to another friend, George King, who was an inmate of the Wincanton workhouse.[15] It is hard to imagine a bleaker world than this. In fact, such was the lowly status of the Newfoundland lads that parishes in Dorset and Devon regarded their or similar jobs as suitable placements for destitute boys in their care.[16] Isaac Peterson, "a poor child of the parish [of Poole]," was packed off to Trinity Harbour in 1737, at the age of fourteen, to be apprenticed to the Reverend Robert Killpatrick until he turned twenty-one.[17] Around thirty years later, John Simmonds, a Poole merchant, offered to take Jack Ash of Puddletown (Dorset) to Newfoundland with him for three years "if the parish will provide him with clothing,"[18] while eighteen years later Wimborne Parish (Dorset) paid the "expenses of apprenticing three poor boys of the [poor] house to Newfoundland," and later provided "clothes for Joshua Penny's boy and William Wheeler going to Newfoundland."[19] But however poor they may have been initially, some boys, with a sense of adventure and an ability to learn new skills, could see a rosy future for themselves, and thus opted to stay.

Judging from the numerous requests for poor relief from those who had taken up summer employment in the Newfoundland fishery when younger, these men had grown used to living at a subsistence level through-out their lives. When just children, Thomas Taylor from Kingsteignton (Devon) and Thomas Leaman from Combeinteignhead (Devon) began to commute every year between Newfoundland and Devon, picking up labouring jobs when they could in the winter, but ending their days dependent on parish assistance.[20] Somerset-born John Deverill had obtained "his meat, drink and clothes" from a local tradesman from the age of nine, and by age twelve worked his summers in Newfoundland and his winters as a servant in Stoke-in-Teignhead (Devon), ending his days as a near-destitute farm labourer in Combeinteignhead.[21]

Apart from the teachers, clergymen, and clerks who came from many parts of England, mainly to work in St. John's, most of Newfoundland's early settlers originated from Devon, Dorset, Somerset, and Hampshire. Unlike the great surge in Irish immigration that had occurred between 1811 and 1815, the English influx was gradual. A family would often clear land, build a house, and run a fishing station, but retire to the West Country, leasing their property to a new arrival who might decide to remain. A combination of temporary and permanent settlement, together with the natural increase in the already-settled population, caused the best fishing harbours in the Old English Shore gradually to fill up with settlers.[22]

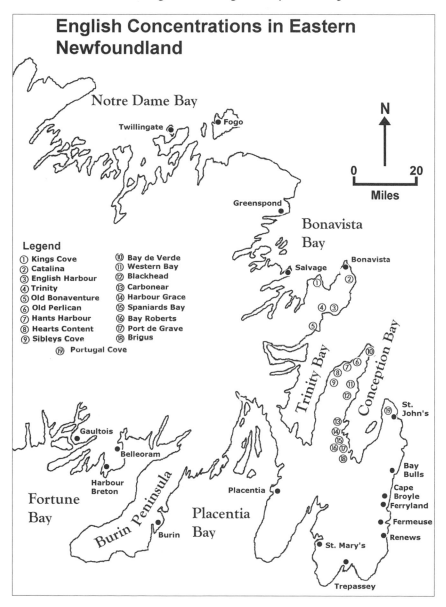

English Concentrations in Eastern Newfoundland

Notre Dame Bay

Twillingate

Fogo

N

0   20
Miles

Greenspond

Bonavista Bay

Bonavista

Salvage

Legend

① Kings Cove
② Catalina
③ English Harbour
④ Trinity
⑤ Old Bonaventure
⑥ Old Perlican
⑦ Hants Harbour
⑧ Hearts Content
⑨ Sibleys Cove

⑩ Bay de Verde
⑪ Western Bay
⑫ Blackhead
⑬ Carbonear
⑭ Harbour Grace
⑮ Spaniards Bay
⑯ Bay Roberts
⑰ Port de Grave
⑱ Brigus

⑲ Portugal Cove

Trinity Bay

Conception Bay

St. John's

Gaultois

Belleoram

Harbour Breton

Burin Peninsula

Burin

Placentia

Placentia Bay

Fortune Bay

Bay Bulls
Cape Broyle
Ferryland
Fermeuse
Renews

St. Mary's

Trepassey

Map 14.

By the beginning of the nineteenth century, new arrivals from the West Country were forced to look to territory in the more outlying areas along the north and south coasts to accommodate their communities.

Because each of the ports in the West Country tended to send men to particular areas of Newfoundland, the fishing trade created distinctive regional settlement patterns.[23] For instance, Bristol merchants generally confined their trade to the St. John's region while their counterparts in the major south Devon ports of Teignmouth and Dartmouth tended to send their workforce to the St. John's region and Conception Bay. On the other hand, the Poole merchants of Dorset operated on a more expansive scale, extending their reach to many areas of Newfoundland.[24] In addition to Conception Bay, their men might have been sent to Trinity Bay, Bonavista Bay, or Notre Dame Bay on the north side of the island, or to Placentia Bay or Fortune Bay on the south (see Map 14). This explains why the St. John's region later acquired a high proportion of Devon residents and why Conception Bay had a mixture of Devon and Dorset settlers.[25]

And because the fishermen who sailed from Poole had originated from a very wide geographical area, extending beyond Dorset to south Somerset and even taking in West Hampshire, men from these three counties who chose to remain became scattered around the various fishing bays. This accounts for the later presence of Dorset, Somerset, and Hampshire residents in Trinity Bay, and Dorset and Somerset residents in Bonavista Bay and Notre Dame Bay. These same regional links also brought Dorset and Somerset settlers to Placentia Bay and Fortune Bay.[26] Their communities must have been among the sixty to seventy settlements that Joseph Bouchette listed in 1832. According to him, the principal ones were to be found along the "old English Shore." Along Conception Bay were Brigus and Harbour Grace, and in the St. John's region were St. John's itself, Bay Bulls, Cape Broyle, Ferryland, Fermeuse, and Renews[27] (see Map 13).

Although St. John's had emerged as the colony's principal fishing centre by 1650, and became its capital, it had more the appearance of a shantytown when Governor William Waldegrave visited nearly 150 years later:

The very first object which attracted my attention on my landing in the town of St. John's was the wretchedness and apparent misery of its inhabitants. It instantly occurred to me that if such were their state in the height of summer whilst money (relatively speaking) must be flowing in upon them from their active labours, what must be their wants in the frigid season.[28]

The Reverend William Hyde, the Congregationalist minister sent to St. John's by the London Missionary Society in 1813, was equally disappointed: "The houses are built of wood; there is not a stone or brick building in the place — not even the parish church, which is a very large one."[29] Finding that the people were either "consigned to the superstitions of Popery or bound up in the ignorance of Methodism," Hyde departed three years later, although he was sorry to leave when the time came.[30] Following him was the Reverend James Rabine, who also felt overwhelmed by the large Catholic population: "Newfoundland is a Little Ireland!" he declared.[31] He was present in the winter of 1816 when a fire swept through St. John's, burning more than 130 homes and merchants' premises: "Families, which at 10 o'clock were in affluent and respectable circumstances, were reduced to poverty and many of them to absolute beggary [later that same day]."[32] Moreover, a Methodist Missionary Society spokesman reported later how the part of the town that was preserved from the fire of November 1816 "was laid in ashes" as a result of a second fire in 1817: "The people [are] totally ruined financially."[33]

Meanwhile, the Anglican congregation of St. John's had petitioned the Bishop of London for help in 1699 after a fire had destroyed a number of its wooden churches, along with most of the town. By then the Society for the Propagation of the Gospel presided over an Anglican mission at the military garrison near St. John's, but despite the Anglican religion's early roots in St. John's, its subsequent churches were slow to materialize. A turning point came with the arrival of the Reverend Aubrey George Spencer, who was appointed first Anglican Bishop of Newfoundland in 1839. With financial help from the Society for the Propagation of the Gospel, the Anglican Church progressed under his leadership, and

Aubrey George Spencer, Newfoundland's first Anglican bishop, 1839–43. He died in Torquay, Devon, in 1872. Lithograph by Francis Theodore Rochard (1798–1858), published by Paul Gauci.

increased both the number of its clergy and church schools by 1843, when Edward Feild succeeded him.

St. Thomas' Anglican Church was built three years before Bishop Spencer's arrival at the east end of St. John's, and was patronized chiefly by the city's mercantile and professional elite. St. Mary the Virgin Church, built in 1859 at the west end, tended to have mainly tradesmen and craftsmen in its congregation.[34] Fortunately St. Thomas's was spared in the great fire of 1846, which "suddenly swept away three-fourths of its [Newfoundland's] wealthy and prosperous capital."[35]

The Cathedral of St. John the Baptist was begun in 1847 by Bishop Feild, who commissioned George Gilbert Scott, the leading Gothic Revival architect of his day, to design the building. The nave, built between 1847 and 1850, served as the entire cathedral church for thirty-five years until

Photograph by Geoff Campey.

St. Thomas' Anglican Church in St. John's, situated at the corner of Military and King's Bridge roads.

the transepts, chancel, and sanctuary were added in 1880–85.[36]

These developments in St. John's reflected well on the success of its sizable business community. By the mid-nineteenth century, men like Benjamin Bowring were expanding their mercantile interests to Liverpool and other British cities. After decades of being treated like an offshoot of Britain, the boot was on the other foot. When Benjamin learned of a promising candidate in Liverpool who might wish to work in St. John's, he asked his brother Charles, who manned the Bowring Company's Liverpool office, to ask him "to state his salary and provide references." He would have his passage provided by the firm "but as they have a vessel of their own which will sail in a fortnight or three weeks [from Liverpool to St. John's] they wish that no delay may occur."[37] The Dartmouth-born Newman Wright Hoyles was another leading merchant in St. John's, fathering one son who became a chief justice and another who became rector of Carbonear (Conception Bay). Mindful of his English ancestry, Hoyles's grandson would later proclaim: "we are

proud of our Devon descent."[38] Another leading merchant was Samuel
Codner of Kingskerswell, near Torquay (Devon); he employed the
young John Bond, also of Kingskerswell, who went on to become a St.
John's merchant himself. Robert, one of Bond's sons, would become the
premier of Newfoundland from 1900 to 1909.[39]

When the Devon-born Azariah Munden went to Brigus (Conception
Bay) in 1760, it was already a bustling centre of fishing and commercial
trade. Becoming agent for a Dorset firm, he married the daughter of
Stephen Percy, a local businessman, eventually taking over Percy's
business and becoming the town's chief merchant.[40] And, in 1819, when
his son William launched himself into the area's profitable seal hunt, the
family's fortunes rose even farther. Brigus became the most prosperous
of the Conception Bay communities. In 1827 a visiting Anglican
minister thought it "beautiful," but noted that it was "chiefly occupied
by Methodists," and that the large Sunday school at nearby Cupids was
"entirely managed by Methodists."[41]

Methodism's popularity in the Conception Bay area can be attributed
to the charismatic Reverend Laurence Coughlan. He arrived at Harbour
Grace in 1766 as a Church of England missionary.[42] Converting to

Photograph by Geoff Campey.

St. George's Anglican Church, built 1876, at Brigus, Conception Bay. It is the second
Anglican church to be built on this site.

Methodism four years later, he reached out to the labouring classes, to the great annoyance of the merchants.[43] Content with having a malleable workforce addicted to rum, the merchants sensed trouble when the Reverend Coughlan preached about public morals and good behaviour: "Before they [the ordinary people] received the Gospel they spent much of their time in rioting and drunkenness; but when the Word took place in their hearts, many of them not only got out of debt but also had [funds] to spare."[44] He helped the people to achieve a greater sense of self-worth and, along the way, gave the region its strong Methodist affiliations.

Coughlan's appeal spread in all directions. By 1768–69, Blackhead, to the north of Harbour Grace, had a Methodist church that was capable of holding four hundred people.[45] By 1816 Methodist missions extended south as far as Port de Grave and beyond Blackhead to Western Bay. And Methodism also took root along Trinity Bay to the west, especially at Island Cove, Old Perlican, Trinity Harbour, and Hants Harbour.[46] The 1857 census would later reveal the extent of Methodism's appeal in this one area. Some 67 percent of the population in the Bay de Verde district, extending from Carbonear on the west shore of Conception Bay to Old Perlican at the northeast end of Trinity Bay, described themselves as Methodists (see Map 14).

Life in these remote areas certainly had its perils. When John Gadis left Bay de Verde for Grates Cove, he collapsed in a snowstorm, and, being found "badly frozen," died soon after. According to the local newspaper he was the fourth person to freeze to death on that route: "There is no road, only extensive barrens, with nothing to guide the traveller."[47] The Congregational minister, William Hyde, had to navigate himself through equally dangerous terrain and, although he did not have Coughlan's charisma and sympathetic attitude, he certainly had his stamina:

I left St. John's on August 8th [1814] for Portugal Cove where I continued till Wednesday, then in an open boat crossed the bay — seven leagues over to Harbour Grace and from thence to Carbonear ... paid the Methodist missionary a visit, On Friday visited Fresh Water Bay,

Crockers Cove, Clowns Cove and High Cliff — from one place to another was a considerable distance ... the path was little more than 18 inches on the edge of a steep rock nearly 300 feet perpendicularly down to the water so that the sea was literally dashing against them under my feet. On Sunday I preached at Carbonear in the morning and in the evening at Harbour Grace (4 miles distant). On Monday left for Bay Roberts, 5 leagues distant ... on Tuesday went across two small bays to Burnt Head and Cabits [Cupids] and from there to Brigus — on Friday to Port de Grave and on Saturday returned to Bay Roberts then crossed the bay to Port de Grave — Monday back to Bay Roberts.... I trust my labour is not in vain.[48]

Like Brigus, Bay Roberts was long-settled, having become a "permanent fishing station" from around 1700: "For a long period the first settlers continued contentedly to occupy their original dwelling places in Juggler's and French Coves, being joined by the Badcocks, Snows, Elms, and Russells, all originally from England [and some from Jersey], who built somewhat further up, yet still below Mercers Cove."[49]

Charles Mercer, one of the early settlers who originated from Ringwood (Hampshire), gave his surname to Mercer's Cove, although he and his family had initially settled at Little Belle Isle. George Vey, a 1790 arrival from Dorset, took charge of the Methodist church at Bay Roberts, while his daughter went on to marry Robert Cranford from Dittisham, near Dartmouth, who immigrated to Bay Roberts in 1819.[50] Working initially as an agent for a firm of Poole merchants, he co-founded Cranford and Cormack ten years later. However, disaster struck the firm when two of his three ships foundered and his uninsured premises were destroyed partially by fire. Clearing his debts, he tried unsuccessfully to re-launch himself as a merchant in Prince Edward Island, but following a later move to New York he did prosper.

Meanwhile, the Reverend James Balfour had been installed as the Anglican minister of Harbour Grace by 1776, occasionally holding services in French's Cove in the house of a Mr. John Loomy.[51] His followers included local planters, who wished "to preserve the memory of the Sabbath and to occupy some of its sacred hours by a semblance, at least, of public worship."[52] The Church of England also had churches at Carbonear and Perry's Cove from 1819, while the Anglican congregation at Bay Roberts had built its St. Matthew's Church by 1824.[53] Another Anglican church was constructed at nearby Port de Grave three years later, and the following year saw the completion of the Newfoundland School Society's sixty-foot-long school, complete with "a dwelling house for the schoolmaster, built by voluntary subscription of the Port de Grave inhabitants."[54] Moved by the lack of educational opportunities on the island and his inability to attract people of an Anglican persuasion to support him, the Devon-born fish merchant Samuel Codner founded the Newfoundland School Society in 1823.[55] Having built its first school at St. John's in 1824, the society had twenty-five schools seven years later, located principally at Conception Bay, Trinity Bay, and in the St. John's area.[56] The Society for the Propagation of the Gospel also had a school in place at Harbour Grace by 1827, but most of its other schools were at Trinity Bay and Bonavista Bay.[57] Disaster struck Harbour Grace in 1858 when a raging fire rendered homeless many families "who a few days [before] were in comparatively comfortable circumstances."[58]

Farther north, Trinity Bay was rapidly increasing its population, and a significant factor in its growth was the business acumen of the Poole merchants, who transformed the fishery at Trinity Harbour into a major industry. Chief among them was Benjamin Lester. Becoming the wealthiest and most influential businessman of both his native Poole and of Newfoundland, his rise had been meteoric.[59] The son of a cooper, he had arrived at Trinity Bay in 1737 at the age of thirteen, taking up employment with his uncle, John Masters, a Poole/Newfoundland merchant. Ten years later Benjamin was himself a leading planter, forming a business partnership with his brother Isaac, who managed the Poole end of the business while he looked after Trinity Bay. His empire grew rapidly, and by the early 1770s Lester owned an ocean-going fleet of twelve vessels and had established mercantile premises at Trinity, Bonavista, Greenspond, and Tilting on Fogo Island.

Portrait of Benjamin Lester, *circa* 1780, artist unknown.

Courtesy of Poole Museums Service.

Courtesy of Dorset County Museum.

Painting of Benjamin Lester's premises at Trinity Harbour, *circa* 1800. Lester's house can be seen in the centre behind the warehouses. Painting by Michael Corne, *circa* 1800.

In Trinity Harbour alone, Benjamin had five fishing establishments, twenty-three houses, a large farm, and a shipyard, and by 1793 owned twenty ships and had shares in more than sixty, many of them built in Trinity. His mansion, the first brick house in Newfoundland, was put up in the 1760s and it remained a striking landmark at Trinity Harbour for two hundred years. A reconstructed building on this same site continues to keep alive his memory.[60] Meanwhile, Lester only lived in Trinity permanently until 1767, after which time he moved his wife and family to Poole; however he continued to travel regularly between both places for a further ten years. Becoming mayor of Poole and a member of parliament, he exercised great influence on both sides of the Atlantic until his death in Poole in 1802.[61]

Table 7

List of Ships, and the Men Taken in Them, from Poole, Waterford, and Cork, in 1810–12, to Work for Merchants at Trinity Bay
[PANL MG204 John Thomas Duckworth collection.]

(1) <u>From January 1, 1810, to July 5, 1811</u>

Benjamin, McCarthy, Master

Passenger Names	Station	For What Term Shipped	For Whose Employ	Wages	From Whence Shipped
Thomas Roach	Youngster	18 month	Geo. Garland	£17.0.0	Waterford
Patrick Casey	"	18 "	"	£17.0.0	"
Jn. Hailey	"	18 "	"	£17.0.0	"
Maurice Scannel	"	18 "	"	£17.0.0	"
John Kinnure	"	18 "	"	£20.0.0	"
Edward Bryan	"	18 "	"	£17.0.0	"
Maurice McCarthy	"	18 "	"	£17.0.0	"
John Cashman	"	18 "	"	£17.0.0	"
Michael Crawley	"	18 "	"	£17.0.0	"
Michael Haven	"	18 "	"	£20.0.0	"
Michael Hearn	"	18 "	"	£17.0.0	"
Michael Hide	"	18 "	"	£20.0.0	"
Michael Lander	"	18 "	"	£17.0.0	"
Owen Bryan	"	18 "	"	£17.0.0	"
John Sheridan	"	18 "	"	£17.0.0	"
William Brenan	"	18 "	"	£17.0.0	"
Patrick Hide	"	18 "	"	£17.0.0	"
Michael Murphy	"	18 "	"	Indentures	"
Patrick Bryan	"	18 "	"	£17.0.0	"

Hope, Bangor, Master

Passenger Names	Station	For What Term Shipped	For Whose Employ	Wages	From Whence Shipped
John Hide	Youngster	18 month	Geo. Garland	£15.0.0	Cork
Andrew Eamond	"	18 "	"	£15.0.0	"

Hope cont'd

Passenger Names	Station	For What Term Shipped	For Whose Employ	Wages	From Whence Shipped
Daniel Dismond	Youngster	18 month	Geo. Garland	£15.0.0	Cork
Patrick Sullivan	"	18 "	"	£15.0.0	"
Daniel Driscol	"	18 "	"	£15.0.0	"

Success, Taylor, Master

Passenger Names	Station	For What Term Shipped	For Whose Employ	Wages	From Whence Shipped
Samuel Garland	Youngster	18 month	Geo. Garland	£30.0.0	Poole
Robert Crawford	"	18 "	"	£30.0.0	"
Reubon Crosby	"	18 "	"	£20.0.0	"
Thomas Baggs	"	18 "	"	Apprentice	"
William Russell	"	18 "	"	Do.	"

Alpha, Hamon, Master

Passenger Names	Station	For What Term Shipped	For Whose Employ	Wages	From Whence Shipped
George Smith	Youngster	18 month	Geo. Garland	£21.10.0	Poole
James Frost	"	18 "	"	£20.0.0	"

(2) <u>From June 1, 1811 to July 5, 1812</u>

John, John Denny, Master

Passenger Names	Station	For What Term Shipped	For Whose Employ	Wages	From Whence Shipped
Henry Bigler	Youngster	4 years	Geo. Garland	£5 at the expiring of the term	Poole
John Best	"	4 "	"	£6 "	"
John Cren	"	4 "	"	£5 "	"
Thomas Fidby	"	4 "	"	£5.5 "	"

John cont'd

Passenger Names	Station	For What Term Shipped	For Whose Employ	Wages	From Whence Shipped
George Wakely	Youngster	4 years	Geo. Garland	£5 "	Poole
John Angel	"	2 Smrs, 1 Wtr	"	£25 "	"
Joseph Young	"	"	"	£25 "	"
Isaac Venson	"	"	"	£25 "	"
Thomas Elsworth	"	"	"	£25 "	"
George Wills	"	4 Smrs, 3 Wtr	"	£5.5 "	"
George Sims	"	"	"	£5.5 "	"

Hope, Richard Bangor, Master

Passenger Names	Station	For What Term Shipped	For Whose Employ	Wages	From Whence Shipped
Paul Mahoney	Sawyer	2 Smrs 1 Wtr	Geo. Garland	£18 at the expiring of the term	Waterford
Philip Cronan	Mason	"	"	£18 "	"
James Power	Youngster	"	"	£16 "	"
Michael Hogarty	"	"	"	£16 "	"
Michael Sweeney	"	"	"	£16 "	"
William Doyle	"	"	"	£16 "	"
Michael Mountain	"	"	"	£16 "	"
William Flattery	"	"	"	£18 "	"
Martin Humphrey	"	"	"	£16 "	"
David Doolin	"	"	"	£16 "	"

Two Brothers, Thos W. Sanders, Master

Passenger Names	Station	For What Term Shipped	For Whose Employ	Wages	From Whence Shipped
Patrick Murphy	Youngster	2 Smrs 1 Wtr	Geo. Garland	£16 at the expiring of the term	Waterford

Two Brothers cont'd

Passenger Names	Station	For What Term Shipped	For Whose Employ	Wages	From Whence Shipped
John Walsh	Joiner	2 Smrs 1 Wtr	Geo. Garland	£18 at the expiring of the term	Waterford
William Mahegan	Youngster	"	"	£16 "	"
John Flinn	"	"	"	£16 "	"
John Mulcahy	"	"	"	£16 "	"
William Walters	"	"	"	£16 "	"
Thomas Ryan	"	"	"	£16 "	"
William Nevil	"	"	"	£16 "	"
Martin Hinefin	"	"	"	£16 "	"
Timothy Mahony	"	"	"	£18 "	"
Patrick Neagle	Joiner	"	"	£17 "	"
William McCan	Joiner	"	"	£17 "	"
William Walsh	"	"	"	£16 "	"
John Caren	"	"	"	£16 "	"
Patrick Ryan	Sawyer	"	"	£17 "	"
Dennis Cowley	Smith	"	"	£29 "	"
David Bronders	"	"	"	£17 "	"
John Savage	Smith	"	"	£3 per mth	"
Philip Troy	Smith	"	"	£17 "	"
Edmund Maddon	"	"	"	£17 "	"
Matthew Harley	"	"	"	£16 "	"
Thomas Courier	"	"	"	£17 "	"

Sally, John Waldron, Master

Passenger Names	Station	For What Term Shipped	For Whose Employ	Wages	From Whence Shipped
William Lovell	Youngster	2 Smrs 1 Wtr	Hope, Sleat & Read	£24 at the expiring of the term	Poole
James Puck	"	"	"	£24 "	"
Thomas Evans	"	3 Smrs 2 Wtrs	"	£37. 10 "	"

Sally cont'd

Passenger Names	Station	For What Term Shipped	For Whose Employ	Wages	From Whence Shipped
Edward Gibbons	Youngster	2 Smrs 1 Wtr	Hope, Sleat & Read	£24 at the expiring of the term	Poole
Joseph Chubb	"	3 Smrs 2 Wtrs	"	£37. 10 "	"
George Stoodley	"	"	"	£37. 10 "	"
James Fifield	"	"	"	£37. 10 "	"
John Ryan	"	2 Smrs 1 Wtr	"	£24 "	"
Andrew Allan	Fisherman	The Summer	"	£24 "	"

Sister, **John Prousy, Master**

Passenger Names	Station	For What Term Shipped	For Whose Employ	Wages	From Whence Shipped
James Clark	Fisherman	monthly	George Garland	40s per month	Poole
Thomas Fiander	Youngster	no term	"		"
Peter Parrot	"	2 Smrs 1 Wtr	"	£21 at the end	"
George Freeman	"	6 years	"	£5. 5 "	"
Jervis Gosling	"	6 "	"	£5. 5 "	"
William Whitty	"	5 Smrs 4 Wtrs	"	£5. 5 "	"
George Crabb	"	Parish Apprentice	"		"
Daniel Lush	"	3 Smrs 2 Wtrs	"	£45 "	"
George Skelton Esq.	Surgeon				
Geo. Garland Jnr.	Gent				
Jas P. Garland	"				
Thos. Robertson	"				
Stephen Roberts	"				
John Anderson	"				

Sister cont'd

Passenger Names	Station	For What Term Shipped	For Whose Employ	Wages	From Whence Shipped
James Collins	Ships Master				
Robert Ash	"				
Miss Baine					

Alpha, Philip Hamon, Master

Passenger Names	Station	For What Term Shipped	For Whose Employ	Wages	From Whence Shipped
James Lanigan	Youngster	2 Smrs 1 Wtrs	Robert Slade	£22. 10 at the end	Poole
John Pitt	"	3 Smrs 2 Wtrs	"	£34 "	"
Edward Waldron	"	2 Smrs 1 Wtr	"	£22. 10 "	"
Anthony Colson	Storekeeper	3 Smrs 2 Wtrs	"	£45 "	"
Joseph Pittman	Youngster	"	"	£32 "	"
Henry Bailey	"	"	"	£31. 10 "	"
William Biggler	"	2 Smrs 1 Wtr	"	£22. 10 "	"
Edward Slade	"	"	"	£22. 10 "	"

Active, Jospeh Pratt, Master

Passenger Names	Station	For What Term Shipped	For Whose Employ	Wages	From Whence Shipped
John Gardiner	Fisherman	1 Summer	Robert Slade	£22. 10 at the end	Poole
Henry Slade	Youngster	2 Smrs 1 Wtr	"	£22. 10 Do.	"

Falcon, Thos Grosland, Master

Passenger Names	Station	For What Term Shipped	For Whose Employ	Wages	From Whence Shipped
Henry Pitcher	Youngster	2 Smrs 1 Wtr	Robert Slade	£20 at the end	Poole
Thomas Pitcher	"	"	"	£20 Do.	"
George Fry	"	3 Smrs 2 Wtrs	"	£27 Do.	"

Lester's vast estates in both Newfoundland and Poole passed to his son-in-law, George Garland, who, although he never set foot in Newfoundland, amassed a fortune several times that of Benjamin Lester's.[62] A surviving list of the 111 men sent from Poole, Cork, and Waterford to work at his and other mercantile establishments in 1810–11 reveals the scale of Garland's operation[63] (see Table 7). However, one of his sons, John Bingley, lived in Newfoundland for many years, being "a merchant and magistrate of Trinity" and later a member of parliament. Becoming the first Speaker of the House of Assembly in 1833, he returned in later life to Poole.[64] Meanwhile, Robert Slade, another Poole merchant, had been challenging the Garland family's supremacy at Trinity for much of the nineteenth century. Acquiring the firms of John Jeffrey and Thomas Street, Slade's business ventures expanded rapidly, but, spending little time in Trinity himself, he managed his affairs almost entirely from Poole.[65] Like the Garland family, Slade employed salaried staff as servants year-round but engaged many others on a seasonal basis, as is revealed by the list of forty-three men, mainly from Poole, who had been recruited in 1811–13 to work for him at Trinity as fishermen, sealers, and in various other trades[66] (see Table 8).

Trinity emerged as the largest trading centre in the northeast, providing excellent job opportunities for agents, clerks, doctors, accountants, craftsmen, and tradesmen, who constituted a sizable proportion of its population, with the servant and labouring classes mainly residing in the surrounding communities. Judging from the census carried out

Table 8

Robert Slade's Servants at Trinity Bay, Fall 1811 [PANL MG504 (1–k–5)]

Name	Capacity	From	Till	Wages	Remarks
William Hiscock	Dockman	7/10/11	20/3/1212	50s. month	Shipped for the Ice
Isaac Sexton	Carpenter	20/10/11	Sch. *Mary* is ready to launch	100s. month	To take all his supplies from R. Slade
Robert Sexton	Carpenter	20/10/11	Ditto	80s. month	"
William Jestican	Dockman	5/11/11	St. Patrick's Day	50s. month payable in goods	
James Wiseman	Carpenter, Icebreaker & Splitter	5/11/11	20/10/12	75s. month and his chance to the ice	
James Dyer	Master of *Cosmopoliti*	20/10/11	20/10/12	£36 and 9d per seal	Sleat & Read give more
William Newhook	Master Shipwright	20/10/11	1/5/12	110s. month	
James White	Dockman, sawyer and Iceman	22/10/11	Schooner fits out for Ice	50s. month and 2 gallons molasses. Wants half chance [to the ice]	
Stephen Perrott	Ditto	24/10/11	Ditto	50s. month, 4 gallons molasses, 2lb tea & 2lb coffee	
James Frost	Fisherman	22/10/11	20/10/12	£21 & 1 pr boots.	
Jno Dollonthy	Master of wood crew & Fisherman	23/10/11	20/10/12	£35	
Robert Dimer	Icehunter and Fisherman	23/10/11	20/10/12	£27 & half his chance to the ice, say ¼.	

Name	Capacity	From	Till	Wages	Remarks
Jno Gardener	Icehunter and ships master	24/10/11	20/10/12	£29 and half his chance to the ice, say ¼.	
Cornelius Sculley	Splitter	24/10/11	20/10/12	£33 & blue jacket	
Michael Sculley	Fisherman	24/10/11	20/10/12	£25 & 1 pr boots.	
Jno Kennedy	Cooper	Since the *Falcon* sails	One twelve month	£50 &, if he drinks grog, to forfeit his wages	
Patrick Curreen	Fisherman	24/10/11	20/10/12	£35 & 3 gallons molasses	
Michael Kennure	Fisherman	24/10/11	20/10/12	£35 & 3 gallons molasses	
Patrick Fitzgerald	Fisherman	24/10/11	20/10/12	£35 & 3 gallons molasses.	
Andrew Kerring	Fisherman & boats master	26/10/11	20/10//12	£32 & 1 pr boots.	
William Gulliford	Mason & Fisherman	25/10/11	20/10/12	£25 & his debt forgiven.	
Jno Brazil	Salter	25/10/11	20/10/12	£33	
Edward Hunt	Cruiser & Icehunter	25/10/11	Schooner	45s. month, 2 galls rum Winter & half a man's share	
Jno Dwyer	Icehunter and Schooners master	25/10/11	20/10/12	£32 & half his chance the summer say 2nd Jan 1812	
Job Phillips	Fisherman	25/10/11	20/10/12	£27	

Name	Capacity	From	Till	Wages	Remarks
William Burrage	Icehunter & Splitter	Time *Mary* fits out	20/10/12	£38 two qtrs fish & half a mans share (A good hand)	
Jno Fitzpatrick	Cooper	30/10/11	1/5/12	40s. month	
Patrick Doyle	Cook & steward in House	31/10/11	20/10/12	£36	
Patrick Lawless	Carpenter	1/11/11	20/10/12	£36	
Jno Hobbs	Cook in the cookroom	9/11/11	20/10/12	£28	
James Cutter	Sailmaker & mate of either of the vessels	15/11/11	15/11/12	£30 Mr. Slade is requested to pay his wife 25s. month only.	
William Walters	Dockman & Ice hunter	4/11/11	Schooner fits out	50s. per month and half his chance	
Daniel Fenton	Ditto	22/4/10	20/11/12	£25 & his passage	
Michael Daly	Youngster	22/4/10	20/10/12	£23 & his passage	
Robert Brown	Cooper	3/5/11	20/11/12	£30 & his passage	
Prince Welsh	Joiner & Carpenter	4/6/11	4/6/12	£32 & his passage	
Edward Slade	(Youngsters	Shipped	20/10/12		
Henry Slade	(assisting		20/10/12		
William Riggler	(in		20/10/12		
Joseph Pittman	(	in	20/10/13		
Jas Lamnigan	(Counting		20/10/12		
Jno Tait	(		20/10/13		
Howard Bailey	(House	Poole	20/10/13		

in 1800–01, the immigrant population was growing rapidly. Of the 54 percent of the population not born on the island, 21 percent originated from Dorset, 14 percent came from Ireland, 12 percent from Somerset and Hampshire, and 7 percent from Devon. The population of Trinity Harbour reached about 1,250 by 1836 and remained at that level until the 1860s.[67]

Predictably, the Society for the Propagation of the Gospel had sent its missionaries into this promising area by 1757. Ninety years later, churches, schools, and preaching stations could be found dotted along the northwest end of Trinity Bay at Old Bonaventure, Trinity Harbour, English Harbour, Catalina, Little Catalina, and Bay Island

Photograph by Geoff Campey

Mansion House, Thames Street, Poole, Dorset. Benjamin Lester's Poole residence. After Lester's death the Garland family lived here. The dining room fireplace is decorated with two marble replicas of salted cod fillets — a reminder of the source of the family's wealth.

Cove, as well as along the eastern shore at Heart's Content and Sibleys Cove[68] (see Map 14). However, Trinity's trade declined from the 1830s, and, according to its Anglican minister, more than one-fifth of the population was destitute in 1855, depending "for subsistence last winter on the government allowance of 4 lbs of Indian meal per head per week." Catalina's minister complained that the "practice of making Catalina Harbour a rendezvous for ice-hunters proceeding to the seal fishery ... causes an unusual variation in the number of my congregation."[69] Trinity's economic life was changing.

Providing good access to the rich fishing and seal-hunting areas farther to the north in Bonavista Bay, Greenspond and Bonavista both developed into important towns and trading centres from which fish, oil, seal skins, lumber, and other products were dispatched. Bonavista's population of "more than 1,000" was already substantial when the Congregationalist missionary John Hillyard visited it in 1800. According to him, some of the inhabitants had "a considerable desire for the gospel ... a missionary could have an extensive circuit taking in Greenspond and Trinity Bay to ply in during the summer season," but given that many of the West Country fishermen returned home in the winter, the missionary would be "more confined" in that season.[70] Moreover, winter was a time of greatest danger. Swain's Island, near Greenspond, on north side of the Bay, lost one of its leading merchants in December 1854 when the English-born William Tiller, his brother George, and two servants perished in a storm when stopping off at Fool's Island to check their vessel. The community was said to have lost its "head man of business."[71]

Having been settled since the 1690s, Greenspond had a sufficient resident population by the early nineteenth century to acquire its first Anglican church in 1812.[72] The Society for the Propagation of the Gospel was particularly active in the Bonavista Bay region, establishing five churches and five preaching stations on the north shore, as well as a school at Greenspond and four churches and six preaching stations on the south shore, together with schools at Bonavista, King's Cove, and Salvage.[73] As happened elsewhere, the trade in Bonavista Bay declined steadily after the 1830s. Twenty-five years later the Reverend John Morton, Anglican minister at King's Cove, reported that "the poverty of the people

Lithograph of Robert Slade by T.H. Maguire, 1849.

Courtesy of Poole Museums Service.

is so extreme that many were only saved from starvation last November by a quantity of Indian meal and molasses sent for their relief by the government.[74] He would know about their hardship, given that some 65 percent of Bonavista Bay's population were supporters of his church.[75]

The Church of England had also built up a considerable following at its northernmost missions at Twillingate and Fogo along Notre Dame Bay.[76] Twillingate had an Anglican congregation from 1815, the church being located on the north side of the harbour and the school on the south side.[77] When Bishop Feild arrived in 1845, he "was welcomed by a splendid display of flags on every side of the harbour, and discharges of the cannon from the establishments of Messrs. Slade & Co and Messrs. Cox & Slade. The church flag of the settlement is a beautiful St. George's ensign presented by three captains of vessels." Robert Slade of Poole also added his support to Twillingate's "capacious and handsome church" by "signifying his wish to furnish funds for the purchase of a complete set of Communion plate to any amount which might be necessary."[78]

West End House in Poole, Robert Slade's former mansion house. The building still survives and remains a lasting symbol of the great wealth he accumulated from the Newfoundland trade.

By contrast, the Congregationalist minister John Hillyard was experiencing "a little opposition" from his parishioners, which he attributed to his admonishments for "Sabbath breaking," but, according to gossip picked up by William Hyde, the Congregationalist minister based at St. John's, "Mr. Hillyard has most grievously fallen" by drinking excessively.[79]

The leading merchant of Twillingate had been John Slade of Poole, Robert's uncle, who founded his initial headquarters there in the late 1750s. Robert had left John Slade & Co. in 1804 to set up his own business at Trinity Bay, while Thomas, another of John's nephews, went into partnership around 1813 with his brother-in-law William Cox, who was based in Shaldon, near Teignmouth (Devon). Owning a number of ships and having three sons who were sea captains, William Cox was a useful ally.[80] The partners' mercantile interests quickly expanded, covering the importing and selling of goods and the exporting of large quantities of fish from Twillingate, Fogo, and Greenspond to southern Europe, Ireland, and England.

However, it is well to remember what life was like at the other end of the social spectrum. It was claimed as early as 1774 that Devon and Dorset supplied "lads from the plough, men from the threshing floor and persons of all sizes, trades and ages from manufactories [who] flock annually in the Spring ... in the hope of returning with £6 or £10 from the land of the fish."[81] George Penney of Wimborne Minster (Dorset) was one of them. "A poor child of the parish," he served his apprenticeship with two Fogo planters until he was twenty-one, and ended up with just five pounds, together with his return passage to England.[82] Back in his native Dorset he would likely find work as an agricultural labourer, but, given the low wages and high unemployment that prevailed, he would remain at the bottom of the social scale for the rest of his life.

With its excellent port and stone-covered beaches, well-suited for drying fish, the town of Placentia, in the southern Avalon Peninsula, developed into yet another important fishing and trading centre, achieving this by the mid-1700s (see Map 14). The town, together with its scattered communities, attracted immigrants until the 1830s, mainly from Ireland, but also from the West Country in England. The Jerseyside community, just to the north of Placentia, is a lasting reminder of the influx from the Channel Islands, which also occurred at this time. As ever, the town had its handful of wealthy merchants — men like John Power, who had "a fine situation" at the north side of Placentia Harbour, having "a dwelling house and gardens, well stocked with fruit trees, a barn and cooperage, two stores and both two stories high, with 50 or 60 acres of land."[83] And of course, Placentia had its many servants — men like Samuel Woodley from Devon and John Adams from Shaftesbury (Dorset), who absconded in 1813 from the service of Joseph Besant Jr., a merchant in Little Placentia. They could be readily recognized because they "walked with knees turned in" — a sure sign of rickets caused by malnourishment.[84]

Burin, another important fishing centre on the west side of the bay, was the home of the Reverend John Lewis, who became Placentia Bay's first Methodist minister in 1819. When he arrived "a roomy chapel" was being constructed. Adjoining it was to be "the house for the missionary," and, over the cliff, a longer schoolroom "capable of containing 210 children at least" was taking shape. Because money was scarce, the building work progressed slowly and, given that he returned home two years later, the Reverend Lewis probably never had a chance to use the new premises.[85] The Society for the Propagation of the Gospel had established its school in Burin by 1827, but both the Methodists and the Church of England came a poor second to the Roman Catholics, who, because of the large Irish population, dominated the area.[86]

With its magnificent land-locked harbour, Harbour Breton was destined to become the principal town of Fortune Bay and the largest fishing centre on the south coast. One of the 1791 arrivals, Joseph Kentisbeer, a seaman born in Chudleigh (Devon), had clearly heard of Fortune Bay's good prospects. Serving as an apprentice to a local tradesman, he "ran away to Fortune Bay" when nineteen years old, but it clearly did not suit him, since he returned to Chudleigh three years later, taking up employment as a labourer.[87] However, the area acquired a regular supply of immigrants from Dorset, Somerset, and the Channel Islands in the following decades as West Country and Jersey merchants established fishing and trading operations in the area.[88] But none would match the Newman family from Dartmouth (Devon), whose involvement with Newfoundland trade spanned three hundred years and many generations of Newmans.

Robert Newman came to realize, after the American Rebellion had ended in 1783, that his company's profits would grow if he ventured into the recently settled and fast-expanding fishing areas along Newfoundland's south coast. Persuading his brothers to invest in this region, the company opened branches on the Burin Peninsula and along Fortune Bay. Harbour Breton was designated as the company's headquarters in 1812, and it was from here that the family directed the economic life of the entire region as the company went from strength to strength.[89] The Anglican minister who visited Harbour Breton in 1846 described it as having "the largest mercantile establishments on the Island."[90] Ten years later it acquired a fresh batch of English workers who were intending to become full-time residents. This was one of the rare occasions when an emigrant group actually sailed together to Newfoundland. However, these were "youngster emigrants," forty-one of them, ranging in age from thirteen to twenty-one. They had been recruited at Sturminster (Dorset) to work for merchants based either at Harbour Breton or at the Newman establishments in Gaultois and Burgeo, farther to the west.[91] All were Anglicans, presumably a requirement of being selected, and most were farm labourers, but the group also included a drover and a railway worker.[92]

Fortune Bay was another Anglican stronghold. In 1857, a staggering 89 percent of the population in Burgeo and La Poile at the west end of the south shore were Anglicans. A church had been built at Belleoram by 1842 and "a school with teacher's house was in progress," while Harbour Breton had its "neat" Anglican church by 1846.[93] These churches were built to serve the religious needs of a population that had grown with the steady intake of male workers from England. The West Country boys and men who came to Newfoundland's shores over many decades supplied the cheap labour that made the fishery so profitable to the merchants. But by the late nineteenth century, when the labour demands of the fishery could be met adequately by the native-born population, the migrations came to an abrupt end. Thus ended a process that had changed the way of life of people on both sides of the Atlantic, but most radically in Newfoundland.

Extreme poverty in Britain had been a factor in encouraging English boys to take up employment in the Newfoundland fishery. The ones who remained in Newfoundland as settlers did so of their own free will. In doing so they gave the colony a large proportion of its immigrants, but because so much immigration went unrecorded, precise figures cannot be given.[94] Another group of juvenile immigrants would not be so fortunate. Thousands of destitute girls and boys from the slums of Liverpool, London, and Birmingham would also end up in the Maritime provinces during the late nineteenth and early twentieth centuries, not by choice, but because they were sent there by well-meaning philanthropic bodies. And nothing could have prepared them for what they actually experienced.

CHAPTER 8

The Home Children

In 1904 my brother and I, Ellen Keatly, were put in the Middlemore Home in Birmingham by our father; the following year we were sent to Nova Scotia. I was about nine when we landed at Scotsburn station in Pictou County, after riding the trains from Halifax, this being the nearest station to where we were to live. The two farmers came with a horse and buggy each to get us. We had tags on the front of our coats like bags of potatoes. Scotsburn is ten miles from Loganville and ten miles from the town of Pictou.[1]

ARRIVING LIKE A parcel in a strange place must have been a terrifying experience for nine-year-old Ellen Keatly. In fact, she was just one of thousands of young immigrants, the so-called "home children," who had been placed in British charitable homes. They came to Canada during the late nineteenth and early twentieth centuries and were expected to work under indentures as farm labourers or domestic servants.[2] The intention was that they would help to alleviate Canada's desperate labour shortages, particularly in rural areas, and in the process benefit themselves by being given the chance of a better life in the New World. Although most settled in Ontario, Quebec, the Prairie provinces, and British Columbia, a substantial number were sent to Nova Scotia and New Brunswick. Given that the Maritime provinces attracted relatively few immigrants at this time, these juvenile immigrants represented a significant supplement to the population of both provinces. Few were sent to Prince Edward Island and almost none went to Newfoundland.

A farm in Loganville would be Ellen's new home. Although she and her brother had been brought to the same region of Nova Scotia, they left in separate buggies, never to see each other again. Not only would she be denied contact with him, but she would also lose touch with the rest of her family in Birmingham. Since the well-intentioned philanthropists who organized such schemes believed that slum children needed to be extricated from the corrupting influences of their home life, a first step was the permanent breakage of parental ties. As a consequence the children felt abandoned and isolated. Hurt feelings might seem unimportant when measured against hunger and deprivation, but the psychological damage would last a lifetime. The organizers, believing that they were saving vulnerable children from unspeakable depravity, subjected them to needless emotional trauma and compounded that sin by failing to protect them from physical mistreatment. However, despite these difficulties, emigration gave hope to children living in desperate, never-ending poverty, and in later life many would reap the benefits that Canada had to offer.

The driving force behind this influx of children had been the harrowing conditions being experienced by Britain's labouring classes. Although the Industrial Revolution, which began in the late eighteenth century, had made Britain the most powerful and wealthy nation on Earth, it had brought untold grief to workers unable to benefit from the rapid economic expansion that was taking place. People had flocked from the country to the cities to fill the new jobs being created in the factories and related industries. However, while this was happening, traditional forms of employment, like handloom weaving, were being destroyed by the increasing growth of mechanization and factory production. As workers found themselves being replaced by machines, they joined a growing pool of unemployed labourers who, if they managed to find work, had to accept pitifully low wages. Even young children had to take paid employment to supplement their families' meagre income. This situation created great misery and squalor in English cities by the late 1860s — especially in London and Liverpool. As conditions deteriorated, the number of deserted and orphaned children entering local authority workhouses and industrial schools began to rise. Many parents and guardians, finding themselves simply unable to cope, began delivering their children to charitable homes, which could offer them food and shelter.

The enveloping humanitarian crisis required an immediate solution, and emigration was seized upon as the most suitable way out for everyone. It was certainly an economic solution. A child's emigration costs were the equivalent of one year's maintenance in a workhouse or industrial school.[3] Thus, a parish could rid itself of an ongoing financial commitment, and, as was hoped, the children could be lifted out of poverty.[4] Emigration was also an obvious escape route for children living in charitable homes, and large-scale plans were devised to relocate them to Canada. However, because the extreme poverty of their parents was thought to have corrupted the children in some way, the self-righteous promoters of such schemes adopted the role of "child savers." Thomas Barnardo, the doyen of the emigration movement, described his work as "philanthropic abduction." It was a case of rescuing children from a degenerate home life and excluding parents from the emigration process that would inevitably follow.[5] Oblivious to the strong family ties and respectability of the labouring poor, he tore countless families apart in his mindless quest for moral correctness. Others, like Maria Rye, Annie Macpherson, and Louisa Birt, would do exactly the same.

In addition to believing that poverty-stricken English children had to be saved at all costs, the organizers of child emigration also fantasized over the virtuous and wholesome future that awaited their charges in Canada. Pallid city boys would be transformed into "brawny sun-burnt" lads. Food would be plentiful, and the "grand Canadian air" would enable "slender, sickly saplings" to thrive. Through agricultural work they would be "depauperised" and "unworkhoused" and would learn to take pride in "honest industry."[6] Such romantic piffle seems absurd today, but it

A sunless alley in Liverpool closed in 1912 by Liverpool City Council.

reflected the idealized picture of rural life that was prevalent at the time in fictional literature. Of course, this muddled thinking bore no relation whatsoever to reality. Andrew Doyle, a senior inspector for the Local Government Board in Britain, first alerted the British and Canadian authorities to the harsh reality he observed during a visit to Ontario and Quebec provinces in 1875. Far from enjoying a pure and joyful life in some rural idyll, Doyle found irrefutable evidence that children were being overworked and physically abused. Despite his recommendation that reforms were needed to ensure that child placements were properly regulated and supervised, little action was taken to remedy the situation until the early twentieth century.[7]

Meanwhile, Canadians were beginning to question whether they really wanted to have young English paupers in their midst. Some Canadian doctors thought that home children might carry diseases such as syphilis, and felt that they would be imbued with anti-social tendencies from birth. The notion was spread that these children would have criminal tendencies and would be morally degenerate.[8] Their unfamiliarity with farming also provoked criticism. They were regarded disparagingly as "the lost men and boys from England's teeming cities, [who] were turned out to work on Canadian farms, many not having the slightest comprehension of rural life or association with farms or farm animals."[9] And well-meaning people back in England believed that "the indescribable workhouse brand needed to be removed from a child's character" before emigrating.[10] Thus, their public persona was at rock bottom, and, in addition to the exploitation and physical hardships they suffered, most home children also had to endure the insults and innuendo that flowed from their poverty and Englishness. Far from taking solace and pride from their cultural identity, as most immigrants did, these children had to repudiate their past.

However, despite misgivings on both sides of the Atlantic, the exodus grew rapidly. About five hundred home children were sent to Canada annually during the late 1870s, and this number more than tripled between 1879 and 1883.[11] More than eleven thousand children arrived in Canada between 1870 and 1914, and this number mushroomed to eighty thousand by 1925.[12] The first two removals were launched in 1870 by Maria Rye and Annie Macpherson, both deeply religious women who had been troubled by the suffering they had witnessed in the slums of London and Liverpool.[13] Miss Rye's children came from workhouses and industrial schools, while Miss Macpherson's youngsters were mainly street waifs gathered from London's east end. In both cases the children were sent mainly to Ontario and Quebec. But their amateurish approach and poor management skills led to unsuitable placements and inadequate supervision, failings that were criticized severely by Andrew Doyle during his later investigations.[14]

It was only when Mrs. Louisa Birt, Annie Macpherson's sister, introduced her emigration scheme that substantial numbers of children began arriving in the Maritime provinces. Nova Scotia was the primary recipient of her children initially. Having received preliminary training in the Liverpool Sheltering Homes, which Mrs. Birt founded in 1872, six groups totalling around 347 children were brought to Nova Scotia between 1873 and 1876.[15] Mrs. Birt dismissed them as "waifs and strays" who were used to being "knocked about and ill-used … as though to make them run away; drunkards' children going through the education which will fit them for the reformatory, prison or penitentiary, as the case may be [and] illegitimate children on whom the sins of their parents are weighing with crushing power."[16] Such a pitiless attitude reveals the prevalent belief that poverty was somehow synonymous with moral degeneracy. Their poverty was actually caused by unpredictable economic cycles that suddenly threw labouring people out of work or denied them a living wage.

In preparing her children for their new life in Nova Scotia, Mrs. Birt turned for help to Colonel John Wimbourne Laurie, a prosperous farmer who lived near Halifax. As inspector of the province's militia and member of its Agriculture Board, Laurie was a powerful and influential figure.[17] He had already taken the initiative in contacting Mrs. Birt, requesting that she direct her charges to Nova Scotia. Persuading the provincial government to pay part of the cost of the emigration and guaranteeing the rest of the funds needed himself, he even accepted full responsibility for placing and supervising the children.[18] Laurie must have seemed a dream come true to Mrs. Birt, who accepted his terms with alacrity.

In a letter published by the *Acadian Recorder* in August 1873, Colonel Laurie notified local people that Mrs. Birt's first group of seventy-six children was on its way to Halifax. Imploring readers not to regard the children as "criminal," but merely "homeless and destitute," he praised Mrs. Birt for having rescued them from "temptation and a probable life of crime."[19] Edwin Clay, the Halifax immigration agent, was soon able to report that the children had all been placed "in good situations; many of them having been adopted into some of our most respectable families."[20] It all seemed very smooth and trouble-free, but by April of the following year, when the second group of Mrs. Birt's children arrived, sixty-seven in all, Laurie's placement strategy had changed. Whereas four counties had been the principal recipients of the first group, this time there was only one winner.[21] Pictou County, one of the province's most industrialized regions, acquired 62 percent of the second group (see Table 9).

Table 9

Placements of Louisa Birt's Children (from Liverpool) in Nova Scotia, 1873–1876
[NSARM RG18 Ser. I Vol. 1 #1: Laurie's List]
(Please note: ages shown in parentheses.)

First Party, August 1873

Mary Hawkins (14)	Saint John, NB
Maggie MacDonald (11)	New Glasgow, Pictou County
Sarah Cunningham (8)	Glengarry, Pictou County
John Stevenson (8)	Little River, Musquodoboit, Halifax County
Robert Jones (10)	Lower Maccan, Cumberland County
Mary E Jones (13)	as above
Amy Ludlow (13)	River Inhabitants
Alice Francis (13)	Richmond, CB
Thos. Robinson (10)	Little River, Musquodoboit, Halifax County
Ellen Maudsley (9)	Paradise, Annapolis County
Henry Hoey (10)	Middle Stewiacke, Cumberland County
Dora McDonald (12)	as above
William Bock (10)	Nictaux Falls, Annapolis County
Robert Laidlaw (11)	Middle Stewiacke, Cumberland County
George W. Hughes (13)	Merigomish, Pictou County
Julia Welch (9)	as above
Elizabeth Maudsley (10)	Lower Maccan, Cumberland County
Henry Profit (14)	Maitland, Halifax County
George Gabriel (12)	Little River, Musquodoboit
Thomas Winstanley (14)	Digby Neck, Rossway, Digby County
Henry McClune (13)	Windsor, Hants County
Anna Taylor (10)	as above
Joseph Roberts (12)	Valley Station, Colchester County
John Marks (13)	Kemptown, Colchester County
John Jones (12)	Middle Manor, Lunenburg County
David Smith (9)	Lower Maccan, Cumberland County
Miriam Caffrey (18)	married
Thos. Williams (11)	Nine Mile River, East Hants County
Ellen Burgess (9)	Douglas, Hants County
John Smith (11)	Lower Ward, Margaree Bay, Inverness County, CB
Mark McSway (12)	Granville, Annapolis County
W.G. Oliphant (11)	Wentworth, Wallace, Cumberland County

Flora Duckworth (7)	123, Barrington St., Halifax
R.H. Edwards (7)	Dartmouth, Halifax County
Catharine Edwards (5)	as above
Sarah Barton (13)	Liverpool, Queens County
Peter Williams (10)	Lower Barneys River, Pictou County
John Carrington (11)	Annapolis, Annapolis County
James Graham (14)	Rossway, Digby County
Robert Kernow (10)	Liverpool, Queens County
Robert Roberts (15)	Truro, Colchester County
Paul Winstone (15)	Three Mile River, Pictou County
John Coleman (14)	Stellarton, Pictou County
James Lewin (11)	Barney's River, Pictou County
Samuel Williams (10)	Scotch Hill, Pictou
Maggie Jones (6)	St. Annes, Cape Breton
E. Jones (9)	St. Annes, Cape Breton
Thomas Williams (9)	Lower Stewiacke, Cumberland County
Sarah Ludlow (8)	River John, Pictou County
Martha Duckworth (11)	Bedford, Halifax County
John Ladybird (11)	Earltown, Colchester County
James Lingforth (15)	Kent Island, Musquodoboit, Halifax County
John Campbell (17)	n/k
M.A. Stafford (6)	Oakfield, Halifax County
M.H. Williams (16)	Clyde River, Shelburne County
Fred G. Williams (13)	as above
Sophy Ludlow (18)	Wallace, Cumberland County
Anne Hawkins and baby (25)	n/k. Baby to orphanage house.
E. Hawkins (7)	Big Brook, Hopewell, Pictou County
Geo. Robinson (8)	Lower Barney's River, Pictou County
Albert Stewart (7)	Kemptown, Colchester County
George Duckworth (3)	Wolfville, Kings County
Charles Teagle (8)	Shubenacadie, Oakfield, Halifax County
David Bell (8)	Middle River, Westville, Pictou County
Thomas Gallagher (5)	Nelson & May Office, New Annan, Colchester County
Charles Ludlow (9)	Earltown, Colchester County
Wm. Fotterdell (9)	Earltown, Colchester County
Joseph Smith (10)	Highland Village Londonderry, Colchester County
Thomas Simpson	Milford, Hants County
Edward Simpson (8)	as above

Henry Brown (8)   Gold Mines Office, Halifax
Mrs Edwards
Mrs Evans

Second Party, April 1874

Mary Burns (12)   Amherst Point, Cumberland County
Agnes Bee (11)   Halifax
Joseph Burton (13)   Chance Harbour, Pictou County
Kate Campbell (16)   24, Creighton St., Halifax
Julia Corkill (11)   Bridgeville, Pictou County
Christina Carl (10)   Little Harbour, Pictou County
Esther Corkil (7)   Cheganois
Mary Cutler (4)   Amherst Point, Cumberland County
Eliza Cutler (4)   Stellarton, Pictou County
John Corkil (5)   French River, Pictou County
John Cosgrove (4)   Middle River, Pictou, Pictou County
Robin Corkhill (3)   New Glasgow, Pictou County
Francis Cullen (15)   Amherst, Cumberland County
Richard Cearns (13)   Merigomish, Pictou County
James Christianson (10)   Merigomish, Pictou County
Thomas Cosgrove (10)   Barney's River, Pictou County
Arthur Cowling (9)   Chance Harbour, Pictou County
John Clifton (8)   Barneys River, Pictou County
John Christianson (6)   Morristown Aylesford, Kings County
Walter Creighton (6)   Barneys River, Pictou County
Frederick W. Cowling (7)   Goshen, Queens County
James Dalton (14)   Annapolis, Annapolis County
John Douglas (6)   Barneys River, Pictou County
Stephen Baniman (5)   Nelson & May Office, New Annan, Colchester
                            County
John H Gimbell (12)   Goshen, Queens County
George Elston (7)   Amherst, Cumberland County
Gabriel Evans (7)   Barney's River, Pictou County
John M Evans (6)   McLellans Brook, N. Glasgow, Pictou County
James Elston (5)   Barneys River, Pictou County
Elizabeth Frederick (12)   Barrington, Shelburne County
Annie Fritz (6)   Chance Harbour, Pictou County
John Fletcher (13)   Lower Onslow, Colchester County

George Frederick (6)	Maitland, Hants County
Sarah Gelling (12)	Upper South River, Antigonish County
Adam Gabriel (9)	Lower Ward, Margaree Bay, CB
Henry Gabriel (5)	Barney's River, Pictou County
William J. Hall (11)	French River, Pictou County
Matthew Hopkins (9)	Fishers Grant, Pictou County
Michael Hopkinson (6)	East River Pictou, Pictou County
James Jones (14)	Ship Harbour, Halifax County
Edward Jessup (13)	Middle Musquodoboit, Halifax County
Grace Hermans (6)	Little Harbour, Pictou County
George Leigh (9)	Piedmont, Pictou County
John Meldon (9)	Upper Clyde River, Shelburne County
Ellen McGuire (13)	St. Pauls, East Branch, East River Pictou County
Margaret Owen (11)	Hopewell, Pictou County
James Owen (13)	Kentville, Kings County
Alice Patten (13)	Frasers Mills, Antigonish County
Elizabeth Parry (10)	East River, Pictou, Pictou County
Mary Patten (10)	Truro, Colchester County
Susie Porter (8)	Hammonds Plains, Halifax County
Sarah Patten (5)	New Glasgow, Pictou County
Robert Porter (8)	Bridgeville, Pictou County
Evan Rutter (11)	Bridgeville, Pictou County
Margaret Smith (14)	166 Lower Road or Holmworth, Aylesford, Annapolis County
Ruth Smith (14)	n/k
Edith Ludlow (5)	S M Dockyard
Gerald Stewart (5)	New Glasgow, Pictou County
James Smith (10)	Upper South River, Antigonish, Antigonish County
John Stanley (6)	Green Hill, West River Pictou, Pictou County
Elizabeth Whitehead (12)	185 Pleasant St. Halifax
Emma Williams (12)	Little Harbour, Pictou County
Susannah Warbrook (8)	New Glasgow, Pictou County
Rosette Williams (6)	Fishers Grant, Pictou County
Margaret Watson (5)	Grand Lake, Enfield, Hants
William Warbrick (11)	West River, Pictou, Pictou County
William Weaver (10)	Little River, Musquodoboit, Halifax County

Third Party, August 1874

George F Moore (8)	Cooks Cove, Guysborough County
Harriet Gallagher (4)	New Minas — Wolfville, Kings County
Hannah Evans (11)	Yarmouth, Yarmouth County
Agnes Hampson (11)	East Rawdon, Hants County
Edward Norton (10)	as above
Edwin Simons (14)	Deer River, Digby, Digby County
Thomas McQuilton (12)	as above
Thomas Hill (14)	n/k
Squire Napier (10)	Beauville, Annapolis, Annapolis County
W.J. Sherburn (10)	Newport, Hants
J. McElvie (14)	Jeddore, Halifax County
Charles Wakefield (14)	Antigonish, Antigonish County
Maggie Stewart (12)	Shelburne, Shelburne County
Albert Napier (10)	Gaberus, Cape Breton
Stanley Lewis (14)	Annapolis, Annapolis County
Thomas Ledder (14)	Little Harbour, Pictou County
E. Anne Libby (10)	Londonderry, Colchester County
Mary E. Gamans (15)	De Berk River, Colchester County
Louisa Hughes (16)	Little Dyke, Londonderry, Colchester County
Andrew Harris (14)	West Branch, River John, Pictou County
Elizabeth Powell (10)	West Brook, Cumberland County
Edwin Howell (14)	West Brook, Cumberland County
Alice Locke (10)	Penford, Cumberland County
Edith Locke (10)	Head of Amherst, Cumberland County
Emma Daniel (12)	n/k
William Gamans (16)	Amherst, Cumberland County
Robert Baird (12)	Avondale, Barney's River, Pictou County
Mary Lewis (7)	n/k
Annie Owens (8)	Merigomish, Pictou County
Mary Anne Saunders (7)	Mount Thom, Pictou County
Robert Latham (10)	Merigomish, Pictou County
Edward Locke (5)	South River Lake, Antigonish County
Edith Pollen (6)	Pictou, Pictou County
Leopold Napier (6)	East Branch Barneys River, Pictou County
Charles Foulkes (9)	East Barneys River, Pictou County
George Pope (9)	French River, Pictou County
Susan Kirkland (10)	Tanner Hill, Pictou County
Edward Tunstall (8)	Barneys River, Pictou County

Maggie McColl (7)	n/k
Donald McColl (7)	n/k
Julia Kirkland (7)	Barneys River, Pictou County
Reginald Colemarsh (6)	Little Harbour, Pictou County
Anne Jones (11)	New Glasgow, Pictou County
Selina Kirkland (5)	Barneys River, Pictou County
Thomas Hollins (10)	Churchville East River, Pictou County
Robert Grugel (4)	Barneys River, Pictou County
Samuel Moore (4)	New Glasgow, Pictou County
John Balfourd (6)	New Glasgow, Pictou County
Charles Whalley (10)	Mount Dalhousie, Pictou County
Robert Carlow (10)	Boat Harbour, Pictou County
George Beck (9)	Fishers Grant, Pictou County
W. Dawson (6)	Little Harbour, Pictou County
Peter Cousins (8)	Upper South River, Antigonish County
Maggie Cooke (16)	Barneys River, Pictou County
Isabella Reynolds (7)	Cape George, Antigonish County
Joseph Whalley (14)	Weavers Mountain, Digby County
Joseph Lewis (14)	McLellans Brook, Pictou County
W.G. Jackson (15)	Upper Settlement, East River, Pictou County
William Brice (7)	Glenelg, St. Mary's Guysborough County
Thomas Dawson (3)	Lane Harbour, Halifax County
Elizabeth Lewis (9)	Two Islands, Parrsboro, Cumberland County
M. Jane Cousins (10)	Kingston, Kings County
Thomas Rodgers (11)	Granville, Annapolis County
Nelie Saunders (4)	Sydney Mines, Cape Breton
William Clucas (13)	Sutherlands River, Pictou County
Maggie Jones (8)	Chance Harbour, New Glasgow, Pictou County
Henry Cousins (12)	Amherst Point, Cumberland County
John Hill (11)	Wallace Bridge, Cumberland County
John Downes (6)	West Chester, Cumberland County
Maggie Porter (15)	Wallace, Cumberland County
Maggie McGuire (17)	Saint John, NB
Elizabeth Carlow (14)	as above
Mary Porter (13)	Wallace, Cumberland County
Elizabeth Owens (4)	New Glasgow, Pictou County
Elizabeth Norton (4)	194 Water St., Halifax
Fanny Pollen (8)	Yarmouth, Yarmouth County
Maria Kelly, G. Maud McCarthy,	Lunenburg, Lunenburg County
Mrs. Birt's children	

Fourth Party, April 1875

Mayflower (2½)	Chief Quarter Master, HMI *Pyraneus*, Dockyard, Halifax
Laura Owens (5)	Stellarton, Pictou County
George Thomson (8)	McLennan's Mount, Pictou County
Jessie Menzies (12)	Aylesford, Annapolis County
Annie Baillie (10)	Central Onslow, Colchester County
Emma Williams (10)	Woodville, Newport, Hants County
Henry Chamberlain (12)	Hardwood Land, Shubenacadie, Hants County
George Nugent (13)	Beech Hill, Horton, Kings County
William Caudle (8)	East Jeddore, Halifax County
James Edward Myers (15)	Lawrencetown, Halifax County
John Fillingham (14)	East Jeddore, Halifax County
George Menzies (8)	Brockington, Middleton Annapolis County
James Mullow (13)	East Jeddore, Halifax County
David Jones (14)	Lower Jeddore East, Halifax County
Elizabeth Eaton (9)	Died
Mary Ann Quinn (6)	Scotsburn, Pictou County
Annie Capper (6)	Stellarton, Pictou County
Richard Wilson (14)	Digby, Digby County
Thomasina Smith (10)	Glenelg, St. Mary, Guysborough County
Esther Henry (16)	Antigonish, Antigonish County
Annie Baker (12)	as above
Henry Williams (15)	Merigomish, Pictou County
George Sibbie (10)	St. Pauls, East Branch, East River, Pictou County
George Duffin (10)	Loading Ground Sound, South Pictou, Pictou County
Mary Jane Thornton (6)	McLellans, Mt. Vale Colliery, New Glasgow, Pictou County
Joseph Fleming (10)	Brookland, Salt Springs, Pictou County
Lewis Davies (8)	Brora Lake, Upper Barney's River, Pictou County
Michael Holland (11)	Merigomish, Pictou County
J. Edward Stanley (11)	Loganville, West Branch River John, Pictou County
John Jones (8)	Wentworth Grant, Pictou County
Lillie Rowling (4)	Pictou, Pictou County
Eliza Laidlaw (13)	Pleasant Valley, Pictou County
Annie Britten (8)	Merigomish, Pictou County
Willie Montrose (2)	Fishers Grant, Pictou County

Enoch Jones (6)	McLellans Brook, New Glasgow, Pictou County
Fred Spencer (15)	Piedmont, Barneys River Pictou County
Alice Parkinson (6½)	Water Vale, Pictou County
Maggie Owens (n/k)	Pictou, Pictou County
Agnes Menzies (10)	Loading Ground, New Glasgow, Pictou County
Mary Green (12)	New Glasgow, Pictou County
John Bales (2½)	Wentworth Grant, Cumberland County; County Creek, Pictou County
Amelia Cotton (n/k)	New Glasgow, Pictou County
Mary Byan (6)	New Glasgow, Pictou County
Thomas Morgan (13)	Wallace Ridge, Cumberland County
David Gerrard (10)	Wallace Malagash, Cumberland County
Frank Clisby (12)	Wentworth, Cumberland County
George H. Faulkner (16)	Wallace Bay, Cumberland County
John O'Brien (12)	Black River, Cumberland County
Andrew Caufman (12)	River Philip, Cumberland County
James Menzies (6)	Victoria Settlement, Cumberland County
Arthur Menzies (6)	as above
James Barlow (13)	Amherst, Cumberland County
Annie Boden (16)	River Hébert, Cumberland County
Elizabeth Strickland (16)	Barton, Digby County
Edward Corlett (11)	Westbrook, Cumberland County
Mary Eaton (11)	Amherst, Cumberland County
Sam Ware (13)	n/k
Willie Owens (11)	Roseway, Shelburne County
Alice Owens (11)	as above
Harriet Jones (11)	Cape Negro Island, Shelburne County
Joseph Ryan (4)	Cross Roads, Upper Stewiacke, Cumberland County
Bernard Lewin (10)	Fort Jollie, Queens County

Fifth Party August, 1875

Amy Lee (4)	Campbell Road, Halifax
Amelia Coram (14)	as above
Lizzie Conway (7)	Pictou Landing, Pictou County
Lily Martin (5)	Diligent River, Parrsboro, Cumberland County
Albert Martin (9)	as above
John Rodgerson (13)	Aylesford, Annapolis County

Peter Manifold (6)	Lower Ward, Margaree Bay, Cape Breton
James Wilson (11)	Aylesford, Annapolis County
James Bridge (13)	Clam Harbour, Halifax County
William England (9)	Breshington, Hants County
Frederic England (13)	Nine Mile River, Hants County
Mary Jane Lee (9)	Pictou, Pictou County
Isabella Wilson (8)	Durham, Pictou County
Lily Smith (6)	Glenelg, St. Mary's, Guysborough County
Agnes Thompson (7)	as above
William J. Plaskett (11)	as above
Mary Stoddart (6)	Westville, Pictou County
Mary Lockley (13)	Pine Tree, New Glasgow, Pictou County
Joseph Lynch (13)	Merigomish, Pictou County
Frederick Trookall (6)	Plymouth, Stellarton, Pictou County
Alfred George Hastie (4)	New Glasgow, Pictou County
Mary Burns (9)	Wallace Bridge, Cumberland County
John Burns (7)	Cape John, River John, Pictou County
Eliza Fairley (16)	Pugwash, Cumberland County (left)
Henry Gerrard (7)	Six Mile Road, Wallace, Cumberland County
Thomas Christian (13)	Gulf Shore, Wallace, Pugwash, Cumberland County
Robert Cearns (11)	Gulf Shore, Pugwash, Cumberland County
Allan G. Wilson (7)	as above
Mary Corkill (15)	Box 47, Amherst, Cumberland County
Annie Rubies (13)	Guysborough, Guysborough County
Alice White (14)	Maccan, Cumberland County
M. E. Baker (6)	Rockford, Shelburne (returned)
Harriett Lee (11)	Churchdown, Shelburne County
Alexander Wilson (13)	Clyde River, Shelburne County
J. Buchannan (11)	Parrsboro, Cumberland County
Robert Rodgerson (12)	Amherst, Cumberland County
A. Thomas Wastie (7)	Clyde River, Shelburne County
Charles Baker (5)	n/k
John Thompson (4)	22 Blower St., Halifax
William Andrews (n/k)	West Brook, Cumberland County (not one of Louisa Birt's)
Mary Jane Hunt (12)	Amherst, Cumberland County

Sixth Party, March 21, 1876

William Hebry Rodgerson (16)	Lockport, Shelburne County
Joseph William Evans (15)	Barrington Head, Shelburne County
Bernard McDonald (14)	Farmers, Digby, Digby County
William Bruce (13)	Watervale, West River, Pictou, Pictou County
Robert James McKettrick (13)	New Glasgow, Pictou County
William Smith (11)	Shelburne, Shelburne County
Thomas Grass (11)	Coldbrook, Cornwallis, Kings County
John Ruddy (10)	Centreville, Digby County
William Henry Davies (10)	Grenville Crossing, Cumberland County
George Gates (9)	Amherst, Cumberland County
Thomas Jones (9)	Advocate Harbour, Cumberland County
William Cooper (8)	Wallace Ridge, Cumberland County
Joseph McDonald (8)	West Jeddore, Halifax County
Samuel Arthur Brown (8)	Thomson Station, Cumberland County
John Maddan (10)	Goose River, Cumberland County
John Burgess (8)	West Jeddore, Halifax County
James Corbett (8)	Whycocomagh, Inverness County, Cape Breton
Thomas Henry Taylor (7)	Blacksmith, New Glasgow, Pictou County
Edward Gates (5)	Diligent River, Cumberland County
Edward Griffiths (5)	West Merigomish, Pictou County
John Devine (5)	South Pictou, Pictou County
Alan O'Neill (5)	New Glasgow, Pictou County
Henry Carter (4)	Stellarton, Pictou County
Willie Ross (4)	Lower Sutherlands River, Pictou County
Jimmy Francis (4)	Acadian Mines, Londonderry, Colchester County
Charlie Mellers (3)	as above (not shown in original)
Patrick Dewer (3)	as above
Jimmy Rigura (2½)	as above
Margaret Bustard (19)	Oakfield, Halifax County
Maggie Anne Colley (14)	Pugwash River, Cumberland County
Catharine Evans (10)	Yarmouth, Yarmouth County
Jessie Bruce (10)	Lockport, Shelburne County
Anne E. Wainwright (11)	Amherst, Cumberland County
May O'Neill (9)	New Glasgow, Pictou County
Margaret Smith (9)	Falmouth, Hants County
Margaret McDonald (9)	Bear River, Digby County
Annie Woodhouse (9)	South River Lake, Antigonish County

Mary Devine (7)	Caribou Island, Pictou County
Margaret McDonald (8)	Parrsboro, Cumberland County
Annie Clifton (6)	Pictou Town, Pictou County
Evangeline Brown (8)	Lower Sutherlands River, Pictou County
Alice Anne Davies (7)	n/k
Winnifred Bularis (5)	Sandy Point, Shelburne County
Emma Jane Davis (5)	Amherst, Cumberland County
Ellen Davis (4)	New Glasgow, Pictou County
Maggie Clifton (4)	Stellarton, Pictou County
Mary Bradbury (4)	Milton, Queens County
Theresa Ross (3)	Lower Sutherlands River, Pictou County
Annie Madden (13)	Goose River, Cumberland County
Elizabeth Philips (7)	Wallace Ridge, Cumberland County
Baby (1)	
M.J. Jordan	Amherst, Cumberland County

Laurie's letter to the *Eastern Chronicle* indicates that he had clearly intended to favour "the eastern part of the province."[22] Selecting the Mechanic's Hall in New Glasgow in the very heart of Pictou's coal-mining operations as the venue for his public meeting, he announced that "the children for allotment" would be present, along with Mrs. Birt, who would give an account of her philanthropic work. Predictably, the children were taken away by people from the immediate area. People living in the towns of Pictou, New Glasgow, and Stellarton, and in other areas within or close to the county's industrial belt had the benefit of this windfall of young immigrant labour.[23] Agricultural counties like Annapolis, Shelburne, and Kings received only a tiny fraction of the total. The inescapable conclusion is that Mrs. Birt's children were being brought to Pictou County to alleviate labour shortages, probably not just on farms but in industry as well, presumably with the full compliance of the provincial authorities.

Overall, Pictou County acquired the greatest proportion of the 347 children in the six groups (37 percent) but Cumberland County's intake, at 19 percent, was also substantial[24] (see Table 9). Doing well out of the placements in this county were the colliery areas of Maccan and

Table 10

County Breakdown of Home Children Placements in Nova Scotia, 1873–76
(taken from Colonel Laurie's list)

County	Aug. 1873 1st Party	Apr. 1874 2nd Party	Aug. 1874 3rd Party	Apr. 1875 4th Party	Aug. 1875 5th Party	March 1876 5th Party	Totals	Percent of Total
Annapolis	5	2	3	3	2	1	15	4
Antigonish		3	4	1		1	9	3
Cape Breton	5	1	2		1	1	10	3
Colchester	9	4	3	1		1	18	5
Cumberland	10	4	11	13	14	14	66	19
Digby	2		3	2		3	10	3
Guysborough			2	1	4		7	2
Halifax	11	7	3	6	4	3	34	10
Hants	6	2	3	2	2	1	16	5
Kings	1	2	2	1		1	7	2
Lunenburg	1		1				2	0.5
Pictou	12	37	30	26	9	15	129	37
Queens	2			1		1	4	1
Shelburne	2	2	1	3	4	5	17	5
Yarmouth			2			1	3	0.5
Total of children placed	66	64	70	60	40	47	347	100
Children not placed	10	3	6	3	1	4		
Total children in party	76	67	76	63	41	51		

River Hébert, and the town of Amherst. Halifax County ranked third in acquiring 10 percent of the total, largely due to the placements in the city of Halifax, where children were presumably expected to learn a trade or work in domestic service. Thus, the three counties of Pictou, Cumberland, and Halifax, having important industrial and urban districts, acquired 66 percent of the total, while the other eleven counties in peninsular Nova Scotia (Annapolis, Antigonish, Colchester, Digby, Guysborough, Hants, Kings, Lunenburg, Queens, Shelburne, and Yarmouth) and the three counties in Cape Breton (Inverness, Richmond, and Victoria) shared the rest[25] (see Table 10).

However, the preference for industrial districts does not in itself mean that any of Mrs. Birt's children necessarily went to commercial enterprises. The rapid growth in the province's mining and other industrial operations from the 1850s created a sudden demand for labour that largely would have been met by attracting workers away from agricultural employment. Thus, hard-pressed farmers in industrial areas could have made the strongest case for acquiring Mrs. Birt's children. However, odd references in Laurie's ledger to children such as Henry Brown, sent to the "Gold Mines Office, Halifax"; Thomas Gallagher and Stephen Baniman, placed at the "Nelson & May Office at New Annan" in Colchester County; Edith Ludlow, placed at a dockyard in Halifax; George Duffin at the "Loading Ground, South Pictou"; Agnes Menzies at the "Loading Ground, New Glasgow"; and Jimmy Francis, sent to the "Acadian Mines, Londonderry" in Colchester County certainly indicate that some children did end up in industrial premises.[26] Oddest of all was the placement of the two-and-a-half-year-old child with the surname of Mayflower (gender unknown), who was sent to the Chief Quarter Master of a naval dockyard in Halifax. Mayflower was the youngest, but an alarming 60 percent of Mrs. Birt's children were under the age of ten.[27] No doubt, children as young as this were being used to carry out menial tasks, but what they were being asked to do is beyond our comprehension!

Another possibility to be considered is whether any of Mrs. Birt's children were dispatched to the mines. Although the use of boys in coal mines had long since been banned in Britain, the practice was widespread in Nova Scotia and Cape Breton. They were sent below ground to drive

Courtesy of Library and Archives Canada, e010764850.

A group of young children brought to Canada by Louisa Birt, *circa* 1902. Taken from the report of G. Brogue Smart, Inspector of British Immigrant Children and Receiving Homes, for the year ending June 30, 1903.

pit ponies, manipulate ventilation doors, and they also assisted in various tasks aboveground.[28] The provincial authorities had spent funds in 1873 to help pay the passages of British immigrants who "had been forwarded to the coal districts in the counties of Pictou and Cape Breton." According to Mather Byles Desbrisay, the provincial immigration agent, they included "45 minors, under 17 years old."[29] Given that the authorities granted funds to Mrs. Birt that same year to bring across her first group, it seems highly likely that the forty-five minors included some of her children. Further arrivals of children brought to Nova Scotia by Mrs. Birt and of families with children under Colonel Laurie's care were reported by the immigration agent in 1875, but no information was given as to their destination.[30]

Colonel Laurie's involvement with emigration schemes came to an abrupt end in 1877 when he apparently fell ill and suddenly withdrew his support.[31] This he did despite the ongoing demand for labour and the deleterious effect his action had in leaving the many young children already placed in Nova Scotia completely stranded. If they were booted out for being unsuitable or inept, or needed to be rescued from real harm, there was no one in the world they could turn to for help.[32] The government of Nova Scotia refused to get involved and, as a result, some children were simply left to fend for themselves.[33] Meanwhile, Mrs. Birt closed down her Nova Scotia operations and opened a distribution centre at Knowlton in the Eastern Townships of Quebec.[34] Perhaps this change in location had been forced upon her. The merest suspicion that she may have allowed some of her children to be exploited as industrial labour would have seemed scandalous back in Liverpool. In giving such high priority to Nova Scotia's economic interests, Mrs. Birt made a mockery of the noble goals that characterized the home-children movement. Children were meant to experience the healthy environment of farms and be treated like members of a family, but instead her charges were treated like commodities in a labour market.

Dr. John Middlemore, a medical doctor and son of a wealthy businessman, founded his emigration home in Birmingham in 1872, but, unlike Mrs. Birt, he retained complete control over the placement of his children. The extensive files kept for each child reveals the care taken to monitor progress and to respond to the regular reports of the Canadian managers who visited the various children at their new homes.[35] Middlemore sent his first contingent of children to Ontario in 1873, but by 1885 he began placing more of his children in New Brunswick, and eight years later Nova Scotia and Prince Edward Island were receiving his children as well.[36] A total of 3,331 children were brought to the Maritime provinces between 1894 and 1932 by Middlemore, with 57 percent being sent to New Brunswick, 38 percent to Nova Scotia, and 5 percent to Prince Edward Island (see Table 11). The children were mainly allocated to farms, and the fairly random nature of the placements would suggest that Middlemore had been more strongly motivated by the suitability of the potential recipients of children than by his children's value to provincial labour markets.

Nevertheless, given the scale of his undertaking, supervision was rudimentary and innumerable cases came to light later of neglect suffered

Table 11

Placements of Middlemore Home Children (from Birmingham) 1885–1930
[BIFHSGO (British Isles Family History Society of Greater Ottawa)
Middlemore Emigration Scheme website]

Year	Vessel Name	New Brunswick	Nova Scotia	P.E.I.	Total
1885	Circassian	17	0	0	17
1886	Lake Superior	24	2	0	26
1887	Lake Ontario	25	0	0	25
1888	Lake Ontario	24	0	0	24
1889	Lake Winnipeg	34	0	0	34
1890	Circassian	36	0	0	36
1891	Parisian	28	0	0	28
1893	Siberian	43	38	6	87
1894	Siberian	14	16	37	67
1895	Carthaginian	23	31	16	70
1896	Corean	63	58	17	138
1897	Assyrian	44	40	19	103
1898	Siberian	65	56	0	121
1899	Siberian	50	30	13	93
1900	Siberian	62	26	15	103
1901	Sicillian	57	40	0	97
1902	Siberian	67	53	0	120
1903	Siberian	51	51	0	102
1904	Carthaginian	74	51	0	125
1905	Siberian	87	60	0	147
1906	Siberian	51	51	0	102
1907	Carthaginian	61	84	0	145
1908	Carthaginian	75	65	0	140
1909	Carthaginian	70	49	0	119
1910	Mongolian	83	46	11	140
1911	Carthaginian	91	63	9	163
1912	Carthaginian	89	62	0	151
1913	Mongolian	83	46	11	140
1911	Carthaginian	91	63	9	163
1912	Carthaginian	89	62	0	151
1913	Mongolian	50	53	6	109
1914	Carthaginian	70	27	0	97
1915	Carthaginian	49	35	0	84

Year	Vessel Name	New Brunswick	Nova Scotia	P.E.I.	Total
1916	*Scandinavian*	57	25	0	82
1920	*Minnedosa*	55	32	0	87
1921	*Minnedosa*	39	18	0	87
1922	*Montcalm*	27	14	0	41
1923	*Scythia*	45	26	1	72
1924	*Franconia*	24	22	0	46
1925	*Andania*	4	6	0	10
1926	*Andania*	8	0	1	9
1927	*Samaria*	10	2	0	12
1928	*Newfoundland*	20	1	1	22
1929	*Newfoundland*	3	2	0	5
1930	*Newfoundland*	12	1	1	14
Totals		**1,909**	**1,266**	**153**	**3,328**

Courtesy of Library and Archives Canada, C-086484.

Middlemore boys taking refreshment during their farming work, location not known.

by the Middlemore children. On her initial placement in 1920 to Kings County, New Brunswick, Winnifred Titus was sexually abused. But after various unsatisfactory placements she found a better life for herself when she moved to the home of Mr. and Mrs. John Titus and later married their nephew.[37] Fred Sanders entered the Middlemore Home in 1923 of his "own free will," with his mother actually paying for his room and board and passage. He was badly treated at his first placement at a farm near Alma in Pictou County and absconded. Returning to the Middlemore Home in Birmingham, he obtained a second placement at a farm near Saint John, where he found himself being treated like one of the family. "I was so happy there. Old Mrs. Smith was just like a mother to me. She knit my mitts and socks and darned them and gave me heck if I didn't change into clean clothes regularly. And could she cook — especially buckwheat pancakes." After travelling to England once again to visit his mother, Fred returned to Saint John and later married an English girl: "I built a log cabin in the woods near the Smiths and they did all they could to help us." Later, the couple owned their own house in the city and raised six children.[38]

Unlike Mrs. Birt, who dished out her children at public meetings like gift tokens, Middlemore adopted a highly bureaucratic system for ensuring that placement procedures were tightly controlled. Following the arrival in 1899 of thirteen Middlemore children to Prince Edward Island, the *Guardian* newspaper reported favourably on "the very superior children" who were being allocated to farms across the island: "The applications have been filled in order as they came and the agent here, Mrs. Hogg, as well as the general agent in Halifax, Mr. J.S. Bough, regret their being obliged to hold so many applications over until next year."[39] What was more, Middlemore offered assurances that he never allowed "any proselytizing of children in religious matters. Roman Catholic children are settled in R.C. homes; Protestants to Protestant homes in every instance."[40] Nor did Middlemore share Mrs. Birt's condescending and stuffy attitude toward destitute children. His daughter remembers being with him at Birmingham Railway Station in 1919 when a big crowd had assembled on the platform to wave goodbye to a group of Middlemore children who were departing for Canada:

> A great yelling and hubbub arose in one of the big
> saloon compartments where a crowd of the young
> children were, and when I went to quell the disorder
> there was my father in among the children playing an
> imaginary fiddle like mad, using his smart, tightly-
> rolled city umbrella as a bow and dancing about to his
> own soundless tune while the children skipped and
> danced with him and shrieked with joy and everyone
> from the matron to the station officials was roaring with
> laughter. He was such fun and his fun was infectious.[41]

Mrs. Birt and Dr. Middlemore ran the major emigration schemes
that brought home children to the Maritime provinces, but there were
many smaller organizations involved in similar work. Between 1885 and
1910, the Bristol Emigration Society sent to Canada around 320 destitute
children, gathered from workhouses and industrial schools, with a
substantial number being placed on farms in New Brunswick. The Society,
having neither Canadian home nor agent, relied on the immigration
agent at Saint John, who clearly could not cope with the extra demands
being placed on him. For instance, one small group of boys who went to
Annapolis, Nova Scotia, in 1885 simply "wandered off."[42]

Poor Law Guardians in cities like Leeds regularly raised funds to assist
orphaned and abandoned children to emigrate. But rather than supervise
their relocation themselves, they sub-contracted the task. The Catholic
Protection Society in Liverpool dealt with Catholic children while
Protestants were placed in the care of Maria Rye or Louisa Birt. Although
Ontario received most of the Leeds children, a few went to New Brunswick.
Two examples were William Lyne and John Borus, who settled in Sussex
Parish and the Chambers settlement respectively, both in Kings County.[43]
Carefully selected phrases from letters written by them to the Leeds
Guardians appeared later in their promotional booklet. William wrote,
"[I] liked the people I am living with, they are very kind to me," while John
thought he had come to "a splendid country" urging them to "show this
letter to the boys who did not want to go to Canada."[44] Their literature
concentrated on the merits of "snatching children from pauperism" and

giving them better prospects, but, because the Leeds Board of Guardians had delegated the bureaucratic arrangements to other institutions, they were oblivious to the perils that lay ahead for their children.

One of the few schemes that actually was sympathetic to the needs of young children was founded in 1904 by Mrs. Ellinor Close. She established a farm near Rothesay (Kings County), New Brunswick, to train small groups of needy children, offering them the option of returning to England on reaching the age of sixteen, although she faced strong opposition from the Canadian authorities in doing so. This was one of the more successful undertakings, but with the outbreak of the First World War it had to be abandoned.[45]

Kingsley Ogilvie Fairbridge, a Rhodesian-born philanthropist, hoped to emulate Mrs. Close's strategy, but had difficulty acquiring suitable land. Founding the Child Emigration Society, he was initially encouraged by the offer of fifty thousand acres of land from Sir Edward Morris, the premier of Newfoundland. However, Lord Northcliffe, the newspaper magnate, soon disabused him of the viability of a farm school in Newfoundland:

> The only people who could possibly succeed in Newfoundland, in my opinion and in that of those who have been working there for five years, are married agriculturalists — preferably Scotsmen — willing to work under very lonely circumstances in a climate that has six months winter and a very intense summer.... As for sending children there, you may not be aware that there is often a considerable amount of starvation among the inhabitants in winter.[46]

Although Fairbridge failed to win support from the Canadian authorities, he did eventually found a training farm in Western Australia, having acquired suitable land in 1912.[47]

Nottingham, like other rapidly expanding English cities, had to cope with rising levels of deprivation. Modelling their ideas on Mrs. Close's concept of a training farm, prominent businessmen founded the Dakeyne

Boys Brigade.[48] Captain Oliver Hind, a local solicitor and magistrate, purchased a farm near Falmouth, Nova Scotia, where young boys could receive training in agricultural work for about one year before being placed with individual farmers in the province.[49] By 1924 a total of 126 boys had benefited from the process. Visiting the farm that year, Mr. G.B. Smart, supervisor of Juvenile Immigration, found that the boys were happy and well cared for.[50] He observed "the large commodious dormitory, in which all the boys sleep — there are thirteen beds, for the thirteen boys continuously in residence at the farm — small, single beds, with plenty of clean bedding and pillows. Next to the dormitory is a large room used as a wardrobe by the boys; the walls of this room are dotted with pegs and each boy has his own peg on which his Sunday suit of clothes was neatly hanging." He noticed "a fine *esprit de corps* amongst all hands" and general satisfaction "with their home life and treatment generally."[51]

By the early twentieth century the child-emigration movement was being motivated more by practical need than by concepts of spiritual salvation. The mass unemployment of the 1920s fuelled rising levels of immigration to the British Dominions — especially Canada and Australia. A new concern for the ruling classes by this time was the rising power of the trade-union movement and its links with the recently formed Communist Party. Alarmed by the growing political and social unrest in the inner cities, clergymen like the Reverend Francis Bacon appealed for public support to fund the emigration costs of destitute children.[52] As vicar of All Saints Anglican Church in Stepney (East London), he appreciated the depths of the economic depression. His leaflet, entitled "Under Which Flag?" invited people to join with him in rescuing local boys from their abysmal surroundings:

> The boys of Slumland are born and reared in the atmosphere of the Red Flag. My problem is, shall I leave them in it to degenerate still further till they become wastrels and criminals, or shall I take them out of their evil surroundings and place them in the Dominions, where they are needed, and where they can grow up to be industrious, loyal and respected citizens of the Empire?[53]

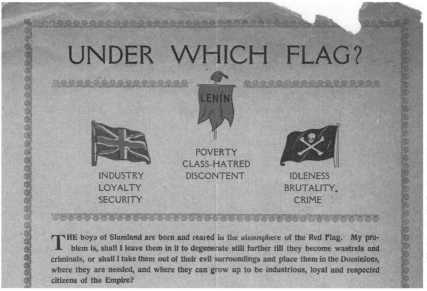

Courtesy of the University of Hull Archives, DBN/27/1.

Part of a pamphlet appealing for donations, produced in 1927 by Reverend Francis Bacon, vicar of All Saints Church, Stepney, London. He argued for assisted emigration and "Empire Development" as a solution to London's social problems.

But few if any of these children came to the Maritimes, since by this time most destitute children were being directed to Ontario, Quebec, and the Prairie provinces.

The philanthropists who organized the emigration of the children described in this chapter were motivated by strong moral convictions. Glowing reports of happily settled children were issued by them, and the immigration authorities in Canada spoke only of success. The world had to wait until 1979 to learn the truth. When social worker Phyllis Harrison published her book *The Home Children*, containing extracts of letters that she had solicited from former home children and their descendants, she provided firsthand evidence of the scale of physical and sexual abuse and exploitation that had been experienced. Joy Parr's doctoral thesis, completed a year later, examined the case papers of every tenth Barnardo's child, and she, too, reached similar conclusions.

Parr found that children's placements were determined solely by economic criteria. Children were moved from poor farming districts to more prosperous regions as they grew older and more experienced, that is, as their market value as workers increased.[54] Although it was intended that home children would be treated as one of the family, they were often shunned and used simply as cheap labour.[55] Invariably they were sent from distribution centres in Canada, on their own with name tags around their necks, to be collected at railway stations. They had to satisfy a farmer's work expectations, but the farmer could do as he pleased with them. A great many failed to provide proper schooling or wages for work, and some mistreated the children under their care. The inescapable conclusion is that the process was profoundly unfair to the children.

Although physical hardship is cruel, it is perhaps not as devastating in the long run as the loss of identity that would have befallen these children. Their English accents, sense of values, and likes and dislikes would have set them apart from other children. Moreover, given that many were discredited because of their background, they had a strong incentive to shed their Englishness as quickly as possible. Generally, most immigrants found solace in meeting up with other people in their part of Canada who shared their ethnic origins, but these children were forced to renounce their identities and become loners. Nor could they take comfort in letters received from home or in being joined by family and friends. But on the positive side, emigration removed them from hopeless situations in England and gave them a chance of a decent livelihood in later life. After serving their indentures most found well-paid work in towns and cities. In achieving this outcome they displayed remarkable resilience and courage and, along the way, graced Canada with their presence, although few people at the time told them so.

In common with other immigrants, the home children had to endure Atlantic crossings, although in their era, when steamships were available, journeys were shorter and safer than was the case with the earlier sailing ships. Sea transport was very basic in the late eighteenth century when the first of the immigrant groups arrived but improved with the growth of the North American timber trade, which greatly increased the availability of transatlantic shipping.

CHAPTER 9

The Sea Crossing

The Secret *has made a move, having been hauled out of her berth, and is now lying abreast of the Quay, presenting her broadside to the High Street, and smilingly welcomes the Sons of Hope on board, to tread her decks once more on her passage over the Atlantic ...*[1]

T HE GOOD PEOPLE of Bideford in Devon were well used to seeing off large groups of emigrants to North America. On this occasion, the *Secret* was preparing to leave for Quebec in the spring of 1849. A cannon was fired, and, "with the cheering of those on board,"[2] the ship was towed out to sea by a steamer. Two years previously the *Secret* had sailed to Charlottetown, and a few years later she went ashore on a sandbar near Bideford and was wrecked. The great perils of the sea were an ever-present reality. Emigrants had to put their faith in a ship and its captain and simply hope for the best. No amount of journalistic hype could disguise the fact that crossing the Atlantic was both dangerous and, at times, unpleasant.

Sea crossings were particularly uncomfortable for steerage passengers, who travelled below deck in the hold. It wasn't that anyone was trying to be deliberately cruel to them. If large numbers of people were to travel together, the only place to put them was in the hold. Nathaniel Smith, who joined 187 other Yorkshire passengers in the 1774 crossing of the *Albion* to Halifax, was probably fairly typical, stoically accepting the cramped and uncomfortable accommodation offered to him, and not complaining when only the basic provisions were provided. He was just glad to have survived the crossing. He and the others had to endure "three weeks of excessive storms and dreadful hurricanes" and the prospect of running aground near Sable Island. Fortunately, their captain, Thomas Perrott, anticipated the danger:

> He began to sound [take soundings] expecting to see we were nigh the shores and about the dead of night could find not bottom. Again about two [p.m.] they sounded on the Starboard side[3] and found only eleven fathoms. All was in uproar expecting we were just upon the rocks. Instantly they sounded on the Port side and found it thirteen fathoms — by that means they knew it right to steer on the left and, as the goodness of God would have it, we escaped the most dangerous place in all the passage from the Land End of England to the Continent of America.[4]

However, ill-luck befell the twenty passengers who sailed in the *Elizabeth* from London for the north shore of Prince Edward Island (then the Island of St. John) the following year. Encountering a gale on her approach to the island, the *Elizabeth* was wrecked after hitting the great sand ridge off Malpeque Bay. The captain and crew helped the passengers into lifeboats and salvaged what they could of the snow's cargo, but most of it was lost. It being November, a top priority was to find shelter. Thomas Curtis, one of the passengers, recorded how they walked a short distance to an area with fir trees and pools of fresh water and immediately built wigwams. Thankfully, Mr. Fry, one of the passengers who resided in North America, "had the presence of mind to put in his pocket instruments for making a fire." The survivors were so cold and wet that they actually "spent their first night standing round the fire." The next day, Fry and two of the sailors left in a small but leaky boat to summon help, using "part of a butter tub" to bail out water as they rowed.[5]

Meanwhile, the raging sea prevented the group from reaching supplies on their stricken ship. Curtis wrote: "[I] did not feel so much for want of food as I did in imagination of the consequences of going many days hungry such as eating the dog and then casting lots [to decide] who should we eat first." The storm did eventually abate, and "six or seven of [the] men got on board the vessel by the help of a rope that was left fast to her which reached the shore." With supplies of oatmeal, meat, and rum having been secured, their mood brightened. Shortly after this, aid arrived. A boat came from Malpeque Bay with food, then came "two whaleboats with four men," then came "Mr. Churchward[6] and the doctor from New London,"[7] and finally a sloop appeared to take them to New London. The survivors had their first experience of the mutual support and kindness that formed a necessary part of pioneer life. But throughout this saga John Russell, the *Elizabeth*'s captain, had remained strangely quiet. Perhaps he felt responsible for the mishap.

At sea, everything depended on the captain's navigational skills and cool head. However, he had almost no technical aids and was at the mercy of the weather. This was a time when captains shouted out their latitude and longitude to each other when their ships passed at sea, simply to get their bearings. Captain John Murray knew from his own harrowing experience of navigating the *Garland* through violent storms just how precarious life at sea could be. He wondered if he would ever see dry land again. Having left Liverpool for the Miramichi in September 1833 to collect a timber cargo, he failed to follow a sufficiently northerly route at the outset, thus inadvertently placing his ship in the path of a never-ending series of westerly gales. He and his crew worked non-stop in manning pumps and repairing the rigging and sails but, despite this, Captain Murray expected they would "be all froze to death." In desperation, he prayed to God: "look down with compassion upon us and if it be thy holy pleasure to bestow upon us thy unworthy servants a favourable wind so as we may be enabled arrive in safety at our port destination Miramichi, I will be ever thankful." The

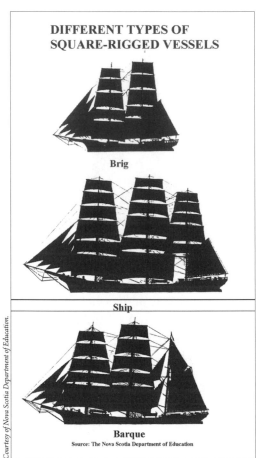

DIFFERENT TYPES OF SQUARE-RIGGED VESSELS

Brig

Ship

Barque

Source: The Nova Scotia Department of Education

Courtesy of Nova Scotia Department of Education.

The brig, or "snow," having two masts and square-rigged on both masts, was the most common vessel to be used on Atlantic crossings during the late eighteenth and early nineteenth centuries. The sails, suspended at right angles to the line of the hull, allowed for maximum propulsion from the prevailing winds. They were gradually replaced by the larger three-masted vessels, rigged as barques or ships.

sight of "the Miramichi pilot boats," that suddenly emerged out of a fog "as thick as it can possibly be," ended his misery.[8] They must have seemed heaven-sent.

In recording "the high sense they entertain of Capt. [Thomas] King's polite and kind attention to them, during their passage from Liverpool,"[9] the people who had sailed in the *Amelia* in 1819 had probably lived through a similar ordeal. No doubt they had been tossed around by mountainous waves and lived to tell the tale. Fourteen years later Thomas King was at the helm of the *George Gordon* when she sailed to Saint John. Long stints of continuous service helped the ship's captains to face the challenges of North Atlantic conditions. Moreover, it was no accident that ships that regularly plied between their home ports in England and ports in the Maritimes often had the same captain.

In addition to the perils of the sea, emigrants had also to face the discomforts of being cooped up for several weeks in the steerage. Their accommodation was basic, to say the least. Wooden planking was hammered over crossbeams and temporary sleeping berths were constructed along each side of the hold. There were no portholes, nor any means of ventilation beyond the hatches. And in stormy seas the hatches could be kept battened down for days. William Fulford, who sailed in 1848 from Bideford in the *Civility*, wrote, "we are so closely situated in our berths" and breathe "much impure air; and [with] the nauseousness [*sic*] of our chamber slops 'tis almost enough to create the plague."[10] Yet shipowners regarded emigrants as just another commodity to be shipped and had little regard for their creature comforts. It would not be until the steamship era, beginning in the 1850s, that custom-built accommodation would become available for passengers. Until then, passenger needs had a low priority, with shipping services being haphazardly run and primarily geared to the stowage requirements of the timber trade. However, for emigrants who could not afford the greater privacy and comforts of a cabin, a berth in the steerage was their only practical means of crossing the Atlantic.

Peter Barrett, one of the 141 Cornish miners who sailed from Liverpool to Halifax as a steerage passenger in the *Mozart* in April 1866, complained bitterly about the poor food and foul-tasting water onboard ship.[11] He and the other passengers suffered dreadfully from bouts of seasickness, made worse by the many gales and stormy seas. The *Mozart*, not being "a regular passenger ship," was woefully inadequate. Neither cooking utensils nor cutlery were provided: "[we had] to cut off the tops of some of our tin cans to make utensils to cook our meat, potatoes, peas, etc." and "to appropriate the use of our shirts, drawers, pants, stockings, etc. to take our supplies for biscuit, flour, mustard, oatmeal, salt, pepper, pork, beef, peas, rice and potatoes." And having improvised receptacles for food, they then had to master the art of cooking their food over an open fire on the deck. "Such a mess of cooking: lands folk never have a chance to see such hardships as we had in consequence, I hope never to be called upon again to suffer."[12]

Travelling in 1833 to Quebec in the *Oscar*, and, soon after this, taking a schooner to St. John's, Newfoundland, the Devon-born Ann Congdon, widow of a prosperous St. John's merchant, was spared such ordeals. Although she was dismayed initially by the sight of her "little room," it was at least a cabin, providing far more privacy and comfort than a berth in the steerage would have done. From time to time members of the crew visited her with supplies of fresh meat — carved from animals slaughtered on the ship — from which she made herself a meat pie or had a roast. Captain Banks regularly dropped by with "a bottle or two" of Porter [beer] and it was "all very neighbourly." Cabin passengers exchanged "a slice of roast beef for a slice of ham and a slice of plum pudding for apple pie, etc." And when the *Oscar* reached the Newfoundland Banks, Ann's mind filled with memories as she recalled the place from "where my dear father, brother, children and friends have so often crossed."[13]

Although steerage passengers had far more basic provisions, William Fulford had no grumbles about his food while sailing in the *Civility*, but wrote that the water "stinked aloud!" To make it palatable, it had to be boiled and flavoured with peppermint.[14] He could purchase a loaf of bread for a penny and "a pie or pudden" at a halfpenny. There were also supplies of "Bacon or Ham dry or in pickle, Salt Herrings or large fish, rice, dry peas, potatoes, good Swede turnips and celery, lump sugar, treacle, currants, honey, currant jelly, pickled onions, coffee, Coco, peppermints ... also cheese ... apples [and] medicine, viz anti-bilious pills, best Epsom salts and Senna ... [also] French Brandy, gin and rum, good cider and vinegar."[15] Of course, resourceful passengers could always put out hooks and lines and catch fish. When the passengers travelling in the *Elizabeth* from London in 1775 reached the Banks of Newfoundland, "a baited line was dragged along ... and when it was hauled up it brought a codfish weighing 42 pounds and a half."[16] No doubt it proved to be a welcome protein supplement to their otherwise meagre diet.

Disease was always a major concern. The captain and crew followed a strict daily routine for cleaning the ship and provided what assistance they could to anyone who fell ill. Although relatively uncommon, deaths from smallpox outbreaks did occur from time to time, as was the case during the *Albion*'s crossing from Hull in 1774, when "Charles Blinkey's wife and three children belonging to other people" perished.[17] The *Eagle*, having arrived at Charlottetown in 1819 from Plymouth with several cases of smallpox onboard, was consigned to the care of Mr. Pope, a local shipbuilder, and allowed to proceed to Bedeque. Although the passengers could land at Charlottetown, the crew was quarantined.[18] But thirteen years later, when the *Royal William* reached Charlottetown from Plymouth, all fourteen of the passengers were required to remain at "the Quarantine Ground."[19] Quarantine measures were once again enforced in October 1849 when cholera was thought to be onboard the *Prince Edward*. The nineteen passengers were sent to the Victoria Hotel in Water Street by order of the island's Board of Health.[20] Still more serious was the loss of life from typhoid fever two years earlier. Some twenty-five of the 444 passengers, probably all Irish, who sailed to the island in the *Lady Constable* from Liverpool succumbed to the disease. Upon arrival the passengers were placed in quarantine and then transferred to a hospital the following day. Eight more deaths followed.[21]

While Charlottetown's quarantine arrangements were largely improvised, Halifax had specially built quarantine facilities in place by the mid-1830s. They were constructed with money raised from the five shillings head tax, payable by each immigrant, which had been introduced in 1832 by the Nova Scotia legislature.[22] Although New Brunswick also levied the same head tax on immigrants the province did not construct a quarantine centre until 1846–47, when a great humanitarian crisis galvanized it into action.[23] Having suddenly to cope with twenty-six thousand starving and disease-ridden immigrants, who were mainly Irish, the authorities built a quarantine station at Partridge Island, a short distance from Saint John.[24] Before then, health checks were fairly rudimentary. One of the ships that reached Partridge Island in 1836 was the *D'Arcy* of Sunderland, with 137 Berwick-upon-Tweed emigrants aboard: "[We] were visited by Dr. Hardy about eight o'clock and he ordered us to wash all our dirty clothes, which we did." The doctor returned at twelve o'clock to see if they had done so, and pronounced that "he had never examined cleaner people."[25] Having been cleared by the doctor, the group travelled in a steamer to Fredericton and then overland to their final destination at Stanley.

Although passengers had many discomforts and problems to contend with, conditions improved significantly in the 1820s with the arrival of the so-called "regular traders."[26] They crossed the Atlantic from the same English port at least twice a year, occasionally three times, and often under the helm of the same captain. The Guernsey-born John Nicholas LePage, who had immigrated to Prince Edward Island in 1807, was one of the earliest shipowners to operate regular passenger services from Plymouth to Charlottetown. His brig, the *John*, carried fifty passengers in 1818, while his other vessel, the *Margaret*, sailed with just over twenty passengers in 1821 and 1822.[27] The Bristol merchant John Cambridge, who had established a flourishing shipyard at Murray Harbour by this time, offered similar services from Bristol. His *John* and *Mary* sailed to the island in the 1820s and the *Amity* and *Felicity* offered continuous runs into the 1830s, the latter being managed by Lemuel Cambridge, his son.[28]

For Prince Edward's Island,
North America.

THE new fast-sailing Brig, MARGARET,
(A. 1.) Burthens 400 tons, Capt. Henry
Reavely, a regular Trader; and will sail
from the Port of *Plymouth*, for CHARLOTTE
TOWN, PRINCE EDWARD's ISLAND, on
the First of April next. She has good ac-
commodations for Passengers, who will be
taken on moderate terms.
    For Freight or Passage, apply to Captain
Reavely, on board the Brig in Sutton Pool,
or to
            FOX, SONS, & Co.
Plymouth, March 14, 1822.

Crossing of the *Margaret* from Plymouth to Charlottetown in 1822. She was one of several vessels owned by John Nicholas LePage. The Plymouth timber merchants Fox, Sons & Co. acted as his agent. From the *West Briton and Cornwall Advertiser*, March 22, 1822.

Although emigrants departed regularly for Prince Edward Island from both Plymouth and Bristol, Plymouth had the far greater passenger trade. Thus, LePage faced serious competition in Plymouth. The Billing family of Plymouth started running the *Bideford* (162 tons) to Charlottetown in 1817, added the *Speculation* (155 tons) in the 1820s, then offered the *Breakwater* (180 tons) in the 1830s, the latter vessel having been built on the island[29] (see Appendix IV). Normally small numbers of passengers were taken on each crossing and the service ran more or less continuously between Plymouth and Charlottetown for around fifteen years. Another Plymouth family, headed by Thomas Pope, who established shipyards on the island, also offered vessels during the 1820s to people wishing to travel from Plymouth to the island.[30]

For NEW BRUNSWICK, AMERICA.
THE Brig BIDEFORD, Thomas Butters, Master, will sail for the above British Settlement in about three Weeks, and has excellent accommodation for Passengers.
Apply to Mr. T. Icely, 5, Prince's-street, or Mr. W. Clark, 93, James-street, Dock.
Dock, 22d July, 1817.

Advertisement in *Trewman's Exeter Flying Post*, July 24, 1817, for the *Bideford*'s crossing from Plymouth. She was owned by the Billing family of Plymouth, probably in partnership with Thomas Butters, the ship's captain.

The leading provider of passenger services from Plymouth was undoubtedly James Ellis Peake, who emigrated to Charlottetown from Plymouth in 1823.[31] His shipyard became one of the most successful on the island and he augmented his earnings by acting as an agent, both for the sale of island-built ships in England and in the provisioning and outfitting of other shipowners' vessels. Between 1828 and 1849, five of his vessels — the *James*, *Mary Jane*, *Royal William*, *Castalia*,[32] and the *Fanny* — regularly carried passengers from Plymouth to Charlottetown. His brother Thomas, having served as captain on the 1828 and 1830 crossings of the *James*, then became captain of the *Royal William* between 1830 and 1831. This really was a family-run business.

It was a similar story for ship crossings from London. Vessels such as the *Amelia*, *Carron*, and *Victoria* attracted a small number of passengers on their westward crossings to Prince Edward Island during the 1830s, while the *Emma Searle*, *Lady Wood*, and *Prince Edward* were favourites in the 1840s and 1850s (see Appendix IV). Designed primarily to handle timber cargoes, they had reasonably sized cabins on the deck capable of accommodating thirty to forty passengers, and frequently carried steerage passengers, who paid reduced fares. The needs of the timber trade were still paramount, but some semblance of a transatlantic passenger service was being offered between London and Charlottetown. The *Prince Edward* was probably fairly typical. Her cabin passengers were accommodated in a "cuddy" about twelve feet long and eight feet wide: "On each were little cupboards, where the berths were fixed. There were six of them, three on a side." In addition, there was a second cabin, about twenty feet long and ten feet wide, also with berths on each side, where passengers ate their meals. Alexander Beazeley, who sailed on *Prince Edward*'s second crossing of 1849, disapproved of the spartan fittings. In his view she was "a lumberer, being built not for a passenger ship."[33]

As Alexander Beazeley correctly observed, the timber trade determined the quality and frequency of the shipping services being offered to passengers.[34] With the introduction of duties on Baltic timber in 1811, making North American timber the cheaper alternative, English ships crossed the Atlantic in ever greater numbers to collect timber cargoes.[35] As they did, shipowners sought emigrants to transport on their vessels' westward crossings. It was essentially a very simple two-way process: timber was loaded into the ship's hold one way, and emigrants were accommodated in the same hold the other way. Because there was a huge shipping capacity, and relatively few people, shippers usually competed with one another, both on the cost of fares and on the quality of the service they offered. The service may have been very basic by modern-day standards, but it was affordable and regular.

Like Plymouth and London, much of Liverpool's regular passenger trade was focused on Prince Edward Island. North of England emigrants were offered a particularly wide choice of regular traders, such as the *Antelope*, *Northumberland*, and *Sir Henry Vere* during the 1840s, and the *Sir Alexander* and *Majestic* in the 1850s, but each carried relatively few passengers. During the 1830s, large numbers of passengers occasionally left Liverpool in vessels such as the *Margaret*, *Mary Ann*, and *Cartha*, but

TIMBER, DEALS, LATHWOOD, & SPARS.

TO BE SOLD BY AUCTION,
By Mr. JOSEPH POPE,

On THURSDAY, the 7th day of March next, at a YARD
adjoining the TOLL GATE, St. Philip's,

THE Entire Cargo now landing ex *Amity,* from St.
John's, New Brunswick, viz. :

219 Pieces PINE TIMBER,
56 Ditto   BIRCH,
4 Fathoms LATHWOOD,
160 Spruce DEALS,
Also a Quantity of SPARS.

The whole of which will be sold in suitable Lots.

Catalogues may be had in due time, by applying to the Auc-
tioneer, at his Office, No. 22, Baldwin-Street, or at Messrs.
J. HARE & Co.'s, Temple-Gate.

Bristol, February 19, 1833.

For PRINCE EDWARD ISLAND,
The Brig AMITY,
300 Tons Burthen,
SAMUEL ANDREWS, Commander.

These Ships are very fast sailers, are being fitted out with great
care and attention, both as to the condition of the Ships, and comfort of the Passengers, the accommodation for whom is very
superior.—For Freight or Passage apply to

Mr. LEMUEL CAMBRIDGE; or to
THOS. CLARK & SON, Brokers, Quay.

Bristol, 27th Feb. 1833.   (*One concern.*)

The *Amity*'s timber cargo, collected from Saint John, was being sold in Bristol in
February 1833. In the following month, the *Amity*'s crossing from Bristol to Prince
Edward Island was being advertised to potential passengers. The *Amity* was owned at
the time by Lemuel Cambridge (*Bristol Mercury*, February 23, March 16, 1833).

these ships had been specially commissioned to transport miners to the coals fields of Pictou and Cape Breton.[36]

When it came to departures for Prince Edward Island, however, the relatively small port of Bideford, in North Devon, surpassed even the mighty Liverpool. Bideford's crucial role in the development of the island's shipbuilding trade had fuelled a steady outflow of West Country people from this one port. At least 850 people emigrated from Bideford to Prince Edward Island between 1830 and 1841, most being labourers, craftsmen, and small farmers from North Devon and North Cornwall.[37] Many more followed over the next decade.

The first arrivals had relied on Thomas Chanter, the nephew of a Bideford merchant, to provide them with safe crossings. Chanter initially offered the *Collina* (156 tons), built in 1827, then the *Calypso* (265 tons), and the *Sappho* (110 tons), constructed two years later. Each had been built on the island by the master shipwright William Ellis, who had been hired by his uncle, Thomas Burnard.[38] Although these three vessels proved popular throughout the 1830s, other shipowners were also vying for emigrant fares. The *Sarah and Eliza,* owned by John How, a Bideford merchant, attracted substantial numbers of passengers, as did the *Civility*, a four-hundred-ton barque owned by Richard Heard, another of the Bideford merchants.

British America.

To sail on *Friday next, the 16th instant.*
FOR ST. JOHN'S. N. B.,

The fine A 1 Brig MARGARET,
Thos. Tweedie, Master;
Burthen per register 160 tons, sails very fast, and is in every respect an excellent conveyance for dry goods.—For freight or passage, apply on board, King's Dock, or to
J. and R. THOMPSON, Salthouse Dock.

Advertisement in the *Liverpool Mercury,* May 9, 1828, for the crossing of the *Margaret,* "a fine A1 brig," to sail from Liverpool to Saint John. She was probably the same vessel that took miners from Liverpool to Pictou and Sydney in 1827 and 1830.

However, when James Yeo arrived from North Cornwall, essentially taking over Chanter's business and becoming a large-scale shipbuilder himself, he dominated the West Country passenger trade to the island. His most popular vessel, the *British Lady*, built in 1836, saw continuous service for ten years. As if to emphasize his personal commitment to his passengers' safety, he appointed his brother William as the captain on many of the fourteen crossings undertaken by the *British Lady*. Eventually, he had a fleet of vessels that included the *Five Sisters*, *Three Brothers*, *Isabella*, *Florida*, and *Malakoff*, and, after extending his North American trading ventures to Bristol, offered passages from both Bideford and Bristol (see Appendix IV).

With the arrival of steamships and railways in 1855, Bideford's trade and shipping boom declined. Because of their greater size and sophistication, steamships could only sail from major ports. Thus, people rejected Bideford and used the North Devon Railway to reach Plymouth.[39] Increasing centralization around fewer ports brought in stricter controls and better enforceability, and because steamships weren't dependent on the vagaries of the weather and wind direction, they generally departed on time. More emigrants opted for their greater speed, safety, reliability, and creature comforts, and by 1870, steam had replaced sail.

Back in the days of the sailing ships, conditions below deck could be grim. Of course, overcrowding and poor sanitary conditions were facts of life at this time. Finding such hardships on a ship was nothing new. Nevertheless, shippers wishing to attract emigrants had to be sympathetic to their needs. For instance, a shipper might offer a more generous floor-to-ceiling height (between-deck) than was required legally. Vessels having six feet between decks were commonly used in the Atlantic passenger trade, even before 1842, when the legal limit was only five-and-a-half feet between decks."[40]

Emigrants also expected to be treated properly. The 132 passengers sailing in the *Calypso* to Prince Edward Island in the spring of 1832 believed they were heading for Charlottetown, but unknown to them, Thomas Chanter, the owner, had instructed the captain, Lewis Grossard, to land them at Princetown. He probably had done this in the hope that the *Calypso* could be released earlier, allowing her to make a second voyage later in the

The *John*'s superior accommodation for passengers wishing to travel from Hull to Saint John is highlighted in this advertisement in the *Hull Packet*, April 15, 1823.

summer. But the emigrants rebelled. Having been deposited on the "wild shores of farmer Hacker's farm in Richmond Bay" (now Malpeque Bay), they forced Grossard to take them to Charlottetown at Chanter's expense.[41]

The provision of a good ship was also very important, setting the overall standard of service for the voyage. Convincing evidence of the quality of shipping used by emigrants can be obtained in the *Lloyd's Shipping Registers*. This documentary source, dating back to the late eighteenth century, records the overall quality of each of the ships listed.[42] As major insurers, Lloyd's of London needed reliable shipping intelligence, which it procured through the use of paid agents in the main ports in Britain and abroad. Vessels were inspected by Lloyd's surveyors and assigned a code according to the quality of their construction and maintenance.[43] An honest and open inspection was vital to the insurer's risk assessment, and the shipowner's ability to attract profitable trade hinged on the classification given to his ships. Shipowners actually complained that the codes were too stringent, particularly in the way a ship's age and place of construction could affect its classification.[44] Today, these codes provide hard data on the quality of construction of the ships which carried English emigrants to ports in the Maritimes during the late eighteenth and nineteenth centuries.

The ships used by emigrants can best be judged by concentrating on those that took the largest numbers of passengers in a single crossing (see Table 12). Taking the eight vessels that carried around nine hundred mainly

Table 12

Selected Emigrant Ships: Ship Quality and Passenger Numbers
[Listed below are vessels that carried fifty or more passengers in a single crossing
and whose Lloyd's Shipping Codes have been found.]

Please note: # denotes a ship built in Prince Edward Island.

Vessel (tonnage)	Year Built	Lloyd's Code	Departure Year	Departure Port	Arrival Port	No. of Passengers
North of England Crossings, 1772–1775						
Duke of York (160 tons)	1762	I1	1772	Liverpool	Halifax	62
Albion (bg, 240 tons)	1762	E1	1774	Hull	Halifax	188
Two Friends (s, 250 tons)	1766	E1	1774	Hull	Halifax	103
Mary (bg, 180 tons)	1771	E1	1774	Stockton-on-Tees	Halifax	34
Prince George (s, 150 tons)	1762	E1	1774	Scarborough	Halifax	170
Providence (s, 170 tons)	1764	E1	1774	Newcastle-Upon-Tyne	Halifax	71
Thomas & William (bg, 300 tons)	1761	E1	1774	Scarborough	Halifax	193
Jenny (s, 450 tons)	1773	A1	1775	Hull	Halifax	80
Crossings to Prince Edward Island, 1821–47						
Valiant (bg, 361 tons)	Prize	E1	1817	Hull	Charlottetown	196
Pitt (320 tons)	1806	E1	1821	Liverpool	Charlottetown	93
# *Collena* (bg, 156 tons)	1827	E1	1830	Bideford	Charlottetwon	74
Venus (bk, 268 tons)	1809	E1	1830	Great Yarmouth	Charlottetown	80
Baltic (bg, 252 tons)	1820	E1	1831	Great Yarmouth	Charlottetown	152

Crossings to Prince Edward Island, 1821–47 cont'd

Vessel (tonnage)	Year Built	Lloyd's Code	Departure Year	Departure Port	Arrival Port	No. of Passengers
Preston (sw, 200 tons)	1823	A1	1832	Great Yarmouth	Charlottetown	152
# *Calypso* (bk, 265 tons)	1829	E1	1832	Bideford	Richmond Bay	197
Sarah and Eliza (bg, 161 tons)	1806	E1	1832	Bideford	Charlottetown	75
# *Breakwater* (bg, 180 tons)	n/k	E1	1832	Plymouth	Richmond Bay	50
# *Calypso* (bk, 265 tons)	1829	E1	1834	Bideford	Charlottetown	56
# *Henrietta* of Exeter (sr, 167 tons)	1841	A1	1842	Bideford	Charlottetown	102
# *Sylvanus* (bk, 298 tons)	1841	A1	1842	Falmouth	Charlottetown	203
# *Mary Ann* (bg, 179 tons)	1842	A1	1843	Bideford	Charlottetown	82
# *British Lady* (bg, 283 tons)	1836	A1	1847	Bristol	Richmond Bay	55

Yorkshire emigrants to Nova Scotia between 1772 and 1775, it becomes clear that this group had mainly sought the less expensive "E1" (second class) vessels. Although the *Albion*, *Two Friends*, *Mary*, *Prince George*, *Providence*, and *Thomas and William* were seaworthy, they would have had some minor defects. However, the group sailing in the *Duke of York*, the first to leave in 1772, had actually been on a vessel judged to be unsuitable for ocean travel (having an "I1" rating). At the other extreme was the *Jenny*. Being the last to leave in 1775, her affluent passengers could afford the very best. Not only did she have an "A1" rating, but she was nearly new at the time of sailing.

What was the overall quality of emigrant shipping later? Given the major gaps in shipping data for Nova Scotia and New Brunswick but relatively complete data for Prince Edward Island, this question can best be resolved by focusing on island crossings. Lloyd's Shipping codes have been located for thirteen of the twenty-one vessels that carried fifty or more passengers to the island between 1791 and 1847.[45] The 196 Yorkshire emigrants who travelled from Hull in the *Valiant* in 1817 and the ninety-three north-of-England passengers who sailed in the *Pitt* from Liverpool four years later had availed themselves of second-class vessels. Both had an "E1" rating, and both were old.[46] They may have deliberately selected them on price grounds, but, given that by this time Hull merchants were mainly sending their ships to Quebec to collect timber cargoes, the choice of departures for Charlottetown was probably very limited. While emigrants travelling to Quebec from Hull and Liverpool would probably have had access to a large number of good quality ships, those going to the Maritime ports had only one or two vessels from which to choose.

Emigrants from East Anglia who sailed from Great Yarmouth during the early 1830s seem also to have chosen mainly "E1" vessels. They, too, had

AMERICA.

For PICTOU (Nova Scotia), PRINCE EDWARD's ISLAND, and NEW BRUNSWICK,

The well-known fast-sailing Ship DIXON, 314 Tons Register, Capt. JAMES ROBERTS, Will take PASSENGERS for the above places, and sail about the 25th March, or with the first Ships.

☞ For particulars, apply to

ROBERT CHATTERTON,

HULL, Feb. 28, 1818. Stewart's-yard.

Advertisement for the crossing of the *Dixon* in 1818 from Hull to the Maritimes. This was the only Maritime crossing being advertised but there were several to Quebec. From the *Hull Packet*, March 3, 1818.

access to only very limited shipping since most of their local timber trade was focused on Quebec by this time. Thus, while the *Preston* was ranked "A1," the *Venus* and *Baltic* were "E1" ships.[47] Meanwhile, competition among shippers for the West Country's burgeoning passenger trade to the island was far brisker, but the standard of shipping remained at an "E1" level until Yeo became involved. For instance, Thomas Chanter's *Calypso*, John How's *Sarah and Eliza*, and the Billing family's *Breakwater* were popular choices in the early 1830s, but they had only an "E1" ranking.[48] By the 1840s, when Yeo entered the scene, West Country emigrants had greater access to "A1" ships. Competing with his *British Lady* for the passenger trade were the *Henrietta* of Exeter, the *Sylvanus*, and the *Mary Ann*, all "A1" vessels. He no doubt competed with his rivals on both quality and price. And given that he eventually cornered the passenger market, he probably drove out the competition by offering the lowest rates.

A good-quality ship does not in itself guarantee a comfortable crossing. Overcrowding was often excessive, particularly in the vessels used by Yorkshire emigrants in the 1770s.[49] While the 1803 legislation did reduce overcrowding for a period, its space requirements were relaxed in 1817 to one-and-one-half tons per person as a result of pressure from shipowners and agents.[50] The passenger to tonnage ratio was set at three passengers for every four tons in 1828, and it was made slightly more generous in 1835 when it was increased to three passengers for every five tons.[51] But instances of overcrowding returned once again with the slackening of space limits. The 197 passengers sailing in the 265-ton *Calypso* in May 1832 found that, although the ship was within its legal limit, space was at a premium: "a considerable part of our luggage was stowed between decks so that we could scarcely stand or sit and were almost compelled either to keep in our miserable berths or stand shivering with wet and cold on the upper decks."[52]

Overcrowding was usually a direct consequence of low fares, since shipowners only offered reduced prices when they could attract a reasonable volume of business. Since the tougher space restrictions of the 1803 Passengers Act reduced the number of passengers they could legally carry, steerage fares soared. For example, fares for the *Thomas and William* crossing in 1774 from Scarborough to Halifax were only five pounds (food supplied by ship) or three pounds, three shillings (food brought by passengers), but they rose to more than double that amount after 1803.[53] Although space restrictions were lessened in 1817, steerage fares remained high. In 1818, a typical crossing to the Maritimes cost ten pounds, ten shillings (with food) or seven pounds, seven shillings (without food).[54] Then, following a further relaxation of space requirements, fares fell as low as three or four pounds by the 1820s for passengers supplying their own food. They decreased again in the following decade to between four and five pounds (with food) or forty to sixty shillings (without food).[55] By 1842, steerage fares from Liverpool to Halifax ranged from three to five pounds without food, but were only two to three pounds to Saint John.[56] In fact, the relatively low fares to Saint John and the Miramichi were seized upon by the Nova Scotia and New Brunswick Land Company as one of the many advantages that New Brunswick offered to potential emigrants.[57]

The stout and sturdy ships which sailed off to the Maritimes to collect timber served their passengers well and usually got to their destinations safely. Of course, the sea voyage was the first step in a long process of relocation. There was the excitement of the new and better life that hopefully lay ahead, but for some there was also great sadness in leaving home. This was a final break for most. Because return journeys were prohibitively expensive, most emigrants would never again see their loved ones.[58] These thoughts were very much in Richard Vicars' mind as he prepared to leave for Newfoundland in the *Orpheus* from the Isle of Wight in 1824:

> If you never quitted England except upon voluntary excursions of pleasure — you can scarcely conceive with what fondness we poor exiles gaze upon her happy shores and how we cling to these to the last — we have undergone the pangs of separation from our friends — but they seem lengthened while we view the land with which our friends are associated, and even the Old Pilot, who is to convey this letter on shore will revive them as being the last tie which connect us with the land. Happy, Happy, Happy England![59]

CHAPTER 10

The English in Atlantic Canada

The English might have chosen anyone to be their national symbol, from a poet to a mariner. Instead, they chose a tradesman.[1]

IT BEFITS A nation of shopkeepers that it should have chosen a minor cloth trader like the fictional John Bull to symbolize itself.[2] John MacGregor took this iconic figure as his benchmark in Atlantic Canada, describing its English settlers as having "honest John Bull bluntness" together with his "other characteristics."[3] Depicted in cartoons as a pot-bellied, middle-aged man, he epitomized energy and determination, was fiercely independent, had a no-nonsense style, and, above all, was a practical man of action. These are traits that English pioneers and their families would no doubt have seen in themselves, especially his never-give-up spirit. Thus, while the English were denied the colourful imagery of the tartans and pipe bands that came to distinguish Scottish and Irish cultural identities in Canada, they did have a superb standard-bearer in the form of John Bull.

Having been constrained by a rigid class system, most ordinary people reacted favourably to the more egalitarian and easygoing social environment prevalent in Atlantic Canada. However, those who saw themselves as superior beings may have taken longer to adjust to the new ways. The English passengers who were shipwrecked off Malpeque Bay in Prince Edward Island in 1775 are a case in point. Having piled into lifeboats, they found a safe place where they could build wigwams as shelters. But, after the first night, John Russell (the ship's captain), Judge Stewart and family, and Mr. Campbell, together with the other cabin passengers, decided that they would "make a separate house [wigwam] for themselves, as they probably would be more comfortable and get a little sleep." In other words, they wished to have a separate cabin-class wigwam. The steerage passengers "readily lent them ... assistance to accomplish it," and when the cabin passengers rushed out in the middle of the night covered in their blankets to escape a fire that engulfed their wigwam, the steerage passengers helped once again in the building of another one.[4] Separate cabin and steerage-class wigwams seemed right in these circumstances, but, as they would all soon discover, top-down social structures that required people to condescend to their so-called betters were an anathema in the New World.

While touring Nova Scotia in 1826, Lord Dalhousie commented disapprovingly on the free and easy attitudes that he observed. Gripped with the delusion that he belonged to a higher order of being, he was extremely condescending toward the province's independent-minded, land-owning farmers. They had the impudence to believe in their own abilities. Because land could be purchased relatively cheaply, he felt that "every man consequently is laird here and the classes of the community known in England as tenantry and peasantry do not exist in these provinces and probably will not be formed until a full stop is put to the system of granting lands." He wondered where were the "gentleman proprietors of land" who could offer leadership and instruction.[5] This outdated, class-ridden ideology had no place in Nova Scotia, although Lord Dalhousie seemed not to notice. And yet the colonies were certainly not free of snobbery or class divisions.

When he toured New Brunswick in 1847, Abraham Gesner observed "a constant struggle between the aristocratic principle and the spirit of freedom and equality characteristic of the Americans." People rising from nothing to affluence and people "with advantages of birth and education" were disapproving of one another, just as they might have been back in England. This caused much bickering, and divided society "into small circles and parties." Each treated the others with aloofness and "a degree of coolness and formality" that was "but too frequently exhibited to strangers"[6] This tendency was confirmed by William Deal Chinery many years later when he visited New Brunswick. Arriving at Saint John on May 1, 1913, he commented on the "dirty, fine horses, everything brown just uncovered from snow, frost, etc., city fine, very hilly, good buildings," but he was "glad to get away," since he found Canadians "coldly polite."[7] Class distinctions were very much alive in Halifax as late as 1884. Two military concerts were held weekly in the Victorian Public Gardens: "on Wednesdays ... people of high degree show their best clothes there, and on Sunday the rest of the population crowd the park, neither class interfering with the other."[8]

Successive waves of immigrants adopted a pick-and-mix attitude to determine what of their cultural baggage to keep and what to reject. When they caught their first glimpse of Nova Scotia in 1774, the Yorkshire-born John Robinson and Thomas Rispin were perplexed by the attire of the New England Planters and their descendents:

> They dress exceedingly gay on a Sunday and they wear the finest cloth and linen. Many of them wear ruffled shirts who, during the rest of the week, go without their shoes and stockings: and there is so great a difference in their dress, that you would scarce know them to be the same people.[9]

Planters were perfectly happy to wear labourers' clothes and dirty their hands for six days a week, but wear the fine clothes of a country squire on a Sunday. A gentleman farmer in England would neither resemble nor act like a common labourer on any day of the week. But this was the Nova Scotia way. Robertson and Rispin also found the social pecking order difficult to fathom. While the Planter generation "may have been stubbornly egalitarian, the rising generation was expected publicly to honour its fathers and mothers and seniors in the good Old Testament way."[10] Old World customs still had a place.

The English experienced real cultural differences when they arrived, although they had less of an adjustment to make in the cities, where lifestyles were essentially British, if not English. According to the 1991 census, Atlantic Canada had Canada's most English cities. Some 77 percent of the inhabitants of St. John's, Newfoundland, claimed to have at least one English ancestor, while the comparable figures for Saint John and Halifax were 61 percent and 57 percent respectively.[11] When he visited Saint John and Fredericton in New Brunswick, Abraham Gesner found that, while most people had adopted what he called "American ways," the "fashions [were] British, with an occasional mixture brought in from the United States.... In summer there are races at Saint John and Fredericton, steamboat excursions, picnics, regattas, shooting, angling and a variety of amusements for those who are not engaged in active business."[12]

Twenty years later, Juliana Ewing, wife of an English army officer, attended a governor's lunch and croquet party in Fredericton, and looked forward to yet another picnic on the following day, when she and her husband would join another couple and go upriver in a canoe.[13] And Charlottetown, with its amateur theatre, "picnic parties, common in summer and winter," and "public subscription library" offered a similar home away from home for its privileged English inhabitants.[14] English lifestyles had been transferred and adapted to meet the demands of the climate, terrain, and local customs.

Having been founded by the English in the mid-eighteenth century, Halifax retained a strong English presence, both numerically and culturally.[15] Merchants, military officers, and government officials formed the Halifax elite, and, together with their families, lived in great opulence. Balls were said to be almost daily occurrences in nineteenth-century Halifax: "The dazzling white shoulders of the Archdeacon's daughters, the bright eyes and elegant figures of the four Miss Cunards, the fair complexions and sweet expressions of the four Miss Uniackes all whirled ... orbiting happily with the arm of a red-coated or blue-jacketed gallant encircling their waist."[16]

REPRESENTATION OF A PICNIC TEA PARTY, AT FREDERICKTON, NEW BRUNSWICK.

A picnic tea party at Fredericton, 1852, attended by officers and soldiers serving in British regiments. A hand-coloured, wood engraving on paper by an unknown artist.

It was much the same a century earlier. At Queen Charlotte's birthday celebrations in 1786, "ladies, with their hair powdered and curled over a frame adorned with feathers, ribbons, lace, flowers and jewels, danced in their high-heeled, buckled slippers peeping out from the folds of rich brocades," as did "the men in their white breeches, embroidered waistcoats, with lace frills at wrists."[17] These frivolities aside, with its fine architecture, Victorian public gardens, and regular British Army parades, Halifax certainly had the outward appearance and many of the customs of an English city.

Despite the appalling poverty suffered by its labouring classes, Newfoundland also had its glitzy side. An army colonel's party held in November 1834, just one of many events to attract the "fashionables" of St. John's, was an elaborate fancy-dress ball. With breathless wonder *The Newfoundlander* described "the tasteful elegance of rooms — the rich display of beauty and the elegant and classic costumes of the various characters," which included King Charles II, Mary Queen of Scots, a French Count, a Spanish peasant, an Albanian Chief, a Bavarian broom girl, "a lame soldier," and an English farmer who was reported to have been "admirably represented."[18] This was very much the wealthy of St. John's at play.

The English obsession with horseracing and hunting with hounds also made its way to Atlantic Canada. Halifax had its first racetrack by 1768, with the impetus for its construction coming mainly from the British garrison stationed there. And fox hunting was highly fashionable in Charlottetown during the early nineteenth century: "Foxes were plentiful and the citizens enjoyed hunting them after the old country fashion." However, because of opposition from farmers and the heavy expense of keeping hounds during long winters, the sport was short-lived.[19]

Rugby, another English passion, found favour in the Maritimes, especially at colleges and private schools. The Wanderers Amateur Club in Halifax formed its first rugby team in 1882, with members drawn mainly from the young professionals who had graduated from local universities. Rugby also attracted support from the English coal miners and their descendents living in Pictou County and Cape Breton, but by the 1940s

Courtesy of Library and Archives Canada, Acc. No. 1970-188-2075. W.H. Coverdale Collection of Canadiana.

Horse-trotting match on the ice, Prince Edward Island, *circa* 1867. The print is by Thomas McLean of a painting by Henry Buckton Laurence (1842–86), sold by Thomas Jefferys, Corner of St. Martins Lane, Charing Cross, London.

the sport's appeal was lost to football.[20] The quintessentially English support of cricket also had its adherents. The Charlottetown Cricket Club, formed in 1850, "became a popular game and local teams often competed against teams from visiting naval vessels."[21] The Saint John Cricket and Athletic Club, founded in 1886, played matches regularly in Toronto, Montreal, New York, Boston, Baltimore, and Philadelphia.[22] Although cricket had strong working-class support in England, in Canada it was always perceived as a bourgeois game that epitomized class privilege, and, because of this, it soon gave way to baseball.[23]

What might be termed English middle-class values and customs were also spread to Atlantic Canada through social networks. The Girl's Friendly Society, founded in England in 1875 to support girls and young women who were employed in domestic service, business, and factories, found a niche for itself in Newfoundland eight years later.[24] Ostensibly

Courtesy of Notman Studio (Halifax) / Library and Archives Canada, PA-028519.

Halifax Cricket Team, 1895–1900, photograph taken by an unknown photographer working for the Notman Studio, Halifax.

the Society was meant to act as a moral shield, "preventing young women from following into vice," but probably its real role in Newfoundland was to encourage female emigration from England. Prospective employers were screened and the girls were given a grounding in "wholesome activities, such as "reading and writing, literary appreciation classes, sewing classes and amateur dramatics."[25] They were essentially being schooled in middle-class ways to suit the needs of the Newfoundland elite who would employ them. Celebrations in 1933 to mark the Society's first fifty years were held in St. John's Cathedral, led by the Anglican bishop, who claimed that the "highest service the Girls Friendly Society can render to girls in Newfoundland" was to help them "maintain their purity, which is threatened today in so many ways."[26] By 1937 the diocese of Newfoundland had 140 associate members (older women), 545 members (girls), and 375 candidates, with most of the membership being concentrated in St. John's.[27]

The Mechanics' Institutes were another English import, but one that was geared primarily to the upwardly mobile working classes. First formed in England in 1823, their aim was to provide vocational education and training to working men.[28] Pushing on an open door in St. John's, Newfoundland, a Mechanics' Institute sprouted as early as 1827, and three years later the Institute had 343 members and funds to purchase scientific apparatus and to acquire a natural history collection. A ceremony held in 1831 acknowledged the valuable services of Mr. Elklis in "stuffing and arranging quadrupeds and birds" and awarded prizes. First prize went to John Neil, apprentice to James Purcell, for "two instruments for taking angles of altitude and perspective drawing"; second prize went to J.P. Adams, apprentice to Alexander Smith, for "a hanging stair[case] cut in free stone; third prize to Lawrence McManus, apprentice to his father, for a cooper's tool; and fourth prize went to Joseph Boyd, apprentice to James McLarty, for a branding iron."[29] Various Mechanics' Institutes were also established by 1847 in cities across New Brunswick, where they were said to "have made an essential improvement in the pursuits of young men of different classes."[30]

Although the English made much less fuss over their ethnicity than did the Scots or Irish, they nevertheless formed ethnic societies in Canada. The first St. George Society, honouring England's patron saint, emerged in Halifax in 1786 and still remains active today. As with other St. George societies, its original aim was to promote and celebrate English culture and to channel funds to needy English people. The St. George Society of Halifax commemorated its bicentenary in more recent times by planting an English oak tree at the entrance to the city's Victorian Public Gardens.[31] And, although St. George's Day (April 23) passes by almost unnoticed in England, it continues to be a provincial holiday in Newfoundland.

However, the largest and most important English cultural society was the Sons Of England, branches of which could be found in most Canadian cities. They were organized by affluent Englishmen with military or professional backgrounds and provided social activities, the highlight of which were social evenings modelled on the English Music Hall. At such gatherings people heard rousing songs, "wept at the evocations of England's green and pleasant land," and savoured the unique pleasure of drinking warm, dark ale.[32] However, there was a philanthropic side, as well, in that the Sons of England Society furnished its members with economic support and held out a special helping hand to newly arrived English immigrants. The need to be English was a sore point though with Walter Couston, who sought to join the newly inaugurated branch at St. John's, Newfoundland, in 1896. Although Walter was "said to be English to the backbone in his ways," he was not of English stock: "My father was a Scotsman, my mother is a native, my grandfather was an Irishman and my grandmother was a Frenchwoman." Yet he was duly granted a "special dispensation by the Grand Session," and became a member.[33] No doubt he regarded the Sons of England as the best club in town through which to further his social and business interests.

As was the case with other immigrants, people of English origin quickly merged into the cultural melting pot that would eventually identify them as Canadians. Even as early as 1851 James Lawson noticed how Prince Edward Islanders "take little or no interest in the changes that have taken place in their parent land, if indeed they are cognizant of them."[34] Thirty years earlier, Walter Johnstone had described these same people as "a motley mixture of almost all nations; yet, various as

Courtesy of The Rooms Provincial Archives of Newfoundland and Labrador. VA 19-112, James Vey, Arthur George Williams Collection.

Sons of England Society members, St. John's, Newfoundland, attending an outing in July 1898. Although many people suffered harsh economic conditions, the fishing industry brought prosperity to some, and such outings formed an important part of the city's social life.

the countries are from whence they emigrated and the customs prevalent in each of them, they are remarkably assimilated here into one form of living, dress, general conduct and manners."[35] Being a substantial component of the population, the English readily adapted to Canadian society. Even in Newfoundland, where they had numeric supremacy, this sometimes meant giving priority to the needs of their new society, rather than fostering a sense of their Englishness for its own sake. The authentic folk songs brought across by early English immigrants were no match for the more tuneful Irish-sounding music that was composed much later. It grew in popularity and Irish songs now dominate Newfoundland music.[36] That is the Canadian way.

The English adapted readily into Canadian society, and, unlike their Scottish and Irish counterparts, did not seek to highlight the distinctive features of what might be termed "English culture." They had not done so in their homeland, so there was no reason why they would seek to wrap themselves in Saint George's flags and dance around maypoles when they became Canadians. First and foremost they saw themselves as being British. They chose Canada over the United States because it offered a British version of the New World. They transformed themselves effortlessly from being British to being Canadians, and along the way helped to reinforce the notion of the English as a "founding people." Unfortunately, this characterization of the English as a founding group came to be perceived as a symbol of British imperialism, and because of this the English came increasingly to be associated with Canada's toffee-nosed elite. This is, of course, a monstrous misrepresentation of the English, as becomes clear when one examines the social and economic diversity of the people who settled in Atlantic Canada.

The English arrived in large numbers over two centuries, not just from England, but from the New England states, and from New York and New Jersey. A few of them were members of the privileged elite, but the majority were ordinary people. While much emphasis has been placed on the former, almost no attention has been paid to the thousands of English tradesmen, craftsmen, agricultural and urban labourers, domestic servants, farmers, and fishermen who originated from many parts of England and made Atlantic Canada their home. The poor Suffolk emigrants, who were packed off to Prince Edward Island by their parishes with a gallon of gin to sustain them on their sea crossings, are an important part of this story, as are the slum children from Liverpool and Birmingham who arrived like parcels at the railway stations. Although many of the new arrivals had been displaced by the sudden economic changes that had taken place in England, they retained a pride in their Englishness but also quickly felt a strong sense of patriotism to their new homeland.

All new arrivals, irrespective of their social and economic status, carried a common sense of their English identity, although it was not expressed in ethnic symbolism. Having originated from an old country that had neither been invaded nor conquered in a thousand years, and which led an Empire that dominated the world, they had a strong sense of self-belief, bordering in some cases on arrogance. Their Englishness did not require any collective displays of nationhood nor did they seek to construct ethnic barriers. Unlike the Scots and Irish, who were at pains to preserve their language, music, and traditions, the English simply became Canadians. They would have missed not seeing snowdrops in February and cowslips in May, and probably longed to see dry-stone walls again and hear church bells, but they were not a sentimental people and instinctively grasped the tenor of pioneer life, albeit after a painful adjustment in some cases. Their self-confidence was their greatest strength. They came with deeply embedded and almost unconscious values that contributed to their strong sense of self-belief and underpinned their enormous tenacity. Because they did not seek to call attention to their ethnic differences they could become the principal unifying force in their communities.

The English came in large numbers to the cities and also surpassed themselves as pioneer farmers, with the Yorkshire settlers being the outstanding example. When Lord Dalhousie viewed their farms in Nova Scotia, he marvelled at "the large fields, extensive crops and gardens about their houses" that far outshone those of their neighbours.[37] Here was the John Bull spirit exemplified, and it came to life in many other ways in all four provinces. He was only an invention, but fits best as the ultimate English stereotype. People of English extraction in Atlantic Canada would treasure more than anything John Bull's indomitable spirit.

APPENDIX I

Yorkshire Passenger Lists,
1774–1775

1. The *Two Friends*, James Watt (master) sailed March 7, 1774, from Hull to Halifax, Nova Scotia. [NAB T47/9 ff. 77–79.]

Name	Age	Occupation	Reason for Emigrating
John Smith	29	farmer	their rents being so high
Mary Smith	25	his wife	they cannot live
John Smith	4		
George Smith	2		
William Smith	1		
Robert Fawceit	30	sail-cloth maker	going on business as agent
Samuel Pickering	23	farmer	going to seek a better livelihood
James Leach	27	farmer	same reason
Francis Layton	29	blacksmith	same reason
Elizabeth Layton	26	his wife and	same reason
Francis Layton	18-months	child	same reason
John Busfield	30	farmer	same reason
George Hayton	32	farmer	same reason
Anthony Hill	57	farmer	on account of his rent being raised by Jno Matthews, his landlord

Two Friends cont'd

Name	Age	Occupation	Reason for Emigrating
John Willison	36	carpenter	going to seek a better livelihood
John Layton	22	husbandman*	same reason
Richard Peck	46	farmer	same reason
William Hodgson	22	husbandman	same reason
John Wilson	46	farmer	same reason
William Ward	24	farmer	same reason
Elizabeth Ward	22	his wife and	
Moses Ward	18-months	child	
Robert Appleby	21	husbandman	same reason
William Brown	22	carpenter	same reason
Jane Brown	21	his wife and	
Jane Brown	1	child	
James Brown	17	husbandman	same reason
Mary Brown	26	servant	same reason
John Webster	25	taylor	same reason
Elizabeth Wrightson	20	servant	same reason
Tomas Yate	22	mason	same reason
Thomas Brigs	28	blacksmith	same reason
John Sedgewick	39	farmer	on acc't of his rent being raised
John Routh	22	husbandman	going to seek a better livelihood
Thomas Harwood	34	farmer	going to seek a better livelihood
George Firth	30	farmer	their rents being raised
William Parker	31	farmer	same reason
Mary Parker	38	his wife	
John Parker	3	& children	
n/k	18-months		
Jane Harrison	20	maid servant	same reason
Mary Parker	74	widow	going to accompany her children
John Lumley	23	husbandman	to seek a better livelihood
Arnistead Fielding	42	farmer	provision, rents and every necessary of life, being so very high they cannot support their family
Elizabeth Fielding	40	his wife	
John Fielding	15		

Two Friends cont'd

Name	Age	Occupation	Reason for Emigrating
William Fielding	15	&	
Nicholas Fielding	12		
Hannah Fielding	8		
Esther Fielding	5		
Joseph Fielding	2	children	
Richard Bare	26	butcher	to seek a better livelihood
William Blinkhorn	33	farmer	on account of their rents being raised
Ann Blinkhorn	29	his wife	
William Blinkhorn	7		
John Blinkhorn	4	&	
Ann Blinkhorn	3		
Eleanor Blinkhorn	1	children	
Abraham Mason	43	husbandman	to seek a better livelihood
Elizabeth Abba	20	servant	same reason
John Watersworth	43	farmer	on account of his rent being raised
Richard Thompson	30	husbandman	to seek a better livelihood
John Bulmer	45	farmer	on account of their rents being raised by Billy Thompson, Esq., their landlord
Grace Bulmer	46	his wife	
James Bulmer	20	children	
George Bulmer	14	to	
Joseph Bulmer	10	John Bulmer	
Ann Bowser	60	shopkeeper	to seek a better livelihood
Richard Bowser	29	farmer	on account of their rents being raised by William Weddell Esq., their landlord
Ann Bowser	26	servant	
Hannah Sterriker	12	servant	
William Routlidge	30	blacksmith	in hopes of a better livelihood
Sarah Routlidge	27	his wife	
Diana Routlidge	2	&	
Joseph Routlidge	18 mo	children	
Richard Stavely	30	husbandman	on account of their rents being raised by William Weddell Esq., their landlord

Two Friends cont'd

Name	Age	Occupation	Reason for Emigrating
Robert Stavely	26	husbandman	
John Linton	28	butcher	
Robert Fenby	26	husbandman	same reason
Andrew Crawford	28	husbandman	same reason
Christopher Harper	40	farmer	same reason
Thomas Harrison	28	husbandman	same reason
William Thursby	28	husbandman	same reason
John Wry	23	weaver	same reason
Pickering Snowdon	22	weaver	going to seek a better livelihood
Mary Suggett	40	widow	same reason
Ann Suggett	14		
Mary Suggett	12	her	
Christopher Suggett	10		
John Suggett	8	children	
William Suggett	18	husband	
Joseph Parker	33	rope maker	same reason
Elizabeth Parker	33	his wife	
William Parker	2	& child	
John Fawceit	29	farmer	on account of their rents being raised
Jane Fawceit	28	his wife	
Mary Fawceit	4	& child	
Thomas Andrews	37	husband	in hope of a better life for himself and family every necessary of life being so dear
Lilley Andrews	37	his wife	
Mary Andrews	7		
John Andrews	4	&	
Mary Andrews	3		
Hannah Andrews	1	children	

* A husbandman was usually a tenant farmer.

2. The *Albion*, Thomas Perrott (master) sailed March 14, 1774, from Hull to Halifax, Nova Scotia. [NAB T47/9 ff. 83–90.]

Name	Age	Occupation	Reason for Emigrating
William Harland	23	farmer	to seek a better livelihood
John Coulson	20	farmer	same reason
Mary Coulson	29	his wife	
Jonathan Patison	19	husbandman	same reason
Nathanial Smith	52	farmer	their rents being raised by his landlord, Mr. Chapman, they have made a purchase of some land in North America
Elizabeth Smith	52	his wife	
Nathaniel Smith	22		
John Smith	18	&	
Robert Smith	9		
Elizabeth Smith	7		
Rachael Smith	22	children	
Mary Veckel	20	maid servant	to seek for better employment
Hannah Veckel	20	maid servant	same reason
Charles Simpson	22	husbandman	same reason
Thomas Scurr	34	farmer	the advance of his rents by Francis Smith Jnr. Esq., his landlord. He is going to purchase land abroad.
Elizabeth Scurr	39	his wife	
Thomas Scurr	9		
William Scurr	7		
Charles Scurr	5	&	
Elizabeth Scurr	3		
Alice Scurr	1	children	
Bryan Kay	28	farmer	to seek for better livelihood
Dorothy Kay	42	his wife	
Robert Kay	42	his brother	same reason
Elizabeth Kay	16		
Hannah Kay	14		
Sarah Kay	12	his	
Ann Kay	9		
Jane Kay	7	children	

Albion cont'd

Name	Age	Occupation	Reason for Emigrating
Anthony Thompson	20	husbandman	same reason
Ann Atkinson	19	servant	same reason
Ann Skelton	18	servant	same reason
William Kay	20	sailor	same reason
Joseph Palister	25	labourer	same reason
John Atkinson	45	labourer	to seek for better livelihood
Frances Atkinson	30	his wife	
Charles Atkinson	8		
Martha Atkinson	4	&	
Michael Atkinson	3		
John Atkinson	1	children	
John Reed	26	husbandman	same reason
George Reed	33	farmer	on account of his rent being raised by his landlord Thomas Walker
Hannah Reed	33	his wife	
Ann Reed	9		
John Reed	6	&	
Isabella Reed	4		
George Reed	1	children	
Mary Simpson	25	servant	to seek a better livelihood
Edward Peckett	11	husbandman's servant	same reason
Lancelot Chapman	49	farmer	on account of their rents being raised by the Duke of Rutland so that they could not live
Frances Chapman	42	his wife	
Thomas Chapman	18		
Rachael Chapman	14		
Frances Chapman	12	&	
Martin Chapman	10		
Ann Chapman	8		
Lancelot Chapman	6		
Hannah Chapman	4	children	
Mary Harrison	17	maid servant	to seek for better livelihood
Paul Cornforth	70	farmer	same reason
Phllis Cornforth	68	his wife	

Albion cont'd

Name	Age	Occupation	Reason for Emigrating
William Cornforth	34	farmer	same reason
Mary Cornforth	26	his wife	
Elizabeth Cornforth	4	&	
Mary Cornforth	1	children	
Michael Taylor	45	husbandman	same reason
Ann Taylor	26	his wife	
Robert Charlton	17	husbandman	same reason
John Slee	22	husbandman	same reason
Thomas Harrison	24	taylor	same reason
George Taylor	25	farmer	same reason
Michael Taylor	23	farmer	same reason
Giles Pickett	41	blacksmith	to seek for a better livelihood
Mary Pickett	38	his wife	
James Pickett	16	children	going with their parents
John Pickett	7		
Margaret Pickett	5	of	
William Pickett	1	Giles Pickett	
John Savage	40	labourer	going to seek a better livelihood
Elizabeth Savage	55	his wife	
Anthony Savage	9	son	
John Dunning	24	farmer	same reason
John Hill	25	farmer	same reason
Jane Hill	28	his wife	
Thomas Hill	2		
Elizabeth Hill	2	&	
Mary Hill	1	children	
James Handwick	34	maltster	on account of his rent being advanced
Elizabeth Handwick	24	his wife	
Robert Appleton	24	husbandman	going to seek a better livelihood
Joseph Stockdale	24	husbandman	same reason
Thomas Lumley	45	farmer	on account of his rent being raised by Mr. Knowsley, his landlord
Ruth Lumley	44	his wife	
Diana Lumley	14	&	
John Lumley	6	children	
Thomas Shipley	31	butcher	to seek a better livelihood

Albion cont'd

Name	Age	Occupation	Reason for Emigrating
Elizabeth Shipley	25	his wife	
Sarah Shipley	3	&	
Thomas Shipley	1	children	
Brian Kay	20	husbandman	same reason
William Truman	52	miller	on account of their rent being raised by Thomas Duncan Esq. their landlord
Ann Truman	58	his wife	
William Truman	22	son, a grocer	
John Beys	24	husbandman	
Sarah Barr	21	servant	a relation being dead they are going to settle their affairs
Richard Dobson	72	gentleman	
William Pipes	49	farmer	on account of their rent being advanced
William Pipes	22	husbandman	
Jonathan Pipes	20	husbandman	same reason
John Smith	28	husbandman	same reason
Mary Smith	20	servant	same reason
George Hunter	40	farmer	in hope of making a purchase
John Watson	33	farmer	same reason
Richard Lowerson	32	husbandman	in hope of making a purchase
John Johnson	27	tanner	to seek a better livelihood
Martha Johnson	23	his wife	
William Johnson	1	& child	
Henry Scott	27	husbandman	same reason
Mary Scott	29	his wife	
Henry Scott	3	&	
Catharine Scott	1	children	
Charles Blinkey	33	farmer	on account of his rent being raised by his landlord Jonothan Wilkinson
Sarah Blinkey	33	his wife	
Jane Blinkey	6	&	
Mary Blinkey	1	children	
William Atkinson	16	tanner	to seek a better livelihood

Albion cont'd

Name	Age	Occupation	Reason for Emigrating
William Chapman	44	farmer	on account of his rent being raised by his landlord, Lord Cavendish, and all necessaries of life being so dear
Mary Chapman	42	his wife	
William Chapman	19		
Thomas Chapman	17		
Jane Chapman	15		
John Chapman	13		
Mary Chapman	9	&	
Henry Chapman	7		
Jonathan Chapman	5		
Sarah Chapman	3		
Ann Chapman	1	children	
Israel Marshall	28	husbandman	rents being high he goes in hope to make a purchase
Henry Hammond	31	farmer	same reason
Margaret Hammond	27	his wife	
Henry Hammond	5		
Jane Hammond	3	&	
Margaret Hammond	1	children	
Tristram Walker	27	husbandman	to seek a better livelihood
William Robertson	15	husbandman	same reason
Alice Dimond	24	servant	same reason
Thomas Wilson	50	joiner	same reason
James Wilson	19	joiner	same reason
David Bennett	30	farmer	his rent being raised by Mr. Bulmer his landlord
Mary Bennett	30	his wife	
Henry Charmick	31	chandler	to seek a better livelihood
John Thompson	32	farmer	on account of the great advance of rents and in the hope of purchasing
Joseph Thompson	26	farmer	same reason
Joshua Gildart	49	husbandman	same reason
Robert Leming	51	husbandman	same reason
Robert Leming Jr.	17	husbandman	same reason

Albion cont'd

Name	Age	Occupation	Reason for Emigrating
John Gildart	19	husbandman	to seek a better livelihood
Eleanor Harrison	48	widow	same reason
Miles Alinson	42	blacksmith	same reason
Mary Alinson	30	his wife	
Miles Alinson	6		
Thomas Alinson	3	&	
Mary Alinson	1	children	
Charles Clarkson	19	husbandman	same reason
Richard Thompson	25	farmer	Lord Bruce having raised his rent
William Sinton	21	miller	to seek a better livelihood
Joseph Jacques	28	farmer	on account of their rent being raised
Elenor Jacques	28	his wife	
Richard Carter	27	farmer	same reason
Robert Atkinson	28	farmer	same reason
Ann Atkinson	21	his wife	
Diana Tatum	25	servant	to seek a better livelihood
Ralph Sidell	29	cartwright	same reason
Ann Weldon	38		going to her husband who is settled abroad
Andrew Weldon	12		
Elizabeth Weldon	8	&	
Thomas Weldon	4		
Ann Weldon	1	children	
Jacob Blackburn	27	servant	to seek a better livelihood
George Gibson	36	miller	same reason
Thomas Little	27	tanner	same reason
Ann Little	24	his wife	
William Winn	27	farmer	same reason
David Winn	17	farmer	same reason
Matthew Fenwick	16	servant	same reason
Mary Lowthier	21	servant	

3. An unnamed ship, probably the *Thomas and William*, Samuel Pattindon (master) sailed April 4, 1774, from Scarborough to Halifax, Nova Scotia. [NAB T 47/9 ff. 120–3.]

Name	Age	Occupation	Reason for Emigrating
Robert Jackson	48	blacksmith	they could not support their families on account of high price of provisions
Wife & 3 children			
William Ellis	24	farmer	
Wife & 1 child			
Thomas Blackburn	28	farmer	same reason
Wife & 2 children			
John Robinson	40	farmer	farm being over rented could not support themselves
John Robinson	41	farmer	
Wife & 6 children			
Robert Jackson	39	ploughwright	to seek for better employment, all necessarys of life being so dear
Wife & 3 children			
Thomas Wilkinson	23	blacksmith	same reason
Wife & child			
Francis Blashell	29	farmer	same reason
William Johnson	22	wheelwright	going with a view to better themselves
William Habishaw	18	farmer	
John Milton (or Millon)	22	farmer	same reason
John Johnson	20	taylor	obliged to quit his farm being so high rented
Henry Huttson	21	taylor	to seek for better employment
Thomas Skelton	35	tallow chandler	same reason
Moses Andrew	34	cooper	same reason
James Dewthwaite	34	farmer	same reason
John Clark	55	farmer	same reason
David Jukes	23	farmer	same reason
Richard Clark	50	farmer	same reason
Thomas Mooring	23	house carpenter	same reason
William Webster	33	house carpenter	same reason
John Lamb	21	farmer	same reason

Thomas and William cont'd

Name	Age	Occupation	Reason for Emigrating
Mary White	20	servant	same reason
Thomas Watson	26	farmer	
John Duke	25	farmer	same reason
Robert Wilson	49	farmer	his rent raised so high obliged him to quit
Wife & 7 children			
William Webster	33	joiner	to seek for better employment
John Witty	32	joiner	same reason
Matthew Walker	24	farmer	all the small farms taken into large ones in his parish, could not get bread
John Steel	46	farmer	to seek for better employment
& son			
John Jaques	36		provisions high could not support their family
Wife & 3 children			
George Sharrow	26	farmer	to seek for better employment
William Wilson	23	farmer	same reason
John Hopper	23	farmer	same reason
Sam Bainbridge	24	farmer	same reason
Adam Hawkworth	34	joiner	same reason
Wife & 4 children			
Richard Garbutt	34	joiner	same reason
Wife & 6 children			
Thomas Gray	31	blacksmith	goes as a hired servant
John Robinson	28	butcher	same reason
William Jarratt	40	farmer	going to see the country and if he like it to settle there
George Cass	19	gardner	goes as a hired servant
Andrew Thompson	40	farmer	to seek employment, provision being so dear in England
Mary Thompson	32	wife	
William Jones	9	son of	
Michael Pickny	42	farmer	turned off his farm, it being turned into a large one
Jonathan Barlow	24	farmer	to seek for better employment
William Hardy	25	farmer	same reason

Thomas and William cont'd

Name	Age	Occupation	Reason for Emigrating
William Gilliat	34	farmer	his farm being over rented, could not live upon it
Rebecca Gilliat	30	his wife	
William Gilliat	3	&	
Elizabeth Gilliat	4		
Mary Gilliat	1	children	
Thomas Hodgson	38	taylor	to seek for better employment
William Sherwood	21	linen weaver	same reason
Clifford Swan	21	joiner & cabinet maker	same reason
Benjamin Jackson Wife & 3 sons	50	mason	same reason
William Moon	25	weaver	same reason
Francis Boast Wife & 5 children	47	farmer	same reason
Richard Topham Wife & child	29	farmer	distressed by his landlord
William Shires	29	farmer	to seek for better employment
Joseph Tranner Wife & child	32	farmer	same reason
Francis Mason	38	butcher	same reason
John Harrison	54	farmer	forced to leave the Kingdom being over rented in his farm
Wife & 9 children			
Robert Mennard	27	taylor	on account of the high price of provision and to seek better employment
George Mennard Wife & child	21	same reason	
William Thomson Wife & 6 children	42	farmer	same reason
Ralph Stibbins & 3 children	40	merchant	same reason
William Reed	30	farmer	same reason
Elizabeth Reed	28	sister to	same reason
Christopher Pearson	20	farmer	same reason
William Pearson	28	gardener	same reason

Thomas and William cont'd

Name	Age	Occupation	Reason for Emigrating
William Hemsel	31	farmer	same reason
Wife and 3 children			
Robert Taylor	28	farmer	same reason
John Richardson	28	smith	same reason
John Holliday	40	shoemaker	same reason
Robert Dean	28	labourer	going to seek better employment
Stapleton	30	physician	gave no reason
Thomas Eison	25	joiner	going to seek better employment
Richard Walker	33	farmer	same reason
Robert Jefferson	24	farmer	same reason
Thomas Gibbin	31	mason	same reason
Matthew Webster	33	taylor	same reason
Wife & 3 children			
John Orkird	30	farmer	same reason
John Holiday	46	farmer	same reason
Wife & 5 children			
John Richardson	28	smith	same reason
Robert Jefferson	24	farmer	same reason
Michael Noddin	n/k	farmer	same reason
John Cole	n/k	farmer	same reason
Jonathan Milner	28	farmer	same reason
Elizabeth Milner	50	farmer	same reason
John Skelton	25	farmer	going to seek better employment
Richard Oliver	19	farmer	same reason
Elizabeth Milner	30	servant	same reason
Hugh Peebles	36	weaver	same reason

4. The *Mary*, John Cathrick (master) sailed April 26, 1774 from Stockton-on-Tees to Halifax, Nova Scotia. [NAB T47/9 ff. 135–6.]

Name	Age	Occupation	Reason for emigrating
William Robinson	32	tallow chandler	to seek better employment
Mary Robinson	35	his wife	
Mary Bentley	65	widow	same reason
Nicholas Pearson	40	shoemaker	same reason
Esther Pearson	36	his wife	
3 children aged 10, 6, 1			
John Greenwood	40	farmer	same reason
Elizabeth Greenwood	36	his wife	
4 children aged 10, 8, 6, 4			
John Teckle	42	staymaker	same reason
Elizabeth Teckle	40	his wife	
Thomas Lancaster	23	linen-draper's apprentice	to dispose of goods
Thomas Elstob	40	farmer	same reason, intends to return
Joshua Luking	41	farmer	intends to return
Ann Luking	39	his wife	
Child	aged 11		
John Old	30	tailor	to seek better employment
William Pashley	70	gardener	same reason
John Latham	32	brewer	same reason
John Hutchinson	22	butcher	same reason
Robert Robinson	23	butcher	same reason
William Hall	40	labourer	same reason
Jane Miller	25	spinster	same reason
John Harland	30	shopkeeper	same reason
William Paterson	34	shopkeeper	same reason
Robert Stavely	26	farmer	same reason
Joseph Pierson	34	ship carpenter	same reason
Thomas Miller	26	shopkeeper	with goods to sell
James Ward	28	ship carpenter	to seek better employment

5. The *Jenny*, William Foster (master) sailed April 10, 1775 from Hull to Halifax, Nova Scotia. [NAB T47/10 ff. 58–60.]

Name	Age	Occupation	Reason for emigrating
William Black	43	linen draper	having made a purchase is going there with his family
Elizabeth Black	36	his wife	
William Black	14		to reside there
Richard Black	11		
John Black	15	&	
Thomas Black	9		
Sarah Black	7	children	
Matthew Lodge	20	servant & house carpenter	going to seek a better livelihood
Elizabeth Redfield	25	servant	same reason
Jane Hurdy	16	servant	same reason
Elizabeth Beaver	30	housekeeper to the governor	same reason
Bridget Sedel	38		going with her children to her husband
Mary Sedel	7	&	
Francis Sedel	6	her	
Sarah Sedel	1	children	
Christopher Horsman	27	farmer	going to seek a better livelihood
Robert Colpits	28	farmer	same reason
Christopher Harper	45	farmer	having made a purchase is going to reside there
Elizabeth Harper	40	his wife	
Hannah Harper	15		
Elizabeth Harper	14		
John Harper	13		
Thomas Harper	12	&	
Catharine	7		
Charlotte	6		
William	4	children	
Thomas King	21	blacksmith	going to purchase or return
William Johnson	28	gentleman	same reason
Mary Lowry	27		going over to her husband
Mary Lowerson	27	same reason	

Jenny cont'd

Name	Age	Occupation	Reason for emigrating
Thomas Wheatley	53	farmer	going to purchase or return
William Clark	42	farmer	same reason
Mary Clark	13		
William Clark	10	his	
Richard Clark	9		
Rachael Clark	3	children	
John Skelton	38	servant	going to seek a better livelihood
Jane Skelton	36	same reason	
Francis Watson	18	taylor	same reason
John Bath	23	servant	same reason
William Johnson	49	farmer	having purchased an estate is going over with his family and servants to reside
Margaret Johnson	48		
George Johnson	26	servant & carpenter to Wm. Johnson	
William Johnson	33	son of Wm Johnson	same reason
Emanuel Johnson	16	son of Wm Johnson	same reason
Joseph Johnson	14	son of Wm Johnson	same reason
James Hutton	15	apprentice to Wm Johnson	same reason
Elizabeth Anderson	36		going over with her children to her husband who is cooper to Wm Johnson
Mary Anderson	9		
Jane Anderson	7	her	
Moses Anderson	5		
William Anderson	4		
John Anderson	1	children	
Thomas Walton	24	husbandman	going to seek a better livelihood
William Robinson	42		having purchased is going over with his family
Elizabeth Robinson	30		

Jenny cont'd

Name	Age	Occupation	Reason for emigrating
Elizabeth Robinson	9	children	
Jonathan Robinson	5		
Francis Robinson	3	of	
William Robinson	2	Wm Robinson	
Thomas Kalin	24	servants to	going with Wm Robinson
Patience Fallydown	22	Wm Robinson	same reason
John Robinson	47	husbandman	to make a purchase or return
Ann Robinson	15	his daughter	going with their father
Jenny Robinson	9	his daughter	same reason
Mary Parker	40		going over to her husband, he having a farm there
Elizabeth Parker	9	her	
James Parker	2	children	
Richard Peek	47	husbandman	having made a purchase is going with his family to reside
Jane Peek	42	his wife	
Mary Peek	20		
Jane Peek	17		
Helen Peek	15		
Isaac Peek	13		
Robert Peek	10		
Rose Peek	7		
Richard Peek	5	children of	
Joseph Peek	2	Richard Peek	
Sarah Fenton	15		going over to their father
Mary Fenton	9		

6. The *Providence*, John Tinker (master) sailed April 24, 1774 from Newcastle-upon-Tyne to Halifax, Nova Scotia. [NSARM RG1 Vol. 44, doc. 37 (Governor Legge's list)]

William Graham
Matthew Malkin
William Blenkinsop
Thomas Franckland
Thomas Graham
Thomas Hall
Michael Silk
John Ramsay
James Remmington
Joseph Jackson
John Oliver
Thomas Watson
Jane Watson
William Watson
Jonothan Watson
James Watson
Thomas Watson
Elizabeth Watson
Robert Watson
Ralph Praid
Rachel Morris
Elizabeth Reed
Robert Ripley
Tobel Ripley
Henry Ripley
Mary Ripley
Robert Ripley
Elias Ripley
John Ripley
Jane Ripley
Jane Calvert
Robert Moon
John Richardson
Mary Richardson
Christopher Richardson

Elizabeth Richardson
Christopher Flintoff
Ann Nelson
George Swinburn
Elizabeth Swinburne
John Jolly
George Ellis
Henry Maughan
James Fairbairn
George Foster
Margaret Foster
Eleanor Foster
Peggy Foster
Polly Foster
Mary Oxley
George Oxley
John Oxley
Matthew Johnson
Ann Johnson
John Johnson
John Atkinson
Martha Atkinson
Ann Atkinson
John Atkinson
Margaret Atkinson
Thomas Atkinson
Henry Atkinson
Robert Atkinson
John Newton
Elizabeth Newton
Foster Turnbull
Thomas Dobson
Joseph Providence Richardson
Robert Wilson
Mrs. Wilson

EXPLANATORY NOTES FOR APPENDICES II TO IV

Ship Crossings from England to Nova Scotia, New Brunswick, and Prince Edward Island

Ship crossing details are organized by province. Vessel information, where known, is provided in each case. The month of arrival in Canada, where known, is shown; where the month of departure from England is given it is marked by (d).

VESSEL NAME
The vessel name often includes the port at which the vessel is registered e.g. *Rebecca* of Saint John. The vessel type and tonnage, where known, appears after the vessel name.

VESSEL TYPE

Brig (bg) is a two-masted vessel with square rigging on both masts.

Barque (bk) is a three-masted vessel, square-rigged on the fore and main masts and for-and-aft rigged on the third aftermost mast.

Ship (s) is a three-masted vessel, square-rigged on all three masts.

Schooner (sr) has fore-and-aft sails on two or more masts. They were largely used in the coasting trade and for fishing, their advantage being the smaller crew than that required by square-rigged vessels of a comparable size.

Snow (sw) rigged as a brig with square sails on both masts but with a small triangular sail-mast stepped immediately toward the stern of the main mast.

TONNAGE

The tonnage was a standard measure used to determine customs dues and navigation fees. Because it was a calculated figure, tonnage did not necessarily convey actual carrying capacity. Before 1836 the formula used to calculate tonnage was based only on breadth and length, but after 1836 it incorporated the vessel's depth as well.

MONTH

Unless otherwise stated, the month shown is the vessel's arrival month; but where the month is followed by (d), it refers to the departure month.

LLOYD'S SHIPPING CODES

Shipping codes have been obtained from the *Lloyd's Shipping Register* in some cases. They were assigned to vessels according to their quality of construction, condition, and age:

A   first-class condition, kept in the highest state of repair and efficiency and within a prescribed age limit at the time of sailing.

AE   "second description of the first-class," fit for safe conveyance, no defects but may be over a prescribed age limit.

E   second-class vessels which, although unfit for carrying dry cargoes, were suitable for long-distance sea voyages.

I   third-class vessels only suitable for short voyages (i.e. not out of Europe).

The letters were followed by the number *1* or *2*, which signified the condition of the vessel's equipment (anchors, cables, and stores). Where satisfactory, the number *1* was used, and where not, *2* was used.

APPENDIX II

Emigrant Ship Crossings from England to Nova Scotia

DOCUMENTARY SOURCES

Because of major gaps in the recording of ship crossings from England to Nova Scotia, this list gives only a partial glimpse of the total volume of shipping involved. For instance, according to Nova Scotia Customs Records and newspaper shipping reports, some nine hundred people sailed from England to Nova Scotia between 1817 and 1819 — and yet, the surviving shipping data reveals only just under five hundred who sailed at this time. While the Customs Records reveal 106 English arrivals in 1824, ship crossing data only survives for thirty people. This pattern of under-recording occurs throughout the entire period.

Documentary sources are shown in the "Comments" column. Some passenger figures are approximate. Uncertainties arise as to whether passenger numbers include all adults (not just heads of households) and children and infants. Where available, passenger list source references are given. Extant passenger lists for the 1774–75 crossings of mainly Yorkshire emigrants appear in Appendix I. Surviving passenger lists for crossings from Liverpool to Halifax in 1862 and 1864 are found in Table 1. See "Explanatory Notes" on pages 303–05 of Appendix I for an explanation of the shipping terms in this listing.

Year	Month	Vessel	Master	Departure Port	Arrival Port	Passenger Numbers
1772	03 (d)	*Duke of York* (160 tns)	Benn	Liverpool	Halifax	62

Seventeen families sailed. Some are named in Cooney, *Emigrants of Yorkshire*. The *Duke of York* was built in 1762 and rated "I1" by Lloyd's (not seaworthy).

Year	Month	Vessel	Master	Departure Port	Arrival Port	Passenger Numbers
1774	03 (d)	*Albion* (bg, 240 tns)	Perrott, Thomas	Hull	Halifax	188

Psgr list: NAB T47/9 83-90 (see Appendix I). The *Albion* was built in 1762 and rated "E1" by Lloyd's. Arrived May 6.

Year	Month	Vessel	Master	Departure Port	Arrival Port	Passenger Numbers
1774	03 (d)	*Two Friends* (s, 250 tns)	Watt, James	Hull	Halifax	103

Psgr list: NAB T47/9 77–9 (see Appendix I). The *Two Friends* was built in 1766 and rated "E2" by Lloyd's. Arrived May 9.

Year	Month	Vessel	Master	Departure Port	Arrival Port	Passenger Numbers
1774	04 (d)	*Mary* (bg, 180 tns)	Cathrick, John	Stockton-on-Tees (Durham)	Halifax	34

Psgr list: NAB T47/9 135–6 (see Appendix I). All from County Durham. The *Mary* was built in 1771, rated "E1" by Lloyd's. Arrived June 11.

Year	Month	Vessel	Master	Departure Port	Arrival Port	Passenger Numbers
1774	04 (d)	*Prince George* (s, 150 tns)	Appleton, Robert	Scarborough (Yorkshire)	Halifax	170

Prince George crossing was not recorded in British Customs Records. Names of some of the passengers appear in "Legge's list" — NSARM RG1 Vol. 44, doc. 37. Number of passengers taken from Robinson and Rispin, *A Journey Through Nova Scotia*, 5. The *Prince George* was built in 1762 and rated "E1" by Lloyd's. Arrived May 16.

Year	Month	Vessel	Master	Departure Port	Arrival Port	Passenger Numbers
1774	04 (d)	*Providence* (s, 170 tns)	Tinker, John	Newcastle-upon-Tyne	Halifax	71

Psgr list: (Legge's list) NSARM Rg1 Vol. 44, doc. 37 (see Appendix I). Passengers consisted of forty-four men, twenty-five women and two children. The *Providence* was built in 1764 and rated "E1" by Lloyd's. Arrived June 1.

Year	Month	Vessel	Master	Departure Port	Arrival Port	Passenger Numbers
1774	04 (d)	*Thomas and William* (bg, 300 tns)	Pattindon, Samuel	Scarborough (Yorkshire)	Halifax	193

Vessel unnamed in Customs Record, but probably *Thomas and William*. Psgr list: NAB T47/9 120–3 (see Appendix I). The vessel was built in 1761 and rated "E1" by Lloyd's. Arrived May 14.

1775	04 (d)	*Jenny* (s, 450 tns)	Foster, William	Hull	Halifax	80

Psgr list: NAB T47/10 58-60 (see Appendix I). Described in *YCWA*, February 3, 1775, as being "a remarkable fine lofty ship, two years old, Hull-built and a fast-sailer." The *Jenny* was built in 1773 and rated "A1" by Lloyd's.

1816	n/k	*Three Brothers* (s)	n/k	Hull	Pictou	n/k

McLaren, *Pictou Book*, 119.

1817	07	*Thomas* (s)	n/k	Bristol	Halifax	40

Carried "between 30 and 40 passengers" (*AR* July 5, 1817). Voyage of 58 days.

1817	09	*Hercules*	n/k	London	Halifax	10

Martell, *Immigration to Nova Scotia, 1815–38*, 44.

1818	07	*Lavinia* (sr, 108 tns)	n/k	Plymouth (Devon)	Halifax	50

Martell, *Immigration to Nova Scotia, 1815–38*, 46. The *Lavinia* was built in 1816 and rated "A" by Lloyd's.

1818	07	*Speculator* (sr)	n/k	Plymouth (Devon)	Halifax	62

Martell, *Immigration to Nova Scotia, 1815–38*, 46.

1818	08	*Commerce* (bg)	n/k	London	Halifax	12

Martell, *Immigration to Nova Scotia, 1815–38*, 46.

Year	Month	Vessel	Master	Departure Port	Arrival Port	Passenger Numbers
1818	08	*Mary* (bg)	n/k	Plymouth (Devon)	Halifax	38

Martell, *Immigration to Nova Scotia, 1815–38*, 46.

1818	08	*Thomas* (s)	n/k	London	Halifax	31

Martell, *Immigration Nova to Scotia, 1815–38*, 46.

1819	04	*Northumber-land* (s)	n/k	London (Isle of Wight)	Halifax	n/k

Martell, *Immigration to Nova Scotia, 1815–38*, 48. Voyage of "fourteen days from the Isle of White."

1819	06	*Integrity* (bg)	n/k	Workington (Cumberland)	Halifax	55

Martell, *Immigration to Nova Scotia, 1815–38*, 48.

1819	07	*Lavinia* (sr, 108 tns)	n/k	Plymouth (Devon)	Halifax	32

Martell, *Immigration to Nova Scotia, 1815–38*, 48. Voyage of seventeen days.

1819	09	*Amelia* (bg, 254 tns)	King, Thos.	Liverpool	Halifax	n/k

AR, September 4, 1819: "The passengers on the Brig *Amelia*, take this public method of expressing the high sense they entertain of Captain King's polite and kind attention to them, during their passage from Liverpool."

1820	06	*Wharton* (bg)	n/k	London	Halifax	n/k

Martell, *Immigration to Nova Scotia, 1815–38*, 50. Voyage of fifty-three days.

1820	08	*Alice* (bg)	n/k	London	Halifax	n/k

Martell, *Immigration to Nova Scotia, 1815–38*, 50. Voyage of forty-nine days.

1820	11	*Fame*	n/k	Liverpool	Halifax	n/k

Martell, *Immigration to Nova Scotia, 1815–38*, 50.

1822	05	*Frindsbury* (s)	n/k	London	Halifax	11

Martell, *Immigration to Nova Scotia, 1815–38*, 53.

Year	Month	Vessel	Master	Departure Port	Arrival Port	Passenger Numbers
1822	n/k	*Mary Anne* (s)	n/k	Whitehaven (Cumberland)	Pictou	39

McLaren, *Pictou Book*, 119. Voyage of fifty-nine days.

1824	06	*Enterprise* (bg)	n/k	Liverpool	Pictou	n/k

Martell, *Immigration to Nova Scotia, 1815–38*, 54. "A number in the steerage."

1824	07	*Trafalgar* (bg)	n/k	Liverpool	Halifax	5

Martell, *Immigration to Nova Scotia, 1815–38*, 54. Five passengers in steerage.

1824	n/k	*Enterprise* (bg)	n/k	Liverpool	Pictou	25

McLaren, *Pictou Book*, 119. In the steerage (English). Voyage of 52 days.

1825	10	*Louisa* (bg)	n/k	Liverpool	Halifax	2

Martell, *Immigration to Nova Scotia, 1815–38*, 55. In steerage.

1826	10	*Aurora* (bg)	n/k	London	Halifax	n/k

Martell, *Immigration to Nova Scotia, 1815–38*, 56; "several in the steerage."

1827	05	*Adelphi*	n/k	Liverpool	Halifax	2

Martell, *Immigration to Nova Scotia, 1815–38*, 58.

1827	06	*Margaret* (bg)	n/k	Liverpool	Pictou	85

Martell, *Immigration to Nova Scotia, 1815–38*, 60. *AR*, June 16, 1827: "with 85 miners and all the necessary engines and machinery to work the Mines at this place."

1827	11	*Mary*	n/k	Liverpool	Pictou	40

Martell, *Immigration to Nova Scotia, 1815–38*, 60. According to the *Novascotian*, October 4, 1827, "A vessel was about being taken up at Liverpool, 24th August, to carry to Pictou, 40 workmen and materials for the Mining Company."

1827	n/k	*Mary* (bg)	n/k	Liverpool	Pictou	n/k

McLaren, *Pictou Book*, 119. Miners (English).

1828	05	*Atlantic* (s)	n/k	Liverpool	Halifax	5

Martell, *Immigration to Nova Scotia, 1815–38*, 61. Voyage of thirty-two days.

Year	Month	Vessel	Master	Departure Port	Arrival Port	Passenger Numbers
1828	05	*Maria* (bg)	n/k	Liverpool	Pictou	8

Martell, *Immigration to Nova Scotia, 1815–38*, 62. "Eight artificers for the mines."

Year	Month	Vessel	Master	Departure Port	Arrival Port	Passenger Numbers
1828	08	*Penelope* (bg)	n/k	Liverpool	Halifax	79

Martell, *Immigration to Nova Scotia, 1815–38*, 61. Voyage of sixty days.

Year	Month	Vessel	Master	Departure Port	Arrival Port	Passenger Numbers
1828	08	*Thomas Battersby* (bg)	n/k	Liverpool	Pictou	n/k

Martell, *Immigration to Nova Scotia, 1815–38*, 62. "Miners and machinery for the Albion Mining Company." Voyage of fifty-one days.

Year	Month	Vessel	Master	Departure Port	Arrival Port	Passenger Numbers
1828	11	*Halifax* (s)	n/k	Liverpool	Halifax	7

Martell, *Immigration to Nova Scotia, 1815–38*, 61. Voyage of thirty-two days.

Year	Month	Vessel	Master	Departure Port	Arrival Port	Passenger Numbers
1828	n/k	*Maria* (bg)	n/k	Liverpool	Pictou	8

McLaren, *Pictou Book*, 120. Miners (English).

Year	Month	Vessel	Master	Departure Port	Arrival Port	Passenger Numbers
1828	n/k	*Thomas Battersby* (bg)	n/k	Liverpool	Pictou	n/k

McLaren, *Pictou Book*, 120. Miners (English). Voyage of fifty-one days.

Year	Month	Vessel	Master	Departure Port	Arrival Port	Passenger Numbers
1829	05	*Ovington* (bg)	n/k	London	Halifax	6

Martell, *Immigration to Nova Scotia, 1815–38*, 63. Voyage of forty-five days.

Year	Month	Vessel	Master	Departure Port	Arrival Port	Passenger Numbers
1830	04	*Atlantic Packet* (s)	n/k	Liverpool	Halifax	2

Martell, *Immigration to Nova Scotia, 1815–38*, 64. Voyage of nineteen days.

Year	Month	Vessel	Master	Departure Port	Arrival Port	Passenger Numbers
1830	05	*Blagdon* (bg)	n/k	London	Halifax	23

Martell, *Immigration to Nova Scotia, 1815–38*, 65. Voyage of fifty-nine days.

Year	Month	Vessel	Master	Departure Port	Arrival Port	Passenger Numbers
1830	05	*Halifax Packet*	n/k	Liverpool	Halifax	10

Martell, *Immigration to Nova Scotia, 1815–38*, 65. Voyage of thirty days.

Year	Month	Vessel	Master	Departure Port	Arrival Port	Passenger Numbers
1830	05	*Justinian* (s)	n/k	London	Halifax	10

Martell, *Immigration to Nova Scotia, 1815–38*, 65. Voyage of forty-two days.

Year	Month	Vessel	Master	Departure Port	Arrival Port	Passenger Numbers
1830	05	*Margaret Ritchie* (bg)	n/k	Liverpool	Halifax	7

Martell, *Immigration to Nova Scotia, 1815–38*, 65. Voyage of forty-eight days.

| 1830 | 08 | *Halifax Packet* | n/k | Liverpool | Halifax | 7 |

Martell, *Immigration to Nova Scotia, 1815–38*, 65. Voyage of forty days.

| 1830 | 09 | *Margaret* (bg) | n/k | Liverpool | Sydney | 37 |

Martell, *Immigration to Nova Scotia, 1815–38*, 65.

| 1830 | 10 | *London* (s) | n/k | Liverpool | Halifax | 5 |

Martell, *Immigration to Nova Scotia, 1815–38*, 65. Voyage of forty days.

| 1830 | 10 | *Thalia* (s) | n/k | London | Halifax | n/k |

Martell, *Immigration to Nova Scotia, 1815–38*, 65. "50 days out of London, bound for Halifax, went ashore near 'Chizencook' on Oct. 23. Two of the passengers arrived at Halifax the next day. The *Thalia* got to sea again and reached Halifax the following week."

| 1830 | 11 | *Atlantic Packet* (s) | n/k | Liverpool | Halifax | 8 |

Martell, *Immigration to Nova Scotia, 1815–38*, 65. Voyage of twenty-four days.

| 1831 | 06 | *Hope* (bg) | n/k | Liverpool | Halifax | 20 |

Martell, *Immigration to Nova Scotia, 1815–38*, 68. Voyage of thirty days.

| 1831 | 09 | *Minstrel* (s) | n/k | London | Halifax | 50 |

Martell, *Immigration to Nova Scotia, 1815–38*, 68. Voyage of fifty-nine days.

| 1831 | 09 | *Polperro* (bg) | n/k | Jersey | Halifax | 6 |

Martell, *Immigration to Nova Scotia, 1815–38*, 68. Voyage of sixty-nine days.

| 1831 | 11 | *Halifax* (s) | n/k | Liverpool | Halifax | 9 |

Martell, *Immigration to Nova Scotia, 1815–38*, 68. Voyage of thirty-five days.

| 1831 | 11 | *Nautilus* (s) | n/k | Liverpool | Liverpool, N.S. | 14 |

Martell, *Immigration to Nova Scotia, 1815–38*, 70. Voyage of fifty days.

Year	Month	Vessel	Master	Departure Port	Arrival Port	Passenger Numbers

1832   05   *Argus* (bg)   n/k   Jersey   Halifax   8
Martell, *Immigration to Nova Scotia, 1815–38*, 71. Voyage of forty-seven days.

1832   05   *Halifax* (s)   n/k   Liverpool   Halifax   4
Martell, *Immigration to Nova Scotia, 1815–38*, 71. Voyage of thirty-four days.

1832   05   *Janet* (s)   n/k   Liverpool   Halifax   8
Martell, *Immigration to Nova Scotia, 1815–38*, 71. Voyage of thirty days.

1832   05   *Jean Hastie* (s) n/k   Liverpool   Halifax   26
Martell, *Immigration to Nova Scotia, 1815–38*, 71. Voyage of twenty-eight days.

1832   05   *Lady Dunmore* n/k   Liverpool   Halifax   32
              (bg)
Martell, *Immigration to Nova Scotia, 1815–38*, 71. Voyage of twenty-three days.

1832   05   *Mary Ann* (bg) n/k   Liverpool   Halifax   44
Martell, *Immigration to Nova Scotia, 1815–38*, 71. Voyage of forty-one days.

1832   07   *Lucas*   n/k   Man-   Antigonish   n/k
                               chester
Martell, *Immigration to Nova Scotia, 1815–38*, 73.

1832   07   *Walker* (bg)   n/k   London   Halifax   4
Martell, *Immigration to Nova Scotia, 1815–38*, 71. Voyage of sixty days.

1833   04   *Halifax*   n/k   Liverpool(?)   Halifax   13
Martell, *Immigration to Nova Scotia, 1815–38*, 74.

1833   04   *Lunenburg* (bk) n/k   Liverpool   Halifax   2
Martell, *Immigration to Nova Scotia, 1815–38*, 74. Voyage of twenty-nine days.

1833   06   *John Porter* (s) n/k   Liverpool   Halifax   2
Martell, *Immigration to Nova Scotia, 1815–38*, 74. Voyage of thirty-five days.

1833   06   *Magdaline* (bg) n/k   Jersey   Halifax   22
Martell, *Immigration to Nova Scotia, 1815–38*, 75. Voyage of fifty-three days.

Year	Month	Vessel	Master	Departure Port	Arrival Port	Passenger Numbers
1833	08	*Castlecalm* (bg)	n/k	London	Halifax	21

Martell, *Immigration to Nova Scotia, 1815–38*, 75. Voyage of sixty-one days.

1833	09	*Corsair* (bg)	n/k	Liverpool	Halifax	6

Martell, *Immigration to Nova Scotia, 1815–38*, 75. Voyage of twenty-seven days.

1833	10	*James* (bk)	n/k	Liverpool	Halifax	5

Martell, *Immigration to Nova Scotia, 1815–38*, 75. Voyage of forty-four days.

1833	10	*Thalia* (s)	n/k	London	Halifax	7

Martell, *Immigration to Nova Scotia, 1815–38*, 75. Voyage of forty-one days.

1834	05	*Damon* (bg)	n/k	Jersey	Halifax	27

Martell, *Immigration to Nova Scotia, 1815–38*, 78. Voyage of twenty-three days.

1834	05	*Elizabeth*	n/k	Newcastle-upon-Tyne	Pictou	1

Martell, *Immigration to Nova Scotia, 1815–38*, 79.

1834	05	*Sceptre* (bg)	n/k	London	Pictou	3

Martell, *Immigration to Nova Scotia, 1815–38*, 79.

1834	05	*Stephen* (bg)		Newcastle-upon-Tyne	Pictou	7

Martell, *Immigration to Nova Scotia, 1815–38*, 79.

1834	n/k	*Elizabeth* (bg)	n/k	Newcastle-upon-Tyne	Pictou	1

McLaren, *Pictou Book*, 121.

1834	n/k	*Sceptre* (bg)	n/k	London	Pictou	3

McLaren, *Pictou Book*, 121.

1834	n/k	*Stephen* (bg)	n/k	Newcastle-upon-Tyne	Pictou	7

McLaren, *Pictou Book*, 121.

Year	Month	Vessel	Master	Departure Port	Arrival Port	Passenger Numbers
1835	05	*Halifax* (s)	n/k	Liverpool	Halifax	3

Martell, *Immigration to Nova Scotia, 1815–38*, 80. Voyage of thirty-three days.

| 1836 | 05 | *Argus* (bg) | n/k | Jersey | Halifax | 18 |

Martell, *Immigration to Nova Scotia, 1815–38*, 82. Voyage of forty-three days.

| 1836 | 06 | *Buchanan* (bg) | n/k | London | Halifax | 7 |

Martell, *Immigration to Nova Scotia, 1815–38*, 82. Voyage of thirty-five days.

| 1836 | 09 | *Elizabeth* | n/k | Liverpool | Pictou | 1 |

Martell, *Immigration to Nova Scotia, 1815–38*, 84.

| 1836 | 10 | *Athabaska* | n/k | Liverpool | Pictou | 4 |

Martell, *Immigration to Nova Scotia, 1815–38*, 84.

| 1836 | 10 | *British Merchant* | n/k | Liverpool | Pictou | 3 |

Martell, *Immigration to Nova Scotia, 1815–38*, 84.

| 1836 | 10 | *Stephen* (bg) | n/k | Newcastle-upon-Tyne | Pictou | 1 |

Martell, *Immigration to Nova Scotia, 1815–38*, 84.

| 1837 | 07 | *Sally* | n/k | Liverpool | Pictou | 3 |

Martell, *Immigration to Nova Scotia, 1815–38*, 87.

| 1837 | 08 | *Exporter* (bk) | n/k | London | Halifax | 4 |

Martell, *Immigration to Nova Scotia, 1815–38*, 85. Voyage of fifty-six days.

| 1837 | 09 | *Peruvian* (s) | n/k | London | Halifax | 7 |

Martell, *Immigration to Nova Scotia, 1815–38*, 85. Voyage of forty days.

| 1837 | 10 | *Des Landries* (sr) | n/k | Guernsey | Halifax | 7 |

Martell, *Immigration to Nova Scotia, 1815–38*, 85. Voyage of thirty days.

Year	Month	Vessel	Master	Departure Port	Arrival Port	Passenger Numbers
1837	10	*Westmoreland* (bg)	n/k	Liverpool	Halifax	8

Martell, *Immigration to Nova Scotia, 1815–38*, 85. Voyage of twenty-eight days.

| 1838 | 05 | *Elizabeth* | n/k | Newcastle-upon-Tyne | Sydney | 3 |

Martell, *Immigration to Nova Scotia, 1815–38*, 90.

| 1838 | 06 | *England* (bk) | n/k | London | Halifax | 3 |

Martell, *Immigration to Nova Scotia, 1815–38*, 88. Voyage of thirty-four days.

| 1838 | 06 | *John Porter* (s) | n/k | Liverpool | Halifax | 4 |

Martell, *Immigration to Nova Scotia, 1815–38*, 88. Voyage of thirty-three days.

| 1838 | 06 | *Speedy Packet* (sr) | n/k | Jersey | Halifax | 4 |

Martell, *Immigration to Nova Scotia, 1815–38*, 88. Voyage of thirty-two days.

| 1838 | 07 | *Neptune* (bg) | n/k | London | Halifax | 8 |

Martell, *Immigration to Nova Scotia, 1815–38*, 88. Voyage of fifty-four days.

| 1838 | 08 | *Lady Paget* | n/k | Liverpool(?) | Halifax | 8 |

Martell, *Immigration to Nova Scotia, 1815–38*, 88.

| 1838 | 10 | *Halifax* (s) | n/k | Liverpool | Halifax | 2 |

Martell, *Immigration to Nova Scotia, 1815–38*, 88. Voyage of fifty days.

| 1838 | n/k | *Mary Ann* (bg) | n/k | Liverpool | Pictou | 100 |

McLaren, *Pictou Book*, 121. Miners (English).

| 1839 | 05 | *Harriet* (bg) | n/k | Liverpool | Halifax | 9 |

Morse, "Immigration to Nova Scotia, 1839–51," 104. Voyage of twenty-eight days.

| 1839 | 06 | *Albion* (bg) | n/k | London | Halifax | 4 |

Morse, "Immigration to Nova Scotia, 1839–51," 104. Voyage of thirty-four days.

Year	Month	Vessel	Master	Departure Port	Arrival Port	Passenger Numbers
1840	05	*Britannia* (bg)	n/k	Liverpool	Halifax	3

Morse, "Immigration to Nova Scotia, 1839–51," 104. Voyage of thirty-seven days.

| 1841 | 07 | *Manchester* (bk) | n/k | London | Halifax | 22 |

Morse, "Immigration to Nova Scotia, 1839–51," 107. Voyage of forty-nine days.

| 1841 | 09 | *Beeline* (bk) | n/k | London | Halifax | 15 |

Morse, "Immigration to Nova Scotia, 1839–51," 107. Voyage of thirty-nine days.

| 1846 | 04 (d) | *Harvest Home* (bk, 750 tns) | Thomp-son, W. | Falmouth (Cornwall) | Pictou | n/k |

RIC ships list

| 1862 | 04 (d) | *British Queen* | Aylward | Liverpool | Halifax | 16 |

Passenger list: NSARM RG1, Vol. 272, 142.

| 1862 | 04 (d) | *Morning Star* | McKenzie | Liverpool | Halifax | 19 |

Passenger list: NSARM RG1 Vol. 272, 141.

| 1862 | 05 (d) | *Frank Flint* | n/k | Liverpool | Halifax | 23 |

Passenger list: NSARM RG1, Vol. 272, 144.

| 1864 | 05 | *Euroclydon* | n/k | Liverpool | Halifax | 43 |

Passenger list: *Journal of the House of Assembly 1865*, Appendix 24, 5.

| 1864 | 06 | *Indian Queen* | n/k | Liverpool | Halifax | 33 |

Passenger list: *Journal of the House of Assembly 1865*, Appendix 24, 6.

APPENDIX III

Emigrant Ship Crossings from England to New Brunswick

DOCUMENTARY SOURCES

Because most of New Brunswick's Customs Records were lost in 1877, in the great fire that engulfed Saint John, ship-crossing details are few and far between. Relevant data does survive for crossings in 1833–34 and 1838, and details of the individual crossings from England are given below. This information, which includes passenger lists, has been extracted from the New Brunswick Genealogical Society's publication *Passengers to New Brunswick: Custom House Records — 1833, 34, 37 & 38* (Saint John, 1987). Passenger lists for crossings involving ten or more passengers appear in Table 2 of this book. Other than this source, most of the other ship-crossing data has been extracted from newspaper shipping reports and advertisements. Another important source is the Royal Institution of Cornwall "Records of Emigrant Ships from Cornwall," which has been abbreviated to *RIC* ships-list.

Passenger figures must be regarded as approximate. Uncertainties arise as to whether passenger numbers include all adults (not just heads of households) and children and infants. In addition, because Saint John was used as a port of transit to the United States, arrival numbers may not necessarily relate to people who actually settled in New Brunswick.

For an explanation of the shipping terms used in the listing, please see the Explanatory Notes on pages 303–05.

Year	Month	Vessel	Master	Departure Port	Arrival Port	Passenger Numbers
1816	08 (d)	*Superior* (s, 400 tns)	Atherdon, Thomas	Liverpool	Saint John	n/k
1817	05	*Trafalgar* (270 tns)	Welburn, John	Hull	Saint John and Quebec	159

Partial reconstructed passenger list appears in Table 3. The list has been compiled from NAB CO 384/1 ff. 127–33. Also see Short, "The 1817 Journey of the Brig Trafalgar with Its Immigrants," 12–16. The *Trafalgar* was described as being "recently refurbished, height between decks of 6 feet" (*HA*, April 26, 1817).

Year	Month	Vessel	Master	Departure Port	Arrival Port	Passenger Numbers
1817	08	*Bideford* (bg, 162 tns)	Butters, Thomas	Plymouth (Devon)	New Brunswick	n/k

Shipping advertisement in *Trewman's Exeter Flying Post* (July 24, 1817) states "excellent accommodation" for passengers.

Year	Month	Vessel	Master	Departure Port	Arrival Port	Passenger Numbers
1818	03(d)	*Ann*	Wilkinson, William	Hull	Miramichi	n/k

According to the *HA* (February 14, 1818) the vessel "has uncommon good height between decks."

Year	Month	Vessel	Master	Departure Port	Arrival Port	Passenger Numbers
1819	03(d)	*Bittern* (s, 281 tns)	Herbert, R.W.	Newcastle	Saint John	n/k

Advertisement in *NC* (March 27, 1819) states that it appeals to "persons desirous of emigrating."

Year	Month	Vessel	Master	Departure Port	Arrival Port	Passenger Numbers
1819	03(d)	*Susanna*	Proctor, John	Exeter (Devon)	St. Andrews	n/k

Advertisement in *TEFP* (March 4, 1819).

Year	Month	Vessel	Master	Departure Port	Arrival Port	Passenger Numbers
1819	04(d)	*Augusta* of Dumfries	n/k	Dumfries (Scotland)	Saint John	286

One of three vessels (*Augusta* of Dumfries, *Thomson's Packet* of Dumfries, and *Jessie* of Dumfries) that took 517 passengers to Saint John in 1819. Passengers also included some Scots from the southwest Borders. See *DWJ*, June 1, 1819. Also see Campey, *Axe and Bible*, 88, 138, 143–45, 152.

Year	Month	Vessel	Master	Departure Port	Arrival Port	Passenger Numbers
1819	04(d)	*Jessie* of Dumfries	Williams, James	Dumfries (Scotland)	Charlotte-twon and Miramichi	n/k

One of three vessels (*Augusta* of Dumfries, *Thomson's Packet* of Dumfries, and *Jessie* of Dumfries) that took 517 passengers to Saint John in 1819. Passengers also included some Scots from the southwest Borders. See *DWJ*, June 1, 1819. Also see Campey, *Axe and Bible*, 88, 138, 143–45, 152.

Year	Month	Vessel	Master	Departure Port	Arrival Port	Passenger Numbers
1819	04(d)	*Thomson's Packet* of Dumfries	n/k	Dumfries (Scotland)	Saint John	150

One of three vessels (*Augusta* of Dumfries, *Thomson's Packet* of Dumfries, and *Jessie* of Dumfries) that took 517 passengers to Saint John in 1819. Passengers also included some Scots from the southwest Borders. See *DWJ*, June 1, 1819. Also see Campey, *Axe and Bible*, 88, 138, 143–45, 152.

Year	Month	Vessel	Master	Departure Port	Arrival Port	Passenger Numbers
1819	06	*Dixon* (314 tns)	Roberts, James	Hull	Charlotte-town	101

Includes passengers who may have gone on to New Brunswick. See Elliott, "English Immigration to Prince Edward Island" (40), 7.

Year	Month	Vessel	Master	Departure Port	Arrival Port	Passenger Numbers
1820	n/k	*Dixon* (314 tns)	n/k	Hull	P.E.I./N.B.	23

Landed 23 passengers for P.E.I. and Bouctouche, N.B. See Elliott, "English Immigration to Prince Edward Island" (40), 7.

Year	Month	Vessel	Master	Departure Port	Arrival Port	Passenger Numbers
1820	n/k	*Prince George*	n/k	n/k	P.E.I./N.B.	n/k

Sailed to the Miramichi. One of the passengers, Mary Hosear, settled at Lot 20. See Donald A. MacKinnon and A.B. Warburton, *Past and Present of Prince Edward Island* (Charlottetown: B.F. Bowen, 1906), 422.

Year	Month	Vessel	Master	Departure Port	Arrival Port	Passenger Numbers
1822	08 (d)	*Swallow*	Davidson, William	Dumfries (Scotland)	Saint John	65

According to *DGC* (August 6, 1822) most of the passengers came from Cumberland.

Year	Month	Vessel	Master	Departure Port	Arrival Port	Passenger Numbers
1823	04(d)	*John*	Ashton, William	Hull	Saint John	n/k

According to the *Hull Packet* (April 21, 1823) the *John* had "exceeding good height between decks" for passengers.

Year	Month	Vessel	Master	Departure Port	Arrival Port	Passenger Numbers
1824	03(d)	*Susan* (sw, 200 tns)	Blackaller, William	Exeter (Devon)	Saint John	n/k
1824	06	*Eddystone* (244 tns)	Dale, J.	London	Charlotte-town	6

One of the passengers was a Mr. Johnston, who was proceeding on to the Miramichi.

Year	Month	Vessel	Master	Departure Port	Arrival Port	Passenger Numbers
1825	03(d)	*Joseph Anderson* (bg, 300 tns)	n/k	Newcastle-upon-Tyne	Saint John	n/k
1825	03(d)	*Mary* (bg, 249 tns)	Lyon, William	Liverpool	Saint John	n/k
1825	03(d)	*Milo* (bg, 277 tns)	Ord	Newcastle-upon-Tyne	Saint John	n/k
1825	03(d)	*Wellington* (bg, 244 tns)	Scott, Luke	Newcastle-upon-Tyne	Saint John & Richibucto	n/k
1826	03(d)	*Henry Arnot* (bg, 245 tns)	Frink, James	Liverpool	Saint John & St. Andrews	n/k
1827	03(d)	*Spring Flower* of Padstow (300 tns)	n/k	Padstow (Cornwall)	Miramichi	n/k

RIC ships-list.

Year	Month	Vessel	Master	Departure Port	Arrival Port	Passenger Numbers
1827	04(d)	*Emma*	Frost, John	Newcastle-upon-Tyne	Saint John	n/k

Year	Month	Vessel	Master	Departure Port	Arrival Port	Passenger Numbers
1830	07(d)	*Unity* (s, 700 tns)	Johnson, John	Bristol	Saint Andrews	n/k

BM (July 27, 1830) reported "English labourers in demand in New Brunswick"; fares in steerage were three pounds.

Year	Month	Vessel	Master	Departure Port	Arrival Port	Passenger Numbers
1832	07	*Amity* (s, 333 tns)	n/k	Bristol	Charlotte-town	28

The *Amity* called at New Brunswick on her way to Charlottetown.

Year	Month	Vessel	Master	Departure Port	Arrival Port	Passenger Numbers
1832	07	n/k	n/k	Bideford (Devon)	Charlotte-town	8

Vessel had sailed from Bideford via Saint John.

Year	Month	Vessel	Master	Departure Port	Arrival Port	Passenger Numbers
1832	07(d)	*Pilot* (s, 500 tns)	Moor, John Denham	Bristol	St.Andrews	n/k

Year	Month	Vessel	Master	Departure Port	Arrival Port	Passenger Numbers
1833	03	*Alchymist* (bk)	Godfrey Wills,	Falmouth (Cornwall)	Saint John	34

The *Alchymist* was due to depart from Restronguet, near Falmouth. According to *RIC* ships-list, fares were three guineas.

Year	Month	Vessel	Master	Departure Port	Arrival Port	Passenger Numbers
1833	04	*Caledonia* of Saint John (s, 497 tns)	McLay, David	Liverpool	Saint John	4

Year	Month	Vessel	Master	Departure Port	Arrival Port	Passenger Numbers
1833	04	*Charlotte Lungan* of Saint John (bk, 543 tns)	Lawrence, Richard	Liverpool	Saint John	7

Year	Month	Vessel	Master	Departure Port	Arrival Port	Passenger Numbers
1833	04(d)	*New Brunswick*	n/k	Falmouth (Cornwall)	New Brunswick & Quebec	n/k

According to *RIC* ships-list the vessel carried "A great number of passengers."

Year	Month	Vessel	Master	Departure Port	Arrival Port	Passenger Numbers
1833	05	*Lord Goderich* (s, 367 tns)	Hopper, John	London	Saint John	29

Passenger list: see Table 2.

Year	Month	Vessel	Master	Departure Port	Arrival Port	Passenger Numbers
1833	05	*Wakefield* (s)	Armstrong, Amos	Liverpool	Saint John	13
1833	06	*Amynta* (s, 214 tns)	Moon, E.	Plymouth (Devon)	Saint John	16

Passenger list: see Table 2.

Year	Month	Vessel	Master	Departure Port	Arrival Port	Passenger Numbers
1833	06	*Anne* (bg, 182 tns)	Davis, William S.	Penzance (Cornwall)	Saint John	2

Passengers were Mr. Beuchant, a merchant settler, and his son.

Year	Month	Vessel	Master	Departure Port	Arrival Port	Passenger Numbers
1833	06	*Augusta* of Saint John (417 tns)	Petrie, William	Liverpool	Saint John	10

Passenger list: see Table 2.

Year	Month	Vessel	Master	Departure Port	Arrival Port	Passenger Numbers
1833	06	*John* (s)	Russell, Thomas	Liverpool	Saint John	4
1833	06	*Margaret* (s)	Munn, William Francis	London	Saint John	22

Passenger list: see Table 2.

Year	Month	Vessel	Master	Departure Port	Arrival Port	Passenger Numbers
1833	06	*Percival* (s)	n/k	Plymouth (Devon)	Saint John	11

Passenger list: see Table 2.

Year	Month	Vessel	Master	Departure Port	Arrival Port	Passenger Numbers
1833	06	*Sarah and Elizabeth*	n/k	Bideford (Devon)	Charlotte-town	40

Fourteen of the passengers left for Bathurst [New Brunswick] and a few left for the U.S.

Year	Month	Vessel	Master	Departure Port	Arrival Port	Passenger Numbers
1833	07	*Branches* (s, 452 tns)	Forsyth, George	London	Saint John	13

Passenger list: see Table 2.

| 1833 | 07 | *Legatus* | Ord, William | London | Saint John | 15 |

Passenger list: see Table 2.

| 1833 | 07 | *Pacific* of Saint John (s, 348 tns) | Johnston, Nicholas | Liverpool | Saint John | 23 |

Passenger list: see Table 2.

| 1833 | 08 | *Caledonia* of Saint John (s, 497 tns) | McLay, David | Liverpool | Saint John | 10 |

Passenger list: see Table 2.

| 1833 | 08 | *Greenhow* (bk) | Aiken, Andrew | Liverpool | Saint John | 1 |

The passenger was Mary Kay.

| 1833 | 08 | *Retrench* (bg, 270 tns) | Turney, Samuel | London | Saint John | 3 |

An advertisement appeared in the *Ipswich Journal* (June 15, 1833) describing the vessel as having "very excellent cabin and steerage accommodation for passengers." An advertisement for lands being offered by the New Brunswick and Nova Scotia Land Company appeared in the same edition.

| 1833 | 09 | *Alchymist* (bk) | Wills, Godfrey | Falmouth Cornwall) | Saint John | 24 |

Passenger list: see Table 2.

| 1833 | 09 | *Sarah* (bk) | Hamen, Joseph | Bristol | Saint John | 20 |

Passenger list: see Table 2.

Year	Month	Vessel	Master	Departure Port	Arrival Port	Passenger Numbers
1833	10	*Bolivar* of Plymouth (s, 356 tns)	Richards, Thomas	Plymouth (Devon)	Saint John	6
1833	10	*John* of Saint John (s, 535 tns)	Russell, Thomas	Liverpool	Saint John	9

Passengers included Hon. William Black, former governor of New Brunswick.

Year	Month	Vessel	Master	Departure Port	Arrival Port	Passenger Numbers
1833	10	*Wakefield* (s)	Armstrong, Amos	Liverpool	Saint John	2
1833	11	*Aurora* (s, 312 tns)	Crowell, Nathaniel	London	Saint John	2
1833	11	*Beverley* (bk)	Lawson, J. S.	Liverpool	Saint John	1

Passenger was William McCameron, aged 29.

Year	Month	Vessel	Master	Departure Port	Arrival Port	Passenger Numbers
1833	11	*Peggy* of Saint John (bk, 268 tns)	Rouland, George	Plymouth (Devon)	Saint John	6
1833	12	*George Gordon* (bg)	King, Thomas	Liverpool	Saint John	1
1834	03(d)	*Dewdrop* (350 tns)	Wade, M.B.	Padstow (Cornwall)	Saint John	n/k

RIC ships-list.

Year	Month	Vessel	Master	Departure Port	Arrival Port	Passenger Numbers
1834	03(d)	*Louisa* (700 tns)	Kunze, C.	Padstow (Cornwall)	Miramichi	n/k

RIC ships-list.

Year	Month	Vessel	Master	Departure Port	Arrival Port	Passenger Numbers
1834	03(d)	*Phoebe* (200 tns)	Luens, W.	Hayle (Cornwall)	Miramichi	n/k

RIC ships-list states "Emigration per Harvey & Co."

Year	Month	Vessel	Master	Departure Port	Arrival Port	Passenger Numbers
1834	05	*Beverley* (bk)	Lawson, J. S.	Liverpool	Saint John	3
1834	05	*Fenwick Keating* (bg, 354 tns)	Atchison, William	Liverpool	Saint John	4
1834	05	*Joseph Anderson* (bg, 300 tns)	Thompson, William	London	Saint John	2
1834	05	*Latona* of Newcastle (bg, 221 tns)	Smith, Thomas	Exeter (Devon)	Saint John	8
1834	05	*William and Robert* of Saint John (bg, 180 tns)	Andrews, George William	Liverpool	Saint John	8
1834	06	*Mercator* (bg)	Mackie, Robert	Sunderland (Durham)	Saint John	12
1834	06	*New Brunswick* of Saint John (bg, 414 tns)	Green, Thomas	Liverpool	Saint John	16

Passenger list: see Table 2.

Year	Month	Vessel	Master	Departure Port	Arrival Port	Passenger Numbers
1834	07	*Breakwater* (bg, 180 tns)	Rowland, R.	Plymouth (Devon)	Saint John	12

Passenger list: see Table 2.

Year	Month	Vessel	Master	Departure Port	Arrival Port	Passenger Numbers
1834	07	*Cassandra* (bk)	Greig, James	Liverpool	Saint John	20

Year	Month	Vessel	Master	Departure Port	Arrival Port	Passenger Numbers
1834	08	*Adelaide* (bk)	Moran, Robert G.	Liverpool	Saint John	10
1834	08	*Liverpool* (bk)	Johnston, Nicholas	Liverpool	Saint John	6
1834	08	*Sir Robert H. Dick* of Saint John (s, 616 tns)	Elder, Alexander	Liverpool	Saint John	16
1834	09	*Beverley* (bk)	n/k	Liverpool	Saint John	6
1834	09	*Frederick* of Saint John (bg, 467 tns)	Westcott, John	Liverpool	Saint John	7
1834	09	*Samuel* of Saint John (s, 558 tns)	Jameson, James	Liverpool	Saint John	8
1834	10	*William and Robert* of Saint John (bg, 180 tns)	Andrews, George William	Liverpool	Saint John	2
1834	11	*Comet* (bk)	Hunt, George C.	London	Saint John	1

The passenger was Caroline Ferguson.

Year	Month	Vessel	Master	Departure Port	Arrival Port	Passenger Numbers
1834	11	*Jennet* (s)	Laidley, David	Bristol	Saint John	1

The passenger was William Howell.

Year	Month	Vessel	Master	Departure Port	Arrival Port	Passenger Numbers
1834	11	*Sir Robert H. Dick* of Saint John (s, 616 tns)	Hamm, Joseph	Liverpool	Saint John	5
1835	10	n/k		Bristol	Charlottetown	2

The vessel had called at the Miramichi.

Year	Month	Vessel	Master	Departure Port	Arrival Port	Passenger Numbers
1836	05(d)	*D'Arcy* of Sunderland (sw, 303 tns)	Phillips, George	Berwick-upon-Tweed	Saint John	110

The safe arrival of the Berwick settlers was reported in *BA* (August 21, 1836). The passengers were taken by steamer from Saint John to Fredericton and then overland to Stanley. The *D'arcy* was built in 1836 (Lloyd's Shipping Code "A1").

Year	Month	Vessel	Master	Departure Port	Arrival Port	Passenger Numbers
1837	06(d)	*Cornelius* of Sunderland	n/k	Berwick-upon-Tweed	Saint John	137

The passengers were taken by steamer from Saint John to Fredericton and then overland to Stanley.

Year	Month	Vessel	Master	Departure Port	Arrival Port	Passenger Numbers
1838	07	*Rebecca* of Saint John (bk, 251 tns)	Pickam, Edward	Liverpool	Saint John	34

Passenger list: see Table 2.

Year	Month	Vessel	Master	Departure Port	Arrival Port	Passenger Numbers
1840	04(d)	*Spring Flower*	n/k	Padstow (Cornwall)	Restigouche	n/k

"Applications to T.R. Avery, Boscastle (Cornwall)." See *RIC* ships-list.

Year	Month	Vessel	Master	Departure Port	Arrival Port	Passenger Numbers
1841	06(d)	*Pero* (bk, 350 tns)	Colenso, C.	Penzance (Cornwall)	Miramichi	n/k

"Applications to Mathews & Co., shipbuilders, Penzance." See *RIC* ships-list.

Year	Month	Vessel	Master	Departure Port	Arrival Port	Passenger Numbers
1841	n/k	*Glengarry* of Saint John	n/k	Liverpool	Saint John	n/k

Thomas Craigs, one of the passengers, was on his way to the Harvey settlement.

Year	Month	Vessel	Master	Departure Port	Arrival Port	Passenger Numbers
1842	03(d)	*Vittoria* (bk, 800 tns)	Simpson, M.	Hayle (Cornwall)	Saint John	n/k

RIC ships-list.

Year	Month	Vessel	Master	Departure Port	Arrival Port	Passenger Numbers
1847	09(d)	*Woodbine* (bk, 600 tns)	Skeach, R.	Falmouth (Cornwall)	New Brunswick	n/k

RIC ships-list.

Year	Month	Vessel	Master	Departure Port	Arrival Port	Passenger Numbers
1861	04(d)	*Dew Drop* (204 tns)	n/k	Padstow (Cornwall)	Miramichi	n/k

"Apply T R Avery, Boscastle." Vessel built Hull, 1820. See *RIC* ships-list.

APPENDIX IV

Emigrant Ship Crossings from England to Prince Edward Island

DOCUMENTARY SOURCES

The table below lists the known ship crossings with emigrants from England to Prince Edward Island from 1774 to 1864. The principal documentary source used is the series of articles written by Orlo Jones and Douglas in *The Island Magazine*, which compiled all recorded crossings under the heading of Those Elusive Immigrants, No. 16 (1984), No. 17 (1985), No. 18 (1985), No. 26 (1989), and No. 27 (1990). The articles record pertinent data from the *Royal Gazette, Royal Herald, Weekly Recorder, Prince Edward Island Gazette, Prince Edward Island Register*, and the Prince Edward Island Customs Records. Any gaps in the listing are due to missing records.

Passenger figures must be regarded as approximate. Uncertainties arise as to whether passenger numbers include all adults (not just heads of households) and children and infants. A partial passenger list for the 1817 crossing of the *Valiant* from Hull appears in Table 6. No other passenger lists have been located.

For an explanation of the shipping terms used in the listing see the "Explanatory Notes" on pages 303–05. Vessels that were owned at the time of sailing by Prince Edward Island merchants are noted (names taken from the *Lloyd's Shipping Register*).

Year	Month	Vessel	Master	Departure Port	Arrival Port	Passenger Numbers
1774	n/k	*Elizabeth* (sw, 200 tns)	n/k	London	Charlottetown	100

Settlers, recruited by Robert Clark, went to New London (Lot 21).

| 1775 | 08 (d) | *Elizabeth* (sw, 200 tns) | Russell, John | London | Charlottetown | 20 |

Wrecked off Lot 11 in 1775. Passengers included Thomas Curtis, Mr. and Mrs. Compton and child, Mr. and Mrs. James Townsend and family, James Campbell (probably son of Robert Campbell, Robert Clark's partner), Mr. Blandruset and servant, Henry Roberts, Mrs. Churchward and two daughters, Mr. Fry, and Judge Stewart and his sons. Passengers went to New London (Lot 21).

| 1791 | 07 | *Charlotte* | Alston, Titus | London | Charlottetown | n/k |

Passengers included Mr. Patterson, J. Webster Sr., and John Townshend. Some came with fruit trees.

| 1791 | 08 | *Speedwell* (bg, 117 tns) | Sughrue, Daniel | London | Charlottetown | 12 |

The *Speedwell* was built in 1787 by John Cambridge (Lloyd's Shipping Code "A1").

| 1791 | 10 | *Minerva* | Fletcher, Alexander | Cowes (Isle of Wight) | Charlottetown | 174 |

The captain was Fletcher "of the Island."

| 1791 | 11 | *Endeavour* (sr, 108 tns) | Perry, Wm. | London | Charlottetown | 12 |

The *Endeavour* was built in 1790 (Lloyd's Shipping Code "A1").

| 1792 | 05 | *Prosperity* (sr, 44 tns) | Baker, Wm. | London | Charlottetown | n/k |

The *Prosperity* was built in 1791 (Lloyd's Shipping Code "A1").

| 1792 | 09 | *Speedwell* (bg, 117 tns) | Sughrue, D. | London | Murray Harbour | 3 |

Passengers: Messrs. Cambridge, Curtis, and Hennessie.

| 1793 | 05 | *Lewis* (bg) | Baker, Wm. | London | Charlottetown | n/k |

Passengers included Robert Shuttleworth, "a gentleman of great opulence and fortune" (*RG*, June 3).

Year	Month	Vessel	Master	Departure Port	Arrival Port	Passenger Numbers
1803	08	*Teresa* (sw, 205 tns)	Murphy, George	Portsmouth (Hampshire)	Charlottetown	>10

Passengers included Edward Walsh, Harry Compton, son Thomas, daughter, servant girl, Mrs. Eleanor Sancy, Mr. Townshend, Mrs. White, Captain Stewart, and his servant maid. See Betty M. Jeffrey and Carter W. Jeffrey, *The Jeffrey Family of the Island of Wight and P.E.I.*; also Edward Walsh and H.T. Holman, "An Account of Prince Edward Island, 1803," *The Island Magazine*, No. 15 (Spring/Summer 1984). The *Teresa* was built in 1801 (Lloyd's Shipping Code "A1").

Year	Month	Vessel	Master	Departure Port	Arrival Port	Passenger Numbers
1806	05	*Neptune* (160 tns)	Messervy, John	Guernsey	Charlottetown	84

Eight families sailed, including the Brehauts, LeLacheurs, Machin/Machons, DeJerseys, Fallows, Taudvins, Marquands, and Robertsons. They settled at Guernsey Cove. The vessel was owned by the settlers.

Year	Month	Vessel	Master	Departure Port	Arrival Port	Passenger Numbers
1807	05	*Elizabeth and Ann* (286 tns)	Wynn, Thos.	Newcastle-upon-Tyne	Charlottetown	n/k
1807	07	*Hope* (342 tns)	Ford, John	Liverpool	Charlottetown	n/k
1808	06	*Devonshire* (300 tns)	Robertson, Peter	Liverpool	Charlottetown	23
1811	06	*Triton* (bg)	n/k	London	Charlottetown	2

Passengers were Mr. and Mrs. Cambridge of Prince Edward Island.

Year	Month	Vessel	Master	Departure Port	Arrival Port	Passenger Numbers
1811	08	*Stag*	Patterson	n/k	Charlottetown (Madeira and England)	2

Passengers were Mrs. Tailor and Mr. Jones from London, via Madeira, and on to Newfoundland.

Year	Month	Vessel	Master	Departure Port	Arrival Port	Passenger Numbers
1811	09	*Sally*		Portsmouth (Hampshire)	Charlottetown	4

Passengers were Robert Stewart and Mrs. Stewart; and Mrs. MacDonald and daughter.

Year	Month	Vessel	Master	Departure Port	Arrival Port	Passenger Numbers
1812	06	*Nancy*	Foster	London	Charlottetown	n/k

Passengers included Charles Wright, Mr. Inns, and William Hollet and family.

Year	Month	Vessel	Master	Departure Port	Arrival Port	Passenger Numbers
1812	09	*Royal Bounty* (s, 360 tns)	Gamble, Henry	Hull	P.E.I.	4

The ship was captured by an American privateer. Passengers included David Moore of Dorset, England, and Milton, P.E.I. (Lot 32), his daughter Mary, and her husband, James Hutton. The passengers eventually made their way to Prince Edward Island.

Year	Month	Vessel	Master	Departure Port	Arrival Port	Passenger Numbers
1817	04	*Valiant* (bg, 361 tns)	Ezard, John	Hull	Charlottetown	196

Passenger list (reconstructed) in Murray, *The "Valiant" Connection*, 6–7 (see Table 6). Passengers were said to include about sixty survivors who had been taken onboard mid-voyage from a wrecked ship that had sailed from Scotland. According to *HA*, February 14, the *Valiant* was to sail to P.E.I., Nova Scotia, and New Brunswick. The *Valiant* was a "Dutch Prize" (Lloyd's Shipping Code "E1").

Year	Month	Vessel	Master	Departure Port	Arrival Port	Passenger Numbers
1818	05	*Dixon* (314 tns)	Roberts, James	Hull	Charlottetown	28

According to *HA*, March 14, the *Dixon* would also call at Pictou and New Brunswick. The *Dixon* was built in 1803 (Lloyd's Shipping Code "E1").

Year	Month	Vessel	Master	Departure Port	Arrival Port	Passenger Numbers
1818	05	*John* (bg)	Carr, G.	Plymouth (Devon)	Charlottetown	50

Year	Month	Vessel	Master	Departure Port	Arrival Port	Passenger Numbers
1818	06	*Horsely Hill* (bg)	Buck	Sunderland (Durham)	Charlottetown	n/k

113 passengers arrived at Quebec. The number disembarking at Charlottetown is not known.

Year	Month	Vessel	Master	Departure Port	Arrival Port	Passenger Numbers
1818	06	*Nancy*	Norman, W.	Hull	Charlottetown	n/k

The number who left at P.E.I. is not known; fifty-six people went on to Quebec. Fares: adults ten guineas (with provisions), to provide themselves, seven guineas, children half price (*HA*, April 11, 1818). See Elliott, "English Immigration to P.E.I." (40), 7.

Year	Month	Vessel	Master	Departure Port	Arrival Port	Passenger Numbers
1818	06	*Valiant* (bg, 361 tns)	Heard, John	Hull	Charlottetown	n/k

Passengers to settle in Churchill (Lots 31 and 65).

Year	Month	Vessel	Master	Departure Port	Arrival Port	Passenger Numbers
1818	09	*John*	n/k	London	Charlottetown	n/k

The passengers included a Mrs. Fanning and daughters.

Year	Month	Vessel	Master	Departure Port	Arrival Port	Passenger Numbers
1818	09	*Peter and Sarah*	n/k	Bideford (Devon)	Canoe Cove	n/k

Vessel came via Pictou. Passengers included William Ellis, Edward Williams, John England, as well as McNeils, MacDonalds, and McPhees. (See Greenhill and Giffard, *Westcountrymen in Prince Edward's Island*, 52–65.)

Year	Month	Vessel	Master	Departure Port	Arrival Port	Passenger Numbers
1818	10	*Britannia* (113 tns)	n/k	Plymouth (Devon)	Charlottetown	2

The passengers were Mr. Smith and Duncan McKay.

Year	Month	Vessel	Master	Departure Port	Arrival Port	Passenger Numbers
1819	04	*Valiant* (bg, 361 tns)	Ashton, William	Hull	Charlottetown	n/k

HA, April 3, 1819, stated that the ship had taken passengers out "for the two last years."

Year	Month	Vessel	Master	Departure Port	Arrival Port	Passenger Numbers
1819	04(d)	*Jessie* of Dumfries	Williams, James	Dumfries (Scotland)	Charlottetown and Miramichi	n/k

One of three vessels (*Augusta* of Dumfries, *Thomson's Packet* of Dumfries, and *Jessie* of Dumfries) that took 517 passengers to Saint John in 1819. Included some Scots from the southwest Borders. See *DWJ*, June 1, 1819. Also see Campey, *Axe and Bible*, 88, 138, 143–45, 152.

Year	Month	Vessel	Master	Departure Port	Arrival Port	Passenger Numbers
1819	06	*Dixon* (315 tns)	Roberts, James	Hull	Charlottetown	101

Includes passengers who may have gone on to New Brunswick. See, "English Immigration to P.E.I." (40), 7.

Year	Month	Vessel	Master	Departure Port	Arrival Port	Passenger Numbers
1819	11	*Jane* (153 tns)	Brown, John	Bristol	Charlottetown	6

Passengers: Charles Wright, Mrs. Wright, T.H. Haviland, and others.

Year	Month	Vessel	Master	Departure Port	Arrival Port	Passenger Numbers
1819	n/k	*Eagle*	n/k	Plymouth (Devon)	Charlottetown	n/k

Several cases of smallpox. Vessel was consigned to Mr. Pope and allowed to proceed to Bedeque.

Year	Month	Vessel	Master	Departure Port	Arrival Port	Passenger Numbers
1819	n/k	*Economy*	[nk]	Hull (probably)	Charlottetown (probably)	>5

To settle in Hampton (Lot 29). Passengers included five Inman brothers from Yorkshire.

Year	Month	Vessel	Master	Departure Port	Arrival Port	Passenger Numbers
1820	05	*Anglian* (215 tns)	Grayson, Thos.	Whitehaven (Cumberland)	Charlottetown	18

Year	Month	Vessel	Master	Departure Port	Arrival Port	Passenger Numbers
1820	05	*Eagle* (bg)	Henley, Edward	Portsmouth	Charlottetown	n/k

The vessel landed fourteen passengers in Quebec, and an unknown number in P.E.I.

Year	Month	Vessel	Master	Departure Port	Arrival Port	Passenger Numbers
1820	05	*George* (225 tns)	Unsworth, James	Liverpool	Charlottetown	9
1820	05	*Indefatigable* (244 tns)	Henzell, J.	London	Charlottetown	26
1820	05	*Margaret*	n/k	Plymouth (Devon)	Charlottetown	21

Mr. J.N. LePage and twenty passengers.

Year	Month	Vessel	Master	Departure Port	Arrival Port	Passenger Numbers
1820	05	*Mary* (374 tns)	Elsdon, Henry	Bristol	Charlottetown	21

The *Mary* was built in 1817 (Lloyd's Shipping Code "A2").

Year	Month	Vessel	Master	Departure Port	Arrival Port	Passenger Numbers
1820	05	*Nautilus* (289 tns)	Mitchell, N.	Plymouth (Devon)	Charlottetown	14
1820	05	*Plymouth Dock Hero*		Plymouth (Devon)	Charlottetown	26
1820	07	*Caldicott Castle* (268 tns)	Hart, Patrick	Newcastle-upon-Tyne	Charlottetown	12
1820	08	*Anglia* (242 tns)	Ord, T.M.	London	Charlottetown	10
1820	08	*Fame* (240 tns)	Robinson, James	London	Charlottetown	17
1820	10	*Commerce* (389 tns)	Chantler, William	Bristol	Charlottetown	8
1820	10	*Jane* (82 tns)	Avery, James (from Bideford)	Bristol	Charlottetown	2

Year	Month	Vessel	Master	Departure Port	Arrival Port	Passenger Numbers
1820	10	*Lord Exmouth* (204 tns)	Barrett, Samuel	Plymouth (Devon)	Charlottetown	11
1820	10	*Mary* (s, 374 tns)	Elsdon, Henry	Bristol	Charlottetown	8
1820	10	*Speculation* (sw, 155 tns)	Richards, Thomas	Plymouth (Devon)	Charlottetown	2

The *Speculation* was a prize (Lloyd's Shipping Code "E1").

Year	Month	Vessel	Master	Departure Port	Arrival Port	Passenger Numbers
1820	n/k	*Anglim*	n/k	Workington (Cumberland)	Charlottetown	n/k
1820	n/k	*Dixon*	Roberts, James	Hull	P.E.I./N.B.	23

Landed twenty-three passengers at P.E.I. and Bouctouche, N.B. See Elliott, "English Immigration to P.E.I." (40), 7.

Year	Month	Vessel	Master	Departure Port	Arrival Port	Passenger Numbers
1820	n/k	*Prince George*	n/k	n/k	P.E.I./N.B.	n/k

Sailed to the Miramichi. One of the passengers, Mary Hosear, settled at Lot 20. See MacKinnon and Warburton, *Past and Present of P.E.I.*, 422.

Year	Month	Vessel	Master	Departure Port	Arrival Port	Passenger Numbers
1821	05	*Caldicott Castle* (268 tns)	Hart, Patrick	Newcastle-upon-Tyne	Charlottetown	16
1821	05	*Carron* (bg, 228 tns)	Short, Ralph	London	Charlottetown	2

Passengers: Mrs. Short, Hon. Wm. Pleace.

Year	Month	Vessel	Master	Departure Port	Arrival Port	Passenger Numbers
1821	05	*Hope*	n/k	Whitehaven (Cumberland)	Charlottetown	16
1821	05	*Lord Exmouth* (204 tns)	Barret, Samuel	Fowey (Cornwall)	Charlottetown	1

Passenger was Francis Bullin.

Year	Month	Vessel	Master	Departure Port	Arrival Port	Passenger Numbers
1821	05	*Margaret* (310 tns)	Reavely, Henry	Plymouth (Devon)	Charlottetown	21

The *Margaret* was built in 1805 (Lloyd's Shipping Code "A1").

Year	Month	Vessel	Master	Departure Port	Arrival Port	Passenger Numbers
1821	05	*Nautilus* (289 tns)	n/k	Plymouth (Devon)	Charlottetown	1

Passenger was Mr. Pope.

Year	Month	Vessel	Master	Departure Port	Arrival Port	Passenger Numbers
1821	05	*Pitt* (320 tns)	Hamilton, J.	Liverpool	Charlottetown	93

Cabin passengers were: Mr. and Mrs. McKay, Mr. R. Brecken, plus ninety steerage passengers. The *Pitt* was built in 1806 (Lloyd's Shipping Code "E1").

Year	Month	Vessel	Master	Departure Port	Arrival Port	Passenger Numbers
1821	05	*Sarah*	Frank	Falmouth (Cornwall)	Charlottetown	1

Passenger was Mr. Seymour.

Year	Month	Vessel	Master	Departure Port	Arrival Port	Passenger Numbers
1821	05	*Speculation* (sw, 155 tns)	Richards, Thomas	Plymouth (Devon)	Charlottetown	6
1821	07	*Friendship* (160 tns)	Williamson, J.	Whitehaven (Cumberland)	Charlottetown	33
1821	07	*Rose* (134 tns)	n/k	Whitehaven (Cumberland)	Charlottetown	10
1821	09	*Nautilus* (289 tns)	Mitchell, A.	Plymouth (Devon)	Charlottetown	9
1821	11	*Relief* (bg, 251 tns)	n/k	Liverpool	Charlottetown	5

Passengers: Alex. Campbell of Bedeque, Dr. Meckieson, plus three other passengers. The *Relief* was built in 1821 (Lloyd's Shipping Code "A1").

Year	Month	Vessel	Master	Departure Port	Arrival Port	Passenger Numbers
1822	05	*Carron* (bg, 228 tns)	Short, Ralph	London	Charlottetown	5

Passengers: Mrs. Short, Mr. J. Brecken Jr., Mr. J. Brecken Sr., Mr. Gates, and his son.

Year	Month	Vessel	Master	Departure Port	Arrival Port	Passenger Numbers
1822	05	*Elizabeth*	Taggart, John	Plymouth (Devon)	Charlottetown	19
1822	05	*John* (bg, 317 tns)	n/k	Bristol	Charlottetown	9

Mr. Blatch and eight steerage passengers.

Year	Month	Vessel	Master	Departure Port	Arrival Port	Passenger Numbers
1822	05	*Margaret* (310 tns)	Reavely, Henry	Plymouth (Devon)	Charlottetown	22
1822	05	*Relief* (bg, 251 tns)	Todd, Simon	Liverpool	Charlottetown	2

James Reilly and one other passenger.

Year	Month	Vessel	Master	Departure Port	Arrival Port	Passenger Numbers
1822	06	*Mary* (s, 374 tns)	Elsdon, Henry	Bristol	Charlottetown	31
1822	08	*John* (bg, 317 tns)	Wall, Richard	Bristol	Charlottetown	11
1822	10	*Mary* (s, 374 tns)	Elsdon, Henry	Bristol	Charlottetown	9
1823	05	*Bideford* (162 tns)	Butters, Thomas	Plymouth (Devon)	Charlottetown	10
1823	09	*Eliza* (204 tns)	Scott, Wm.	Liverpool	Charlottetown	n/k

Passengers included Reverend Mr. Adin and daughters.

Year	Month	Vessel	Master	Departure Port	Arrival Port	Passenger Numbers
1823	10	*Eclipse* (136 tns)	Carr, G.	Plymouth (Devon)	Charlottetown	4
1823	10	*Speculation* (sw, 155 tns)	Richards, T.	Plymouth (Devon)	Charlottetown	17
1823	11	*Amity* (s, 333 tns)	Johnson, John	Bristol	Charlottetown	1

Passenger was William Pope. The *Amity* was built in 1823 (Lloyd's Shipping Code "A").

Year	Month	Vessel	Master	Departure Port	Arrival Port	Passenger Numbers
1824	05	*Amity* (s, 333 tns)	Johnson, John	Bristol	Charlottetown	12

Passengers were Mr. Lewellin and family, plus ten carpenters and sawyers.

Year	Month	Vessel	Master	Departure Port	Arrival Port	Passenger Numbers
1824	05	*Carron* (bg, 228 tns)	Strachan, H.	London	Charlottetown	44

Passengers: Hon. Thomas Haviland, Miss Haviland, John Brecken, plus forty-one others.

Year	Month	Vessel	Master	Departure Port	Arrival Port	Passenger Numbers
1824	05	*King David* (276 tns)	Robinson, J.	Bristol	Charlottetown	34

Passengers: Captains Young and Pearce, Mr. Douse, Lemuel Cambridge, plus thirty workmen for shipbuilding (to Souris).

Year	Month	Vessel	Master	Departure Port	Arrival Port	Passenger Numbers
1824	05	*Medusa* (217 tns)	Hutchinson, J.	London	Charlottetown	n/k
1824	05	*Relief* (bg, 251 tns)	Morison, J.	Liverpool	Charlottetown	34

Passengers: Alex. Campbell, Mr. Pollock, Joseph Higgins, Captain James and wife, Mr. Martin, Mr. Cooksey, Captain Crowther, plus twenty-six workmen.

Year	Month	Vessel	Master	Departure Port	Arrival Port	Passenger Numbers
1824	05	*Speculation* (sw, 155 tns)	Browning	Plymouth (Devon)	Charlottetown	n/k
1824	06	*Douglas* (146 tns)	Eales, Samuel	Liverpool	Charlottetown	1

Passenger was Charles Worrell.

Year	Month	Vessel	Master	Departure Port	Arrival Port	Passenger Numbers
1824	06	*Eddystone* (244 tns)	Dale, J.	London	Charlottetown	6

One of the passengers was Mr. Johnston, who was proceeding on to the Miramichi.

Year	Month	Vessel	Master	Departure Port	Arrival Port	Passenger Numbers
1824	06	*Rover* (92 tns)	Brown, James	Bideford (Devon)	Charlottetown	21

Passengers: T.B. Chanter plus twenty shipwrights and mariners.

Year	Month	Vessel	Master	Departure Port	Arrival Port	Passenger Numbers
1824	08	*Liberty* (156 tns)	n/k	Plymouth (Devon)	Charlottetown	1

Passenger was Mr. Peake.

Year	Month	Vessel	Master	Departure Port	Arrival Port	Passenger Numbers
1824	09	*Brisk* (155 tns)	Holliday, John	Liverpool	Charlottetown	n/k

Passengers included Messrs. Kempts.

Year	Month	Vessel	Master	Departure Port	Arrival Port	Passenger Numbers
1824	10	*Jane Hatton* (124 tns)	Gale, Samuel	Liverpool	Charlottetown	1

Passenger was Duncan MacKay.

Year	Month	Vessel	Master	Departure Port	Arrival Port	Passenger Numbers
1824	10	John (bg, 317 tns)	Chantler, Wm.	Bristol	Charlottetown	>10

Passengers: Mrs. L. Cambridge and family, Miss McDonald, Captain John Stewart, John Hurdis, private secretary, and a number in the steerage.

1825	05	Amity (s, 333 tns)	Johnson, John	Bristol	Charlottetown	11

"To Three Rivers" (near Georgetown).

1825	05	Carron (bg, 228 tns)	Strachan, H.	London	Charlottetown	2

Passengers: Samuel Welsford, Captain Spencer.

1825	05	Idas (243 tns)	Ramsden	Liverpool	Charlottetown	3

Passengers: Angus MacDonald, Mrs. MacDonald, and Lt. Colin MacDonald.

1825	05	John (bg, 317 tns)	Raye, Richard	Bristol	Charlottetown	1

Passenger was Hon. George Wright.

1825	05	Sovereign (110 tns)	n/k	Dartmouth (Devon)	Charlottetown	1

Passenger was Mr. Curtis.

1825	06	Speculation (sw, 155 tns)	Codnor, Richard	Plymouth (Devon)	Charlottetown	16

Passengers: Thomas Peake, Mr. Walker, plus fourteen others in the steerage.

1825	09	Loyalist (311 tns)	Rames, James	London	Charlottetown	1

Passenger was Theo. Stewart.

1825	10	Amity (s, 333 tns)	Johnson, John	Bristol	Charlottetown	1

Passenger was Charles Wright, Surveyor General.

1826	05	Amity (s, 333 tns)	n/k	Bristol	Charlottetown	2

Passengers: Mr. Lewellin, Mr. Douse.

Year	Month	Vessel	Master	Departure Port	Arrival Port	Passenger Numbers
1826	05	*Argus*	n/k	Plymouth (Devon)	Charlottetown	3

Passengers: William Pope, Jonathan Pope, Captain Lash.

Year	Month	Vessel	Master	Departure Port	Arrival Port	Passenger Numbers
1826	05	*Bideford* (bg, 162 tns)	n/k	Plymouth (Devon)	Charlottetown	8

| 1826 | 05 | *Carron* (228 tns) | Strachan, H. | London | Charlottetown | 5 |

Passengers: Miss Brecken, Mr. Brecken, Mr. Dodd, Mr. C.D. Rankin, Captain Blake.

| 1826 | 05 | *Hannah* (238 tns) | Scott, Wm. | Liverpool | Charlottetown | >10 |

Passengers: Mr. J. McGregor, Samuel Braddock, James Jackson, Miss Jackson, and several passengers in steerage.

| 1826 | 05 | *Mary* (414 tns) | Findlay, Alexr. | Plymouth (Devon) | Charlottetown | 1 |

Passenger was Frederick LePage.

| 1826 | 06 | *Bellona* (bg, 271 tns) | England, Richard | Bideford (Devon) | Charlottetown | 1 |

Passenger was Thomas Burnard Chanter.

| 1826 | 06 | *Catherine McDonald* (bg, 302 tns) | Williams, Joseph | Liverpool | Charlottetown | 2 |

Passengers: Mr. and Mrs. Hugh McDonald.

| 1826 | 06 | *Restitution* (s, 317 tns) | Fox, Wm. | Plymouth (Devon) | Charlottetown | 1 |

Passenger was Mr. Billing.

| 1826 | 06 | *William* (bg, 161 tns) | Newell, Jas. | Liverpool | Charlottetown | >10 |

Passengers: Ewen Cameron, Captain Thomson (on his way to Pictou), Mr. Morrison, and several in steerage.

Year	Month	Vessel	Master	Departure Port	Arrival Port	Passenger Numbers
1826	08	*Pretty Lass* (sr, 113 tns)	Eales, Saml.	Plymouth (Devon)	Charlottetown	3

Passengers: Mr. Peake, Mr. Hodge, George Winslow.

Year	Month	Vessel	Master	Departure Port	Arrival Port	Passenger Numbers
1826	12	*Mary* (374 tns)	Toms, John	London	Charlottetown	16

Passengers: Lt. Governor Ready and two daughters, Donald MacDonald of Glenaladale, Mr. Lewis, Mr. and Mrs. Dunk and five servants, Lieutenant Ridge, a sergeant and two privates of the Royal Staff Corps on their way to Canada.

Year	Month	Vessel	Master	Departure Port	Arrival Port	Passenger Numbers
1827	05	*Carron* (bg, 228 tns)	Strachan, H.	London	Charlottetown	12

Passengers: Mr. Stone and son, Mr. Davies, Messrs. Mawley, Spalding, Coates, and Mills, and William Cooper, and four others. Mr. Cooper was an island resident returning from selling his vessel, the *Hackmatack*, in Britain.

Year	Month	Vessel	Master	Departure Port	Arrival Port	Passenger Numbers
1827	05	*Dungallon* (bg, 233 tns)	James, J.W.	Liverpool	Charlottetown	1

Passenger was Colin McDonald.

Year	Month	Vessel	Master	Departure Port	Arrival Port	Passenger Numbers
1827	05	*Felicity* (bk)	Gyles	Bristol	Murray Harbour	5

Passengers: Mr. Owen, Mr. Lewellin and son, Mr. Weir, Mr. Sargent.

Year	Month	Vessel	Master	Departure Port	Arrival Port	Passenger Numbers
1827	05	*John Thomas* (bk)	Reavely, Henry	Liverpool	Charlottetown	4

Passengers: Frederick and Elizabeth LePage, Henry Palmer, and Mrs. Smith.

Year	Month	Vessel	Master	Departure Port	Arrival Port	Passenger Numbers
1827	06	*Bellona* (bg, 271 tns)	England, Richard	Bideford (Devon)	Richmond Bay	1

Passenger was Mr. Chanter.

Year	Month	Vessel	Master	Departure Port	Arrival Port	Passenger Numbers
1827	06	*New Bideford* (bg)	Babb	Plymouth (Devon)	New London	1

Passenger was Mr. Nicholls.

Year	Month	Vessel	Master	Departure Port	Arrival Port	Passenger Numbers
1827	09	*Relief* (bg, 251 tns)	Burton	Liverpool	Richmond Bay	4

Passengers: Mr. and Mrs. Hutchinson, Mr. Christopher Cross, Miss Mary Johnson

Year	Month	Vessel	Master	Departure Port	Arrival Port	Passenger Numbers
1828	05	*New Bideford* (bg)	Mathewson	Plymouth (Devon)	Charlottetown	n/k
1828	06	*Elizabeth* (bg)	Codner	Liverpool	Cascumpec	n/k
1828	06	*Thorntons* (bk)	Brown	Liverpool	Charlottetown	1

Passenger was Angus McDonald of Three Rivers, P.E.I.

Year	Month	Vessel	Master	Departure Port	Arrival Port	Passenger Numbers
1828	09	*Speculation* (sw, 155 tns)	Newman	Plymouth (Devon)	Charlottetown	n/k
1828	10	*Amity* (s, 333 tns)	Younger	Bristol	Charlottetown	n/k
1828	10	*James* (bg)	Peake, Thomas	Liverpool	Charlottetown	4

Vessel owned by the Peake family.

Year	Month	Vessel	Master	Departure Port	Arrival Port	Passenger Numbers
1829	05	*Argo* (bg)	Walker	Liverpool	Georgetown	n/k
1829	05	*Felicity* (bk)	n/k	Bristol	Murray Harbour	>10

Passengers: John Campbell, Captain Younger, plus several in steerage.

Year	Month	Vessel	Master	Departure Port	Arrival Port	Passenger Numbers
1829	05	*James* (bg)		Plymouth (Devon)	Charlottetown	4

Passengers: Messrs. Peake, Sharpe, Duchemin, and Davis.

Year	Month	Vessel	Master	Departure Port	Arrival Port	Passenger Numbers
1829	05	*New Bideford* (bg)	Matthewson	Plymouth (Devon)	Charlottetown	n/k
1829	06	*Amelia* (bg, 254 tns)	n/k	Liverpool	Charlottetown	n/k

The *Amelia* was built in 1828 in P.E.I. (Lloyd's Shipping Code "E1").

Year	Month	Vessel	Master	Departure Port	Arrival Port	Passenger Numbers
1829	06	*Calypso* (bk, 265 tns)	Lowther	Liverpool and Bideford	Charlottetown	5

Passengers: Charles Ready, son of His Excellency the Lt. Governor, Mr. and Mrs. Chanter, Miss Hodgson, and Miss Griffiths. The *Calypso* was built in 1829 (Lloyd's Shipping Code "E1").

Year	Month	Vessel	Master	Departure Port	Arrival Port	Passenger Numbers
1829	06	*Collina* (bg, 156 tns)	Martin	London	Charlottetown	2

Passengers: Edward Holland and Mr. Hele. The *Collina* was built in 1827 (Lloyd's Shipping Code "E1").

Year	Month	Vessel	Master	Departure Port	Arrival Port	Passenger Numbers
1829	06	*Minerva*	n/k	Great Yarmouth (Norfolk)	Charlottetown	12

"Settlers."

Year	Month	Vessel	Master	Departure Port	Arrival Port	Passenger Numbers
1829	06	*Nancy* (sr)	n/k	Liverpool	Charlottetown	32

"32 settlers from Kent County." They mainly settled at Lot 33. The group included Alfred Horne from Canterbury.

Year	Month	Vessel	Master	Departure Port	Arrival Port	Passenger Numbers
1829	06	*New London* (bg)	Redmore	Plymouth (Devon)	Charlottetown	n/k
1829	08	*Thomas*	n/k	London	Charlottetown	n/k
1829	09	*Felicity* (bk)	Dugdale	Bristol	Charlottetown	19

Passengers: Hon. George Wright, William Hodges, Miss Folkstone, plus sixteen in steerage.

Year	Month	Vessel	Master	Departure Port	Arrival Port	Passenger Numbers
1829	09	*Three Sons*	Smith	Liverpool	Charlottetown	7

Passengers: Mr. Cavendish, John and Abercrombie Willock, Mrs. Willock and servant, plus two steerage passengers.

Year	Month	Vessel	Master	Departure Port	Arrival Port	Passenger Numbers
1829	12	*Brothers*	n/k	Liverpool	Charlottetown	n/k
1829	12	*Isabella*	n/k	Liverpool	Charlottetown	n/k
1830	05	*Collina* (bg, 156 tns)	Martin, W.	Bideford (Devon)	Charlottetown	74

Men, women, and children. "The men consist of farmers and mechanics and are chiefly from the counties of Devon and Cornwall."

Year	Month	Vessel	Master	Departure Port	Arrival Port	Passenger Numbers
1830	05	*Felicity* (bk)	n/k	Bristol	Charlottetown	2

Passengers: John S. Smith, Mr. Sharpe.

Year	Month	Vessel	Master	Departure Port	Arrival Port	Passenger Numbers
1830	05	*James* (bg)	Peake, Thomas	Plymouth (Devon)	Charlottetown	4

Passengers: Mr. John T. Thomas, Miss Moyer, and two in steerage. "Loss of her main top mast and the life of a man …."

Year	Month	Vessel	Master	Departure Port	Arrival Port	Passenger Numbers
1830	05	*Mary Jane*	Pile	Plymouth (Devon)	Charlottetown	6

Steerage passengers. Ship owned by the Peake family.

Year	Month	Vessel	Master	Departure Port	Arrival Port	Passenger Numbers
1830	06	*Amelia* (bg, 254 tns)	Davies	London	Charlottetown	n/k

Year	Month	Vessel	Master	Departure Port	Arrival Port	Passenger Numbers
1830	06	*Bacchus* (bg)	How	Bideford (Devon)	Richmond Bay	n/k

Year	Month	Vessel	Master	Departure Port	Arrival Port	Passenger Numbers
1830	06	*Breakwater* (bg, 180 tns)	Newman, W.	Plymouth (Devon)	New London	8

The *Breakwater* was built in P.E.I. (Lloyd's Shipping Code "E1").

Year	Month	Vessel	Master	Departure Port	Arrival Port	Passenger Numbers
1830	06	*Calypso* (bk, 265 tns)	Lowther	Falmouth (Cornwall)	Richmond Bay	n/k

Year	Month	Vessel	Master	Departure Port	Arrival Port	Passenger Numbers
1830	06	*Cornwallis* (bg)	McLeod	Liverpool	Charlottetown	n/k

Year	Month	Vessel	Master	Departure Port	Arrival Port	Passenger Numbers
1830	06	*Elizabeth* (bg)	Lang	Liverpool	Cascumpec	n/k

Year	Month	Vessel	Master	Departure Port	Arrival Port	Passenger Numbers
1830	06	*Euphemia*	n/k	Falmouth (Cornwall)	Charlottetown	n/k

Year	Month	Vessel	Master	Departure Port	Arrival Port	Passenger Numbers
1830	06	*New Bideford* (bg)	Mathewson	Plymouth (Devon)	Richmond Bay	70

Passengers: Mrs. P. Duchemin and family, Mrs. Miller, and sixty-three settlers.

Year	Month	Vessel	Master	Departure Port	Arrival Port	Passenger Numbers
1830	06	*Sappho* (bg, 110 tns)	Day, W.	Bideford (Devon)	Charlottetown	4

The *Sappho* was built in 1829 (Lloyd's Shipping Code "A").

Year	Month	Vessel	Master	Departure Port	Arrival Port	Passenger Numbers
1830	07	*Doris* (bg)	Roberts	Liverpool	Charlottetown	n/k

Year	Month	Vessel	Master	Departure Port	Arrival Port	Passenger Numbers
1830	07	*Hibernia* (s)	Owston	Chatham (London)	Charlottetown	n/k
1830	08	*Brothers* (bg)	Poland	Teignmouth (Devon)	Charlottetown	n/k
1830	08	*Minerva*	[nk]	Great Yarmouth (Norfolk)	Charlottetown	80

"Settlers."

Year	Month	Vessel	Master	Departure Port	Arrival Port	Passenger Numbers
1830	08	*Venus* (bk, 268 tns)	Simmons	Great Yarmouth (Norfolk)	Charlottetown	80

Immigrants from Norfolk and Suffolk. The *Venus* was built in 1809 (Lloyd's Shipping Code "E1").

Year	Month	Vessel	Master	Departure Port	Arrival Port	Passenger Numbers
1830	09	*Mary Jane*	Pile	Plymouth (Devon)	Charlottetown	n/k

A Peake family vessel.

Year	Month	Vessel	Master	Departure Port	Arrival Port	Passenger Numbers
1830	10	*Bacchus* (bg)	Howes	Bideford (Devon)	Charlottetown	n/k
1830	11	*Amelia* (bg, 254 tns)	Davies	Plymouth (Devon)	Charlottetown	n/k
1830	11	*Collina* (bg, 156 tns)	Martin, W.	Bideford (Devon)	Charlottetown	n/k
1830	11	*Elizabeth* (bg)	Lang	Dartmouth (Devon)	Charlottetown	14
1830	11	*Royal Edward* (bk)	Harrison	Liverpool	Charlottetown	n/k

Year	Month	Vessel	Master	Departure Port	Arrival Port	Passenger Numbers
1830	n/k	*Rosa*		Great Yarmouth (Norfolk)	Charlottetown /Quebec	50

Passengers from Suffolk. A total of 160 passengers had sailed to Quebec, but fifty decided to settle in P.E.I. (See Elliott, "English Immigration to Prince Edward Island" (41), 5.

| 1831 | 04 | *Mary Jane* | n/k | Plymouth (Devon) | Charlottetown | n/k |

Owned by Peake family.

| 1831 | 05 | *Adelaide* | n/k | Plymouth (Devon) | Charlottetown | n/k |

| 1831 | 05 | *Amelia* (bg, 254 tns) | n/k | London | Charlottetown | 10 |

Passengers: Mr. and Mrs. Gates and children, Miss Mary Stewart, Mr. Sabine.

| 1831 | 05 | *Breakwater* (bg, 180 tns) | n/k | Plymouth (Devon) | New London | 29 |

Passengers: Thomas Billing and twenty-eight settlers to go to New London.

| 1831 | 05 | *Brothers* | n/k | Teignmouth (Devon) | Charlottetown | n/k |

| 1831 | 05 | *Preston* (sw, 200 tns) | Woodthorpe, Thomas | Great Yarmouth (Norfolk) | Charlottetown | n/k |

The *Preston* was built in 1823 (Lloyd's Shipping Code "A1").

| 1831 | 05 | *Restitution* (s, 317 tns) | n/k | Plymouth (Devon) | Charlottetown | 41 |

Passengers: Lieutenant Bolman, R.N., Mrs. Bolman, plus thirty-nine others.

| 1831 | 06 | *Baltic* (bg, 252 tns) | Ebbage, Thomas | Great Yarmouth (Norfolk) | Charlottetown /Quebec | 152 |

The *Minerva* sailed with the *Baltic* and together they carried 274 passengers of whom 160 landed at P.E.I. and 114 at Quebec. Ship departure for *Baltic* was advertised in the *Norwich Mercury* April 9, 1831. The *Baltic* was built in 1820 (Lloyd's Shipping Code "E1").

Year	Month	Vessel	Master	Departure Port	Arrival Port	Passenger Numbers
1831	06	*Collina* (bg, 156 tns)	n/k	Bideford (Devon)	Charlottetown	n/k
1831	06	*Minerva*	n/k	Great Yarmouth (Norfolk)	Charlottetown /Quebec	122

Chiefly farm labourers and their wives and families. They included John Birt, John Cook, William Smith, Charles Gibbs, and Samuel Mayhew. Also see entry for the *Baltic* (1831). The *Suffolk Chronicle* of March 1, 1832, carried an advertisement for the crossing of *Minerva* to P.E.I. and Quebec, but there is no evidence of any passengers being taken by her that year.

Year	Month	Vessel	Master	Departure Port	Arrival Port	Passenger Numbers
1831	06	*Sappho* (bg, 110 tns)	n/k	Bideford (Devon)	Charlottetown	33
1831	09	*Adelaide*	n/k	Bristol	Charlottetown	n/k
1831	09	*Felicity* (bk)	n/k	Bristol	Murray Harbour	n/k
1831	09	*George & Henry*	n/k	Liverpool	Charlottetown	n/k
1831	09	*Mary Jane*	n/k	Plymouth (Devon)	Charlottetown	n/k

Peake family vessel.

Year	Month	Vessel	Master	Departure Port	Arrival Port	Passenger Numbers
1831	09	*Royal William* (bk, 340 tns)	Peake, Thomas	Plymouth (Devon)	Charlottetown	2

Passengers: Mr. and Mrs. Murray, on their way to Quebec.

Year	Month	Vessel	Master	Departure Port	Arrival Port	Passenger Numbers
1831	10	*Amelia* (bg, 254 tns)	n/k	London (Downs)	Orwell Bay	8

Passengers: Mr. and Mrs. Mearns and four children, Mrs. Riddell, Captain C.D. Rankin.

Year	Month	Vessel	Master	Departure Port	Arrival Port	Passenger Numbers
1831	10	*Ellen*	n/k	Bideford (Devon)	Charlottetown	n/k

Passengers: Mrs. Westacott and family, Mr. Gavraut.

Year	Month	Vessel	Master	Departure Port	Arrival Port	Passenger Numbers
1831	10	*William Pitt*	n/k	London	Charlottetown /Quebec	2

Passengers: Mr. and Mrs. Murray.

Year	Month	Vessel	Master	Departure Port	Arrival Port	Passenger Numbers
1831	11	*Sappho* (bg, 110 tns)	n/k	Bideford (Devon)	Charlottetown	n/k
1832	05	*Amelia* (bg, 254 tns)	Davies	London	Charlottetown	6

Passengers: Mr. and Mrs. E. Holland and four others.

Year	Month	Vessel	Master	Departure Port	Arrival Port	Passenger Numbers
1832	05	*Amyntas* (bg)	Matthewson, John	Plymouth (Devon)	Charlottetown	17

Passengers: Mr. William Compton and sixteen others.

Year	Month	Vessel	Master	Departure Port	Arrival Port	Passenger Numbers
1832	05	*Baltic* (bg, 252 tns)	Ebbage, Thomas	Great Yarmouth (Norfolk)	Charlottetown /Quebec	46

The *Baltic* carried ninety-six passengers (Mr. and Mrs. Worthy and son plus ninety-three in the steerage), fifty of whom went on to Quebec.

Year	Month	Vessel	Master	Departure Port	Arrival Port	Passenger Numbers
1832	05	*Calypso* (bk, 265 tns)	Grossard, Lewis	Bideford (Devon)	Richmond Bay	197

Mainly mechanics and labourers.

Year	Month	Vessel	Master	Departure Port	Arrival Port	Passenger Numbers
1832	05	*Fame*	n/k	Bideford (Devon)	Richmond Bay	n/k
1832	05	*Mary Jane*	n/k	Liverpool	Charlottetown	3

Passengers: Lieutenant Colin McDonald, Mr. Francis Longworth Jr., Mr. Irving.

Year	Month	Vessel	Master	Departure Port	Arrival Port	Passenger Numbers
1832	05	*Preston* (sw, 200 tns)	Waters, J.	Great Yarmouth (Norfolk)	Charlottetown /Quebec	79

A total of 152 passengers sailed; seventy-nine disembarked at Charlottetown and seventy-three went on to Quebec.

Year	Month	Vessel	Master	Departure Port	Arrival Port	Passenger Numbers
1832	05	*Royal William* (bk, 340 tns)	Peake, Thomas	Plymouth (Devon)	Charlottetown	24

Passengers: Mr. James Peake, Mr. Bell, Surgeon, Mr. Perkins, Captain Nicholls, and twenty in steerage. The *Royal William* was built in 1831 (Lloyd's Shipping Code "A1").

Year	Month	Vessel	Master	Departure Port	Arrival Port	Passenger Numbers
1832	06	*Breakwater* (bg, 180 tns)	n/k	Plymouth (Devon)	Richmond Bay	50
1832	06	*Calypso* (bk, 265 tns)	Grossard, Lewis	Bideford (Devon)	Charlottetown	n/k
1832	06	*Fame*	Cowell, Wm. J.	Plymouth (Devon)	Charlottetown	n/k
1832	06	*Sarah and Eliza* (bg, 161 tns)	n/k	Bideford (Devon)	Charlottetown	75

All in good health. Passengers include Mr. Bartlett and family, who were on their way to Canada. The *Sara and Eliza* was built in 1806 (Lloyd's Shipping Code "E1").

Year	Month	Vessel	Master	Departure Port	Arrival Port	Passenger Numbers
1832	07	*Amity* (s, 333 tns)	Andrews, Samuel	Bristol	Charlottetown	28

The *Amity* called at New Brunswick on her way to Charlottetown.

Year	Month	Vessel	Master	Departure Port	Arrival Port	Passenger Numbers
1832	07	*Ellen*	n/k	Bideford (Devon)	Charlottetown	20
1832	07	n/k	n/k	Bideford (Devon)	Charlottetown	8

Vessel had sailed from Bideford via Saint John.

Year	Month	Vessel	Master	Departure Port	Arrival Port	Passenger Numbers
1832	07	*Norma*	n/k	Liverpool	Charlottetown	n/k
1832	10	*Amelia* (bg, 254 tns)	Davies	Plymouth (Devon)	Charlottetown	4

Passengers: Mr. and Mrs. Livett, Mrs. Charles Stewart, Miss Ellen Stewart.

Year	Month	Vessel	Master	Departure Port	Arrival Port	Passenger Numbers
1832	10	*Amyntas* (bg)	Matthewson, John	Penzance (Cornwall)	Charlottetown	n/k

Year	Month	Vessel	Master	Departure Port	Arrival Port	Passenger Numbers
1832	10	*Bollina* (bg)	Heay	Bideford (Devon)	Charlottetown	n/k
1832	10	*Royal William* (bk, 340 tns)	Peake, Thomas	Plymouth (Devon)	Charlottetown	14

At the Quarantine Ground. Passengers: Mr. Pethick, Mr. Nicholl, Mr. Smardon, Mr. Small and two Misses Smalls, and eight others.

1833	05	*Amelia* (bg, 254 tns)	n/k	London	Charlottetown	1

Passenger was Mrs. Monckton.

1833	05	*Breakwater* (bg, 180 tns)	n/k	Plymouth (Devon)	Charlottctown	11

Passengers: Charles and Thomas Connery, and nine in the steerage.

1833	05	*Royal William* (bk, 340 tns)	Peake, Thomas	Plymouth (Devon)	Charlottetown	n/k
1833	06	*Amity* (s, 333 tns)	n/k	Bristol	Charlottetown	7

Passengers: Mr. and Mrs. Stewart of Mount Stewart, Mr. W. Douse, and four in steerage.

1833	06	*Baltic* (bg, 252 tns)	Freeman, James	Great Yarmouth (Norfolk)	Charlottetown	24

In all, sixty-three passengers: twenty-four landed at Charlottetown, thirty-nine went on to Quebec.

1833	06	*Ellen*	n/k	Bideford (Devon)	Charlottetown	2
1833	06	*Sarah and Eliza* (bg, 161 tns)	n/k	Bideford (Devon)	Charlottetown	40

Fourteen of the passengers left for Bathurst, New Brunswick, and a few left for the U.S

1833	09	*Royal William* (bk, 340 tns)	n/k	Plymouth (Devon)	Charlottetown	3

Passengers: Mr. and Mrs. Connelly and Mr. F. Goodman.

Year	Month	Vessel	Master	Departure Port	Arrival Port	Passenger Numbers
1833	10	*Amelia* (bg, 254 tns)	n/k	London	Charlottetown	5

Mrs. Walpole and three children, and Edward Rotson.

| 1833 | 10 | *Amity* (s, 333 tns) | n/k | Bristol | Murray Harbour | n/k |

| 1833 | 10 | *Ellen* | n/k | Bideford (Devon) | Charlottetown | n/k |

| 1834 | 05 | *Britannia* | n/k | London | Charlottetown | 1 |

Passenger was Captain Davis.

| 1834 | 05 | *Calypso* (bk, 265 tns) | n/k | Bideford (Devon) | Charlottetown | 56 |

Passengers: Hon. T.H. Haviland, Miss Brecken, Captain Marshal, Mr. R.W. Rennels, and fifty-two in steerage.

| 1834 | 05 | *Eliza* | n/k | Plymouth (Devon) | Charlottetown | n/k |

| 1834 | 05 | *Royal William* (bk, 340 tns) | n/k | Plymouth (Devon) | Charlottetown | 9 |

Passengers: John Peake, Colin MacDonald, William Nichol, and six in the steerage.

| 1834 | 05 | *Temperance* | n/k | Liverpool | Charlottetown | 2 |

Passengers: Mr. Andrew Duncan and Captain Snell.

| 1834 | 08 | *Sappho* (bg, 110 tns) | n/k | Liverpool | Charlottetown | n/k |

| 1834 | 08 | *Superb* | n/k | Liverpool | Three Rivers | 5 |

Passengers: Hon. Robert Hodgson, Attorney General of this island, Major Burrows , his two sons, and Miss MacDonald.

| 1834 | 08 | *Unity* | n/k | Liverpool | Charlottetown | 1 |

Passenger was Mr. Dennis Reddin.

Year	Month	Vessel	Master	Departure Port	Arrival Port	Passenger Numbers
1834	09	*Eliza*	n/k	Newport (Isle of Wight?)	Charlottetown	1

Passenger was Miss Edwards.

1834	09	*Royal William* (bk, 340 tns)	n/k	Plymouth (Devon)	Charlottetown	12

Passengers: Mr. and Mrs. Hurdis, Mr. George Tanton, Miss A. Davis, and eight others.

1834	10	*Britannia* (bg)	Roxby	London	Charlottetown	2

Passengers: Daniel Brenan, James Ritson.

1834	10	*Ebenezer*	Marshall, James	Bideford (Devon)	Charlottetown	n/k

1835	05	*Amelia* (bg, 254 tns)	n/k	London	Charlottetown	4

Passengers: Lieutenant Charles Young, R.A. (son of His Excellency, the Lieutenant Governor), George and Chester Woolner, Miss Mary Ashley.

1835	05	*Eliza*	n/k	Gloucester	Charlottetown	2

Passengers: Mr. Kelly, Mr. Bovyer.

1835	05	*Mary Jane*	n/k	Bridgewater (Somerset)	Charlottetown	n/k

Mary Jane owned by Peake family. *Royal Gazette*, May 19, 1835, states passengers were on their way to Ohio. They were William Haine, Stephen and John Syms, and John West.

1835	05	*Royal William* (bk, 340 tns)	n/k	Plymouth (Devon)	Charlottetown	n/k

1835	06	*Cato* (bk)	Crossman	Plymouth (Devon)	Charlottetown	4

1835	06	*Sarah and Eliza* (bg, 161 tns)	Marshall, James	Bideford (Devon)	Charlottetown	20

Total of sixty passengers: Twenty disembarked at Charlottetown. The remaining forty sailed on to Quebec.

1835	09	*Eliza*	n/k	Penzance (Cornwall)	Charlottetown	n/k

Year	Month	Vessel	Master	Departure Port	Arrival Port	Passenger Numbers
1835	09	*Mary Jane*	n/k	Plymouth (Devon)	Charlottetown	10

Passengers: Mr. and Mrs. Buckston and three children, plus five in steerage. A child was killed in a mishap during the crossing.

1835	09	*Royal William* (bk, 340 tns)	n/k	Liverpool	Charlottetown	n/k

1835	09	*Welsford*	n/k	Bristol	Three Rivers, Richmond Bay	n/k

Unknown number of passengers disembarked at Richmond Bay (included Miss MacDonell) Also included Lemuel Cambridge and family. Remaining passengers sailed on to Quebec.

1835	10	*Despatch*	n/k	Bideford (Devon)	Charlottetown	5

Passengers: Reverend Mr. Lloyd, Mrs. Lloyd, and three children.

1835	10	n/k	n/k	Bristol	Charlottetown	2

Vessel had called at the Miramichi.

1836	05	*Ardent*	n/k	Liverpool	Charlottetown	10

Passengers: Mr. Joseph Hodgson, wife and child, Messrs. Duncan, Hope, James, Captain Long of Cocagne, New Brunswick, and three in steerage.

1836	05	*Castalia* (bk)	Massey	Plymouth (Devon)	Charlottetown	10

Passengers: James Peake, merchant, Henry Shearman and family, Miss Newton.

1836	05	*Priam*	n/k	Plymouth (Devon)	Charlottetown	1

Passenger was Isaac Nicholas.

1836	05	*Victoria* (bk)	nk	London	Charlottetown	21

Passengers: J. Woodman, Thomas and Henry Woodman, John MacGowan, Mr. Green, J.W. Hopkins and son, Mr. Woolner and three children, Mr. and Mrs. Dix and three children, Miss Mawley; four in steerage.

1836	06	*Lady Young*	n/k	London	Charlottetown	4

Passengers: Robert Gray, Misses Elizabeth and Stukeley Gray and servant.

Year	Month	Vessel	Master	Departure Port	Arrival Port	Passenger Numbers
1836	06	*Magnes*	n/k	Plymouth (Devon)	Charlottetown	n/k

Vessel owned by James Peake.

Year	Month	Vessel	Master	Departure Port	Arrival Port	Passenger Numbers
1836	06	*Marina*	n/k	Bideford (Devon)	Charlottetown	2

The vessel called at Egmont Bay on June 15 where Mr. and Mrs. Grigg disembarked, then proceeded to Charlottetown.

Year	Month	Vessel	Master	Departure Port	Arrival Port	Passenger Numbers
1836	06	*Mary Jane*	n/k	Plymouth (Devon)	Charlottetown	n/k
1836	06	*Sappho* (bg, 110 tns)	n/k	Bristol	Charlottetown	n/k
1836	06	*Sarah and Eliza* (bg, 161 tns)	n/k	Bideford (Devon)	Charlottetown	30
1836	08	*Emeline*	n/k	London	Charlottetown	12

Passengers: Col. Sir John Harvey, Lieutenant-Governor, Lady Harvey and daughter, Captain Harvey, 70th Regiment, and two "other of His Excellency's sons, together with 3 men and 3 women servants."

Year	Month	Vessel	Master	Departure Port	Arrival Port	Passenger Numbers
1836	08	n/k	n/k	London	Charlottetown	3

Passengers: Mr. and Mrs. Levitt and child. Vessel had called at Halifax before sailing to P.E.I.

Year	Month	Vessel	Master	Departure Port	Arrival Port	Passenger Numbers
1836	09	*Castalia* (bk)	Massey	Plymouth (Devon)	Charlottetown	10

Passengers: Mr. and Mrs. Hall and family, Miss Dalbien, Mr. W.C. Monckton.

Year	Month	Vessel	Master	Departure Port	Arrival Port	Passenger Numbers
1836	09	*Margaret*	n/k	Bideford (Devon)	Charlottetown	n/k
1836	10	*Magnes*	n/k	Bristol	Charlottetown	n/k
1836	10	*Solo*	n/k	Liverpool	Bedeque	n/k

Year	Month	Vessel	Master	Departure Port	Arrival Port	Passenger Numbers
1836	10	*Victoria* (bk)	n/k	London	Charlottetown	14

Passengers: Mr. and Mrs. Fanning and servant, Chester Woolner, Mrs. Woolner and three children, Mrs. Webby and five others. John Allerington, from Suffolk, died October 12, aged 72 (during the crossing).

1837	05	*Castalia* (bk)	Massey	Plymouth (Devon)	Charlottetown	2

Passengers: Miss Margaret Jenkins, Theophilus Chappell Jr.

1837	05	*Crystal* (bk)	Gladson	Liverpool	Charlottetown	2

Passengers: Andrew Duveen and Mr. J. Longworth.

1837	05	*Merino*	n/k	Bideford (Devon)	Charlottetown	3

Passengers: Captain Emanuel (late of the French Army), wife and son.

1837	06	*British Lady* (bg, 283 tns)	Yeo, William	Bideford (Devon)	Richmond Bay	26

The *British Lady* was built in 1836 (Lloyd's Shipping Code "A1").

1837	06	*Royal George* (s. 477 tns)	Wilson	London	Charlottetown	n/m

Passengers: Colonel Sir C.A. Fitz Roy, Lady Mary Fitz Roy, family and suite. Vessel left from West Indian Docks, London.

1837	06	*Victoria* (bk)	n/k	London	Charlottetown	3

Passengers: William Douse and two in steerage.

1837	06	*William Alexander*	n/k	London	Cascumpeque	n/k
1837	07	*Collina* (bg, 156 tns)	n/k	Bideford (Devon)	Charlottetown	n/k
1837	09	*British Lady* (bg, 283 tns)	n/k	Bideford (Devon)	Richmond Bay	n/k
1837	09	*Brothers*	n/k	Liverpool	Charlottetown	5

Passengers: Mr. and Mrs. Monk and three sons.

Year	Month	Vessel	Master	Departure Port	Arrival Port	Passenger Numbers
1837	09	*Castalia* (bk)	n/k	Plymouth (Devon)	Charlottetown	4

Passengers: Mrs. Mason, Mr. W. Pope, and two in steerage.

1837	10	*Victoria* (bk)	n/k	London	Charlottetown	12

Passengers: J.P. Collins, lady and two children, Mr. and Mrs. Metcalf, Mrs. Abel, Captain Hubbard, Benjamin Davis, and three in steerage.

1838	05	*Bravo*	n/k	Gloucester and Bideford	Cascumpeque	n/k

1838	05	*British Lady* (bg, 283 tns)	Yeo, William	Bideford (Devon)	Richmond Bay	20

Passengers: Mr. W. Pethick and family, plus fourteen others. Vessel "had been 10 days in the ice off Cape North in company with many other vessels."

1838	05	*Brothers*	n/k	Liverpool	Charlottetown	n/k

1838	05	*Castalia* (bk)	n/k	Plymouth (Devon)	Charlottetown	>10

Passengers: James Peake, William Nicholl, Mr. Ducheman, and the crews for two vessels.

1838	05	*Industry* (bk)	n/k	Plymouth (Devon)	Charlottetown	1

Passenger: Thomas J. Pope.

1838	05	*Queen* (s)	n/k	Liverpool	Charlottetown	8

Passengers: Messrs. Brennan, Longworth, Prentice, Moody, Dodd, Lord, Hartel, and Waters.

1838	05	*Victoria* (bk)	n/k	London	Charlottetown	1

Passenger: Joseph Hopkins.

1838	06	*Ebenezer*	n/k	Bideford (Devon)	Charlottetown	n/k

1838	08	*Halifax Packet* (bk)	Head	London	Charlottetown	13

Passengers: Mr. and Mrs. Woodman; John H. and William Woodman; Misses Eliza and Jane Woodman; Messrs. Dernier, Frederick, Charles, Septimus and Alexander Woodman; Dr. Hobkirk and Mrs. Hobkirk.

Year	Month	Vessel	Master	Departure Port	Arrival Port	Passenger Numbers
1838	09	*British Lady* (bg, 283 tns)	n/k	Bideford (Devon)	Richmond Bay	n/k
1838	10	*British Union* (bg, 189 tns)	Purvis	Plymouth (Devon)	Bedeque	8

Passengers: Eight workmen for Mr. Pope at Bedeque.

Year	Month	Vessel	Master	Departure Port	Arrival Port	Passenger Numbers
1838	10	*Castalia* (bk)	n/k	Plymouth (Devon)	Charlottetown	n/k
1838	10	*Julia* (sch)	n/k	Plymouth (Devon)	Charlottetown	n/k
1838	10	*Victoria* (bk)	Davies	London	Charlottetown	n/k
1839	05	*British Lady* (bg, 283 tns)	Yeo, William	Bideford (Devon)	Richmond Bay	41
1839	05	*Ono* (sr, 181 tns)	Williams	Plymouth (Devon)	Charlottetown	n/k
1839	05	*St. George*	n/k	Liverpool	Charlottetown	4

Passengers: Mr. A. Duveen and three others.

Year	Month	Vessel	Master	Departure Port	Arrival Port	Passenger Numbers
1839	05	*Symmetry*	n/k	London	Charlottetown	7

Passengers: Captain Jackson and six others.

Year	Month	Vessel	Master	Departure Port	Arrival Port	Passenger Numbers
1839	09	*British Lady* (bg, 283 tns)	n/k	Bideford (Devon)	Richmond Bay	n/k
1839	09	*Industry* (bk)	Gilpin, G.	Plymouth (Devon)	Bedeque	n/k
1839	10	*Britannia*	n/k	Liverpool	Charlottetown	5

Passengers: Francis and Robert Auld of Covehead, Mr. Edwards of Greenock, Miss Townshend, Dennis Reddin.

Year	Month	Vessel	Master	Departure Port	Arrival Port	Passenger Numbers
1839	10	*Bruno*	n/k	Bideford (Devon)	Cascumpeque	n/k

Year	Month	Vessel	Master	Departure Port	Arrival Port	Passenger Numbers
1839	10	*Ono* (sr, 181 tns)	n/k	Gloucester	Charlottetown	2

Passengers: Messrs. Heath and Frederick Haviland.

Year	Month	Vessel	Master	Departure Port	Arrival Port	Passenger Numbers
1839	11	*Alice*	n/k	Plymouth (Devon)	Charlottetown	n/k
1840	05	*Alice*	n/k	Plymouth (Devon)	Charlottetown	n/k
1840	05	*Ambassador* (bk, 299 tns)	Tale, J.S.	Liverpool	Charlottetown	30

Passengers: Messrs. W.W. Irving, Bonshaw, John Longworth, Charles Wright and Captain Morgan, Francis and Robert Auld of Covehead, Mr. Edwards of Greenock, and Miss Townshend, the remainder in steerage.

Year	Month	Vessel	Master	Departure Port	Arrival Port	Passenger Numbers
1840	05	*British Queen*	n/k	Bideford (Devon)	Charlottetown	1

Passenger was Hon. Samuel Cunard.

Year	Month	Vessel	Master	Departure Port	Arrival Port	Passenger Numbers
1840	05	*John Craig* of London (bk, 375 tns)	Pettengel	London	Charlottetown	20

Passengers: Captain Swaby, R.A. and lady, ten children, six servants. The *John Craig* was built in 1826 (Lloyd's Shipping Code "AE1").

Year	Month	Vessel	Master	Departure Port	Arrival Port	Passenger Numbers
1840	05	*Minerva* (bg, 125 tns)	Heard, R.	Bideford (Devon)	Charlottetown	c.16

Passengers: Captain W.A. Marshall, Mr. George Hard, Mrs. Grossard, Mr. and Mrs. Ellis and family, eight in steerage. The *Minerva* was built in 1837 (Lloyd's Shipping Code "A1").

Year	Month	Vessel	Master	Departure Port	Arrival Port	Passenger Numbers
1840	05	*Symmetry*	n/k	Dartmouth (Devon)	Charlottetown	n/k
1840	06	*Ann*	n/k	London	Charlottetown	n/k
1840	06	*Helen Stuart*	n/k	Liverpool	Charlottetown	n/k

Year	Month	Vessel	Master	Departure Port	Arrival Port	Passenger Numbers
1840	06	*Thomas and Elizabeth*	n/k	Bideford (Devon)	Charlottetown	24

Passengers: Mr. and Mrs. Hooper, Thomas Howe, and twenty-one in steerage.

Year	Month	Vessel	Master	Departure Port	Arrival Port	Passenger Numbers
1840	09	*Alice*	n/k	Plymouth (Devon)	Charlottetown	n/k
1840	09	*Ambassador* (bk, 299 tns)	Tale, J.S.	Liverpool	Charlottetown	1

Passenger: Lawrence MacLaren, surgeon.

Year	Month	Vessel	Master	Departure Port	Arrival Port	Passenger Numbers
1840	09	*British Queen*	n/k	Gloucester	Charlottetown	n/k
1840	09	*Collina* (bg, 156 tns)	n/k	Bideford (Devon)	Charlottetown	n/k
1840	09	*Lady Wood*	n/k	Plymouth (Devon)	Three Rivers	n/k
1840	10	*Mary Ann*	n/k	Plymouth (Devon)	Georgetown	n/k
1840	10	*Minerva* (bg, 125 tns)	Heard, R. (Devon)	Bideford	Murray Harbour	n/k

The Heard family owned the vessel (shipbuilders).

Year	Month	Vessel	Master	Departure Port	Arrival Port	Passenger Numbers
1840	11	*Huzza* (sr, 160 tns)	Hall	London	Charlottetown	n/k
1840	11	*Royal Mail Steamship Britannia*	n/k	Liverpool	Charlottetown	1

Passenger was Reverend A. McIntyre, recently appointed to the Church of Scotland, Charlottetown.

Year	Month	Vessel	Master	Departure Port	Arrival Port	Passenger Numbers
1841	05	*Isabella* (bg)	Day, W.	Bideford (Devon)	Charlottetown	37

Year	Month	Vessel	Master	Departure Port	Arrival Port	Passenger Numbers
1841	05	*John Craig* of London (bk, 375 tns)	Pettengel	London	Charlottetown	46

Passengers: Mr. Hensley and servant, Mr. and Mrs Grub, Mary C., Elizabeth and Louisa Grub, Robert, Edward, Arthur, and Charles Grub, plus housekeeper and eight servants, Miss Abbott, Mr. and Mrs. Ridge and two children, Mr. Ainsley, and twenty in steerage.

1841	05	*Lady Wood*	Salmon	London	Charlottetown	6

Passengers: Mr. And Mrs Parker, four in steerage.

1841	05	*Northumber-land* (bk)	n/k	Liverpool	Charlottetown	32

Passengers: Miss Pope, Mr. and Mrs. W. Lord, R. Longworth, James Kelly and son, Donald and John Mathewson, and twenty-four in steerage.

1841	05	*Pocohontas*	n/k	Bideford (Devon)	Charlottetown	22

Passengers: Lieutenant Hensley, R.N., and wife, ten sons and daughters, governess, and five servants. Mrs. Faulkner and son, Mr. J. Jury, and one in steerage.

1841	05	*Spec* (sr, 149 tns)	Marshall, J.	Bideford (Devon)	Charlottetown	81

1841	05	*William*	Larmer	Plymouth (Devon)	Charlottetown	3

Passengers: Messrs. Pope, Stumbles, Penny.

1841	06	*Emily B Heard*	n/k	Bideford (Devon)	Charlottetown	n/k

Vessel came via New York.

1841	06	*Florida* (bg, 186 tns)	Hillman	Bideford (Devon)	Port Hill	29

Vessel owned by Yeo & Co.

1841	07	*Shannon*	n/k	Liverpool	Charlottetown	n/k

1841	08	*Matilda*	n/k	Plymouth (Devon)	Charlottetown	3

Passengers: Mr. and Mrs. J.T. Thomas and child.

Year	Month	Vessel	Master	Departure Port	Arrival Port	Passenger Numbers
1841	08	*Minerva* (bg, 125 tns)	Heard, R.	Bideford (Devon)	Charlottetown	15
1841	09	*William*	n/k	Plymouth (Devon)	Charlottetown	n/k
1841	10	*Emily B. Heard*	n/k	Bideford (Devon)	Charlottetown	18

Passengers: Reverend Mr. Pickings, three Messrs. Heard, fourteen in steerage.

1841	10	*Glenburnie* (bk, 238 tns)	Day, W.	Bideford (Devon)	Charlottetown	n/k

Passengers: R. Haythorne and the crew for a new vessel.

1841	10	*Lady Wood*	n/k	London	Charlottetown	>10

Passengers: John Mayne, R.N., Mrs. Mayne and family plus a servant, Messrs. Gurney, R.C.H. Tims, C. Birch Bagster, Captain Riddle, Captain and Mrs. R. Mearns, Mrs. Seaman, Mrs. Wigmore.

1841	10	*Northumber-land* (bk)	n/k	Liverpool	Charlottetown	n/k

Vessel called at Three Rivers before reaching Charlottetown. Passengers at Charlottetown were Ralph Brecken and Peter Macgowan.

1841	11	*True Brothers*	n/k	Liverpool	Charlottetown	n/k
1842	05	*Antelope* (bg)	Griffiths, William	Liverpool	Charlottetown	18

Passengers: Miss Binns, Mrs. Blackstone of Bathurst, New Brunswick, Captain Williams, Mr. Murray of Nova Scotia, and thirteen in steerage.

1842	05	*Five Sisters* (bk)	Williams	Bristol	Charlottetown	9

Voyage of thirty-three days. Passengers: Samuel Green and eight in the steerage.

1842	05	*Henrietta* of Exeter (sr, 167 tns)	Glover, T.	Bideford (Devon)	Charlottetown	102

The *Henrietta* was built in 1841 (Lloyd's Shipping Code "A1").

Year	Month	Vessel	Master	Departure Port	Arrival Port	Passenger Numbers
1842	05	*John Bromham* (bk)	n/k	Plymouth (Devon)	Charlottetown	5

Voyage of forty-two days. Passengers: Hon. J. Brecken and Lady, John Livett, his wife and daughter.

1842	05	*Lady Wood*	n/k	London	Charlottetown	15

Passengers: Dennis Reddin, William Millar (of England) and servant, and twelve in steerage.

1842	05	*Spray*	n/k	Carlisle (Cumberland)	Charlottetown	n/k

1842	06	*Ann*	n/k	Bristol	Charlottetown	c.50

Voyage of forty days. Passengers: Mr. Gurney, family and servants, Henry Woodman of Amherst, N.S., Messrs. Merrit, Perry, Wilks, Batt, Pearse, Willis, and thirty-seven in steerage. They were principally from Devizes in Wiltshire, "and intend settling on the Earl of Selkirk's property, in the New Wiltshire Settlement."

1842	06	*British Lady* (bg, 283 tns)	n/k	Bideford (Devon)	Charlottetown	n/k

1842	06	*Diadem* (bk, 294 tns)	Robertson	London	Charlottetown	39

1842	06	*Five Sisters* (bk)	Williams	Bristol	Princetown	n/k

1842	06	*Sylvanus* (bk, 298 tns)	Lang, W.	Falmouth (Cornwall)	Charlottetown	203

Passengers: C.B. Bagster, Mr. Bourdie, Mr. Tims, and two hundred in the steerage. The *Sylvanus* was built in 1841 (Lloyd's Shipping Code "A").

1842	06	*William*	n/k	Plymouth (Devon)	Charlottetown	n/k

1842	08	*St. George*	n/k	Liverpool	Charlottetown	10

Vessel was a steamship "touching at Cork and St. John's Newfoundland." Passengers: Francis Longworth Jr. , Mr. Pope, Reverend Mr. Boone, Captain and Miss Cook, Mr. and Mrs. Clift, Messrs. J.H. Dunscombe, Johnston, and Duncan.

Year	Month	Vessel	Master	Departure Port	Arrival Port	Passenger Numbers
1842	09	*Elizabeth*	n/k	Plymouth (Devon)	Charlottetown	1

Passenger was James Gardiner.

Year	Month	Vessel	Master	Departure Port	Arrival Port	Passenger Numbers
1842	10	*Ann Kenny*	n/k	n/k (England)	Charlottetown	1

Edward Nash, a passenger in the *Ann Kenny*, was killed falling between the vessel and the Queen's Wharf. "He came here with a view of providing a home for his family, which he left in England" (Fraser, "More Elusive Emigrants," *Island Magazine* [26], 37).

Year	Month	Vessel	Master	Departure Port	Arrival Port	Passenger Numbers
1842	10	*Antelope*	n/k	Liverpool	Charlottetown	n/k

Year	Month	Vessel	Master	Departure Port	Arrival Port	Passenger Numbers
1842	10	*Lady Wood*	n/k	London	Charlottetown	29

Voyage of fifty days. Passengers: Mr. and Mrs. Broderick and five children, Alfred Nicholson, Henry A. Brooking, and twenty in the steerage. The principal of the latter are to be employed in erecting houses, etc. for the Fishing Company lately formed in London for carrying on the fisheries at Cascumpec in this island.

Year	Month	Vessel	Master	Departure Port	Arrival Port	Passenger Numbers
1842	10	*Mary Ann* (bg, 179 tns)	n/k	Bideford (Devon)	Charlottetown	n/k

The *Mary Ann* was built in 1842 (Lloyd's Shipping Code "A1").

Year	Month	Vessel	Master	Departure Port	Arrival Port	Passenger Numbers
1843	05	*Ann Kenny*	n/k	London	Charlottetown	4

Passengers: Mrs. Holloway and three children.

Year	Month	Vessel	Master	Departure Port	Arrival Port	Passenger Numbers
1843	05	*Antelope* (bg)	n/k	Liverpool	Charlottetown	21

Passengers: Masters John and William Smith, Mrs. Mary Bradwell and three children; fifteen in the steerage.

Year	Month	Vessel	Master	Departure Port	Arrival Port	Passenger Numbers
1843	05	*British Lady* (bg, 283 tns)	n/k	Bideford (Devon)	Charlottetown	30

Passengers were three crews for new vessels.

Year	Month	Vessel	Master	Departure Port	Arrival Port	Passenger Numbers
1843	05	*Civility* (bk, 400 tns)	n/k	Bideford (Devon)	Charlottetown	1

Passenger was Christopher Cross.

Year	Month	Vessel	Master	Departure Port	Arrival Port	Passenger Numbers
1843	05	*Emma Searle* (bk)	n/k	London	Charlottetown	20

Voyage of forty days. Passengers: Hon. J. Brecken and Lady, Miss Hodgson, Lieut. Orlebar, Lady, three children and servant, Mr. Daniel Davies, Mr. and Mrs. Hubbard and two children; Steerage: Mr. and Mrs Holliday and two children, Miss Crouch, Mr. Riggs.

| 1843 | 05 | *John Bromham* (bk) | n/k | Plymouth (Devon) | Charlottetown | 11 |

Passengers: Mr. Smardon plus ten in steerage.

| 1843 | 05 | *Mary Ann* (bg, 179 tns) | Saunders, W.H. | Bideford (Devon) | Charlottetown | 82 |

Passengers: Dr. Boswell and family, and seventy-five in the steerage.

| 1843 | 06 | *British Lady* (bg, 283 tns) | n/k | Bideford (Devon) | Charlottetown | 29 |

One of the passengers was Samuel Green .

| 1843 | 06 | *William* | n/k | Liverpool | Charlottetown | 1 |

Passenger was Mr. Russell of Pictou.

| 1843 | 08 | *Brothers* | n/k | Plymouth (Devon) | Charlottetown | n/k |

| 1843 | 09 | *Sir Henry Vere Huntley* | n/k | Liverpool | Charlottetown | n/k |

| 1843 | 10 | *Constance* | n/k | London | Charlottetown | 3 |

Passengers: Daniel Davies, Master Dickson, A. Gutters.

| 1843 | 10 | *John Bromham* (bk) | n/k | Plymouth (Devon) | Charlottetown | 11 |

Passenger: Mrs. Smardon, and ten in the steerage.

| 1843 | 10 | *John Hawkes* | n/k | Bideford (Devon) | Cascumpec | n/k |

Voyage of thirty days.

| 1843 | 10 | *Lady Huntley* | n/k | Liverpool | Charlottetown | n/k |

Year	Month	Vessel	Master	Departure Port	Arrival Port	Passenger Numbers
1843	10	*William* (bg)	Griffiths, William	Liverpool	Charlottetown	n/k
1843	10	*William Wilberforce*	n/k	Ilfracombe (Devon)	Charlottetown	n/k

Vessel to sail on to Quebec.

Year	Month	Vessel	Master	Departure Port	Arrival Port	Passenger Numbers
1844	05	*Constance*	n/k	London	Charlottetown	n/k
1844	05	*Emma Searle* (bk)	n/k	London	Charlottetown	8

Voyage of forty-two days. Passengers: D. Davies, E. Carey, James Davies, Mrs. Howlett, plus three in steerage — Mr. Jacobs, Mr. Spence, Mr. Scott.

Year	Month	Vessel	Master	Departure Port	Arrival Port	Passenger Numbers
1844	05	*John Bromham* (bk)	Barrett	Plymouth (Devon)	Charlottetown	10

Voyage of fifty-three days.

Year	Month	Vessel	Master	Departure Port	Arrival Port	Passenger Numbers
1844	05	*Lady Sale*	n/k	Bideford (Devon)	Charlottetown	n/k

Passengers: Mr. and Mrs. Heard and others.

Year	Month	Vessel	Master	Departure Port	Arrival Port	Passenger Numbers
1844	05	*Mary Jane*	n/k	Liverpool	Charlottetown	c. 20

Voyage of thirty days. Passengers: Mr. and Mrs. Holroyd, Miss Watson, Captain Eales and family, plus fourteen in steerage.

Year	Month	Vessel	Master	Departure Port	Arrival Port	Passenger Numbers
1844	05	*Sir Henry Vere Huntley* (bg)	Gourlay	Liverpool	Charlottetown	4

Voyage of fifty-six days. Passengers: W.N. Boyer, Mrs. Boyer, Mrs. Smallwood, E.G. Smallwood, John Sutton.

Year	Month	Vessel	Master	Departure Port	Arrival Port	Passenger Numbers
1844	08	*Florida* (bg, 186 tns)	Hillman	Bideford (Devon)	Port Hill	1

Passenger: Mrs. Widgery. Vessel owned by Yeo & Co.

Year	Month	Vessel	Master	Departure Port	Arrival Port	Passenger Numbers
1844	09	*British Lady* (bg, 283 tns)	Redmond, George	Bideford (Devon)	Bedeque	7

Voyage of twenty-four days. Passengers: Mrs. Humphreys and two children, Reverend Mr. Harris and Lady, Reverend Mr. Carravay and Lady.

Year	Month	Vessel	Master	Departure Port	Arrival Port	Passenger Numbers
1844	09	*Constance*	n/k	London	Charlottetown	n/k
1844	09	*Emma Searle* (bk)	n/k	London	Georgetown	6

Voyage of twenty-eight days.

1844	09	*Helen* (sr)	Smith	Plymouth (Devon)	Charlottetown	n/k
1844	09	*John Bromham* (bk)	n/k	Plymouth (Devon)	Charlottetown	6

Passengers: L.Y. Nash, lately appointed Barrack Master and Ordnance Storekeeper for this place — Lady and four children.

1844	09	*Lady Sale*	n/k	Bideford (Devon)	Charlottetown	n/k
1844	09	*Mary Jane*	n/k	Bristol	Port Hill	n/k

Vessel came via Dublin.

1844	09	*Northumberland* (bk)	Baldwin	Liverpool	Charlottetown	n/k
1844	09	*Wellington*	n/k	Liverpool	Charlottetown	1

Voyage of thirty-five days. Passenger was A. Leslie.

1844	10	*Civility* (bk, 400 tns)	n/k	Bideford (Devon)	Charlottetown	n/k
1844	10	*Isabella* (bg)	n/k	Bideford (Devon)	Port Hill	n/k

Voyage of thirty-one days.

1844	11	*Mariner*	n/k	Liverpool	Charlottetown	n/k

Voyage of sixty days.

1845	05	*Antelope*	n/k	Liverpool	Charlottetown	n/k

Year	Month	Vessel	Master	Departure Port	Arrival Port	Passenger Numbers
1845	05	*British Union* (bg, 189 tns)	n/k	London	Charlottetown	4

Passengers: Miss Buxton plus three in steerage.

| 1845 | 05 | *Civility* | n/k | Bideford (Devon) | Charlottetown | 46 |

Passengers: Mr. and Mrs. Widgery and servant, Master Nott and Miss Nott, Miss Williams, Miss Webb, thirty-nine in steerage, part of whom proceed with the vessel to Quebec.

| 1845 | 05 | *Fanny* (bg) | n/k | Liverpool | Charlottetown | n/k |

| 1845 | 05 | *Florence* (bk) | n/k | Plymouth (Devon) | Charlottetown | 1 |

Vessel called at Liverpool. Passenger was William Cooper of Fortune Bay (Newfoundland).

| 1845 | 05 | *John Bromham* (bk) | Barrett | Plymouth (Devon) | Charlottetown | 5 |

Passengers: Mr. and Mrs. Jenkin, Mr. Aitkins, Mrs. Lethbridge, Master Whiteway.

| 1845 | 05 | *Juventas* (bg) | Job | Sunderland (Durham) | Charlottetown | n/k |

| 1845 | 05 | *Mary Jane* | n/k | Liverpool | Charlottetown | 7 |

Passengers: John McGill and son plus five others.

| 1845 | 05 | *Northumber-land* (bk) | n/k | Liverpool | Charlottetown | n/k |

| 1845 | 05 | *Sir Henry Vere Huntley* | n/k | Liverpool | Bedeque | n/k |

Vessel called at Halifax.

| 1845 | 05 | *Walmsey* | n/k | London | Charlottetown | n/k |

Voyage of forty-seven days.

| 1845 | 06 | *Grendon* (bg) | Hianmarch | Sunderland (Durham) | Charlottetown | n/k |

Voyage of fifty-two days.

Year	Month	Vessel	Master	Departure Port	Arrival Port	Passenger Numbers
1845	08	*Antelope*	n/k	Liverpool	Charlottetown	27

Passengers: Colour Sergeants Mitchell and Macgowan, plus twenty five others.

| 1845 | 08 | *Sir Edward* | Ellis | Liverpool | Charlottetown | n/k |

Voyage of thirty-nine days.

| 1845 | 08 | *Sir Henry Vere Huntley* | n/k | Liverpool | Crapaud | n/k |

Voyage of thirty-seven days from Liverpool.

| 1845 | 09 | *Civility* (bk, 400 tns) | n/k | Bideford (Devon) | Charlottetown | n/k |

| 1845 | 09 | *John Bromham* (bk) | n/k | Plymouth (Devon) | Charlottetown | n/k |

| 1845 | 10 | *Fanny* (bg) | Smith | Liverpool | Charlottetown | n/k |

| 1845 | 10 | *Jewess* (bg) | Elles | Liverpool | Charlottetown | n/k |

| 1845 | 10 | *Mary Lyall* | Jones | Liverpool | Charlottetown | n/k |

| 1845 | 11 | *British Union* (bg, 189 tns) | n/k | London | Charlottetown | 2 |

Passengers: Mr. James Reddin, Captain Harris. Vessel also carried a horse purchased in Britain for the Royal Agricultural Society.

| 1846 | 05 | *Agitator* | n/k | London | Charlottetown | n/k |

| 1846 | 05 | *Antelope* (bg) | Jones | Liverpool | Charlottetown | 43 |

Voyage of forty-one days. Passengers: Francis Longworth, Joseph Macdonald, W.W. Lord, the owner, R.C.H. Tims of Millvale, Captain Ellis, Mr. James Caffray, Wm. Marshall (who intends settling at DeSable), has imported for farm stock, one short-horned Durham bull, one heifer, and five pigs of a superior breed; two Misses Marshall. Thirty-four in steerage, the latter principally from Northern Ireland.

| 1846 | 05 | *British Lady* (bg, 283 tns) | Scott | Bideford (Devon) | Port Hill | n/k |

Passengers: Masters and outfits for five new vessels and two families, passengers (to James Yeo).

Year	Month	Vessel	Master	Departure Port	Arrival Port	Passenger Numbers
1846	05	*Elizabeth* (bk)	Watson	London	Charlottetown	n/k
1846	05	*Florence* (bk)	Brummage	Plymouth (Devon)	Charlottetown	n/k
1846	05	*Heart of Oak* (bk)	Stoker	London	Charlottetown	n/k
1846	06	*Scio*	n/k	London	Richmond Bay	n/k
1846	07	*Spartan*	n/k	Liverpool	Charlottetown	n/k
1846	08	*Bravo*	n/k	Sunderland (Durham)	Charlottetown	n/k
1846	09	*Antelope* (bg)	n/k	Liverpool	Charlottetown	45

Passengers: Mr. W.G. Stron, wife and two children; Captain Salmond and forty Irish emigrants in steerage.

Year	Month	Vessel	Master	Departure Port	Arrival Port	Passenger Numbers
1846	09	*Civility* (bk, 400 tns)	n/k	Bideford (Devon)	Charlottetown	n/k

Voyage of thirty-eight days. "To W. Heard."

Year	Month	Vessel	Master	Departure Port	Arrival Port	Passenger Numbers
1846	09	*Fanny* (bg)	n/k	Plymouth (Devon)	Charlottetown	n/k
1846	09	*Lady Sale*	n/k	Bideford (Devon)	Charlottetown	n/k

Voyage of thirty-five days. Passengers: Two passengers and "the crew of a vessel landed here on the way to Quebec."

Year	Month	Vessel	Master	Departure Port	Arrival Port	Passenger Numbers
1846	09	*Mary Jane*	n/k	Liverpool	Richmond Bay	n/k
1846	09	*Three Brothers* (bg)	Pugsley	Bristol	Charlottetown	n/k

Passengers: A crew for a new barque, to James Yeo.

Year	Month	Vessel	Master	Departure Port	Arrival Port	Passenger Numbers
1846	10	*Iodone*	n/k	Portsmouth (Hampshire)	Charlottetown	n/k

Year	Month	Vessel	Master	Departure Port	Arrival Port	Passenger Numbers
1846	10	*Themis*	n/k	Liverpool	Charlottetown	n/k
1846	10	*Zitella* (bk)	n/k	Liverpool	Charlottetown	22

Voyage of thirty-six days. Passengers: John Sutton, Mr. Rossiter, Captains Evans, Grig, Campbell, and Bell. Sixteen in the steerage.

| 1846 | 11 | *Idas* (bg) | n/k | London | Charlottetown | n/k |

Passengers: Mr. and Mrs. Birnie, Mr. John H. Gates, Mr. G.T. Haszard and others. There had been a death at sea — Mr. James Robertson, son of James Robertson of St. Peter's Road.

| 1846 | 11 | *Spartan* | n/k | Liverpool | Charlottetown | 5 |

Voyage of fifty-nine days. Passengers: Alfred Firth, H.J. Massey, Messrs. Ricket, H. McLean, Michell.

| 1847 | 05 | *Fanny* (bg) | n/k | Plymouth (Devon) | Charlottetown | 26 |

Passengers: Captains Barrett, Campbell, and Moore. Messrs. James Reddin, W. Matthewson, Orr, plus twenty in steerage.

| 1847 | 05 | *Florence* (bk) | Brummage | Plymouth (Devon) | Charlottetown | 19 |

Passengers: Mrs. Stumbles, James and Thomas Stumbles, Mr. Sampson, wife, and fifteen others.

| 1847 | 05 | *Lady Constable* (bk) | n/k | Liverpool | Charlottetown | 444 |

Passengers: "419 emigrants." There were 444 passengers (probably all Irish), of whom twenty-five died on the passage. A further eight died after arriving at the port.

| 1847 | 06 | *Annabell* (a) | n/k | London | Charlottetown | 4 |

Passengers: R.H.C. Tims, Mr. Daniel Davies, Captains Nowlan and Fawcette.

| 1847 | 06 | *Fellowship* | n/k | Liverpool | Charlottetown | 3 |

Passengers: John Furnace and daughter, John Malcolm.

| 1847 | 06 | *Secret* (bk, 600 tns) | n/k | Bideford (Devon) | Charlottetown | n/k |

Year	Month	Vessel	Master	Departure Port	Arrival Port	Passenger Numbers
1847	06	*William Wilberforce*	n/k	Liverpool	Charlottetown	n/k
1847	09	*Fanny* (bg)	n/k	Plymouth (Devon)	Charlottetown	n/k
1847	10	*British Lady* (bg, 283 tns)	n/k	Bristol	Richmond Bay	55

Passengers: Forty sailors, twelve passengers, Mr. and Mrs. Winsloe, Miss Veale.

Year	Month	Vessel	Master	Departure Port	Arrival Port	Passenger Numbers
1847	10	*Fellowship*	n/k	Liverpool	Charlottetown	n/k
1847	10	*Protector*	n/k	Liverpool	Charlottetown	n/k
1847	11	*Annabella* (bg)	Bennett	London	Charlottetown	13

Passengers: Captain Burns, Mrs. Burns, and seven children, Mrs. Moore, Miss Coates, Captains Hogan and Clarkin.

Year	Month	Vessel	Master	Departure Port	Arrival Port	Passenger Numbers
1847	11	*Conquest* (bg)	Marshall, J.	Bideford (Devon)	Charlottetown	n/k
1847	11	*Mary Jane*	n/k	Gloucester	Charlottetown	n/k

Voyage of forty-three days. Passengers: Captain Broaders, crew and nine passengers of the brig *Racer* from Liverpool, bound for Richibucto. "The *Mary Jane* fell in with the *Racer* in latitude 44 in a water-logged state, and after laying by her for 3 days, succeeded in taking the crew and passengers who were in such an exhausted state as to be unable to launch their own boat." (Douglas Fraser, "More Elusive Emigrants," *Island Magazine*, No. 26 [Fall/Winter 1989], 40).

Year	Month	Vessel	Master	Departure Port	Arrival Port	Passenger Numbers
1848	05	*Concordia* (bg)	n/k	Liverpool	Charlottetown	5

Passengers: Lady Campbell, son and daughter; Mrs. Campbell, His Excellency Sir Donald Campbell's mother; Robert Longworth.

Year	Month	Vessel	Master	Departure Port	Arrival Port	Passenger Numbers
1848	05	*Jessie*	n/k	Liverpool	Charlottetown	4

Voyage of thirty-five days. Passengers: Captains James, McDonald, and Laing; Mr. W. Hayden.

Year	Month	Vessel	Master	Departure Port	Arrival Port	Passenger Numbers
1848	05	*Mary Jane*	n/k	Bristol	Port Hill	11

Voyage of thirty-seven days.

Year	Month	Vessel	Master	Departure Port	Arrival Port	Passenger Numbers
1848	05	*Mary McWhinnie*	n/k	London	Charlottetown	n/k

Voyage of forty-one days.

Year	Month	Vessel	Master	Departure Port	Arrival Port	Passenger Numbers
1848	05	*Prince Edward*	n/k	London	Georgetown	n/k

Passengers: Miss Douse, C. Birch Bagster, and others.

Year	Month	Vessel	Master	Departure Port	Arrival Port	Passenger Numbers
1848	05	*Princess Victoria*	n/k	London	Richmond Bay	n/k
1848	06	*Conquest* (bg)	n/k	Bideford (Devon)	Charlottetown	7
1848	09	*Concordia* (bk)	n/k	Plymouth (Devon)	Charlottetown	n/k
1848	09	*Conquest* (bg)	n/k	Bideford (Devon)	Charlottetown	n/k
1848	09	*Fanny* (bg)	n/k	Liverpool	Charlottetown	8

Passengers: Mr. Badge, wife and three children, Mrs. Austen, Mr. Jardine.

Year	Month	Vessel	Master	Departure Port	Arrival Port	Passenger Numbers
1848	09	*Midas*	n/k	Fleetwood (Lancashire)	Charlottetown	n/k
1848	10	*Mary McWhinnie*	n/k	London	Charlottetown	n/k
1848	11	*Sophia*	n/k	Liverpool	Charlottetown	n/k
1849	04	*Fanny* (bg)	n/k	Plymouth (Devon)	Charlottetown	n/k
1849	05	*Douglas*	n/k	Liverpool	Charlottetown	26

Voyage of thirty-eight days. Passengers: Mr. and Mrs. Hunter, Mr. and Mrs. Wilkinson and five children, Messrs. McGregor, Lawson, Captain Smith, and fourteen in steerage.

Year	Month	Vessel	Master	Departure Port	Arrival Port	Passenger Numbers
1849	05	*Minerva* (bg)	Murchison	Liverpool	Charlottetown	12

Passengers: Major William McIntosh, Lady, four Misses McIntosh and four Masters McIntosh; Mr. William Mathieson.

Year	Month	Vessel	Master	Departure Port	Arrival Port	Passenger Numbers
1849	05	*Prince Edward*	n/k	London	Charlottetown	14

Voyage of thirty-four days. Passengers: Mr. Brown, Mr. and Mrs. Williams, Mrs. Blatch, and ten in steerage.

Year	Month	Vessel	Master	Departure Port	Arrival Port	Passenger Numbers
1849	05	*Union*	n/k	Liverpool	Charlottetown	n/k
1849	06	*Civility* (bk, 400 tns)	Bale, John	Bideford (Devon)	Charlottetown	8

Passengers: Mr. and Miss Trown, Mrs. S. Widgery and son, three in steerage.

Year	Month	Vessel	Master	Departure Port	Arrival Port	Passenger Numbers
1849	07	*Canada*	n/k	n/k (England)	Charlottetown	1

Passenger: Reverend John McLennan.

Year	Month	Vessel	Master	Departure Port	Arrival Port	Passenger Numbers
1849	08	*Douglas*	n/k	Liverpool	Charlottetown	n/k
1849	08	*Vixen*	n/k	Liverpool	Charlottetown	5

Passengers: Mr. Henry of Nova Scotia, two Messrs. Thomson, two Messrs. Norton.

Year	Month	Vessel	Master	Departure Port	Arrival Port	Passenger Numbers
1849	09	*Arthur*	n/k	Liverpool	Charlottetown	n/k
1849	09	*Civility* (bk, 400 tns)	n/k	Bideford (Devon)	Charlottetown	n/k

Passengers: Thomas Tanton and family, Captain Smith.

Year	Month	Vessel	Master	Departure Port	Arrival Port	Passenger Numbers
1849	09	*Fanny* (bg)	n/k	Plymouth (Devon)	Charlottetown	n/k
1849	09	*Gleaner*	n/k	Bristol	Port Hill	n/k

Voyage of thirty days. Passengers: Robert Boswall and others.

Year	Month	Vessel	Master	Departure Port	Arrival Port	Passenger Numbers
1849	10	*James*	n/k	Liverpool	Richmond Bay	n/k
1849	10	*Prince Edward*	Chambers	London	Charlottetown	19

Voyage of thirty days. Passengers: George Beazley, Lieutenant R.N., his Lady, Miss Simeona and Margaret Beazley, Alexander and Michael Beazley, Mr. and Mrs. Aldous and three children, John Holl Griffith, Miss Mackie, Captain Nowlan and five others.

Year	Month	Vessel	Master	Departure Port	Arrival Port	Passenger Numbers
1850	05	*Civility* (bk, 400 tns)	Bale, John	Bideford (Devon)	Charlottetown	9

Voyage of twenty-three days. Passengers: Mrs. Hebbes, Mrs. Browne and two children, Reverend Jacob Gale and Lady, three in steerage.

Year	Month	Vessel	Master	Departure Port	Arrival Port	Passenger Numbers
1850	05	*Fancy*	n/k	Plymouth (Devon)	Charlottetown	n/k

Year	Month	Vessel	Master	Departure Port	Arrival Port	Passenger Numbers
1850	05	*Hornet* (bg)	n/k	Liverpool	Charlottetown	8

Passengers: Hon. Charles Worrell, Lieut. Lane, Captain Michael Walsh, Captain Jones, David Mutch, Charles McDonald, one in steerage.

Year	Month	Vessel	Master	Departure Port	Arrival Port	Passenger Numbers
1850	05	*Lochiel*	n/k	Liverpool	Charlottetown	n/k

Voyage of sixty days.

Year	Month	Vessel	Master	Departure Port	Arrival Port	Passenger Numbers
1850	05	*Pink*	n/k	Liverpool	Charlottetown	2

Passengers: Mr. and Mrs. David Lawson.

Year	Month	Vessel	Master	Departure Port	Arrival Port	Passenger Numbers
1850	05	*Prince Edward*	n/k	London	Charlottetown	c.23

Passengers: Cabin: Miss Haviland, Mr. R. Haviland, Mr. R. Hensley, Mr. Agazis, Mr. Hales, Mr. Broad, Mr. Johnston, Captain Lickis, Captain Hogan, Captain Knowlan, Captain Mackay. Steerage: Mr. Webster, wife and family, Mr. Skinner, Henry J. James, Mr. and Mrs. Amoy.

Year	Month	Vessel	Master	Departure Port	Arrival Port	Passenger Numbers
1850	06	*Five Sisters* (bk)	n/k	Bristol	Richmond Bay	n/k

Year	Month	Vessel	Master	Departure Port	Arrival Port	Passenger Numbers
1850	06	*Zetus* (bk)	n/k	Liverpool	Charlottetown	n/k

Vessel called at Boston.

Year	Month	Vessel	Master	Departure Port	Arrival Port	Passenger Numbers
1850	09	*Fancy*	n/k	Liverpool	Charlottetown	n/k

Year	Month	Vessel	Master	Departure Port	Arrival Port	Passenger Numbers
1850	10	*Hornet* (bg)	n/k	Liverpool	Charlottetown	n/k

Passengers: Captains Salmond, McMillan, Master John Gill and others.

Year	Month	Vessel	Master	Departure Port	Arrival Port	Passenger Numbers
1850	11	*Prince Albert*	n/k	Great Yarmouth (Norfolk)	Charlottetown	n/k

Year	Month	Vessel	Master	Departure Port	Arrival Port	Passenger Numbers
1851	05	*Gleaner*	n/k	Liverpool	Richmond Bay	n/k

Year	Month	Vessel	Master	Departure Port	Arrival Port	Passenger Numbers
1851	06	*Prince Edward*	n/k	London	Charlottetown	8

Passengers: Messrs. Shepherd, Stubbs, Tubs, Driver, G. Davies, Mr. and Mrs. Conroy, Captain Lockyer.

Year	Month	Vessel	Master	Departure Port	Arrival Port	Passenger Numbers
1851	09	*Fancy*	n/k	Liverpool	Charlottetown	n/k
1851	09	*James Hill* (bk)	Rigby	Bristol	Port Hill	n/k

Passengers and general cargo for James Yeo with masters and crew for new ships.

Year	Month	Vessel	Master	Departure Port	Arrival Port	Passenger Numbers
1851	09	*Regina*	n/k	Liverpool	Charlottetown	n/k
1851	09	*Vernon*	n/k	Liverpool	Charlottetown	1

Passenger: Miss Margaret Binns from Scotland.

Year	Month	Vessel	Master	Departure Port	Arrival Port	Passenger Numbers
1851	10	*Civility* (bk, 400 tns)	n/k	Bideford (Devon)	Charlottetown	n/k
1852	05	*Falcon* (bg)	Chambers	London	Charlottetown	n/k

Passengers: F. Longworth and Joseph McDonal, W. Nelson and Mr. Kilner.

Year	Month	Vessel	Master	Departure Port	Arrival Port	Passenger Numbers
1852	05	*Mancred*	n/k	Liverpool	Charlottetown	n/k
1852	05	*Sir Alexander* (bk, 340 tns)	Blackburn	Liverpool	Charlottetown	16

Passengers: Misses Lord, Watson, Dousell, Hodgson; Captain Jones, Mr. James, D. Lawson; Messrs. Grey, Nicholson, Hunter, and Canclus bound for Pictou; five others in steerage. The *Sir Alexander* was built in 1851 (Lloyd's Shipping Code "A1").

Year	Month	Vessel	Master	Departure Port	Arrival Port	Passenger Numbers
1852	06	*William*	n/k	Liverpool	Charlottetown	n/k
1852	08	*Banner* (bg)	Dunsford	Bideford (Devon)	Charlottetown	n/k
1852	08	*Trinidad*	n/k	Great Yarmouth (Norfolk)	Charlottetown	n/k
1852	09	*Closina* (bk)	Welsh	Liverpool	Charlottetown	n/k

Voyage of thirty-five days.

Year	Month	Vessel	Master	Departure Port	Arrival Port	Passenger Numbers
1852	09	*Henrietta* of Liverpool (bg, 198 tns)	Williams, W.	Liverpool	Charlottetown	n/k

The *Henrietta* was built in 1851 (Lloyd's Shipping Code "A").

Year	Month	Vessel	Master	Departure Port	Arrival Port	Passenger Numbers
1852	09	*Margaret*	n/k	Liverpool	Charlottetown	n/k
1852	09	*Trinidad*	n/k	Great Yarmouth (Norfolk)	Charlottetown	n/k
1852	09	*William*	n/k	Plymouth (Devon)	Charlottetown	n/k
1852	10	*Acastus*	n/k	Liverpool	Charlottetown	n/k
1852	10	*Sir Alexander* (bk, 340 tns)	Walsh, M.	Liverpool	Charlottetown	n/k
1853	05	*Sir Alexander* (bk, 340 tns)	n/k	Liverpool	Charlottetown	19

Voyage of forty-two days. Passengers: Mrs. Goff, Captains Walsh, Taylor, and English, T. Harrison, James Kelly, and thirteen in steerage.

Year	Month	Vessel	Master	Departure Port	Arrival Port	Passenger Numbers
1853	06	*Attwood*	n/k	London	Charlottetown	13

Passengers: John Douse, Mrs. William Newman, eleven in steerage.

Year	Month	Vessel	Master	Departure Port	Arrival Port	Passenger Numbers
1853	07	*Nugget*	n/k	Bideford (Devon)	Charlottetown	n/k

Voyage of forty-three days.

Year	Month	Vessel	Master	Departure Port	Arrival Port	Passenger Numbers
1853	10	*Margaret*	n/k	Liverpool	Charlottetown	n/k
1853	11	*Ellen*	n/k	Liverpool	Charlottetown	n/k

Passengers: Masters and crew for two vessels.

Year	Month	Vessel	Master	Departure Port	Arrival Port	Passenger Numbers
1853	11	*Nugget*	n/k	Bideford (Devon)	Charlottetown	n/k

Year	Month	Vessel	Master	Departure Port	Arrival Port	Passenger Numbers
1853	11	*Sir Alexander* (bk, 340 tns)	Walsh, M.	Liverpool	Charlottetown	43

Passengers: J. M. and Mrs. Stark, Miss Rigg, Miss Watson, Captain E. McMillan, John Lea, and fourteen in steerage. "The Sir Alexander … fell in with the Brigantine *Banner* from Liverpool for Arichat, dismasted and in a sinking condition; took off Captain Dewolfe, crew and 14 passengers, 23 in all, and brought them to this port" (Fraser, "More Elusive Emigrants," 41).

Year	Month	Vessel	Master	Departure Port	Arrival Port	Passenger Numbers
1854	05	*Challenge*	n/k	Bristol	Charlottetown	n/k
1854	05	*Peeping Tom* (bg)	Hamilton	Liverpool	Charlottetown	13

Passengers: Mrs. Southey, five children and servant, Captains Grossard, James, and MacPherson, plus three steerage passengers.

Year	Month	Vessel	Master	Departure Port	Arrival Port	Passenger Numbers
1854	05	*Sir Alexander* (bk, 340 tns)	Walsh, M.	Liverpool	Charlottetown	n/k

Voyage of thirty-seven days.

Year	Month	Vessel	Master	Departure Port	Arrival Port	Passenger Numbers
1854	06	*John*	n/k	London	Charlottetown	n/k

Voyage of fifty-four days.

Year	Month	Vessel	Master	Departure Port	Arrival Port	Passenger Numbers
1854	06	*Princeton*	n/k	Liverpool	Charlottetown	n/k

Voyage of forty-four days.

Year	Month	Vessel	Master	Departure Port	Arrival Port	Passenger Numbers
1854	07	*Grace*	n/k	Liverpool	Charlottetown	n/k

Voyage of fifty-eight days.

Year	Month	Vessel	Master	Departure Port	Arrival Port	Passenger Numbers
1854	07	*Kjeltstad*	n/k	Liverpool	Charlottetown	n/k

Voyage of fifty-six days.

Year	Month	Vessel	Master	Departure Port	Arrival Port	Passenger Numbers
1854	10	*Annie*	n/k	Liverpool	Charlottetown	n/k
1854	10	*Cicily*	n/k	London	Charlottetown	n/k

Voyage of forty-two days.

Year	Month	Vessel	Master	Departure Port	Arrival Port	Passenger Numbers
1854	10	*Nugget*	n/k	Bideford (Devon)	Charlottetown	n/k

Year	Month	Vessel	Master	Departure Port	Arrival Port	Passenger Numbers
1855	10	*Majestic* of Liverpool (s, 659 tns)	Walsh	Liverpool	Charlottetown	34

Passengers: Hon. W.W. Lord; Captains Beaton, James, Atkinson, and Sleator; A. Lord; Chas. McDonald; Chas. Stanfield; Messrs. Watson, Bryson, and Fraser; and twenty-three steerage passengers (emigrants). The *Majestic* was built in 1838 (Lloyd's Shipping Code "AE1").

1856	05	*Majestic* of Liverpool (s, 659 tns)	n/k	Liverpool	Charlottetown	21

Passengers: The Lady of the Hon. W.W. Lord, Miss Lee, Artemas Lord, Richard, and John Milford, Captains Hobs, Messrs. Atkinson, R. Walsh, and Frantz. About a dozen steerage passengers.

1856	05	*Malakoff* (bk)	Martin	Bristol	Richmond Bay	n/k

Some passengers and the masters and crews for three new vessels, to James Yeo.

1856	10	*Isabel* (bk)	n/k	Liverpool	Charlottetown	c. 30

Passengers: Hon. T.H. Haviland, Miss Haviland, Miss Matilda Haviland and servant; Mr. and Mrs. Harris, five children and servant; Mr. and Mrs. Stretch, six children and servant; Mr. and Mrs. R.P. Hodgson, Mr. and Mrs. Gibson and family, and Mrs. Hogan.

1857	05	*Majestic* of Liverpool (s, 659 tns)	n/k	Liverpool	Charlottetown	18

Passengers: Mrs. Barker and two children, Captain Bromley, Captain Lang, Mr. Nelson, Joseph Kaye, Captain Gorden, Allan Reid; Mr. J. Knight, wife and three children, Mr. Joseph Knipe, Mr. Griffiths and wife, Mr. J. Gibson.

1857	10	*Majestic* of Liverpool (s, 659 tns)	Johnson, J.	Liverpool	Charlottetown	24

Passengers: the Lady of the Hon. P. Walker; ____ Edwards and five children, Mrs. Miller; J. Foster, wife and three children; A. Lord, Wm. Yorster, J. Vaniderstine, Joseph Nelder, P. Hughes; and six emigrants.

1858	06	*Aurora* (bk)	n/k	Liverpool	Charlottetown	6

Passengers: Hon. G.R. Goodman, Miss Caroline Goodman, Mrs. Harvey, son and servant, and John Douse.

Year	Month	Vessel	Master	Departure Port	Arrival Port	Passenger Numbers

1860 05   *Garland* (bk)   Holman   Bristol   Richmond Bay   n/k
Passengers: crews for new vessels, arrived at Richmond Bay May 8, for Hon. James Yeo.

1860 05   *Gazelle* (bk)   n/k   Liverpool   Charlottetown 20
Passengers: 1st Cabin: Stephen Swabey, William W. Balls, John Lea, James Bassett. 2nd Cabin: Mrs. Carr, Mrs. Clibborn and two children, Mrs. McCann and daughter, Miss Connors; Messrs. Ronald McDonald, and James McQuillan; Bridget Foy, Also: Mrs. Heard, Miss Anne Heard, Mrs. Benjamin Davies, Mrs. Dixon, Miss Balfor, H.D. Martin, M.D.

1860 10   *Garland* (bk)   Kelly   Bristol   Port Hill   n/k
Passengers: Crews for new vessels for Hon. James Yeo.

1860 11   *Gazelle* (bk)   Cameron, R. Liverpool   Charlottetown 11
Passengers: 1st Class: Captain Murchison, S. Howatt, and D. McDougall; 2nd Class: Miss C. Morrison, Mr. and Mrs. James Groon, Mr. and Mrs. George Brenan, Mrs. and two Misses Brenan.

1861 08   *Gazelle* (bk)   Lord, W.W. Liverpool   Charlottetown 7
                              (owner)
Passengers: A. Mawley, J. Mawley, J. Stockman, Master Matthison, Captain Welsh, Neil Sutherland, Sarah Hughes.

1861 08   *Gazelle* (bk)   Cameron, R. Liverpool   Charlottetown 9
Passengers: Messrs. Dalgleish, Hopwood, Calder, J.W. Daniels, Joseph Davies, Adam Ness, and three in the steerage.

1862 05   *Gazelle* (bk)   Cameron, R. Liverpool   Charlottetown 13
Passengers: Mrs. Sutherland, two Misses Mullen, Mrs. Molesin, Messrs. J. Lea, McPhee, and seven in the steerage.

1862 06   *Malakoff* (bk) Holman   Bristol   Port Hill   n/k
Passengers: crews for new ships of Hon. James Yeo.

1864 05   *Superb* (bk)   Elliott   Liverpool   Richmond Bay   n/k
The *Superb* has eighty hands onboard, all told, captains and crews for new vessels.

NOTES

CHAPTER 1: LEAVING ENGLAND

1. John MacGregor, *Historical and Descriptive Sketches of the Maritime Colonies of British America* (London: Longman, Rees, Orme, Brown and Green, 1828), 68.
2. *Ibid.*, 68
3. In the introduction to an edition of the *British Journal of Canadian Studies* (Vol. 16:1, 2003), dealing exclusively with English emigration, Philip Buckner discusses the factors behind the neglect of the English as an immigrant group. See pages 1–5.
4. The colonies did not all join Confederation at the same time. While Nova Scotia and New Brunswick joined in 1867, Prince Edward Island waited until 1873, and Newfoundland delayed joining until 1949.
5. Philip Buckner, *Peoples of the Maritimes: English* (Tantallon, NS: Four East Publications, 2000), 16–19. The English also formed a majority of the British immigrants who came to Canada during the 1920s and after the Second World War.
6. For details of yearly emigration from England and Wales, Scotland, and Ireland to the United States, British North America, and Australia between 1815 and 1930, see N.H. Carrier, and J.R. Jeffrey, *External Migration: A Study of the Available Statistics 1815–1950* (London: HMSO, 1953), 95–96.
7. LAC MG23–J3: "Narrative of a Voyage Onboard the *Elizabeth* from England to the Island of St. John, 1775–1777," 44. This diary has been published in Daniel Cobb Harvey, *Journeys to the Island of Saint John or Prince Edward Island, 1775-1832* (Toronto: MacMillan, 1955), 1–72.
8. Anon, *A True Guide to Prince Edward Island, Formerly St. John's in the Gulph of*

St. Laurence, North America. (Liverpool: printed by G.F. Harris for Woodward and Alderson, booksellers, 1808), 14.

9. *Ibid.*, 19.

10. John Robinson and Thomas Rispin, *A Journey Through Nova Scotia: Containing a Particular Account of the Country and Its Inhabitants; With Observations on the Management in Husbandry, the Breed of Horses and Other Cattle, and Every Thing Material Relating to Farming; To Which Is Added an Account of Several Estates For Sale in Different Townships of Nova-Scotia, with Their Number of Acres and the Price at Which Each Is Set.* (York: Printed for the authors by C. Etherington, 1774), 33.

11. MacGregor, *British America*, 68.

12. Walter Johnstone, "Letters Descriptive of P.E.I.," in Harvey, *Journeys to the Island of Saint John or Prince Edward Island, 1775–1832*, 142–43.

13. LAC MG19–F10, Edward Walsh fonds: Journal of a Voyage from Portsmouth to Quebec, 1803, 112, 116. Walsh was a passenger on the *Teresa*, which sailed from Spithead (channel between Portsmouth and the Isle of Wight). He served as an assistant surgeon to the 29th (Worcestershire) Regiment from 1797 to 1800, and as surgeon to the 49th (Hertfordshire) regiment from 1800–*circa* 1807, the 62nd (Wiltshire) Regiment from *circa*1807 to 1809, and the 6th Regiment of Dragoon from 1809 to 1814.

14. John Stewart, *An Account of Prince Edward Island in the Gulph of St. Lawrence, North America: Containing Its Geography, a Description of Its Different Divisions, Soil, Climate, Seasons, Natural Productions, Cultivation, Discovery, Conquest, Progress and Present State of the Settlement, Government, Constitution, Laws, and Religion.* (London: Printed by W. Winchester, 1806), xii–xiii. According to Stewart, the number of English who had immigrated to the United States far exceeds the number of Scots who had immigrated to Canada.

15. By the second half of the nineteenth century the English had formed a majority of the British immigrants coming to Canada, and by the twentieth century they were an overwhelming majority. However, before 1907, the preferred destination of the English was always the United States.

16. Philip Buckner, "The Transformation of the Maritimes: 1815–1860," *The London Journal of Canadian Studies*, Vol. 9 (1993), 13–30.

17. Some Acadians escaped deportation in 1755 by fleeing to Île Royale (renamed Cape Breton) and the Island of St. John (renamed Prince Edward Island), then still under French control. But when Britain acquired these islands, another round of deportations followed in 1858. With the ending of hostilities in 1763, many Acadians returned to the eastern Maritimes, although they were confined to mainly remote areas and to relatively poor land. S. MacNutt, *The Atlantic Provinces: The Emergence of Colonial Society, 1712–1857* (London: McClelland & Stewart, 1965), 62–63, 113; Phillip Buckner and John G. Reid (eds.), *The Atlantic Region to Confederation: A History* (Toronto: University of Toronto Press, 1993), 144–47, 164–65, 198–99.

18. The Mi'kmaq declared war on Britain in 1749, in retaliation for the creation of a British military presence and settlement at Halifax. Despite attempts by the British

to bring this war to an end by treaty, the conflict continued until 1760, when a series of treaties finally brought peace. Meanwhile, with the defeat of the French at Louisbourg in 1758, the Mi'kmaq had been forced to surrender to British control, and from then on they were progressively removed from their hunting grounds to make way for European settlers and to accommodate Britain's defence needs.

19. "Planter" is an old English term for colonist.

20. A total of forty-thousand Loyalists had been relocated from the United States at this time. The Maritimes acquired the majority with thirty-five thousand, while the remaining five thousand were mainly sent to stretches along the St. Lawrence River, with some also going to the Gaspé Peninsula, Prince Edward Island, and Cape Breton.

21. Canadian census-takers insisted that a person's ethnicity should be defined by the ethnicity of the first antecedent from Europe on the male side to have set foot on North American soil.

22. This compares with 49.5 percent of the population of Prince Edward Island who claimed at least one English ancestor in 1991, while the comparable figures for Nova Scotia and New Brunswick were 54 percent and 43 percent respectively. Bruce Elliott, "The English," *The Encyclopedia of Canada's Peoples*, edited by Paul Robert Magosci (Toronto: Published for the Multicultural History Society of Ontario by the University of Toronto Press, *circa* 1999), 463–65.

23. New Brunswick and Nova Scotia Land Company, *Practical Information Respecting New Brunswick: For the Use of Persons Intending to Settle Upon the Lands of the New Brunswick and Nova Scotia Land Company* (London: Pelham Richardson, 1843), 31.

24. LAC MG29 A62: John Laing Diary, 6. John Laing kept a diary of his impressions of the New Brunswick countryside during a visit in 1885.

25. John Lewellin, "Emigration, P.E.I., 1832," in Harvey, *Journeys to the Island of Saint John or Prince Edward Island, 1775–1832*, 206.

26. J.F.W. Johnston, *Notes on North America: Agricultural, Economical and Social*, 2 Vols. (Edinburgh: William Blackwood & Sons, 1851), Vol. 2, 58.

27. Joshua Marsden, *The Narrative of a Mission to Nova Scotia, New Brunswick and the Somers Islands with a Tour to Lake Ontario*. (Plymouth-Dock, England: Printed and sold by J. Johns, 1816), 23.

28. DRO 219/29/22a-c #132.

29. Under the Poor Law Amendment Act (1834) English parishes were able to raise funds to pay the emigration costs of poor people to the British colonies, although some had been doing so long before the Act was passed. Ireland had no similar provision until 1838 and neither did Scotland, which did not have a compulsory Poor Law until 1845. Local authorities were under pressure to keep emigrants in the Empire, rather than allowing them to supplement the population of the United States.

30. Captain Swing, the alleged leader of the 1830–31 riots, has never been identified. The rioters were repressed and the worst offenders transported to Australia. See E.J. Hobsbawn and Rudé George, *Captain Swing* (London: Lawrence & Wishart, 1969), 60, 121, Appendix I. Suffolk had very few reported incidents. The counties with the greatest number of incidents were: Hampshire, 208; Wiltshire, 208; Kent, 154;

Berkshire, 165; Norfolk, 88. There were a total of 1,475 recorded incidents during the Swing riots.

31. PP 1831–2 (724) XXXII.

32. William Cobbett, *The Emigrant's Guide in 10 Letters Addressed to the Taxpayers of England: Containing Information of Every Kind, Necessary for Persons About to Emigrate; Including Several Authentic and Most Interesting Letters from English Emigrants, Now in America, to Their Relations in England*. (London: the author, 1829), 40–41. Cobbett disapproved of Canada's "miserable colonies." He described them as "the offal of North America; they are the head, shins, the shanks and hoofs of that part of the world; while the United States is the sirloins, the well-covered and well-lined ribs and the suet."

33. *Ibid*. During a visit to the Salisbury area, Cobbett was furious to learn that an Emigration Committee "was sitting to devise the means of getting rid not of the idlers, not of the pensioners, not of the dead-weight ... but to devise means of getting rid of these working people, who are grudged even the miserable morsel that they get!" William Cobbett, *Rural Rides*, Ian Dyck, ed. (London: Penguin Books, 2001), 287, 463. First published 1830.

34. SROI Education File 26: Extract from *Gentleman's Magazine* (May 1832), 457.

35. The 1841 census of Great Britain, which recorded the extent of emigration by county, reveals that Cornwall and Devon lost relatively large numbers in that one year. Although Atlantic Canada acquired a relatively large number of immigrants from these two counties, they were only a small fraction of the number who went to the United States and Upper Canada. Charlotte Erickson, *Leaving England: Essays on British Emigration in the Nineteenth Century* (Ithica, NY: Cornell University Press, 1994), 37–38.

36. Elliott, "The English," 462–69.

37. Andrew Hall Clark, *Three Centuries and the Island: A Historical Geography of Settlement and Agriculture in Prince Edward Island, Canada* (Toronto: University of Toronto Press, 1959), 48–52; F.W.P. Bolger, ed., *Canada's Smallest Province: A History of Prince Edward Island* (Halifax: Nimbus, 1991), 38–42. J.M. Bumsted, *Land Settlement and Politics in Eighteenth Century Prince Edward Island* (Kingston, ON: McGill-Queen's, 1987), 16–26.

38. WRO CR 114A/562: Charles Morris to John Butler, January 12, 1767. The proprietors were to get land, upon payment of a quit rent assessed at rates ranging from two shillings to six shillings per one hundred acres, and had to agree to settle their lands within ten years, at the rate of one hundred people per township. It was also agreed that the quit rent revenues would be used to finance the island's government, which was established on the island some two years later, in 1769. The condition that the new government's expenses would be paid from the proceeds of quit rents was not honoured by the proprietors in spite of repeated attempts to force them to pay. Bolger, *Canada's Smallest Province*, 42–43.

39. *BA*, March 4, 1843.

40. Johnston, *Notes on North America*, Vol. II, 173–74.

CHAPTER 2: LAYING THE FOUNDATIONS: YORKSHIRE EMIGRATION

1. *Charles Dixon's Memoir*, September 21, 1773, in Bernard Bailyn, *Voyagers to the West: Emigration from Britain to America on the Eve of the Revolution* (New York: Alfred A. Knopf, 1986), 384.

2. *Ibid.*

3. The *Duke of York* arrived in Halifax on March 16, 1772. There is no surviving passenger list, but the following names are known: James Metcalf; Charles and Sussanah Dixon and family; William Freeze Sr., William Freeze Jr, wife and two children; Richard, Mary, Elizabeth, Ann, Thomas, Joseph, and Mary Lowerison; William, Elizabeth, and Valentine Wood and two females; Ralph Siddall plus wife, Ralph and Francis Siddall, and three females; George Bulmer, Thomas Coates. See Michael F. Cooney, *Emigrants of Yorkshire, 1774–1775* (Kingston-upon-Hull: Abus, *circa* 1994); Reginald Burton Bowser, *A Genealogical Review of the Bowser Family: Researches with Particular Reference to Thomas Bowser of Yorkshire, England and Sackville, New Brunswick, Canada* (Moncton, NB: R.B. Bowser, *circa* 1981), 2, 13; Bailyn, *Voyagers from the West*, 379–87.

4. At this time Cumberland included not only the present County of Cumberland in Nova Scotia, but also the counties of Westmorland and Albert in New Brunswick.

5. James B. Dixon, *History of Charles Dixon* (Sackville, NB: 1891), 3.

6. James Snowdon, "Footprints in the Marsh Mud: Politics and Land Settlement in the Township of Sackville, 1760–1800," unpublished MA thesis, University of New Brunswick (1974), 54–55.

7. Birdsall is fifteen miles northeast of the city of York. Thomas Bowser's two sisters sailed in the *Two Friends* in 1774.

8. In 1777, Bowser acquired the tract for £125. Robinson and Rispin, *A Journey Through Nova Scotia*, 39. Reginald Bowser, *The Bowser Family*, 3.

9. Bailyn, *Voyagers to the West*, 384.

10. James Metcalf to Ann Gill, August 1772 — Webster Collection (Mount Allison University Archives) printed in full in W.C. Milner, "The Records of Chignecto," *Collections of the Nova Scotia Historical Society*, Vol. 15 (1911), 62–64.

11. *Ibid.*, 64.

12. Bailyn, *Voyagers to the West*, 379–84.

13. *DCB*, Michael Francklin, Vol. 4.

14. Advertisement placed by Michael Francklin in the *York Courant*, May 19, 1772.

15. *Ibid.*

16. Bailyn, *Voyagers to the West*, 373–74, 376, 379.

17. Between 1772 and 1775, at least 1,400 British emigrants (eight hundred from northern England and six hundred from Scotland) sailed on thirteen vessels to Nova Scotia and the Island of St. John (later Prince Edward Island).

18. John Bartlet Brebner, *The Neutral Yankees of Nova Scotia: A Marginal Colony During the Revolutionary Years* (New York: Columbia University Press, 1937), 114–20.

19. Eagleson to SPG Committee, December 27, 1773, quoted in Snowdon, "Footprints in the Marsh Mud," 52.

20. *York Chronicle and Weekly Advertiser*, October 8, 1773.

21. *Ibid.*

22. NAB T/47/9 and /10: Register of emigrants, 1773–1776. The individual passenger lists are printed in Appendix I.

23. NAB T 47/9 ff. 120–23.

24. *Ibid.*

25. WYAS WYL 219/305/5: William Lister to Lord Dartmouth, June 14, 1774.

26. *Ibid.*

27. WYAS WYL 219/305/5: Edward Elmsall to Lord Dartmouth, May 30, 1774.

28. However, a decline in the cloth trade in the Leeds area was causing great distress. WYAS WYL 219/305/5: Edward Elmsall to Lord Dartmouth, April 8, 1773.

29. STRO D(W)1778/II/2507: Francis Legge to Lord Dartmouth, August 18, 1775.

30. NSARM RG1 Vol. 32, doc 22.

31. NAB T/47/9 ff. 77–79.

32. *YCWA*, August 26, 1774.

33. NSARM MG 1 Vol. 1854 F3: C.B. Fergusson papers. Nathaniel Smith in Hull to his brother, March 5, May 29, 1774.

34. *Ibid.*

35. *YCWA*, March 18, 1774.

36. The agents were: William Thompson in Sherborn; John Lancaster in Wilton, near Thornton; Mr. Grant in Skeldergate; John Burton at the Pack Horse, in Micklegate, York; Mr. Weatherhead or Mr. Hague in Malton; and Mr. Cook, at the post office in Bridlington.

37. *YCWA*, March 18, 1774.

38. The agents were Robert Appleton in Bridlington; John Baxter in Setterington; William Porter in Driffield; William Stavley in Thornby; Richard Sheppard in Kirby; Andrew Loughhead in Pickering; and Jonathan Milner in Burrow.

39. *YCWA*, February 18, 1774.

40. *YCWA*, April 15, 1774.

41. NAB T 47/9 ff. 120–3.

42. The customs list contains all of the people known to have sailed in the *Thomas and William* but none of the *Prince George*'s passengers. Most of the names in the customs list can be found in a single sequence in the list provided by Legge, which was organized by ship.

43. NSARM RG1 Vol. 44, doc 37: An account of the number of passengers from Great Britain April 5 to July 5, 1774.

44. Robinson and Rispin, *A Journey Through Nova Scotia*, 5.

45. The 1803 Passenger Act specified a minimum space allocation for passengers and daily food requirements. Lucille H. Campey, *"Fast Sailing and Copper-Bottomed": Aberdeen Sailing Ships and the Emigrant Scots They Carried to Canada* (Toronto: Natural Heritage Books, 2002), 105–06.

46. The tonnage to passenger ratio for the *Thomas and William* was better, since she had a tonnage of three hundred.

47. *YCWA*, August 26, 1774.

48. *YCWA*, September 23, 1774.

49. *YCWA*, April 15, 1774. Harrison was said to be worth three thousand pounds but eight hundred pounds had been left "on security" in England.

50. Fares: adults, five pounds; two to ten years old, two pounds, ten shillings; under two years, gratis. Providing their own provisions: adults, three pounds, three shillings; under ten years, two pounds, two shillings. Cabin passengers: ten pounds (see *Newcastle Chronicle* or *Weekly Advertiser*, April 1, 1775).

51. A traveller from Kent who also stayed at the inn reported his encounter with the group to the *Canterbury Journal*. See Mildred Campbell, "English Emigration on the Eve of the American Revolution," *American Historical Review*, Vol. 61 (1955), 16. See also Bailyn, *Voyagers to the West*, 408–11.

52. Robertson and Rispin, *A Journey through Nova Scotia*, 3–4.

53. The shipping agents were Robert Swann in Sunderland and William Robinson in Stockton-on-Tees. See *YCWA*, March 18, 1774.

54. Steerage fares cost five pounds, five shillings for adults, and two pounds, two shillings and sixpence for children under ten. See *Newcastle Chronicle*, April 1, 1775.

55. Louise Ryder Young, *The Yorkshire Antecedents and American Descendents of the William H.A. Richardson Family of Sackville, New Brunswick, Canada and Reading, Massachusetts* (Ellicott City, MD: Author, 1984), 1, 7. The Richardson's baby born during the crossing was named Joseph Providence.

56. NAB T47/9 ff. 135–36.

57. NSARM RG1 Vol. 44, doc 37: An account of the number of passengers from Great Britain April 5 to July 5, 1774.

58. *YCWA*, January 27, 1775.

59. NSARM RG1 Vol. 44, doc 37: Governor Legge to Lord Dartmouth, July 6, 1774.

60. *Ibid.*, Vol. 44, doc 44: Legge to Dartmouth, Sept. 13, 1774.

61. Robinson and Rispin, *A Journey Through Nova Scotia*, 19–20.

62. The shipping agents were: Christopher Laybourn of Hull; Christopher Harper of Barthorpe-Bottoms; John Robinson of Bewholm, in Holderness, an intended passenger and author of the late *Journey Through Nova Scotia*, who lately bought an estate there, and whose books are to be sold at Mr. Etherington's, York; Mr. Holtby at Bridlington; and Mr. Hudson at Weighton. See *YCWA*, February 3, 1775.

63. *YCWA*, February 3, 1775

64. Robinson and Rispin, *A Journey Through Nova Scotia*, 6, 8, 14, 15.

65. *Ibid.*, 17.

66. Snowdon, "Footprints in the Marsh Mud," 89–107.

67. NSARM MG 1 Vol. 427 (m/f 14920) Harrison family papers, No. 188: Luke to William Harrison, June 30, 1774.

68. *Ibid.*, No. 190: Luke to William Harrison, January 1, 1803. By then the Harrisons had re-established themselves along the Maccan River.

69. PANB MC1 Trueman family; Bailyn, *Voyagers to the West*, 423–25.

70. NSARM MG 1 Vol. 1854 F3: C.B. Fergusson papers. Nathaniel to his brother Benjamin, May 29, 1774.

71. Fort Lawrence, located just to the northwest of Amherst, Nova Scotia, had been built by the British in 1750 but was later destroyed. In response to the building of Fort Lawrence, the French had built Fort Beauséjour (renamed Fort Cumberland) in 1751 (see Map 2). The French had also built Fort Gaspereau (renamed Monckton by the British) on the other side of the isthmus at Baie Verte, in 1751. It, too, was destroyed by the British in 1756.

72. NSARM MG 1 Vol. 1854 F3: C.B. Fergusson papers. Nathaniel to his brother Benjamin, July 30, 1775.

73. Gildart's other business interests required him to return to England from time to time. Bailyn, *Voyagers to the West*, 413–14.

74. G. Barlow, *Family Genealogy of Jonathan Barlow...* in Snowdon, *Footprints in the Marsh Mud*, 53.

75. Young girl's letter to her parents in Yorkshire, in *YCWA*, August 26, 1774.

76. NSARM MG 100 Vol. 263 No. 13: Nathaniel to Benjamin, June 20, 1774.

77. NAB CO 217/52: Massey to Lord George Germain, Halifax, June 27–28, 1776.

78. Biographical details of the Yorkshire settlers who came to Nova Scotia between 1772 and 1775 can be found in: Howard Trueman, *The Chignecto Isthmus and Its First Settlers* (Toronto: William Briggs, 1902), 217–59.

79. Legge to Dartmouth, May 10, 1774, in Brebner, *Neutral Yankees*, 102.

80. Snowden, "Footprints in the Marsh Mud," 53–60.

81. Robinson and Rispin, *A Journey through Nova Scotia*, 25.

82. William Black was the son of a prosperous linen draper from Huddersfield, *DCB*, Vol. 6.

83. *Ibid.*, Robinson and Rispin, *A Journey through Nova Scotia*, 32–34.

CHAPTER 3: THE LOYALISTS WHO FOLLOWED

1. PANB MC80/2579: Nathaniel Smith to Benjamin Smith, January, 25, 1777, in Pat Finney, *Nathaniel Smith: A Stranger in a Strange Land* (Sackville, NB: Tantramar Heritage Trust, 2000), 22–23.

2. Trueman, *Chignecto Isthmus*, 225, 228–29.

3. For a detailed description of Eddy's rebel army and its attempted siege of Fort Cumberland, see Peter L. McCreath and John G. Leefe, *A History of Early Nova Scotia* (Tantallon, NS: Four East Publications, 1990), 272–90.

4. The Royal Fencible Americans were disbanded at Fort Cumberland and granted land in the parish of St. George on Passamaquoddy Bay in New Brunswick.

5. Snowdon, "Footprints in the Marsh Mud," 63–88; Milner, "Records of Chignecto," 45–57.

6. DHC D/LEG/F8: Diary and ledger of Benjamin Lester, August 11, 1782.

7. *DCB*, Vol. 4. See also G.A. Rawlyk, ed., *Henry Alline: Selected Writings* (New York: Paulist Press, *circa* 1987), 336–38.

8. *Ibid.*

9. Samuel Delbert Clark, *Church and Sect in Canada* (Toronto: University of Toronto Press, 1948), 18–19.

10. They settled in what became Upper Canada, when the separate provinces of Upper and Lower Canada were created in 1791.

11. Buckner and Reid, *Atlantic Region*, 184–209.

12. Bolger, *Canada's Smallest Province*, 60.

13. The British Army consisted of British regulars (professional soldiers who served wherever they were needed, usually for life), the provincial corps, and the militia (non-professional soldiers who were responsible for local defence in times of emergency). The soldiers in the provincial corps were organized and trained much like the British regulars but were recruited in North America for service only in that region.

14. Esther Clark Wright, *The Loyalists of New Brunswick* (Fredericton, NB: Moncton Publishing, 1955), 4–6, 151–55.

15. Neil MacKinnon, *This Unfriendly Soil: The Loyalist Experience in Nova Scotia, 1783–1791* (Montreal: McGill-Queen's University Press, 1986), 57–66. Wright, *Loyalists of New Brunswick*, 155–56, 159.

16. They were mainly runaway slaves from Virginia and South Carolina. G. Wynn, "A Region of Scattered Settlements and Bounded Possibilities: Northeastern America 1775–1800," *Canadian Geographer*, Vol. 31, No. 4 (1987), 319–38.

17. Quoted in C.W. Vernon, *Bicentenary Sketches and Early Days of the Church in Nova Scotia* (Halifax: Chronicle Printing, 1910), 137.

18. Some men of the 60th Regiment settled at Falmouth. MacKinnon, *This Unfriendly Soil*, 21, 43, 47.

19. Marion Gilroy, *Loyalists and Land Settlement in Nova Scotia* (Halifax: PANS Publication No. 4, 1937).

20. Wynn, "A Region of Scattered Settlements," 319–38.

21. Men from the disbanded Royal Highland Emigrants Regiment (84th) were allocated land along both sides of the Nine Mile River and the Kennetcook River, but few remained.

22. Loyalist concentrations along the north shore at Pictou and Merigomish were principally Scottish. They were formed from two disbanded Scottish regiments: the Duke of Hamilton's (82nd) and the Royal Highland Emigrants (84th), who mainly settled on their allocations. A militia regiment from Westchester County, New York, had been granted land near Tatamagouche, to the west of Pictou, and in Cumberland County, but most of them opted for Westmorland County (New Brunswick) or the city of Saint John.

23. MacKinnon, *This Unfriendly Soil*, 42–47, 54–56, 171–73.

24. Timothy Hierlihy, their former commander, led about eighty-six officers and men to Antigonish Harbour. A number of units serving in the Island of St John had been merged with Timothy Hierlihy's group to form the Nova Scotia Volunteers.

25. MacKinnon, *This Unfriendly Soil*, 44.

26. Scots who had served with the Royal Highland Regiment (42nd) were allocated land along the Nashwaak River, to the north of Fredericton, but they left and moved northwards to the Miramichi region to take advantage of its lumbering opportunities. They were joined in the Miramichi by other Scots from the Macdonald Highlanders Regiment (76th), the North Carolina Volunteers, and the Queen's Rangers. See Lucille H. Campey, *With Axe and Bible: The Scottish Pioneers of New Brunswick, 1784–1874* (Toronto: Natural Heritage Books-Dundurn Group, 2007), 16–32.

27. The blocks of land which were assigned to the Loyalist Regiments in the St. John Valley are shown in Robert Dallison, *Hope Restored: The American Revolution and Founding of New Brunswick* (Fredericton: Goose Lane Editions and the New Brunswick Military Heritage Project, 2003), 28.

28. Wynn, "A Region of Scattered Settlements," 324–25.

29. The group from Maine had settled on the Penobscot River in 1775, but a boundary change in 1783 required them to move to their new location at St. Andrews so they could remain in British-held territory. The group's leading members were Glasgow-born Robert Pagan and his two brothers, William and Thomas, who were timber exporters and shipbuilders. D. Gallant, "Early Settlers in Southwestern New Brunswick," unpublished BA thesis, Mount Allison University, 1959, 50–52.

30. For details of the Charlotte County Loyalist settlements, see Campey, *Axe and Bible*, 29, 30, 32, 34, 37, 38.

31. The Royal Fencibles settled mainly in Cumberland and Sackville townships, in the Chignecto Isthmus (later Westmorland County, New Brunswick) and along the Passamaquoddy Bay near the Maine boundary. Chester Martin, "The Loyalists in New Brunswick," *Ontario Historical Society, Papers and Records*, Vol. 30 (1934), 160–70.

32. *The Winslow Papers* quoted in Wynn, "A Region of Scattered Settlements," 324.

33. Robert Fellows, "Loyalists and Land Settlement in New Brunswick," *Canadian Archivist*, Vol. 2 (1971), 5–13.

34. MacKinnon, *This Unfriendly Soil*, 137–38, 146.

35. Wilbur Henry Siebert, "The Loyalists in Prince Edward Island," *Transactions of the Royal Society of Canada*, Series 3, Vol. 4, Section 2, 113–17.

36. MacKinnon, *This Unfriendly Soil*, 62–64, 137–38, 151–55.

37. Patrick Cecil Telford White, ed., *Lord Selkirk's Diary 1803–04: A Journal of His Travels Through British North America and the Northeastern United States* (Toronto: The Champlain Society, 1958), 17–18.

38. LAC MG24 F89: Colin Campbell's letter-book, August 4, 1783.

39. MacKinnon, *This Unfriendly Soil*, 154–55.

40. *Ibid.*, 136, 174–75.

41. SOAS MMS/North America/Correspondence/FMB 1 (hereafter SOAS MMS), letter dated November 16, 1804.

42. LAC M-1352: Glasgow Colonial Society Correspondence, Reverend Gavin Lang to Reverend Robert Burns, December 24, 1829.

43. Following the discord in Digby, Amos Botsford moved to Dorchester, New Brunswick, and later represented Westmorland County in the House of Assembly.

44. Taunya Jean Padley, "The Church of England's Role in Settling the Loyalists in the Town of Digby 1783–1818," unpublished MA thesis, Acadia University, 1991.

45. MacKinnon, *This Unfriendly Soil*, 137, 174–75.

46. NAB CO 700: Nova Scotia, No. 60: Digby township plan, 1786.

47. Isaiah W. Wilson, *A Geography and History of the County of Digby, Nova Scotia* (Belleville, ON: Mika Studio, 1972), 152. Originally published by the author in 1893.

48. *New Brunswick Gazette*, May 26, 1802.

49. MacKinnon, *This Unfriendly Soil*, 43.

50. *Ibid.*, 89–117, 158–79.

51. Wynn, "A Region of Scattered Settlements," 321–25.

52. MacKinnon, *This Unfriendly Soil*, 27–36.

53. *Ibid.*, 158–79. Wynn, "A Region of Scattered Settlements," 324–26.

54. The original settlers also included Swiss and French Huguenots.

55. Anglican ministers at Loyalists settlements reported that their congregations represented less than one-half of the total population. Judith Fingard, *The Anglican Design in Loyalist Nova Scotia* (London: SPCK, 1972), 39–53.

56. The mission was established on the false premise that Cape Breton would attract many Loyalists, but this never happened. It attracted few Loyalists and eventually became a major Scottish enclave.

57. Arthur Wentworth Hamilton Eaton, *The Church of England in Nova Scotia and the Tory Clergy of the Revolution* (London: J. Nisbet & Co., 1892), 215–16.

58. Ross N. Hebb, *The Church of England in Loyalist New Brunswick, 1783–1825* (Madison, NJ: Farleigh Dickinson University Press, 2004), 31–41; Herbert G. Lee, "An Historical Sketch of the First Fifty Years of the Church of England in the Province of New Brunswick" (Saint John, NB: Sun Publishing Co., 1880), 27–40, 55–86.

59. *Ibid.*, 27.

60. MacKinnon, *This Unfriendly Soil*, 33–34

CHAPTER 4: NOVA SCOTIA'S ENGLISH SETTLERS: TWO TYPES OF ENGLISH

1. NSARM MG1 Vol. 1897: C.B. Fergusson papers F1 Immigration to N.S. 1773–1837, Folder 1, F1/5 Wentworth to Castlereagh, February 3, 1806.

2. Robinson and Rispin, *A Journey Through Nova Scotia*, 34–36.

3. Lucille H. Campey, *An Unstoppable Force: The Scottish Exodus to Canada* (Toronto: Natural Heritage Books-Dundurn Press, 2008), 1–16.

4. Most immigrants sailed in timber ships that initially did most of their trade with Maritime ports. Since they included immigrants destined for either the United States or Upper Canada, arrival numbers at Maritime ports do not necessarily signify permanent settlers.

5. Scots made up 56 percent of the total and the Irish 33 percent. Martell, *Immigration to Nova Scotia, 1815–38*, 91–95, 100.

6.   J.S. Martell, *Immigration to and Emigration from Nova Scotia, 1815–1838* (Halifax, NS: PANS 1942), 8–9.

7.   *Ibid.*, 44, 46, 48.

8.   The *Integrity* sailed to Halifax from Workington in 1819 with fifty-five people and the *Mary Anne* from Whitehaven to Pictou in 1822 with thirty-nine passengers. Martell, *Immigration to Nova Scotia, 1815–38*, 48; George MacLaren, *The Pictou Book: Stories of our Past* (New Glasgow, NS: Hector Pub. Co., 1954), 119.

9.   Martell, *Immigration to Nova Scotia, 1815–38*, 61, 68, 71, 75, 78, 82.

10. A total of 13,500 British immigrants came to Nova Scotia during this period, with around 60 percent arriving between 1839 and 1843. The Irish ranked third at 17 percent of the total. Susan Longley Flewwelling (Morse), "Immigration to and Emigration from Nova Scotia 1839–51," *Nova Scotia Historical Society (Collections)*, Vol. 28 (1949), 121.

11. The largest group of settlers came from the east end of London. McCreath and Leefe, *Early Nova Scotia*, 196–203.

12. Around 45 percent of the 2,547 settlers who arrived in 1749 were reported to have left the area. Esther Clark, Wright, *Planters and Pioneers* (Wolfville, NS: the author, 1982), 8–11.

13. Lilliam Gertrude Best Hallam, *When You Are in Halifax: Sketches of Life in the First English Settlement in Canada* (Toronto: Church Book Room, 1937), 30–38. St. Matthews, the Congregational Church, was built in 1754, but it was destroyed by fire in 1857.

14. DRO 219/29/22a-c #18, 89, 163, 187: Devonian families resident abroad.

15. MacGregor, *British America*, 145.

16. Marjorie Whitelaw, ed., *The Dalhousie Journals* (Ottawa: Oberon, 1978–82), Vol. 1, 75.

17. British public opinion was opposed to emigration, since it would mean the loss of people to the colonies who would otherwise be in its labour force or armed services.

18. Wright, *Planters and Pioneers*, 11–12.

19. Society for the Propagation of the Gospel in Foreign Parts (hereafter described as SPG) *Annual Report*, 1845, xxxiii–xxxvii.

20. Whitelaw, *Dalhousie Journals*, Vol. 1, 42.

21. *SPG Annual Report*, 1855, xxxvi–xlii. New Dublin had acquired Ulster settlers in 1762, led by the enterprising Alexander McNùtt, although most moved out. McNutt's colonizing efforts were more successful in the Cobequid Bay area, when fifty New Hampshire families who originated from Ulster, together with around 250 immigrants who came directly from Ulster, settled at Truro, Onslow, and Londonderry (see Map 8).

22. In 1752, the Acadian population was estimated to be between ten and fifteen thousand. Buckner and Reid, *Atlantic Region*, 131, 144–47, 164–65, 198–99.

23. *Ibid.*, 151–52, 162–63; J.M. Bumsted, *The Peoples of Canada: A Pre-Confederation History*, Vol. 1 (Toronto: Oxford University Press, 1992), 140–44.

24. Bailyn, *Voyagers to the West*, 366–67.

25. STRO D (W) 1778/II/446: William Gerard de Brahm to Lord Dartmouth; n/d but received October 1772.

26. Wright, *Planters and Pioneers*, 12–13.

27. NSARM MG 100 Vol. 263 #13 (m/f 22,346): Nathaniel Smith to Benjamin Smith, April 1789.

28. *Ibid.*

29. The first Baptist church was built at Horton in 1778, while the second was built at Halifax in 1795. By 1800, additional Baptist churches had been built at Upper Granville, Lower Granville, Digby, Digby Neck, Yarmouth, Cornwallis, and Newport. J.M. Cramp "The Centenary of Baptists in Nova Scotia," *General Report of the Nova Scotia Baptist Education Society* (Halifax: Christian Message Office, 1860) No. 18, 4–6, 32–35.

30. Whitelaw, *Dalhousie Journals*, Vol. 1, 84. The Anglican church was probably located at present-day Wolfville.

31. *Ibid.*, 86.

32. Joseph Bouchette, *The British Dominions in North America: A Topographical and Statistical Description of the Provinces of Lower and Upper Canada, New Brunswick, Nova Scotia, the Islands of Newfoundland, Prince Edward Island and Cape Breton*, Vol. 2 (London: 1832), 30–31, 36–37.

33. Whitelaw, *Dalhousie Journals*, Vol. 1, 62–73.

34. NSARM MG 1 1739 #19: Kennedy B. Wainwright fonds, extracts from Bishop Inglis's diary, August 14, 1791.

35. Aylesford had been settled initially by Loyalists. In 1832, Kings County contained the four townships of Horton, Cornwallis, Aylesford, and Parrsboro.

36. NSARM MG 1 1739 #19: Kennedy B. Wainwright fonds, extracts from Bishop Inglis's diary, August 14, 1791.

37. SOAS MMS William Black, October 10, 1804.

38. Whitelaw, *Dalhousie Journals*, Vol. 1, 37–38.

39. SOAS MMS J. Mann, January 30, 1817.

40. *Ibid.*

41. Yarmouth would become a major shipbuilding centre and one of the province's leading ports.

42. LAC MG25–G404: Bond family fonds. Joseph Norman Bond, *DCB*, Vol. 6.

43. The townships (Falmouth, Newport, and Windsor) would later lie in Hants County (see Map 5).

44. WYAS WYL 109: Rockingham letter books, 70. Inglis to Sir John Wentworth, November 23, 1801.

45. Whitelaw, *Dalhousie Journals*, Vol. 1, 62–63.

46. By 1856, Anglicans were mainly concentrated at Rawdon, Kennetcook, and Five Mile River. RHL USPG Series E, 1856 (LAC m/f A221).

47. King's College moved to Halifax in 1922.

48. SOAS MMS John Mann, September 18, 1804.

49. *Ibid.*, W. Croscombe, June 24, 1818.

50. Whitelaw, *Dalhousie Journals*, Vol. 1, 41.

51. Cumberland was settled first in 1759 by families from Connecticut. Sackville (New

Brunswick) had its first New England settlers by 1761. In addition to the New Englanders, the isthmus also attracted disbanded soldiers who had served in the large British garrison at Fort Cumberland. Milner, "Records of Chignecto," 1–40.

52. In 1767 the isthmus had 868 settlers: Amherst had 125 (eighty-five Irish, twenty-nine Americans), Cumberland had 334 (twenty-eight Irish, 269 Americans), Moncton had sixty (forty-nine Germans), and Sackville had 349 (343 Americans). Brebner, *Neutral Yankees*, 60–66. Louise Walsh Throop, "Early Settlers of Cumberland Township, Nova Scotia," *National Genealogical Society Quarterly*, Vol. 67 (September 1979), 182–92.

53. Thomas Chandler Haliburton, *An Historical and Statistical Account of Nova Scotia*, 2 Vols. (Halifax: J. Howe, 1829), Vol. 2, 64. Joseph Bouchette also extolled the great agricultural potential of this region. See Bouchette, *The British Dominions in North America*, Vol. 2, 24–25.

54. Whitelaw, *Dalhousie Journals*, Vol. 1, 83–84.

55. NSARM: MG1 Vol. 427, No. 191: John Harrison, Junior to William Harrison, June 24, 1810. The Harrisons had left Yorkshire in 1774, having first settled at the River Hébert. They moved to the Maccan River in 1787.

56. *Ibid.*, No. 190: Luke Harrison to William Harrison, January 1, 1803.

57. John MacLean, *William Black: The Apostle of Methodism in the Maritime Provinces of Canada* (Halifax: Methodist Book Room, 1907), 14.

58. Memoirs of William Black, quoted in Snowdon, "Footprints in the Marsh Mud," 58.

59. *DCB*, William Black, Vol. 4.

60. Bailyn, *Voyagers to the West*, 421–26.

61. The Wesleyan Methodist Missionary Society was founded in Britain in 1786 to support missionary activities overseas.

62. Methodist congregation numbers were highest at Halifax (153), Liverpool (120), Annapolis (105), Shelburne (96), Cumberland (95), and Windsor (60). SOAS MMS W. Lowry, March 20, 1804.

63. SOAS MMS, T. Payne, May 7, 1817.

64. According to the 1871 census returns, Methodism was strongest at Advocate Harbour (58 percent), Maccan (46 percent), River Philip (41 percent), and Wallace (35 percent).

65. In 1845, the Amherst minister, George Townsend, reported that he served two churches and four outlying preaching stations serving a total congregation of 330: Amherst (100), Pugwash (100), Wallace (80), head of Amherst (50). RHL USPG Series E, 1845 (LAC m/f A221).

66. Whitelaw, *Dalhousie Journals*, Vol. 1, 47–49.

67. *Report of the Wesleyan Methodist Missionary Society*, 1838, 89.

68. *Acadian Recorder*, June 16, 1827. The *Mary* sailed from Liverpool that same year with forty miners, the *Maria* in 1828 with "8 artificers for the mines," the *Thomas Battersby* that same year with an unknown number of miners, and the *Mary Ann* in 1838 with one hundred miners. Martell, *Immigration to Nova Scotia, 1815–38*, 60–62; McLaren, *Pictou Book*, 121.

69. Martell, *Immigration to Nova Scotia, 1815–38*, 92–93; Susan Longley Morse, "Immigration to Nova Scotia 1839–51," unpublished MA thesis, Dalhousie University (1946), 115–20.

70. Large concentrations of Scots had become established in Pictou County, in mainland Nova Scotia, and throughout most of Cape Breton by 1800. See Lucille H. Campey, *After the Hector: The Scottish Pioneers of Nova Scotia and Cape Breton, 1773–1852* (Toronto: Natural Heritage Books, 2004), 56–84.

71. Whitelaw, *Dalhousie Journals*, Vol. 1, 58.

72. Perhaps Augustus Frederick, Duke of York (1773–1843), was an unlikely person to have had gambling debts. He promoted benevolent schemes and was noted for his library, which amounted to over fifty thousand volumes, including one thousand editions of the Bible.

73. The jewellers established an office for the General Mining Association in Ludgate Hill in the city of London near their premises. The firm also speculated in mining stock in South America with disastrous results. Paul Storr, *The Last of the Goldsmiths* (London: Batsford, 1954), 76–77.

74. The General Mining Association established the Albion Foundry at Albion Mines in 1828. The enterprise brought Nova Scotia its first steam engine and first steam-powered sawmill, along with the capacity to build more steam engines. Barbara Robertson, *Sawpower: Making Lumber in the Sawmills of Nova Scotia* (Halifax: Nimbus Pub. Ltd. and the Nova Scotia Museum, 1986), 59, 147.

75. J.S. Martell, "Early Coal Mining in Nova Scotia," *Cape Breton Historical Essays*, edited by Don MacGillivray and Brian Tenyson (Sydney, NS: College of Cape Breton Press, 1981), 165–71.

76. Stephen J. Hornsby, *Nineteenth Century Cape Breton: A Historical Geography* (Montreal: McGill-Queen's University Press, 1992), 15–18. The French had mined coal at Sydney in the early eighteenth century, and the mine was reopened in the mid-1780s, when Loyalists arrived, to supply the naval yards at Halifax and St. John's, Newfoundland. Anxious to protect its coal-mining interests in Cape Breton, the British government tried to limit colonization initially. It introduced restraining orders that restricted freehold grants to Loyalists and fish merchants. But, ignoring government regulations, Scots arrived in their thousands from 1790, taking their land by squatting. See Campey, *After the Hector*, 71–74.

77. The 142 English immigrants who arrived in Cape Breton in 1830 and 1832 had almost certainly been recruited for the Sydney mines. One hundred and five of them had sailed to Sydney from Liverpool in the *Cartha* in 1832. See Martell, *Immigration to Nova Scotia, 1815–1838*, 73, 93.

78. Hornsby, *Nineteenth Century Cape Breton*, 95–107, 169–83. R. Brown, *The Coal Fields and Coal Trade of Cape Breton* (London: Sampson, Low, Marston, Low & Searle, 1869), 76. C. Ochiltree Macdonald, *The Coal and Iron Industries of Nova Scotia* (Halifax: Chronicle Publishing Co., 1909), 189–90.

79. NSARM MG 1 Vol. 3371: Thomas Neville fonds, No. 46, Albion Mines September 19, 1844.

80. *Ibid.*, No. 47. Thomas Neville purchased a farm from Hugh H. Ross on the Tatamagouche Road. It was to be divided in two. Neville purchased "the upper part" for sixty pounds and rented the "lower part with buildings valued at £100" for four pounds per annum.

81. NSARM MG 1 Vol. 3371, No. 9, Joseph Bridgen to his brother (Thomas Neville) and sister Annie, who live at Albion Mines, July 25, 1842.

82. *Ibid.*

83. *Ibid.*, No. 15, Simon and Christinah Neville in Quebec to Thomas Neville (their brother), January 1841.

84. *Ibid.*, No. 24, Simon Neville to Thomas Neville, April 1841.

85. NSARM MG 1 Vol. 3196A: Peter Barrett fonds, 1–5.

86. These primitive conditions were similar to those experienced during the early stages of coal mining, when men lived, slept, and ate in communal cook-rooms.

87. By 1842 the Albion Mines had ninety-one well-finished dwelling houses, twenty-one smaller, and 110 "old log houses" — altogether providing "more than a house for every man." Martell, "Early Coal Mining in Nova Scotia," 169–71.

88. NSARM MG 1 Vol. 3196A, 6–7.

89. *Ibid.*, 13–15, 17.

90. The General Mining Associations' monopoly on coal production was broken by 1858, and after this new companies were formed.

91. Cornishmen working at the mine who were unhurt included James Dunstan, Edward Burns, and Abraham Guy.

92. NSARM MG 1 Vol. 3196A, 19–20, 39.

93. *Ibid.*

94. LAC MG25 G271, Vol. 16. Adam Bousfield had initially immigrated to Boston in the late nineteenth century, moving on to the Pictou area sometime later.

95. Reverend D. MacDonald, *Cape North and Vicinity: Pioneer Families, History and Chronicles: Including Pleasant Bay, Bay St. Lawrence, Aspy Bay, White Point, New Haven and Nell's Harbour* (Nova Scotia: Port Hastings, 1933), 46. Dixon was taken to the home of Neil MacPherson, who lived near the scene of the wreck.

96. The London Missionary Society, founded in 1795, represented the various non-conformist religions — especially the Methodist and Congregationalist faiths. Their missionaries were sent from England to various parts of the world.

97. SOAS CWM/LMS/ Continent of America/Incoming correspondence/Box 1A, (hereafter LMS), Jacket B, Folder 5 /1, November 1, 1819. The householders listed were: Nicholas Paint Junior, Angus Grant, Nathaniel Clough, George B. Carter, Chandler Martin, James Grant, Stephen Reynolds, John Stewart, George Holland, Joseph Carter, John Reeves.

98. *Ibid.*

99. SOAS LMS, Jacket B, Folder 5/6, John Mitchell, April 1, 1815.

100. Reverend D.C. Moore, Rector of Christ Church, Albion Mines, *Letters and Facts Concerning the Church of England in the County of Pictou* (Halifax: Baillie and Anderson, 1879).

101. Reverend Forsyth also provided religious services at Baddeck. *SPG Annual Report*, 1855, 1856; RHL USPG Series E (LAC m/f A221).

102. RHL USPG Series E, 1855 (LAC m/f A221).

103. *Cape Breton News*, July 1, 1852.

104. A timber Anglican church was built at South Head, east of Sydney, in 1846. Susan Ann Hyde and Michael Bird, *Hallowed Timbers: The Wooden Churches of Cape Breton, Nova Scotia* (Erin, ON.: Boston Mills Press, 1995), 109–10.

105. RHL USPG Series E, 1845 (LAC m/f A221). The 1871 census reveals that the English were concentrated in and around Sydney and Sydney Mines, Cow Bay, Main-à-Dieu, Louisburg, and Gabarus.

106. Some disbanded English soldiers and New Englanders had been employed in the fisheries at Main-à-Dieu, Louisbourg, and Gabarus. Hornsby, *Nineteenth Century Cape Breton*, 5, 12.

107. Report of a debate in the House of Assembly on emigration in 1848 printed in *The Nova Scotian*, January 5, 1852.

108. The Canada Company, a land company founded in 1826 by the Scottish novelist John Galt with financial backing of British entrepreneurs (Galt was the first commissioner sent to Upper Canada), advertised Upper Canada with great gusto and attracted large numbers of immigrants to the province. For details of its formation see Robert C. Lee, *The Canada Company and the Huron Tract, 1826–1853* (Toronto: Natural Heritage Books, 2004).

109. Canada Company advertisement printed in the *Acadian Recorder*, January 26, 1849.

110. The Londonderry iron works, owned by the Acadian Charcoal Iron Company, was opened in 1850. *The Nova Scotian*, January 26, February 9, 1857.

111. *Acadian Recorder*, February 14, 21, 1857.

112. NSARM RG1 Vol. 272, Doc. 141 (m/f 15,360). In 1862 the *Morning Star* arrived with thirty passengers, including a farmer and seven miners; the *Frank Flint* with twenty-three passengers, nineteen of whom were single labourers; and the *British Queen* with twenty passengers, including seven single females, six labourers, and two farmers.

113. *Journals of the House of Assembly*, 1865, Appendix 24, 5–6. The *Euroclydon* disembarked forty-three passengers (twenty from Ireland), including sixteen English labourers; the *Europa* disembarked ten passengers, mainly one family; and the *Indian Queen* came with thirty-three passengers (nine from Ireland), including two couples and two families. The ten passengers who sailed in the *Europa* were assisted by the wealthy Angela Georgina Burdett-Coutts, daughter of a British banker. All quickly found employment and were said to be "in comfortable circumstances." See Terrence Punch, "Nova Scotia Arrivals by Sea in 1864," *Nova Scotia Genealogist*, Vol. 22/2 (2005), 93–95.

114. *Journals of the Assembly of Nova Scotia, 1867*, Immigration Report of 1866, Halifax arrivals, Appendix 7, entitled "Immigration Report."

115. Nova Scotia's gold mines were located mainly in Guysborough, Halifax, and Queens counties.

116. The *Mozart* carried 267 passengers, the *Havelock* 365 passengers, and the *Queen* thirty-six passengers.

117. "Immigration Report," *Journals of the Assembly of Nova Scotia, 1867*, 4.

118. See Chapter 8.

119. *Nova Scotia Legislative Council, Journal and Proceedings*, 1874, Appendix 9: Report of Mather Byles Desbrisay, December 31, 1873. The children, described as "minors," were probably going to work in the mines. Presumably the women were wives. The possible use of immigrant child labour in coal-mining areas is discussed further in Chapter 8.

120. LAC RG17 Vol. 139, No. 14579. They were organized by Nicholas Bryant of St. Agnes and his son, Captain John Bryant. Edward Jenkins, the agent general in London for the Dominion of Canada, organized some financial help for the Cornish group.

121. Nova Scotia House of Assembly, Proceedings, 1875, Appendix 17.

122. WYAS LLD3/719 [197]: Records of all persons aided to emigrate, 1906–1912. The families sailed in the *Norseman* from Liverpool.

123. The heads of household were: James Jordan, a labourer; James Bower, a baker; Charles Midgley, a rough cutter; George Smith, a labourer; John Atkinson, a plumber; John Thomas Gargin, a miner; Joseph Watson, an electrician; Harry Young, a joiner; James Schofield, a brick drawer; Herbert Cox, a mason; Charles Green, a joiner and electrician; Frank Spurr, a brass founder; Charles A. Wadsworth, an engineer and whitesmith; and Walter Wormald, a plasterer. Each family received between thirty and fifty pounds, depending on the number of children.

CHAPTER 5: SCATTERED FAR AND WIDE IN NEW BRUNSWICK

1.   Anon, *Practical Information to Emigrants Including Details Collected from the Most Authentic Accounts Relating to the Soil, Climate, Natural Productions, Agriculture etc. of the Province of New Brunswick* (London: John Richardson, Royal Exchange, 1832), 79.

2.   The Loyalist settlements extended from the mouth of the St. John River to above Woodstock (now Carleton County). For a detailed account of Loyalist settlements, see W.F. Ganong, "Monograph of Origins of Settlements in the Province of New Brunswick," *Transactions of the Royal Society of Canada*, second series (10) sections 1–2 (1904), 52–73.

3.   Bouchette, *The British Dominions in North America*, 235.

4.   J. Hannay, *History of New Brunswick: Its Resources and Advantages*, Vol. 1 (Saint John: John A. Bowes, 1909), Vol. 1, 282–92.

5.   PP 1828 (148) XXI, Appendix to Colonel Cockburn's Report, 86.

6.   Hannay, *History of New Brunswick*, Vol. 1, 282–90.

7.   Norman MacDonald, *Canada, Immigration and Settlement 1763–1841* (London: Longmans & Co., 1939), 512–25.

8.   Ganong, "Settlements in New Brunswick," 73–94.

9.   Hannay, *History of New Brunswick*, Vol. 1, 353.

10. Abraham Gesner, *New Brunswick with Notes: for Emigrants, Comprehending the Early History, Settlement, Topography, Statistics, Natural History, etc.* (London: 1847), 316.

11. Graeme Wynn, *Timber Colony: An Historical Geography of Early Nineteenth Century New Brunswick* (Toronto: University of Toronto Press, 1981), 11–53.

12. Peter Fisher, *History of New Brunswick* (Saint John: reprinted under the auspices of the New Brunswick Historical Society, 1921, 85. Originally published in 1825.

13. Between 1829 and 1838, some 94 percent of the 41,195 immigrants who landed at Saint John had sailed from Ireland. Elliott, "The English," 467–69. J.S. Buckingham, *Canada, Nova Scotia, New Brunswick and Other British Provinces in North America: With a Plan of National Colonization* (London, Paris: Fisher & Sons, 1843), 428.

14. Most of the Customs Records were lost in 1877 in the great fire of Saint John. They only survive for 1815, 1832, 1833–34, and 1837–38.

15. Campey, *Axe and Bible*, 3–94.

16. Ganong, "Settlements in New Brunswick," 73–94. Immigrant numbers peaked in 1847 at 14,879, the overwhelming number being Irish.

17. *Ibid.*, 76.

18. In 1871 the Scots accounted for 14 percent of the total population and the Acadians 16 percent.

19. Albert County was created from Westmorland County in 1845. It contains the original parishes of Hillsborough and Hopewell, part of Salisbury, and the later parishes of Coverdale and Harvey.

20. New Brunswick Genealogical Society, *Passengers to New Brunswick: Custom House Records — 1833, 34, 37 and 38* (Saint John: 1987).

21. They sailed from Falmouth, Plymouth, Bristol, Penzance, and Exeter.

22. *Newcastle Courant*, March 27, July 31, 1819.

23. *Bristol Mercury*, July 27, 1830.

24. The *Pilot*, due to sail from Bristol to Boston and St. Andrews, offered passengers "a height between decks of seven feet" (*BM*, July 14, 1832).

25. DRO 219/29/22a-c: Devonian families resident abroad, Nos. 102, 139, 234. John Sheppard came in a "man of war" ship while serving in the navy. He married Jane Crawford and had five children. The family moved later to Minnesota. Henry Stentiford emigrated with his brothers, who settled in Fredericton. Sarah Bradford and her husband moved later to Boston.

26. They were only a fraction of the much larger group of New Englanders who went to the Annapolis Valley and the south shore of the Nova Scotia peninsula (see Chapter 4).

27. Jane Elizabeth Holmes, *The Pre-Loyalist Emigration from New England and Resettlement of Nova Scotia* (Sackville, NB: Mount Allison University Archives, 1973), 17–18. New Englanders also went to the townships of Moncton, Hillsborough, and Hopewell from 1765, but their numbers were very small.

28. Snowdon, "Footprints in the Marsh Mud," 14–15.

29. *Ibid.*, 39–62.

30. Hillsborough had acquired a substantial number of Pennsylvania Germans by 1765.

31. Hopewell also attracted settlers from Colchester County (Nova Scotia) who had originated from Northern Ireland.

32. Trueman, *Chignecto Isthmus*, 220–21, 224–25.

33. Ganong, "Settlements in New Brunswick," 126, 127, 130, 138, 139, 151, 170.

34. *DCB*, Vol. 7. Ganong, *Ibid.*, 171–72. William Hanington was an entrepreneur, having interests in the fur trade, fishing, lumbering, shipbuilding, and land speculation. He controlled the economic life of the Shediac Bay for nearly forty years.

35. For example, the Yorkshire-born George Dobson moved from Westmorland to Cape Tormentine (Botsford) in 1795. See Trueman, *Chignecto Isthmus*, 245–47).

36. Eldon Hay, *The Chignecto Covenanters: A Regional History of Reformed Presbyterianism in New Brunswick and Nova Scotia, 1827–1905* (Montreal: McGill-Queen's University Press, 1996), 37. Ganong, "Settlements in New Brunswick," 152.

37. The shipping advertisement stated that the *Trafalgar* would sail to Halifax and Saint John, when it actually went to Saint John and Quebec (*Hull Advertiser*, April 26, 1817).

38. For details of the *Valiant* crossing, see Chapter 6.

39. PP 1836 (567) XVII: Report of the 1836 Select Committee appointed to inquire into the causes of shipwreck. See also *www.theshipslist.com/ships*.

40. *New Brunswick Courier*, quoted in Al Short, "The 1817 Journey of the Brig *Trafalgar* with Its Immigrants," *Generations* (Journal of the New Brunswick Genealogical Society) (Spring 2006), 12–16.

41. Nelda Murray, ed., *The Valiant Connection: A History of Little York* (Charlottetown: York History Committee, 1993), 6–7. John Rennison went to Albert County while John Millner and John Towse settled at Sackville. Having gone initially to Covehead (Prince Edward Island), Thomas Fawcett moved to Salisbury Parish in 1817.

42. Table 3 contains a partial passenger list for the *Trafalgar* crossing, showing the fifty-two heads of household who were due to sail. The source is NAB CO 384/1 ff. 127–33: Hugh Cochran (ship's owner) to Lord Bathurst, May 22, 1817.

43. SOAS LMS Jacket B Folder 5/3, September 1, 1804.

44. Trueman, *Chignecto Isthmus*, 70–86.

45. Milner, "Records of Chignecto," 74, 78.

46. W.C. Milner, *History of Sackville, New Brunswick*, (Sackville, NB: Tribune Print Co., 1934), 61.

47. *Ibid.*, 62.

48. Charles H.H. Scobie and John Webster Grant, eds., *Contribution of Methodism to Atlantic Canada* (Montreal: McGill-Queen's University Press, *circa* 1992), 108–09.

49. RHL USPG Series E, 1845–1855 (LAC m/f A221).

50. G. Herbert Lee, *Historical Sketch of First Fifty Years of Church of England in New Brunswick* (Saint John: Sun Publishing Co., 1880), 120–23.

51. SOAS MMS, W. Bennett, November 16, 1804. He reported that the London-based Methodist Missionary Society had about ninety members "in the city and its suburbs — both whites and blacks," who were generally "in middling circumstances."

52. Buckner and Reid, *Atlantic Region*, 295–96, 337–38.

53. Ganong, "Settlements in New Brunswick," 76.

54. RHL USPG Series E, 1845–1855 (LAC m/f A221). The Anglican church at Saint John was built by Loyalists in 1789. Another Anglican church was built in 1824.

55. Ganong, "Settlements in New Brunswick," 148. The other townships along the St. John River (Conway, Amesbury, Gagetown, Jemseg, Burton, Sunbury, Newton, and Francfort) attracted few New Englanders (see Wright, *Planters and Pioneers*, 24–25.

56. Ganong, "Settlements in New Brunswick," 172. PANB RS108 (m/f F1035): land petitions for Sunbury County. For example, see George Hayward's petition of 1788.

57. PANB RS108 (m/f F1035): Entry in 1819 for English Emigrants. This part of Blissville Parish fell within Gladstone Parish from 1874.

58. SOAS LMS, Jacket C, Folder 6 /27: David Bewpe, October 28, 1823.

59. Gesner, *New Brunswick with Notes for Emigrants*, 155–56. H.W. Barker, "The Maugerville Church and the American Revolution," *Church History: Studies in Christianity and Culture*, Vol. 7, No. 4 (December 1938), 371–72.

60. *SPG Annual Report*, 1846, ciii. Sunbury County had two Anglican churches by 1847 (Gesner, *New Brunswick with Notes for Emigrants*, 316.) The Maugerville church also served nearby Burton.

61. Ganong, "Settlements in New Brunswick," 133.

62. *Ibid.*, 130.

63. Information taken from the Crealock family database (see *freepages.genealogy.rootsweb.ancestry.com*) and William Gamblin website (*www.gamblinfamily.org*). Samuel Grimshaw, probably from Leeds in Yorkshire, also went to the English settlement. See *www.grimshaworigin.org*, the Grimshaw website.

64. The English settlement is on the boundary with Studholm Parish in Kings County.

65. This article, appearing in the *British Colony*, was reprinted in Anon, *Practical Information to Emigrants, New Brunswick*, 79, to promote the province's attractiveness to potential emigrants.

66. Annie E. Elder, *The History of New Jerusalem* (Fredericton: Ubsdell Printing Ltd., 1953), 1–13.

67. Ganong, "Settlements in New Brunswick," 155. Although significant English immigration had taken place to Queens County, the fact that they accounted for 35 percent of the population in 1871 is probably more attributable to the large numbers of Loyalist descendents who later claimed English ancestry.

68. RHL USPG Series E, 1845–1855 (LAC m/f A221).

69. Johnston, *Notes on North America*, Vol. 1, 117.

70. *Ibid.*, 124–25.

71. Gesner, *New Brunswick with Notes for Emigrants*, 148.

72. Ganong, "Settlements in New Brunswick," 175.

73. Reverend W. Christopher Atkinson, *An Historical and Statistical Account of New Brunswick British North America with Advice for Emigrants* (Edinburgh: Printed by Anderson & Bryce, 1844), 88, 93.

74. In 1871, the English accounted for 34 percent of the population of Kings County.

75. RHL USPG Series E, 1845–1855 (LAC m/f A221).

76. By 1846 an Anglican minister presided over churches at Hampton and Upham and preaching stations at Gondola Point (Rothesay Parish) and Londonderry (Hammond Parish).

77. Westfield had an Anglican church by 1793, but it had been damaged by fire and was rebuilt later. The church at Greenwich was built in 1825. See RHL USPG Series E, 1845–1855 (LAC m/f A221).

78. *SPG Annual Report*, 1846, ciii.

79. Charlotte county acquired 20 percent of the Loyalists in the newly created colony by 1785. See T.W. Acheson, "A Study in the Historical Demography of a Loyalist County," *Social History*, No. 1 (April 1968), 55.

80. The indentured servants had been advanced their fares and agreed to pay them back by working for several years. The New Warrington place name suggests that some of the settlers might have had connections with Warrington in Cheshire.

81. Ganong, "Settlements in New Brunswick," 155.

82. RHL USPG Series E, 1845–1855 (LAC m/f A221).

83. Wynne, *Timber Colony*, 162.

84. Ross, *Church of England in Loyalist New Brunswick*, 27. St. Andrew's had its first Anglican church built by 1786.

85. Thomas Baillie, *An Account of the Province of New Brunswick Including a Description of the Settlements, Visitations, Soil and Climate of That Important Province with Advice to Emigrants* (London: J.G. & F. Rivington, 1832), 112.

86. Wynn, *Timber Colony*, 20, 95, 97. Timber was exported to both the West Indies and Britain.

87. Atkinson, *An Historical and Statistical Account of New Brunswick*, 50–51.

88. The highly diversified small family businesses that dominated the timber trade in its early stages gradually declined in importance from the 1830s. The arrival of large steam-powered sawmills, higher licence fees, and rising transport costs favoured the few large, well-funded concerns that quickly acquired a monopolistic control over the trade. Wynn, *Timber Colony*, 84–86, 110–11, 113–37.

89. Wynn, *Timber Colony*, 100–01, 106.

90. *Ibid.*, 162–63.

91. SOAS MMS, W. Lowry, March 20, 1804. St. George had its first Anglican church by 1822, while St. Stephen was reported to have "a neat wooden church of the Establishment" by 1832 (see Thomas Baillie, *An Account of the Province of New Brunswick Including a Description of the Settlements, Visitations, Soil and Climate of That Important Province with Advice to Emigrants* (London: J.G. & F. Rivington, 1832), 112. St. David's Anglican Church was located at Oak Bay.

92. Kent and Gloucester counties were created from Northumberland County in 1826.

93. Bouchette, *The British Dominions in North America*, Vol. 1, 132.

94. PANB MC1: Some Accounts of Early Settlers in Salisbury Parish, Westmorland County, NB.

95. *SPG Annual Report*, 1855, xliii. Richibucto's first Methodist church was built in 1838.

96. PANB MC3 No. 340: "Early History of Kent County" by W.C. Milner. Later

petitioners included Thomas and William Nickerson, Andrew Holmes, Jonathan Call, William Little, John Wood, and Richard Leech.

97. Campey, *Axe and Bible*, 88–94.

98. A total of 517 people sailed in the *Augusta*, *Thomson's Packet*, and *Jessie* in 1819. Most were from Cumberland, but some were from the southwest of Scotland. They included former hand-loom weavers, farmers, and labourers. The first two vessels sailed to Saint John, while the third went to the Miramichi and Prince Edward Island. See *Dumfries and Galloway Courier*, June 1, 1819; New Brunswick *Royal Gazette* May 26, June 2, 1819.

99. *DGC*, April 13, 1819.

100. They had sailed in the *Swallow*, *DGC*, August 6, 1822.

101. Bruce S. Elliott, "English Immigration to Prince Edward Island," *The Island Magazine*, No. 40 (1996), 7. The Newcastle crossings were discussed above. The *Dixon* sailed from Hull to Prince Edward Island and New Brunswick in 1819 and 1820, while the *Prince George* sailed with twenty-three passengers to Prince Edward Island and Bouctouche, New Brunswick, in 1820.

102. "English, P.E.I." is shown as an ethnic designation in the 1851 census.

103. Wynn, *Timber Colony*, 36–38.

104. The Cumberland immigrants included Thomas Cale and Daniel Roberston, both farmer/lumberers; Rachel Murray, a housekeeper; Robert Jackson, a butcher/farmer; Andrew Hudson and William Robertson, both farmers; and William Glenross, a farmer/surveyor. Westmorland immigrants included Isaac Sowerby and John Farrah, both farmers.

105. RHL USPG Series E, 1845–1855 (LAC m/f A221).

106. PANB MC 80/730: *History of Westmorland County: Emersons and Descendents*, by Randall Emmerson (Wolfville, NS: author, nd).

107. My thanks to John MacDougall of the Miramichi for providing this information. Sewell died in 1826.

108. RHL USPG Series E, 1845–1855 (LAC m/f A221).

109. Fredericton had been selected as the capital because it was the highest point on the St. John River, which was navigable for ocean-going vessels.

110. Sheffield Record Office (HAS 41/12), Gatting correspondence quoted in Donna McDonald, *Illustrated News: Juliana Horatia Ewing's Canadian Pictures, 1867–1869* (Toronto: Dundurn Press, 1985), 36. Married to an army officer who served in the 22nd (Cheshire) Regiment, Juliana returned later to Yorkshire.

111. W.S. MacNutt, *New Brunswick, A History: 1784–1867* (Toronto: Macmillan of Canada, 1984), 199–201.

112. *SPG Annual Report*, 1857, xliv.

113. Sheffield Record Office (HAS 65/37) quoted in McDonald, *Illustrated News*, 69.

114. Thomas Baillie, the New Brunswick commissioner of crown lands and surveyor-general, had the initial idea of forming a land company. Capital was provided by London merchants who were encouraged and assisted by Lord Stanley, the colonial secretary. See MacNutt, *New Brunswick*, 231–32.

115. For details of the company's prospectus, see NAB CO 384/41 ff. 319–20. The land company published extensive publicity. For more information see New Brunswick and Nova Scotia Land Company, *Sketches in New Brunswick: Taken Principally with the Intention of Shewing the Nature and Description of the Land in the Tract Purchased by the New Brunswick and Nova Scotia Land-Company in the Year 1833, and Illustrating the Operations of the Association During the Years 1834 and 1835* (London: Ackerman, 1836). See also New Brunswick and Nova Scotia Land Company, *Practical Information Respecting New Brunswick for the Use of Persons Intending to Settle Upon the Lands of the New Brunswick and Nova Scotia Land Company* (London: Pelham Richardson, 1843).

116. For an analysis of the British American Land Company's role as a settlement promoter see John Irvine Little, *Nationalism, Capitalism and Colonization in Nineteenth Century Quebec, the Upper St. Francis District* (Kingston, ON: McGill-Queen's University Press, 1989), 36–61.

117. The British American Land Company also experienced similar problems in attracting settlers to its St. Francis Tract in Lower Canada.

118. See for example "Prospectus of the New Brunswick Company," Bouchette, *The British Dominions in North America*, Vol. 2, 287–88.

119. The company was never profitable. It had to sell much of its land below the original price it had paid, and, by 1872, the company finished trading.

120. The English settlement was previously known as Lime Kiln. Ganong, "Settlements in New Brunswick," 130.

121. But its ham-fisted efforts to turn Skye crofters into settlers at another site near Stanley had a calamitous outcome. See Campey, *Axe and Bible*, 105–13.

122. Marjorie Kohli, *The Golden Bridge: Young Immigrants to Canada, 1838–1939* (Toronto: Natural Heritage Books, 2003), 68–70.

123. However, according to Bruce Elliott, the children actually came from an asylum at Hackney Wick, run by the Society for the Suppression of Juvenile Vagrancy, founded in 1830, and later renamed the Children's Friend Society. He claims that the boys re-branded themselves later on as having originated from the socially superior Blue Coat School to distance themselves from the notoriety associated with the home children, who arrived later in the century. Elliott, "Emigrant Recruitment by the New Brunswick Land Company," *Generations* (Winter 2004), 50–4.

124. The boys sailed to Saint John in June 1836, from London, in the *Hinde*, Captain Custard master.

125. *NBC* (January 22, 1834) claimed that the scheme would attract "the most depraved and vicious of the human race" — quoted in Elliott, "Emigrant Recruitment by the New Brunswick Land Company," *Generations* (Winter 2004), 52.

126. *The Times*, May 14, 1839. The spelling had been altered to assist readability. J. Charles Forss had accompanied the boys from London and became a settler at Stanley.

127. Reverend Frank Baird, *History of the Parish of Stanley and its Famous Fair* (Fredericton: Printed by McMurray Book & Stationery, 1950), 89–91. Other boys

who have been identified were: Henry Bendell, Bloom, Cooper, George Howell, Chris Kelly, and George Linnell.

128. Article reprinted in the *Berwick Advertiser*, August 21, 1836. A company agent had gone to Northumberland to recruit settlers. See *BA*, May, 14, 21, 1836.

129. People in the area had shown interest in immigrating to Upper Canada but not the Maritimes. Around three hundred people had sailed from Berwick for Quebec in the *William Shand* in 1831, and, a year later, 227 sailed in the *Dalmarnoch* to Quebec. See *Quebec Mercury,* July 2, 1831, and July 5, 1832. In 1835, the *Caroline*, with "a large and elegantly fitted-up cabin," and the *Berwick on Tweed*, with a captain highly recommended by "those who have gone out with him," were preparing to leave Berwick for Quebec (*BA*, March 28). The Berwick Record Office shipping database records many shipping advertisements for crossings from Berwick to Quebec from 1833 to 1837.

130. *BA*, September 24, 1836.

131. They had been promised lots of one hundred acres, with five acres cleared, and a log house (NAB CO 188/60 ff. 147–48).

132. NAB CO 188/61 ff. 147–48, 388–89: Petition, dated April 1838.

133. NAB CO 188/60, ff. 149–50: Petition to R. Haynes, Commissioner New Brunswick and Nova Scotia Land Company, June 15, 1838.

134. *Ibid.*, ff. 153–54.

135. *Ibid.*, ff. 149–50, 155–56.

136. New Brunswick and Nova Scotia Land Company, *Practical Information Respecting New Brunswick*, 31–32.

137. PANB MC 80/695: History of Stanley pioneers by Mrs. Arthur Pringle, 1934, 19–20.

138. "Notes of Mrs. Arthur Pringle," quoted in Baird, *History of the Parish of Stanley*, 86.

139. PANB RS 9 Executive Council meeting, December 9, 1871: Inhabitants were: John Hanley, George Packen, John Spencer Sr., Thomas McDonald, Alexander Smith, Joseph Culhoom, John Weors, Angus Boies, John Fairley, Robert Snow, Thomas Boies, Alexander and John McDonald, David McGemel, John Spencer Jr., James Fairley, John, Joseph, and Roderick Conroy, William McNeile, John Linscott, Alexander Moir, Thomas Palmer, Ebinezer and John Stickner, Richard and George Palmer, Robert and William Hanley, William Scott, (Mr.) Miles, John Lines, Thomas Hunter, Giles Standish, Robert McKay, William Carson, William Mins, and John and Peter Hayes.

140. *NBC,* July 15, 1837, quoted in Elliott, "Emigrant Recruitment by the New Brunswick Land Company," (Summer 2005), 11–17.

141. PANB RG 637 26d: Records of the Surveyor General. The settler list (see Table 5), produced in 1837, contains 146 names — slightly more than the number given for the crossing of the *Cornelius* that same year. The settler list omits Henry Craigs, who was known to be in the 1837 group.

142. *BA*, August 19, 1837.

143. Later expanded to Tweedside, Wooler, Little Settlement, Goss Settlement, and Harvey or York Mills. See Ganong, "Settlements in New Brunswick," 138.

144. PANB RS 24 1838 re/1 Assembly Sessional Papers 1838: Report of Thomas Baillie, A. Wilmot and James Taylor, commissioners appointed for locating sundry English emigrants in York County, February 16, 1838.

145. John Thompson, "An Account of the Original Settlement of Harvey" (manuscript), quoted in Elliott, "Emigrant Recruitment by the New Brunswick Land Company," (Summer, 2005) 15.

146. PANB RS 24 1839 re/5 Assembly Sessional Papers 1839: Report of the commissioners for locating the Northumberland emigrants, March 5, 1839.

147. PANB RG 637 #26d: Records of the Surveyor General.

148. PANB RS 24 1838 re/1.

149. Atkinson, *An Historical and Statistical Account of New Brunswick*, 68.

150. Helen C. Craig, *The Craigs of Harvey Settlement, Red Rock and the Pontiac* (Fredericton: author, 1999).

151. Most Harvey people had a Presbyterian background and were served by Presbyterian ministers. PANB MC 80/818; History of Harvey Settlement by Reverend William Randall (1972), 39.

152. BRO C4/27: *Sketch of the Life of Thomas Craigs*, 11.

153. The Ambleton, Hutchison, Moffat, and Robinson families are shown in the 1851 census for Kingsclear Parish as having arrived in 1842. Further families arrived in ones and two until 1853. The original Harvey families still present in Kingsclear Parish in 1851 were: Ambleton (Embleton), Cockburn, Craigs, Grieve, Hay, Herbert, Kay, Messer, Mowet, Nesbit, Piercy, Thompson, Wightman. See also Elliott, "Emigrant Recruitment by the New Brunswick Land Company," (Fall, 2005) 7–12.

154. PANB RS 24: Journal of the House of Assembly 1843, xciii–xcv: Report of Hon. L.A. Wilmot, Commissioner for Harvey settlement.

155. *Ibid.*

156. Carleton County was created from York County *circa* 1831.

157. PANB RS24 1837/pe File 7, No. 22: Petition to Sir John Harvey, July 6, 1837. Names: John Bedwin, JP; Richard Witcham, JP; John Dibbler, JP; James Kitchen, JP; A.I. Garden, JP; A.I. Carman, JP; (?) Garden; Joseph Phillips; Laban Stoddard; Daniel Foster; Ralph Kitchener; Hezekiah Stoddard; Richard Dibbler; Joseph Haney; John Harper; (?) Jenning; (?) Grosvenor; John Bustin; George Williams; (?) Dibbler; Samuel D. Lee Street, Rector of Woodstock; Richard English; Thomas G Cunliffe; Charles Raymond; William Suly; John Winchan; (?) Newham; John Bedell, JP; Avner Bull; George Bedell; Walter Bedell; and A.K. Medislertrudy.

158. NAB CO 188/75 ff. 177–82: Edward Villiers to Colonial Land and Emigration Office, November 10, 1841.

159. PP 1852–53 (1647) XV.

160. PP 1854 (1833) XXVIII.

161. In an attempt to encourage emigration, the Saint John Mechanics' Institute announced a prize competition in 1859 for essays on New Brunswick's suitability "as a home for emigrants," with the three top essays eventually being published. One of these was written by James Brown.

162. Born in Forfarshire, Brown had immigrated to New Brunswick in 1810 and eventually settled in St. David, Charlotte County. He was elected to the House of Assembly in 1830 and became surveyor general in 1850–54 and in 1861–62.

163. PANB MC 80/319: "Report of Mr. Brown's Mission to Great Britain and Ireland for the Promotion of Emigration to the Province" (Fredericton, NB: *Royal Gazette*, 1863). Martin Hewitt, "The Itinerant Emigration Lecturer: James Brown's Lecture Tour of Britain and Ireland, 1861–62," *The British Journal of Canadian Studies*, Vol. 10, No. 1 (1995), 103–19.

165. J. Edgar et al., *New Brunswick As a Home for Emigrants: With the Best Means of Promoting Immigration and Developing the Resources of the Province* (Saint John, NB: Barnes & Co., 1860), 13. This quote is taken from James Brown's essay.

CHAPTER 6: WITH SHIPS TO LAUNCH: THE PRINCE EDWARD ISLAND ENGLISH

1. *North Devon Journal*, April 14, 1831.

2. Lucille H. Campey, *"A Very Fine Class of Immigrants": Prince Edward Island's Scottish Pioneers, 1770–1850* (Toronto: Natural Heritage Books, 2001), 16–31.

3. Even by as late as 1841, less than a quarter of the land in over half of the townships was freehold. The leasehold system was only completely abolished in 1873 when Prince Edward Island entered the Canadian Confederation. Bumsted, *Land Settlement and Politics*, 196–200; Clark, *Three Centuries and the Island*, 91–95.

4. There were settlements at Charlottetown, Malpeque (Lot 18), Covehead (Lot 34), New London (Lot 21), Tryon and Cape Traverse (Lot 28), Tracadie (Lot 36), and Three Rivers (Lot 59). See Harvey, *Journeys to the Island of Saint John or Prince Edward Island 1775–1832*, 76–77.

5. Ian Ross Roberston, "Highlanders, Irishmen and the Land Question in Nineteenth-Century Prince Edward Island," in *Interpreting Canada's Past*, J.M. Bumsted, ed., Vol. 1 (Toronto: Oxford University Press, 1986), 359–73.

6. Census data reveals that large numbers of immigrants arrived from Britain between 1821 and 1832 but few of their ship crossings were recorded (see the introduction to John Lewellin's "Emigration" in Harvey, *Journeys to the Island of Saint John or Prince Edward Island, 1775–1832*, 177.)

7. Clark, *Three Centuries and the Island*, 83–91.

8. The English were second to the Scots in Lots 20, 23, 24, 25, 28, and 31, and second to the Irish in Lot 26.

9. Acadians were concentrated primarily in Lots 1, 2, 5, 6, 14, 15, 16, and 17 (Prince County) and Lots 23 and 24 (Queens County).

10. The Channel Island influx began in 1806 (see below). In 1881, 53 percent of Lot 64's population claimed English ancestry. The English were greatly outnumbered by the Scots and/or Irish in the rest of Kings County. Their best showing was in Lot 59 (Montague) and Sturgeon (Lot 61), where they represented around 16 percent of the population.

11. Scottish proprietors promoted emigration from Perthshire, Argyll, Inverness-shire, and the Western Isles. Bumsted, *Land Settlement and Politics*, 45–64. Campey, *A Very Fine Class of Immigrants*, 16–31. Lieutenant Governor Thomas Desbrisay attempted to recruit settlers from Northern Ireland to Lots 31 and 33 in Queens County, which he partly owned, but because he provided no assistance and his terms were extortionate, little came of his initiative.

12. Peter Gallant and Nelda Murray, *From England to Prince Edward Island* (Charlottetown: P.E.I. Genealogical Society, 1991).

13. Robert Campbell, another Londoner, was a co-owner with Robert Clark of Lot 21, but he died soon after arriving on the island. *DCB*, Robert Clark, Vol. 4.

14. Elizabethtown's location can be seen on a map drawn by John Stewart in 1806 (see Stewart, *An Account of Prince Edward Island*.) By January 1775, the place had 129 inhabitants.

15. Indentured servants received their passage and provisioning in return for four years' service.

16. Cameron, "P.E.I. Methodist Prelude," in Scobie and Grant, *Contribution of Methodism to Atlantic Canada*, 127–28; John T. Mellish, *Outlines of the History of Methodism in Charlottetown, Prince Edward Island* (Charlottetown: 1888), 3–4.

17. *DCB*, Vol. 4. Chappell later became the island's deputy postmaster.

18. Quoted in D.C. Harvey, "Early Settlement and Social Conditions in Prince Edward Island," *Dalhousie Review*, Vol. 11, (1931/32), 452.

19. Mellish, *Methodism in Charlottetown*, 65–73.

20. On his return to London, Robert Clark leased Lot 49 to John Adams and Joseph Smith Jr., who sent Quaker Edward Allen to Derbyshire to find settlers, but once they arrived on the island they sought other property because of the unfavourable terms being offered.

21. PAPEI Acc 2277: Daybooks of Benjamin Chappell, Vol. 1.

22. The diary kept by Thomas Curtis, one of the passengers, reveals that twenty people arrived at Charlottetown.

23. Harvey, *Journeys to the Island of Saint John or Prince Edward Island, 1775–1832*, 10, 11, 38, 39, 46.

24. *Ibid.*, 56–59.

25. *Ibid.*, 64–65.

26. Stewart, *An Account of Prince Edward Island*, 168–70.

27. The Billings group sailed from Plymouth in the *Breakwater*. J. Orlo and Fraser D., "Those Elusive Immigrants, Parts 1 to 3," *The Island Magazine*, No. 16 (1984), 36–44; No. 17 (1985), 32–37; No. 18 (1985), 29–35; No. 17 (1985), 34. New London also acquired Louise Montgomery from Surrey in 1827 and Maria Parsons from Stepney (London) in 1841.

28. John Lawson, *Letters on Prince Edward Island by John Lawson, Esq., Barrister at Law and Judge Advocate* (Charlottetown: G.T. Haszard, 1851), 43.

29. James Townsend, his wife Elizabeth, and their five children sailed in the *Elizabeth* in 1775, together with their servant Thomas Edmonds (see NAB T 47/10/139). James,

one of their sons, also remained. Park Corner survives as an island place name.

30. The Loyalist influx included around 120 families who had originally gone to Shelburne (Nova Scotia), but, becoming disappointed with it, moved to the island. However, many of these families probably left the island as well. Siebert, "The Loyalists in Prince Edward Island," 109–17; Bumsted, *Land, Settlement and Politics*, 106–07, 115, 119–20, 191–92.

31. See Chapter 3.

32. Clark, *Three Centuries and the Island*, 57–58, 61. Bolger, *Canada's Smallest Province*, 59–64.

33. W.H. Crosskill, *Prince Edward Island: Garden Province of Canada: Its History Interests and Resources with Information for Tourists etc.* (Charlottetown: Murley & Garnhum, 1906), 18.

34. S.S. Hill, *A Short Account of Prince Edward Island Designed Chiefly for the Information of Agriculturist and Other Emigrants of Small Capital by the Author of the Emigrant's Introduction to an Acquaintance with the British American Colonies* (London: Madden, 1839), 15.

35. RHL USPG Series E, (LAC m/f A-221). St. Eleanors' first Anglican church was built in 1825–28. Burning down in 1835, the church was rebuilt in 1838. In 1851 John Lawson commented on the new church organ that had come from England. See Lawson, *Letters on Prince Edward Island*, 44.

36. In 1881 Bedeque had a tiny Church of England congregation, while Methodism was its second most popular religion after Catholicism. The area between Bedeque and Tryon (Lots 25, 26, 27, 28) was strongly Methodist. Cameron, "P.E.I. Methodist Prelude," in Scobie and Grant, *Contribution of Methodism to Atlantic Canada*, 127–28.

37. Orlo and Fraser, *The Island Magazine*, No. 16 (1984), 37. *Royal Gazette and Miscellany of the Island of Saint John*, October 21, 1791.

38. Bumsted, *Land, Settlement and Politics*, 145–46, 149, 151, 162, 171–72.

39. Island tombstones and death notices reveal Isle of Wight arrivals from 1807. James Jeffrey and his son George immigrated to the island from the Isle of Wight shortly before 1809. They were joined by Stephen, George's brother, in 1810. James returned to England in 1812 much disappointed with the island. He tried to persuade his sons to follow his example but they remained and prospered. See Betty M. Jeffrey and Carter W. Jeffrey, *The Jeffrey Family of the Island of Wight and P.E.I.* (Alberton, PE: Therles Press, 1998), 1–30.

40. Orlo and Fraser, *The Island Magazine*, No. 16 (1984), 37. Gallant and Murray, *From England to P.E.I.* They included the following eight families: Brehaut, Machin, DeJersey, Lelacheur, Captain Fallow, Tuadvin, Marquand, and Robertson. Mary LeMessurier arrived in 1810. Some Cornish-born left from Guernsey two years later for Murray Harbour.

41. A Methodist chapel was built at Murray Harbour in 1815 — the first to be built on the island. The island's first ordained minister was the Reverend James Bulpitt, who arrived in Charlottetown in 1807.

42. Cambridge benefited from Robert Clark's financial demise and gained control of

his assets and land, thus establishing himself as a substantial merchant by the 1790s. When he died in 1831, Cambridge held 102,000 acres, being the proprietor of Lots 14, 21, 27, 32, 46, 48, 49, 63, and 64.

43. William Townsend, Charles Worrell, and John Cambridge claimed to have brought out six hundred settlers in the period from 1798–1805 (Harvey, *Journeys to the Island of Saint John or Prince Edward Island, 1775–1832*, 76–77).

44. Walter Johnstone, "Letters Descriptive of P.E.I.," written in 1820–21, in A.B. Warburton, *History of Prince Edward Island* (Saint John: Barnes & Co., 1923), 354.

45. *The Irish Unitarian Magazine (and Bible Christian)* (Belfast: 1846), 256–58.

46. Murray Harbour, which comprised Lots 63 and 64, had a combined population of nine hundred in 1839. By 1881 Lot 63 was dominated by people of Scottish origin, while Lot 64 was equally dominated by people of English and Scottish origin.

47. Hill, *Short Account of Prince Edward Island*, 11.

48. Lawson, *Letters on Prince Edward Island*, 37.

49. *DCB*, John Cambridge, Vol. 6. He returned to Bristol in 1814, leaving his sons to manage his firm's combined timber and shipbuilding activities on the island.

50. Basil Greenhill and Anne Gifford, *Westcountrymen in Prince Edward's Isle* (Toronto: University of Toronto Press, 1967), 28, 47.

51. Cambridge initially recruited boys from London to work as indentured servants at his sawmill.

52. The *Felicity*, one of John Cambridge's ships, arrived at Murray Harbour from Bristol in 1829 with steerage passengers.

53. In common with other merchants, John Cambridge suffered severe business reverses from time to time but always managed to begin again. The key factor in his success was his ability to maintain control over much of his land.

54. Murray, *The "Valiant" Connection*, 5–21. Some of the emigrants originated from Lincolnshire. During the voyage the *Valiant* took on the passengers and crew from a stricken Scottish ship.

55. The *Dixon* carried twenty-eight emigrants from Hull and the *Nancy* an unknown number. See Elliott, "English Immigration to Prince Edward Island," No. 40, 7. There were other emigrant ship arrivals from Hull in 1819, such as the *Economy*, with an unknown number of passengers who were due to settle at Hampton (Lot 29). The *Dixon* sailed from Hull in 1820 with twenty-three passengers who were destined for the island and Bouctouche, in Kent County, New Brunswick.

56. PAPEI Acc 2277: Benjamin Chappell's diary, July 15, 1817.

57. Murray, *The "Valiant" Connection*, 8.

58. Sir James Montgomery established a flax plantation at Stanhope using labour recruited from Perthshire. Campey, *A Very Fine Class of Immigrants*, 20–21, 136–37.

59. McGregor, *British America*, 480.

60. The first two years were free, the third year they paid sixpence, the fourth ninepence, and afterward an annual rent of one shilling.

61. Family heads at Little York included Robert Vesey, George West, George Hardy, Thomas Hardy, and Thomas Best.

62. Warburton, *History of Prince Edward Island*, 347.

63. Warburton, *Past and Present of Prince Edward Island*, 355–56.

64. *Ibid.*, 356–57.

65. Extracts from essays on rural life on the island in 1864, submitted to a Women's Institute essay competition in 1964. A summary is printed in Murray, *The "Valiant" Connection*, 104–05.

66. The Yorkshire family heads who settled at Crapaud include Christopher Smith, William Hodgson, George Wiggington, Thomas Carr (single), William Pearson, Joseph Trowsdale, Thomas Best, and William Lowther.

67. Elliott, "English Immigration to Prince Edward Island," No. 40, 7.

68. Anon., *The History of Crapaud*, Vol. 3 (1957–1991.) (Crapaud: Women's Institute, nd), 6, 33–36, 44–68. In 1881 Methodism was second only to Catholicism at Crapaud.

69. The sale of several of Cross's Yorkshire cottages to Sir Tatton Sykes, a Yorkshire baronet, took place through an agent. UHA DDSY Syke family papers: DDSY 23/88 — declaration of William Turner as to property to be sold by Christopher Cross in Charlottetown, October 27, 1840.

70. UHA DDSY 23/89.

71. UHA DDSY 23/92: Christopher Cross to his brother Thomas in Melsonby (North Riding), November 23, 1840.

72. Orlo and Fraser, *The Island Magazine*, No. 16 (1984), 38.

73. They sailed in the *Anglian, Hope, Friendship, Rose*, and *Mary Anne* (see Appendix 4). Westmorland emigrants might also have sailed from Workington. For details of the influx of Dumfriesshire emigrants to Prince Edward Island, see Campey, *A Very Fine Class of Immigrants*, 66–79.

74. The *Dictionary of Prince Edward Island English* by T.K. Pratt reveals that 8 percent of the non-standard English words used on the island were north of England in derivation, suggesting that a significant part of the island's population had northern roots.

75. For example, William Profit and his wife, both from North Shields (Durham), settled at Lot 21, while William Evans, also from North Shields, settled at Lot 18. Joseph Atkinson from Broughton (Lancashire) settled at Lot 31, while David Johnson from Carlisle (Cumberland) settled at Lot 64. See Gallant and Murray, *From England to P.E.I.*

76. John Hill, a major timber exporter, told the 1820 Foreign Trade Select Committee of the House of Lords (in London) that the timber trade financed four-fifths of the island's total imports from Britain. His evidence was published in the *Prince Edward Island Gazette*, September 8, 1821.

77. LAC MG24–D99: George and Alexander Birnie fonds, April 30, 1820.

78. *Ibid.*, December 16, 1820.

79. Because of the large amounts of credit needed to finance the Atlantic timber trade, merchants were always one step away from bankruptcy, and unexpected downturns in trade could spell disaster.

80. John Bradley, *Letter-Books of John and Mary Cambridge of Prince Edward Island, 1792–1812* (Devizes [Wiltshire], UK: the author, 1996), 278–79, 322.

81. LAC MG55/24–No. 299: John Hill fonds. Hill purchased Lot 3 in 1809 and Lot 4 in 1806. *DCB*, John Hill, Vol. 7.

82. Advertisement in the *Western Luminary*, quoted in Greenhill and Gifford, *Westcountrymen in Prince Edward's Isle*, 132–33.

83. For example, in 1824 the *King David* and *Amity* arrived from Bristol and the *Rover* from Bideford with workmen to build ships. The *Castalia* came from Plymouth in 1838 with the crews for two vessels, the *Glenburnie* came from Bideford in 1841 with the crew for a new vessel, and in 1846 the *Lady Sale* did the same. In 1853 the *Ellen* arrived from Liverpool with the crews for two vessels. Orlo and Fraser, "Elusive Immigrants," *The Island Magazine*, No. 16: 39; No. 18: 33, 35; No. 26: 39; No. 27: 41.

84. Greenhill and Gifford, *Westcountrymen in Prince Edward's Isle*, 123–24, 132–33, 179–80.

85. Alison Grant and Peter Christie, *The Book of Bideford* (Buckingham, UK: Barracuda Books Ltd., 1987), 38.

86. Greenhill and Gifford, *Westcountrymen in Prince Edward's Isle*, 42–43.

87. Having left Lot 13, the Acadians became concentrated in Lot 15.

88. George Hardy, who originated from East or West Knighton in Dorset, arrived from New York with a large family. He claimed that, if the land was good, he intended to bring ten families from New York to join him. Thomas Curtis described him as "a remarkable, good-natured man" (*DCB*, George Hardy, Vol. 5).

89. Hugh Edward Conway Seymour, 8th Marquess of Hertford, had obtained Lot 13 by 1793. WRO CR 114A/568: sketch map of part of Lot 13.

90. Greenhill and Gifford, *Westcountrymen in Prince Edward's Isle*, 52–65.

91. WRO CR 114A/564: Robert Gray to Lord Seymour, 1793.

92. Greenhill and Gifford, *Westcountrymen in Prince Edward's Isle*, 101. Elliott, "English Immigration to Prince Edward Island," No. 40: 9–11; No. 41: 4.

93. Gallant and Murray, *From England to P.E.I.*

94. Reverend L.C. Jenkins to Reverend A. Hamilton, *SPG Journal*, Vol. 36: 59–62, quoted in Greenhill and Gifford, *Westcountrymen in Prince Edward's Isle*, 71. See also PAPEI Acc 3067: Port Hill Parish fonds.

95. H.M. Scott Smith, *Historic Churches of Prince Edward Island* (Halifax: SSP Publications, 2004), 96. Anglican churches were also built at Milton (Lot 32) and Rustico (Lot 24).

96. *DCB*, James Yeo, Vol. 9.

97. *DCB*, William Ellis, Vol. 8.

98. Greenhill and Gifford, *Westcountrymen in Prince Edward's Isle*, 79–94.

99. The *Three Brothers* arrived in 1846 from Bristol with the crew for yet another of Yeo's new ships, as did the *James*, which came in 1851. Orlo and Fraser, "Elusive Immigrants," No. 26: 37, 39; No. 27: 41.

100. Greenhill and Gifford, *Westcountrymen in Prince Edward's Isle*, 216–17.

101. *Royal Gazette* (Charlottetown), June 1, 1830.

102. Orlo and Fraser, "Elusive Immigrants," No. 17: 33–35. In 1832, seventy-five people

sailed from Bideford in the *Sarah and Eliza* and fifty sailed from Plymouth in the *Breakwater*, and in 1834, fifty-six sailed from Bideford in the *Calypso*.

103. LAC MG25–G345: Dyment family collection. Humphrey's brother John and his family emigrated at this time, but they settled near Hamilton in Upper Canada.

104. WRO CR 114A/565: 1846 rental of Lot 13, showing Lord Seymour's forty-six tenant holdings.

105. WRO CR114A/565: Yeo to Seymour, October 9, 1846.

106. NAB CO 226/52 f. 252: Henry Shearman to Robert Hay, 1835. See also MacGregor, *British America*, 51.

107. Orlo and Fraser, "Elusive Immigrants," *The Island Magazine*, No. 18: 30.

108. Henry to his sister Marian in London, May 4, 1840, published at *www.islandregister. com*.

109. DRO 219/29/22a-c #66 1/2: Devonian families resident abroad.

110. Greenhill and Gifford, *Westcountrymen in Prince Edward's Isle*, 176.

111. In 1841 the *Speculation* (81 passengers); in 1842, the *Henrietta* (102), and the *Sylvanus* (203); in 1843, the *Mary Ann* (82). Orlo and Fraser, "Elusive Immigrants," *The Island Magazine*, No. 18: 34; No. 19: 36–37. The Quebec immigration agent stated that twenty-two of the eighty passengers who sailed in the *Mary Ann* in 1843 landed at Quebec. See PP 1844 (181) XXXV.

112. Greenhill and Gifford, *Westcountrymen in Prince Edward's Isle*, 101.

113. Between 1840 and 1900, 434,806 people left from ports in Devon for overseas destinations with an overwhelming 86 percent going to Australia and New Zealand. However, the majority of Bideford departures for this period were to British North America. Official records show that 363 people left from Bideford for Prince Edward Island between 1844 and 1856. This is far lower than the 2,080 people who sailed from Bideford to Quebec between 1841 and 1856, reflecting the greater popularity of Upper Canada. Mark Brayshay, "The Emigration Trade in Nineteenth Century Devon," in Michael Duffy et al., *The New Maritime History of Devon*, Vol. 2, (London: Conway Maritime Press, 1994), 108–18.

114. Sherreall Branton Leetooze, *A Corner for the Preacher*, with the introductory chapter by Elizabeth Howard and a preface by Colin Short (Bowmanville, ON: L. Michael-John Associates, *circa* 2005), 18–22, 27–28, 31, 36.

115. John Harris, *The Life of Francis Metherall and the History of the Bible Christians in Prince Edward Island* (Toronto: Bible Christian Bookroom, 1883), 33–36.

116. Leetooze, *Corner for the Preacher*, 71–74. Metherall's preaching circuit also included Miminegash (Lot 2), Cascumpec (Lots 5 and 6), Cape Wolfe (Lot 7), and Bethel, Knutsford, and Milburn (Lot 8). However, the 1871 census reveals that the Bible Christians were chiefly concentrated in Lots 7 and 8.

117. LAC MG25–G345: Dyment family collection.

118. As revealed by cemetery transcriptions in Gallant and Murray, *From England to P.E.I.*

119. The first Bible Christian house of worship was built in 1834 on the Princetown (or Malpeque) Road. Leetooze, *Corner for the Preacher*, 72–74

120. Gallant and Murray, *From England to P.E.I.*
121. The Bible Christian circuit also extended to nearby Wheatley River (Lot 24).
122. Isaac's father, Hugh, who originated from Milton Damerel (Devon), died at Lot 23. The other Devon families who sailed in 1832 also included Brimacombes, Darkes, Wayes, Furzes, Harrises, Pounds, Cooks, Esserys, Nichols, and Brooks.
123. DRO 219/29/22a-c #182: Devonian families resident abroad. Gallant and Murray, *From England to P.E.I.*
124. The Bible Christian movement attracted small numbers, having only 369 members in 1855. Wesleyan Methodism attracted three times as many members. See Cameron, "P.E.I. Methodist Prelude," in Scobie and Grant, *Contribution of Methodism to Atlantic Canada*, 129–30.
125. Cephas Barker was transferred to Ontario in 1865. D.W. Johnson, *History of Methodism in Eastern British America Including Nova Scotia, New Brunswick, Prince Edward Island* (Sackville, NB: Tribune Printing, 1925), 239–40.
126. Pidgeon was accused of bouts of drunkenness. These St. Peters' men vouched for his sobriety: James McEwen, Charles Sanderson, David McEwen, David McLaren, Kimball Coffin, James Anderson, Benjamin Coffin, James Baker, (Elder), Elisha Coffin, William Mcewen, John Patience, and David Anderson.
127. SOAS LMS, Jacket B, Folder 6.
128. *SPG Annual Report*, 1855, xli.
129. As was the case elsewhere in Kings County, the Roman Catholic Church and Presbyterianism predominated at Lots 49 and 50.
130. *Report of the Wesleyan Methodist Missionary Society, 1821* (London: The Society, 1821). Also see reports for 1824, 1838, and 1856.
131. PAPEI Acc4362#2: Mark Butcher fonds. Mark Butcher, William's son, became the island's most prolific and successful cabinetmaker.
132. Gallant and Murray, *From England to P.E.I.*
133. A Poor Law Union included several parishes. Unions were created to enable parishes to share the costs of building and supporting a workhouse within the union area.
134. NAB MH 12/11837, Hoxne Poor Law Union letter December 18, 1834.
135. However, poor people had been assisted to immigrate to British North America by parishes, local organizations, and private individuals long before 1834, without approval from Parliament. The act was merely legitimizing a practice that was already widespread.
136. Parishes drew the necessary emigration funds by borrowing from local sponsors against the security of the poor rates. The payments were organized and administered at a local level by elected boards of guardians and overseen by Poor Law commissioners.
137. The controversy aroused by the assisted emigration schemes adopted in East Anglia is discussed in Gary Howells, "Emigration and the New Poor Law: Norfolk Emigration Fever of 1836," *Rural History*, Vol. 11, No. 2 (October 2000), 145–64.
138. *Suffolk Chronicle*, March 9, 1833 (unnamed author, Edgeware Road, London).
139. Workhouses were made as unpleasant as possible in the hope that inmates would wish to leave and find work.

140. They sailed in the *Minerva* (80), *Venus* (80), and *Rosa* (50). See Elliott, "English Immigration to Prince Edward Island," No. 41, 4–6.

141. SROL 124/A3/99/35: Halesworth Parish records. Holland received four pounds for the passage, two pounds for provisions, one pound spending money and five shillings for a hammock to be provided for him by the captain.

142. John E. Archer, *By a Flash and a Scare: Incendiarism, Animal Maiming and Poaching in East Anglia, 1815–1870* (Oxford: Clarendon Press, 1990), 50.

143. In 1836, the ratepayers of Covehithe Parish paid sixty-six pounds to assist their poor to travel to Quebec (SRO[L] 119/G5/1). In 1837, Halesworth was preparing to spend ninety pounds, two shillings, and eightpence on assisted immigration to Upper or Lower Canada, while similar schemes were being planned by Benacre, Kelsale, and Uggleshall parishes. See MH 12/11731 ff. 211, 214–18, 221.

144. SROI FC 131/G14/1: Benhall Parish records, 1831. John Birt had six children, John Cook also six, William Smith two, while Charles Gibbs and Samuel Mayhew each had one child. Thomas Pair and the Fleming and Mannel families were shown on the list of people due to emigrate, but they did not receive funds.

145. For example, the cost of maintaining John Cook's family was calculated to be twenty-six pounds, eleven shillings, and sixpence. The final emigration bill was expected to be £150. In 1836, the parish of Brandeston (Plomesgate) agreed to borrow £220 to fund immigration to Upper or Lower Canada. See SROI FC 105/G7/1/4.

146. They included Edward Robertson from South Elmham St. James Parish and George Robertson from Mettingham Parish (both in Wangford), Samuel Aldridge from Laxfield Parish, and Sarah Wright, wife of Samuel, from Dennington Parish (both in Hoxne).

147. The *Suffolk Chronicle* of March 1, 1832, carried an advertisement for the fourth crossing of the *Minerva* to Charlottetown and Quebec but there is no evidence that passengers were carried.

148. PP (1835) XXXV: First Annual Report of the Commissioners under the Poor Law Amendment Act.

149. Elliott, "English Immigration to Prince Edward Island," No. 41, 5. York was renamed Toronto in 1834.

150. Bruce Elliott, "Regional Patterns of English Immigration and Settlement in Upper Canada," in Barbara J. Messamore, ed., *Canadian Migration Patterns from Britain and North America* (Ottawa: University of Ottawa Press, 2004), 51–90.

151. Elliott, "English Immigration to Prince Edward Island," No. 41, 5.

152. SROL 124/G1/19/1: letter dated February 29, 1832.

153. SROL 455/4: S. Woolnough to her father, November 9, 1830.

154. *Ibid.*, 455/7: July 2, 1832.

155. Anon, *Emigration: Extracts from Various Writers on Emigration, with Authentic Copies of Letters from Emigrants from Norfolk, Suffolk, and Sussex, Now Settled in Upper Canada, Containing Useful Information Respecting That Country* (Norfolk: Bacon and Kinnebrook, 1834), 11–13.

156. The increasing poverty of farm workers stimulated much assisted emigration from

Wiltshire during the 1830s, but it was directed at Upper and Lower Canada.

157. The Selkirk estate of around a hundred thousand acres had been acquired by the 5th Earl, who died in 1820.

158. *Colonial Herald*, Charlottetown, September 21, 1839. David Haystead was married at Diss, in Norfolk. By 1881 he had moved to Dundas, Ontario. He denied that his emigration expenses had been paid by his parish in England.

159. *Royal Gazette* (Charlottetown), October 13, 1840.

160. They sailed as steerage passengers in the *Ann* from Bristol (Orlo and Fraser, "Elusive Immigrants," No. 26, 36). Cabin passengers included Mr. Gurney, family and servants; Henry Woodman of Amherst, Nova Scotia; and Messrs. Merrit, Perry, Wilks, Batt, Pearse, and Willis.

161. Gallant and Murray, *From England to P.E.I.*

162. James Waylen, *A History, Military and Municipal of the Ancient Borough of the Devizes: And Subordinately of the Entire Hundred of Potterne and Cannings* (London: Longman, 1859), 595.

163. They sailed in the *Nancy* from Liverpool. See Orlo and Fraser, "Elusive Immigrants," No. 16, 41.

164. Gallant and Murray, *From England to P.E.I.*

165. Sidney Smith, *The Settler's New Home, or, Whether To Go, and Wither?: Being a Guide to Emigrants in the Selection of a Settlement, and the Preliminary Details of the Voyage, Embracing the Whole Fields of Emigration, and the Most Recent Information Relating Thereto* (London: John Kendrick, 1850), 46–48.

166. *Ibid.*, 48.

167. Bungay was named after Bungay in Suffolk by settlers who probably arrived *circa* 1830.

168. PAPEI Acc 4561: James Cross fonds. Letter to Mary Ann (Cross) Carew, August 18, 1860.

169. SROL Acc. No. 868: Letter dated November, 1841. The Grubb(e) letters (uncatalogued) are contained in the papers of John's son, John Eustace Grubbe of Southwold in Suffolk. It appears that John Grubb dropped the *e* from his name when he reached the island but later generations re-established it.

170. Grubb acquired Falcon Wood, a 280-acre estate situated two-and-a-half miles from the banks of the Hillsborough River. The house was not completed until 1850, four years after Grubb's death. The estate was leased by the Grubb(e) family over many decades, with the most prominent tenant being Sir John A. Macdonald, who occupied it as he recovered from the discomforts of a gallstone during the summer of 1870.

171. SROL Acc. No. 868: Mrs. Shard to John Grubb, April 25, 1843.

172. *Ibid.*, Grubb to Mrs. Shard, October 30, 1843.

173. Eric J. Evans, *The Forging of the Modern State: Early Industrial Britain, 1783–1870* (Harlow, UK: Pearson Education, 2001), 177–78.

174. Hill, *Short Account of Prince Edward Island*, 62.

175. Clark, *Three Centuries and the Island*, 120–32.

176. The SPG clergymen were based at Charlottetown, St. Eleanors (Lot 17), the combined mission at Milton (Lot 32) and Rustico (Lot 24), and the combined mission of Georgetown (Lot 54) and Cherry Valley (Lots 49 and 50). The Reverend Merick Lally noted that some of the congregation at Georgetown and Cherry Valley were Germans or were of German descent. RHL USPG, Series E, 1845–1885 (LAC m/f A-221). For details of the churches see Smith, *Historic Churches of P.E.I.*, 58, 74, 101–02.

CHAPTER 7: NEWFOUNDLAND'S WEST COUNTRY SETTLERS

1. Keith Matthews, *Lectures on the History of Newfoundland, 1500–1830* (St. John's: Maritime History Group, 1973), 160.
2. The importance to merchants of being able to exercise total control over Newfoundland's affairs is discussed in David J. Starkey, "Devonians and the Newfoundland Trade," in Michael Duffy et al., eds., *The New Maritime History of Devon*, Vol. 1 (London: Conway Maritime Press in association with University of Exeter, 1992), 163–71.
3. Keith Matthews, "A History of the West of England-Newfoundland fishery," unpublished Ph.D. thesis, University of Oxford, 1968, 14.
4. UHA DDSY 101/48, Syke family papers: Henry de Ponthieu, a London merchant, to Reverend Sir Mark Sykes, September 10, 1761.
5. By the early eighteenth century the French and British components of the resident population were roughly equal. Bumsted, *The Peoples of Canada*, 56–59. Buckner and Reid, *Atlantic Region*, 53–56.
6. Buckner and Reid, *Atlantic Region*, 55–77. W.G. Handcock, "English Migration to Newfoundland," in John H. Mannion, ed., *The Peopling of Newfoundland: Essays in Historical Geography* (St. John's: Institute of Social and Economic Research, Memorial University of Newfoundland, 1978), 15–48.
7. Matthews, "A History of the West of England-Newfoundland Fishery," 334–39.
8. DHC D.1822/1: (Douch collection): John Tilley to his sister Susan in Boston, February 5, 1776. Some men enlisted in the Newfoundland Volunteers, a militia group, organized partly to provide government assistance for the unemployed and impoverished. Bumsted, *The Peoples of Canada*, 150–52.
9. STRO D3388/23/3: William Dyott to his brother Richard in Lichfield, Staffordshire, July 1787.
10. Mannion, *The Peopling of Newfoundland*, 1–13.
11. Planters had to pay for supplies at prices determined by the merchants, and their earnings were also controlled by the merchants.
12. SORO DD\SAS\C/795/SW/21: Sweetman collection, "Will of Abra Targett," 88. Targett returned to Somerset in later life.
13. DRO 3137A/PO40/2 (Hemyock).
14. SORO DD\S\ST/23: Stradling family papers, letter book of R. Anstice, September 30, 1769; June 20, 1771; October 30, 1771.

15. SORO DD\SAS\C/795/SW/22: Notes by George Sweetman of Wincanton," n.d., 127.

16. At least twenty-seven Dorset parishes placed boys out with Poole merchants and planters in the Newfoundland fishery. See W. Gordon Handcock, *So Longe As There Comes Noe Women: Origins of English Settlement in Newfoundland* (St. John's: Breakwater, 1989), 191–93).

17. DHC PE/Pl/OV 3/30 (Poole): Indenture, March 8, 1737.

18. DHC PE/PUD/OV7/2 (Puddletown).

19. The Overseers of the Poor Account Books (Wimborne), quoted in Handcock, *So Longe As There Comes Noe Women*, 191–93.

20. DRO 2565A/P051/5 (Kingsteignton); DRO 3419A/P09/30 (Combeinteignhead).

21. DRO 3419A/P19/45 (Combeinteignhead).

22. The Old English Shore extended between Trepassey on the south to Greenspond on the north.

23. Handcock, *So Longe As There Comes Noe Women*, 145–53.

24. The smaller number of fishermen who left from the North Devon ports of Devon and Barnstaple tended to go to the St. John's region, settling between Trepassey and Cape Broyle.

25. Conception Bay also attracted fishermen from the Channel Islands.

26. Handcock used parish registers to reveal the regional origins of the Newfoundland English.

27. Bouchette, *The British Dominions in North America*, Vol. 2 (1832), 184–85, 187.

28. Waldegrave to St. John's Magistrates, August 31, 1797, quoted in Matthews "A History of the West of England-Newfoundland Fishery," 593.

29. According to John Hillyard, who preceded him, the London Missionary Society congregation at St. John's numbered four hundred at this time. SOAS LMS, Box 1A Jacket A, Folder 1/1, June 24, 1799.

30. SOAS LMS, Jacket C, Folder 1/15, /22; Jacket A, Folder 2/36. The following people expressed their gratitude to William Hyde when he left in 1816: William Ryall, George Bate, Samuel Toms, Daniel Lawrence, Susan Warne, Sarah England, Thomas Brown, Richard Vicars, John McNaughton, Robert Watt, William Teul, William Shore, Catherine Brown, Thomas Williams, William Hall, Ronald Cole, Jolson Coulby, Mary Finan, James S. Lilly, Mary Hume, James Gill, Elizabeth Calvers Eford, John Partridge, William Brown, Mary Ann Parsons, Emilia Parsons, Phillip Knight, Mary Dinah Chancey, E. Chancey, George Woolcott, Maria Woolcott, Joosap Ward, Joseph Taylor, William Wood, Abraham Adams, Rich Wamsley, Benjamin Barton, Joseph Mills, William Foote, and E. MacNab.

31. SOAS LMS, Jacket B, Folder 2/43, July 31, 1817.

32. *Ibid.*, /45, March 4, 1818.

33. SOAS MMS St. John's, November 19, 1819.

34. Sean T. Cadigan, *Newfoundland and Labrador: A History* (Toronto: University of Toronto Press, 2009), 58, 144.

35. DHC PE/LAH/IN 5/1 (Langton Herring): receipts for money collected by the Society for Propagation of the Gospel in Foreign Parts (and other societies) with

printed circulars asking for help for St. John's, Newfoundland, 1846.

36. The cathedral was restored following the great fire of 1892.

37. LCA 380 BOW 1/2: Benjamin Bowring's letter book, Benjamin to Charles Bowring, August 19, 1840. The Bowring firm established a branch at Liverpool in the 1820s.

38. DRO 219/29/22a-c: Devonian families resident abroad, No. 136. Sir Hugh William became chief justice and the Reverend William John Hoyles was rector, but he moved in later life to Newton Abbot (Devon). Hoyles's grandson became principal of Osgoode Hall Law School in Toronto.

39. *Ibid.*, No. 18. The Honourable Robert Bond, one of Bond's sons, became the premier and colonial secretary of Newfoundland. A cousin became a merchant in Montreal.

40. *Ibid.*, No. 173. This information was supplied by a distant descendent — William Azariah Munn of St. John's. His letterhead reveals a logo for MUNN'S GENUINE COD-LIVER OIL.

41. *An Account of the State of the Schools in the Island of Newfoundland, Established or Assisted by the Society for the Propagation of the Gospel in Foreign Parts*, (London: Printed for the Society and sold by C. and J. Rivington, 1827), 7.

42. RHL USPG, Series E, 1845–55 (LAC m/f A221). An Anglican mission was established at Harbour Grace in 1766.

43. A plaque at Harbour Grace commemorates the beginnings of Methodism in North America. DHC D/LEG/Z31: Eleanor McKim, "Newfoundland Claims First Methodist Preacher," *Newfoundland Quarterly*, Vol. 65, No. 2 (1966), 31–32.

44. Hans Rollmann, "Laurence Coughlan and the Origins of Methodism in Newfoundland," in Scobie and Grant, *Contribution of Methodism to Atlantic Canada*, 53–78.

45. *DCB*, Laurence Coughlan, Vol. 4.

46. There was also a substantial Methodist presence at Bonavista Bay and Fortune Bay. Johnson, *Methodism in Eastern British America*, 243–47.

47. PANL Mildred Howard Collection (hereafter MHC), Vol. 1, 166.

48. SOAS LMS, Box 1A, Jacket C, Folder 1/21, September 12, 1814.

49. PANL MG 367 (R1–K-4): Reverend M. Blackmore, lecture on the history of Bay Roberts, delivered January 24, 1865.

50. DRO 219/29/22a-c: Devonian families resident abroad, No. 58.

51. In addition to the church at Harbour Grace, Anglican chapels were also built at Bryant's Cove, Bishop's Cove, and Island Cove.

52. PANL MG 367 (R1–K–4).

53. RHL USPG, Series E, 1845–55 (LAC m/f A221).

54. PANL MHC, Vol. 1, 85.

55. The Newfoundland Society was also known as the Newfoundland and British North America Society. Although it claimed to be interdenominational, the society became increasingly identified with the Church of England. The Society won the support of the British government, which provided free grants of land on which to build schools and financial help for teachers.

56. PANL MHC, Vol. 1, 96.

57. *An Account of the State of the Schools in the Island of Newfoundland*, 4–12. DHC D/LEG/

Z26: Reverend Lewis Amadeus Anspach (late a magistrate of that island and missionary for the district of Conception Bay), *History of the Island of Newfoundland: Containing a Description of the Island, the Banks, the Fisheries, and Trade of Newfoundland, and the Coast of Labrador* (London: printed for the author, 1819), 478–80.

58. PANL MHC, Vol. 5, 44.

59. Given the fluctuations in the fishing trade, some merchants struggled, leading to a regular turnover of dominant merchant families. Benjamin Lester was fortunate in being able to retain his fortune and pass it on to the next generation.

60. Lester's house was pulled down in the 1960s but, having remained in ruins for thirty years, it was reconstructed on the same site and now accommodates a museum.

61. In addition to Benjamin Lester, other leading merchants at Trinity included John Jeffrey, Thomas Street, and Samuel White.

62. Apart from George Garland, the main firms in Trinity at this time were Robert Slade, Sleat and Read of Christchurch (Hampshire), and Parker and Knight of St. John's. W. Gordon Handcock, *Merchant Families and Entrepreneurs of Trinity in the 19th Century* (St. John's: Government of Newfoundland and Labrador, 1981), 1–12.

63. Of the 111 men, forty-nine came from Waterford, five from Cork, and the remainder from Poole. All were to be employed by George Garland, apart from nine men who would work for Messrs. Hope, Sleat, and Read. Most were described as "youngsters" and were employed for eighteen months (two summers and a winter). Wages generally varied from fifteen to eighteen pounds per year.

64. DHC D/LEG/Z13.

65. *DCB*, George Garland, Vol. 6.

66. PANL MG 504, Robert Slade, Folder No. 1. Two of the men on the list were Edward and Henry Slade, who were presumably being sent to Newfoundland to learn about the business. Wages were paid in money, sometimes supplemented by molasses or clothing, and in one case tea and coffee. The usual wage was twenty-five to thirty-five pounds per year. The cooper was paid fifty pounds, "and if he drinks grog (alcohol) to forfeit his wages."

67. W.G. Handcock, "The Poole Mercantile Community and the Growth of Trinity, 1700–1839," paper read before the Newfoundland Historical Society, January 26, 1984, 3.

68. RHL USPG, Series E, 1845–55 (LAC m/f A221).

69. *SPG Annual Report*, 1855, lxviii, lxix. *An Account of the State of the Schools in the Island of Newfoundland*, 4–12.

70. SOAS LMS, Box 1A, Jacket A, Folder 1/2, July 18, 1800.

71. PANL MHC, Vol. 2, 90.

72. Evidence from parish registers shows that the permanent settlement of the central Bonavista Bay area only began in earnest during the nineteenth century. Alan G. Macpherson, "A Model Sequence in the Peopling of Central Bonavista Bay, 1676–1857," in John Mannion, ed., *The Peopling of Newfoundland: Essays in Historical Geography* (St. John's: Memorial University of Newfoundland, Institute of Social and Economic Research, 1978), 102–35.

73. RHL USPG, Series E, 1845–55 (LAC m/f A221).

74. *SPG Annual Report*, 1855, lxviii.

75. Census of Newfoundland, 1857.

76. According to the 1857 census, 64 percent of the population at Twillingate and Fogo were Anglicans.

77. RHL USPG Series E, 1845–1855 (LAC m/f A221).

78. *SPG Annual Report*, 1845, xlviii–l.

79. SOAS LMS, Box 1A, Jacket C, Folder 1/15, June 25, 1813.

80. DRO 2386 Madd 2/C/ letters from Captain William Fox papers, 1816–17.

81. Jean M. Murray, ed., *The Newfoundland Journal of Aaron Thomas, Able Seaman in HMS Boston: A Journal Written During a Voyage from England to Newfoundland and from Newfoundland to England in the Years 1794 and 1795, Addressed to a Friend* (London: Longmans, 1968), 173, quoted in Handcock, *So Longe As There Comes Noe Women*, 256.

82. DHC PE/WM/OV/11/1/181: April 20, 1801 (Wimborne Minster).

83. PANL *MHC*, Vol. 1, 10.

84. PANL MIIC, Vol. 1, 37–38.

85. PANL MG 252 (folder R1–K–3) letter, dated November 15, 1819, to someone in Wimborne (Dorset), a facsimile, the original is in Bodleian Library, University of Oxford.

86. The 1857 census reveals that the Roman Catholic church commanded support from 86 percent of the combined population of Placentia Bay and St. Mary's Bay. The proportion of Methodists at Burin was a respectable 33 percent, probably reflecting the pastoral work undertaken by the Reverend Lewis in his short time there.

87. DRO 3009A-99/PO12/455 (Chudleigh).

88. Jersey Harbour, just to the north of Harbour Breton, probably marks the place where Jersey immigrants settled.

89. *DCB*, Robert Newman, Vol. 5.

90. *SPG Annual Report*, 1846, xlviii.

91. RHL SPG E1 (1856). See quarterly report, June 30, 1856, of the Reverend William Kepple White. The children arrived May 2, 1856. Details of the boys (without names) appear on page 273. Only fifteen of the children could read and write.

92. One of the men originated from Shaftesbury (Dorset). They sailed from Dartmouth to Harbour Breton in the *Chanticlear*. One-third were to remain in Harbour Grace while the remainder would go farther west.

93. *SPG Annual Report*, 1846, xlviii.

94. The 1857 census reveals that the Protestant to Catholic ratio (virtually synonymous with English to Irish) was around 64,500 Protestants compared with around fifty-seven thousand Catholics, suggesting that they were present in nearly comparable numbers at that time.

CHAPTER 8: THE HOME CHILDREN

1. Phyllis Harrison, ed., *The Home Children: Their Personal Stories* (Winnipeg: Watson & Dwyer Publishing Ltd., 1979), 77–79.
2. Joy Parr, *Labouring Children* (London: Croom Helm, 1980), 11–14.
3. The Poor Law Act was amended in 1850 to allow Poor Law Guardians to send orphaned and deserted children abroad.
4. Parr, *Labouring Children*, 27–44.
5. *Ibid.*, 62–81.
6. Comments made by various child emigration promoters quoted in Parr, *Labouring Children*, 46.
7. Parr, *Labouring Children*, 45–61.
8. *Ibid.*, 142–57; Roy Parker, *The Shipment of Poor Children to Canada, 1867–1917* (Bristol, UK: University of Bristol, The Policy Press, 2008), 277–82.
9. LAC R11550–8–E: Richard Robertson fonds. Richard Robertson arrived in New Brunswick from Ontario in the 1930s as "a boy farm labourer."
10. WYAS PL/3/7/1–3: *Liverpool Daily Post*, May 14, 1887.
11. Parr, *Labouring Children*, 324.
12. Thomas Barnardo was the principal promoter of child emigration, but few of his children went to the Maritime provinces. Between 1882 and 1905 the Barnardo homes sent twenty-seven thousand children to Canada, nearly all to Ontario and the Prairie provinces (see Kohli, *The Golden Bridge*, 143–68). Some Barnardo children arrived at Halifax from Liverpool in 1887 in the *Parisian* and *Siberian*, and in 1892 in the *Carthaginian* and *Labrador*. See NSARM MG 100, Vol. 97, No. 27: home children — list of ships and ports of arrival and departure, 1870–99.
13. The major exodus only began from the 1870s, but before this small groups were being sent from Liverpool to Canada. One example is the group of eighteen children sent in 1868 from Industrial Schools in Liverpool to Newfoundland. See Kay Parrott, "The Apprenticeship of Parish Children from Kirkdale Industrial Schools, Liverpool, 1840–70," *The Local Historian*, Journal of the British Association of Local History, Vol. 30, No. 2 (May 2009), 131.
14. Kohli, *The Golden Bridge*, 71–104. In 1870, Miss Rye organized the relocation of 253 children. They went mainly to Ontario, but some were also sent to Nova Scotia and New Brunswick. Many more were sent to Ontario in the next two years. Annie Macpherson brought over 2,500 children to Ontario and Quebec between 1870 and 1875, establishing three reception homes in Canada, which offered training in farming.
15. Kohli, *The Golden Bridge*, 119–31. The Liverpool Sheltering Home was first located on Byrom Street, between Gerrard and Circus streets. A new site was found ten years later on Myrtle Street.
16. Lilian M. Birt, *The Children's Home Finder* (London: J. Nisbit, 1913), 114, quoted in Kohli, *The Golden Bridge*, 120.
17. Having emigrated from England, Colonel Laurie had acquired a large estate at Oakfield, near Halifax, by the early 1870s.

18. Five dollars a head was remitted to the Liverpool Committee, which paid the passages, while an average cost of about $1.50 per head was paid to maintain the children until their placements were agreed. Laurie claimed that his "cost of correspondence, stationery, postage, telegraphing and incidental travelling" amounted to seventy-five dollars. See *Eastern Chronicle*, May 28, 1874.

19. *AR*, August 7, 1873, quoted in Kohli, *The Golden Bridge*, 121–22.

20. Halifax immigration agent's report quoted in Kohli, *The Golden Bridge*, 123.

21. Just over 60 percent of the children had gone to Pictou, Halifax, Cumberland, and Colchester counties, with each getting similar numbers.

22. *EC*, April 30, 1874 (New Glasgow newspaper).

23. NSARM RG18, Ser. 1, Vol. 1, No. 1: Laurie's list. The August 1873 group was the "1st party," while the April 1874 group was the "2nd party."

24. Although the ledger kept by Colonel Laurie only contains around 347 placements, Mrs. Birt claimed in her own literature to have placed five hundred children in Nova Scotia before 1886. See WYAS PL/3/7/1–3, No. 17, No. 113, Leeds Board of Guardians papers, which provides extracts from reports of the Sheltering Home in Liverpool.

25. Although Cape Breton's coal-mining industry expanded greatly from the 1860s, it was able to recruit most of its workforce from the large pool of surplus rural labour that was available at the time. See Hornsby, *Nineteenth Century Cape Breton*, 169–83.

26. NSARM RG18, Ser. 1, Vol. 1, No. 1: Laurie's list. Jimmy was only four years old, Thomas, Stephen, and Edith were aged five, Henry was aged eight, while George and Agnes were both ten.

27. Thirty-five percent of Mrs. Birt's sixth group were below the age of five.

28. Robert McIntosh, "'Grotesque Faces and Figures': Child Labourers and Coal-Mining Technology in Victorian Nova Scotia," *Scientia Canadensis: Canadian Journal of the History of Science, Technology and Medicine*, Vol. 12, No. 2 (1988), 97–112.

29. *Nova Scotia Legislative Council, Journal and Proceedings*, 1874, Appendix 9: Report of Mather Byles Desbrisay, December 31, 1873. The 1873 group of immigrants consisted of 221 men, thirty-five women, and forty-five minors. The immigration agent also referred to families with children under Colonel Laurie's' care who received help to emigrate.

30. *Nova Scotia House of Assembly, Proceedings*, 1875, Appendix 17: Immigration Report Assistance. The following groups were assisted financially in 1875 by the provincial authorities: Mrs. Birt: In April, ten adults and sixty-three children under fourteen years of age; in August, twenty-two adults and sixty children under fourteen years. Colonel Laurie: In April, four men, two women, and three children under seventeen years; in May, a married couple and seven children; in July, five adults and seven children; in September, four adults and three children; in December, four adults.

31. Although Colonel Laurie helped Mrs. Birt place her 347 children, he was clearly involved with other schemes. He is known to have placed a total of about 550 children in Nova Scotia between 1873 and 1876 — two hundred of whom were apparently unconnected with Mrs. Birt. See Kohli, *The Golden Bridge*, 123.

32. Gillian Wagner, *Children of the Empire* (London: Weidenfeld and Nicholson, 1982), 78–79.

33. They joined the band of unsupervised home children who had been abandoned by Maria Rye. She had placed her children vaguely in the care of two friends who were unable to cope with their problems. Failing to obtain help from the government of Nova Scotia, Miss Rye took no further action. See *ibid.*, 78–79.

34. Mrs. Birt continued to send a small number of children to Nova Scotia. For instance, in 1888 the Halifax immigration agent reported that eighteen of her children were being placed in the province. (See Kohli, *The Golden Bridge*, 125–27.) A letter sent to her by Mary Jane Fletcher in 1896 from the premises of "Anthony Johnson, manufacturer of all descriptions of lumber," in Bouctouche, New Brunswick, indicates that some of her charges had been sent even farther afield. The Young Immigrants to Canada: Envelopes from Mrs. Birt's Children website gives details of the place names recorded on the envelopes used by the children when writing to Mrs. Birt. The envelopes were acquired by an English stamp collector some years later.

35. BCL MS 517/20 Annual Reports, 1897–1902; MS 517/107 Letters from the Halifax manager; MS 517/262 Settlements and Reports of Children sent to Canada. A large ledger was kept for each child, recording parental consents, progress reports, and other snippets of information. Detailed information was recorded of each child's placement. Judging from the cryptic nature of some managers' reports, there were many instances when visits had taken place, but the children had not been seen. Presumably visits were informal and unannounced in advance.

36. It is estimated that between 1873 and 1932 a total of five thousand children were brought to various parts of Canada by John Middlemore. Kohli, *The Golden Bridge*, 131–37.

37. Harrison, *The Home Children*, 183–85.

38. *Ibid.*, 208–14.

39. Charlotte Hunt went to West River, Alfred Henry Heckett to Orwell, Mary Rabbitt to Baldwin's Road, John S. Ruddick to Kinross, William Smith to Rustico, and James Rabbitt was sent to Mr. James Baldwin.

40. *Guardian*, June 21, 1899, quoted in "Middlemore Home Children in P.E.I.," in *P.E.I. Genealogical Society Newsletter*, No. 93, Vol. 24, No. 2 (April 2000), 17–9.

41. Anon., *One Hundred Years of Child Care: The Story of Middlemore Homes, 1872–1972* (Birmingham: The Middlemore Homes Committee, 1972), 7, quoted in Kohli, *The Golden Bridge*, 136.

42. Kohli, *The Golden Bridge*, 192–94.

43. WYAS PL 3/7/5: Leeds Board of Guardians Register of Emigrant Children, 1888–95. William Lyne and John Borus sailed in May 1890 in the *Sardinian*. In addition, James and George Harker, William Burke, and Thomas King, all Roman Catholics, sailed to Halifax from Liverpool in August 1888.

44. WYAS PL 3/7/4: *Emigration of Children from the Leeds Union, Report Upon the Scheme* (Leeds: Joseph Rider, 1891), 8–10.

45. Kohli, *The Golden Bridge*, 194–97.

46. Wagner, *Children of the Empire*, 194–95.
47. Kohli, *The Golden Bridge*, 206–07.
48. The Boys Brigade is a Christian youth organization that acquired a world-wide organization by the early 1890s. The Dakeyne name was taken from the Dakeyne Street Lad's Club in Sneinton (Nottinghamshire), just to the south of the city of Nottingham.
49. Parr, *Labouring Children*, 144.
50. LAC RG76–1–A-1, Vol. 615, file 911684 (m/f C-10435): Young English emigrants sent to Dakeyne Training Farm. The children staying at the farm at the time of Mr. Smart's inspection were: William Banham, William Bennett, Fred Cutler, Albert Glover, William Eaton, William Easton, Frank Porter, Cyril Potts, Perry Starbuck, Cyril Sunderland, Sydney J Dayton, and David Wilkinson.
51. LAC RG76–1–A–1: Cutting from Halifax newspaper, no date, but probably May 1924.
52. There is a long tradition of clergymen helping to organize the emigration of children from the English slums to Canada. Dr. Thomas Bowman Stephenson, a Methodist minister who founded the National Children's Home, relocated just over three thousand children to Canada from many parts of England between 1873 and 1933, while the Catholic Emigration Association and the Church of England Waifs and Strays sent six thousand and three thousand children respectively over this period. See Kohli, *The Golden Bridge*, 137–43, 156–63, 260.
53. HUA DBN/27/1: Emigration Papers, 1927.
54. Parr, *Labouring Children*, 82–98.
55. Parker, *Shipment of Poor Children*, 290–94.

CHAPTER 9: THE SEA CROSSING

1. Inkerman Rogers, *Ships and Shipyards of Bideford, Devon, 1569 to 1938: A Record of Wooden Sailing Ships and Warships Built in the Port of Bideford from 1568 to 1938, with a Brief Account of the Shipbuilding Industry in the Town* (Bideford, UK: Gazelle Printing Service, 1947), 27–28.
2. *Ibid.*
3. Starboard is the right hand side of a vessel. It was usually reserved for the captain, who used the starboard ladder when going ashore or returning, while all others used the port ladder. His cabin was normally on the starboard side.
4. PANB MC80/2472: Nathaniel Smith to his brother Benjamin, May 29, 1774.
5. LAC MG23-J3: Narrative of a voyage onboard the *Elizabeth* from England to the Island of St. John, 1775–1777, 28–42. Thomas Curtis travelled in the steerage.
6. Mrs. Churchward and her two daughters were among the passengers.
7. LAC MG23-J3: Narrative of a voyage onboard the *Elizabeth*.
8. LCA 387 MD 35: Journal of brig *Garland*, Liverpool to Miramichi, 1833, kept by Commander John Murray.

9. *AR*, September 4, 1819.

10. William Fulford's diary, described in Grant and Christie, *The Book of Bideford*, 38–39.

11. *Journals of the Assembly of Nova Scotia, 1867*, Immigration Report of 1866, Halifax arrivals, Appendix 7. The *Mozart* carried a total of 267 passengers.

12. NSARM MG 1, Vol. 3196A: Peter Barrett fonds, 4–5.

13. PANL MG 316: Duder family fonds, "Transcript of a Diary of an Atlantic Crossing Kept by Ann Congdon Duder, Aug. 5 to Sept. 13, 1833." Ann Congdon was the widow of Thomas Duder. Her relatives lived in St. Marychurch Parish (near Newton Abbot) in Devon.

14. The *Civility* carried her passengers to Quebec in 1848 but in the following year sailed with "a large number of emigrants for Prince Edward Island," Rogers, *Ships and Shipyards of Bideford Devon*, 28.

15. Grant and Christie, *The Book of Bideford*, 38–39.

16. LAC MG23–J3: Narrative of a voyage onboard the *Elizabeth*, 30.

17. PANB MC80/2472: Nathaniel Smith to his brother Benjamin, May 29, 1774.

18. Executive Council Minutes, June 14, June 22, 1819, microfilm #M-562.

19. Orlo and Fraser, "Elusive Immigrants," No. 17: 35.

20. The Island Register website, *www.islandregister.com*. Letters from/to P.E.I.: Alexander Beazeley to Miss Nicholson, at Thornton Bank, near Berwick-upon-Tweed, November 23, 1849.

21. *Royal Gazette*, May 25, May 28, 1847.

22. Martell, *Immigration to Nova Scotia, 1815–38*, 23–29.

23. The Fredericton Emigrant Society, formed in 1820 to help destitute immigrants, was the first institution of its kind in the province. See Ganong, "Settlements in New Brunswick," 75–77.

24. Two thousand of the 1846–47 arrivals died later. See MacNutt, *New Brunswick*, 303–04.

25. Letter by anonymous writer in *BA*, September 24, 1836.

26. The physical characteristics of a vessel greatly affected sailing performance as well as passenger comfort and safety. For an analysis of the different types of Aberdeen-registered vessels that were used to take emigrants to North America, see Campey, *Fast Sailing and Copper-Bottomed*, 80–98.

27. Elliott, "English Immigration to Prince Edward Island," (No. 40), 9.

28. Greenhill and Gifford, *Westcountrymen in Prince Edward's Isle*, 41–42, 123, 158.

29. Thomas Billing Jr. immigrated to the island and established a shipyard. Becoming a prominent public figure, he later returned to England. See Elliott, "English Immigration to Prince Edward Island," (No. 40), 9.

30. The Pope family's *Elizabeth* carried nineteen passengers to Charlottetown in 1822 and the *Nautilus* did the same between 1820 and 1821, carrying a total of twenty-five passengers. Thomas Pope, a timber merchant, remained in Plymouth, while his sons, William, John, and Joseph, ran operations on the island. Joseph Pope, whose farm and shipyard were in Bedeque, became one of Prince Edward Island's most important merchants. He served as a member of the legislative assembly from 1830 to 1853. See *DCB*, Vol. 12.

31. The Plymouth firm of Peake & Sons was managed by George Peake. James Peake returned to England in 1860, where he died.

32. The *Castalia*'s time as a regular trader came to an abrupt end in 1838 when she was driven ashore near the mouth of Bedeque Bay in a heavy storm. After being adrift in ice, she was eventually brought to Charlottetown and put ashore by means of a trench. James Peake had the ground levelled around her and had a roof built over the deck, thus converting the stricken vessel into a warehouse and rigging loft. See Lorne C. Callbeck, *The Cradle of Confederation: A Brief History of Prince Edward Island from Its Discovery in 1534 to the Present Time* (Fredericton: Brunswick Press, 1964), 215. Known affectionately as "Peake's Ark," it is featured in George Hubbard's painting shown on the book's front and back covers.

33. The *Island Register* website, *www.islandregister.com*. Letters from-to P.E.I.: Alexander Beazeley to Miss Nicholson, at Thornton Bank, near Berwick-upon-Tweed, November 23, 1849 (unfinished letter enclosed with another letter of the same date to Miss Nicholson). For details of the passengers see Appendix 4.

34. Arthur R.M. Lower, *Great Britain's Woodyard: British America and the Timber Trade, 1763–1867* (Montreal: McGill-Queen's University Press, 1973), 67–75.

35. Ralph Davis, *The Industrial Revolution and British Overseas Trade* (Leicester: Leicester University Press, 1979), 48–49. Tariffs increased from twenty-five shillings per load in 1804 to fifty-four shillings and sixpence per load in 1811. Between 1814 and 1843, Baltic timber was sometimes shipped to North America and then back to Britain, as the saving of duty more than compensated for the double freight. Despite widespread complaints in Britain over the high cost of timber, the protective tariffs remained in place until 1860.

36. The *Margaret* brought eighty-five miners from Liverpool to Pictou in 1827 and thirty to Pictou in 1830. The *Mary Ann* took one hundred miners to Pictou in 1838 while the *Cartha* carried 105 miners from Liverpool to Sydney in 1832. See Martell, *Immigration to Nova Scotia, 1815–38*, 60, 65, 73.

37. In that period, a total of 2,250 people sailed from Bideford to North America. Phillip Payton, *The Cornish Overseas* (Fowey, UK: Alexander Associates, 1999), 80.

38. Greenhill and Gifford, *Westcountrymen in Prince Edward's Isle*, 95–122.

39. *North Devon Journal*, April 16, 1857.

40. Anon., *Information Published by His Majesty's Commissioners for Emigration Respecting the British Colonies in North America* (London: Charles Knight, publisher to the Society for the Diffusion of Useful Knowledge, 1832), 6, 7.

41. Letter from George Beer in *Royal Gazette*, March 5, 1833, quoted in Greenhill and Gifford, *Westcountrymen in Prince Edward's Isle*, 109.

42. The *Lloyd's Shipping Register* is available as a regular series from 1775, apart from the years 1785, 1788, and 1817.

43. Still in use today, and run by a Classification Society with a worldwide network of offices and administrative staff, the *Lloyd's Register* continues to provide standard classifications of quality for shipbuilding and maintenance.

44. The number of years that a ship could hold the highest code varied according to where

it was built. In time, rivalries developed between shipowners and underwriters and this led to the publication of two registers between 1800 and 1833 — the *Shipowners Register* (Red Book) and the *Underwriters Register* (Green Book). Their coverage was similar but not identical. By 1834, with bankruptcies facing both sides, the two registers joined forces to become the *Lloyd's Register of British and Foreign Shipping*.

45. To locate a ship's code from the *Register* it is usually necessary to have the vessel name, the tonnage, and/or captain's name. Such data is not always available and is highly problematic to locate. Some vessels may not have been offered for inspection, particularly in cases where a shipowner could rely on his personal contacts for business. The lack of a survey might arouse our suspicions but is not necessarily conclusive proof of a poor-quality ship.

46. The *Valiant* was a Dutch Prize. Prize was normally the name given to an enemy vessel captured at sea by privateers.

47. The *Rosa* and *Minerva* between them carried more than 250 passengers from Great Yarmouth to the island, but their shipping codes have not been located.

48. Overall the *Calypso* carried at least 260 passengers, the *Sarah and Eliza* at least 165 passengers, and the *Breakwater* took at least 110 passengers.

49. See Chapter 2.

50. However, the absence of any regulatory body meant that space limitations were largely unenforceable and they were frequently ignored. But shipowners had to treat their passengers well to attract repeat business. Their desire for a good personal recommendation from satisfied passengers kept them in check far more than did the legislation. That was the emigrant's principal weapon. Emigrant transport legislation is discussed in Oliver Macdonagh, *A Pattern of Government Growth, 1800–1860: The Passenger Acts and Their Enforcement* (London: Macgibbon & Kee, 1961), 54–62, 80–89, 148–51, 216–19, 237–45, 337–49.

51. Edwin C. Guillet, *The Great Migration: The Atlantic Crossing By Sailing Ships Since 1770* (Toronto, 1963), 13–19.

52. Letter from George Beer in *Royal Gazette*, March 5, 1833, quoted in Greenhill and Gifford, *Westcountrymen in Prince Edward's Isle*, 109.

53. *YCWA*, March 18, 1774.

54. See the fares for the *Nancy* crossing from Hull to Charlottetown in *HA*, April 11, 1818.

55. Anon., *Information Published By His Majesty's Commissioners for Emigration*, 4–5. In his "Emigration, P.E.I.," printed in Harvey, *Journeys to the Island of St. John or Prince Edward Island, 1775–1832*, John Lewellin states that the steerage fare from Liverpool to North America in 1826 was three pounds (see page 203).

56. Anon., *Information for Emigrants to British North America* (1842), 7–8.

57. The land company's promotional literature stated that "owing to the number of ships which go out in ballast for timber, passages are generally more moderate to Saint John or Chatham on the Miramichi than to any other part of America."

58. Shippers had space to fill going from east to west and offered cheap steerage rates. But in going from west to east, ships were packed with timber, thus restricting opportunities for travelling in the steerage.

59. DRO 1148M/Box 11 (i)/3: Richard Vicars to Sir Thomas Acland, February 28, 1824.

CHAPTER 10: THE ENGLISH IN ATLANTIC CANADA

1.   Jeremy Paxman, *The English: The Portrait of a People* (London: Michael Joseph, 1998), 184.
2.   John Bull was invented in 1712 by John Arbuthnot, a Scot. He went through many modifications and by the twentieth century was usually depicted wearing a Union Jack waistcoat and having a bulldog by his side.
3.   MacGregor, *British America*, 68.
4.   LAC MG23–J3: Narrative of a voyage onboard the *Elizabeth* from England to the Island of St. John, 1775–1777, 48.
5.   Whitelaw, *Dalhousie Journals*, Vol. 1, 62, 73.
6.   Gesner, *New Brunswick with Notes for Emigrants*, 329.
7.   LAC R3151–0–8–E: William Deal Chinery fonds.
8.   *AR*, July 10, 1884, quoted in Carrigan, "The Immigrant Experience in Halifax, 1881–1931," 36.
9.   Robinson and Rispin, *A Journey Through Nova Scotia*, 26–27.
10. *Ibid.*, 206.
11. Elliott, "The English," 463. In each case, single and multiple origin responses have been added together.
12. Gesner, *New Brunswick with Notes for Emigrants*, 330–32.
13. Blom and Blom, *Canada Home*, 194–95.
14. Warburton, *History of Prince Edward Island*, 348.
15. The 1991 census revealed that 57 percent of Halifax's population claimed at least one English ancestor.
16. Hallam, *When You Are in Halifax*, 73. Joseph Cunard had a great shipbuilding empire, while Richard Uniacke was the Nova Scotia attorney general.
17. *Ibid.*, 64–65.
18. DHC D/LEG/X26: *The Newfoundlander*, February 13, 1834.
19. Callbeck, *The Cradle of Confederation*, 164–65.
20. Colin D. Howell, *Blood, Sweat and Cheers: Sport and the Making of Modern Canada, Themes in Canadian Social History* (Toronto: University of Toronto Press, 2001), 17–18, 47–49.
21. Callbeck, *The Cradle of Confederation*, 164–65.
22. Anon., *The Cricketer* (Saint John: George A. Knodell, 1886).
23. Neil Tranter, *Sport, Economy and Society in Britain, 1750–1914* (Cambridge: Cambridge University Press, 1998), 13–31.
24. Kohli, *The Golden Bridge*, 333–38.
25. LAC MG28–I349 (m/f A-1193): Girls' Friendly Society fonds. The quotations are from the Finding Aid, 2–5.
26. *Ibid.*, *The Diocesan Magazine*, Girl's Friendly Society Jubilee Service, October 1933.

27. Apart from St. John's, the principal branches were at Harbour Grace (Conception Bay), Trinity, and Bonavista. In 1952, there were Girls' Friendly Society branches at St. John's, Bonavista, Catalina, Trinity, Fogo, Harbour Grace, Gander, Yorris Point, Howley, Badger's Quay, Queenspond, Petty Harbour, St. Phillips, Salryon Cove, and Lamaline.

28. The London Mechanics' Institute was founded by George Birkbeck in London in 1823. By the mid-nineteenth century, there were over seven hundred institutes in towns and cities across Britain and overseas, some of which were the foundations of later colleges and universities.

29. PANL MHC, Vol. 2, 58.

30. Gesner, *New Brunswick with Notes for Emigrants*, 330–32.

31. The Halifax St. George Society continues to promote English traditions and now satisfies its philanthropic role in contributing money to good causes in Halifax.

32. Ross McCormack, "Cloth Caps and Jobs: The Ethnicity of English Immigrants in Canada," in *Ethnicity, Power and Politics in Canada*, edited by Jorgen Dahlie and Tissa Fernando, (Toronto: Methuen, 1981), 38–55.

33. *Evening Telegram* (St. John's), July 23, 1896.

34. Lawson, *Letters on Prince Edward Island*, 38.

35. Johnstone, *A Series of Letters Descriptive of P.E.I.*, 52.

36. Terry McDonald, "Where Have All the (English) Folk Songs Gone?" *British Journal of Canadian Studies*, Vol. 14, No. 2 (1999), 180–92.

37. Whitelaw, *Dalhousie Journals*, Vol. 1, 83–84.

BIBLIOGRAPHY

PRIMARY SOURCES (MANUSCRIPTS)

Berwick-upon-Tweed Record Office (BRO)
C4/27: Sketch of the Life of Thomas Craigs.

Birmingham Central Library (BCL)
MS 517: Middlemore Home Children Archive.

Devon Record Office (DRO)
219/29/22a-c: Roper–Lethbridge Letters, Devonshire families resident abroad.
1148M: Acland of Broadclyst papers.
2386M: Fox family papers.
2565A/P051/5: Parish of Kingsteignton.
3009A-99/PO12/455: Parish of Chudleigh.
3137A/PO40/2: Parish of Hemyock.
3419A/P09/30, 3419A/P19/45: Parish of Combeinteignhead.

Dorset History Centre (DHC)
D.1822/1: Douch collection.
D/LEG: Lester and Garland families archive.
PE/LAH/IN 5/1: Parish of Langton Herring.
PE/Pl/OV 3/30: Parish of Poole.
PE/PUD/OV7/2: Parish of Puddletown.

PE/WM/OV/11/1/181: Parish of Wimborne Minster.

Library and Archives Canada (LAC)
M-1352: Glasgow Colonial Society Correspondence (microfilm reel).
MG17–B1: United Society for the propagation of the Gospel fonds Series E (m/f A-221). Originals held at Oxford University.
MG17–C2: Wesleyan Methodist Missionary Society, 1791–1819 (copies on microfiche — originals at University of London).
MG17–F6: London Missionary Society fonds, 1799–1840 (copies on microfiche — originals at University of London).
MG19–F10: Edward Walsh fonds, 1776–1807.
MG23–J3: Thomas Curtis' narrative of a voyage onboard the *Elizabeth* from England to the Island of St. John, 1775–1777.
MG24–D99: George and Alexander Birnie fonds.
MG24 F89: Colin Campbell's letter-book.
MG24–I131: (m/f M-5567) William Peters and family fonds.
MG25–G271: Descendants of Adam Bousfield (1839–*circa* 1905), who emigrated from Yorkshire to Nova Scotia via Boston.
MG25–G345: Dyment family collection.
MG25–G404: Bond family fonds.
MG28–I349 (m/f A-1193): Girls' Friendly Society fonds (Newfoundland).
MG28–I492: Middlemore Children's Emigration Home fonds, 1873–1975 (originals at Birmingham Central Library).
MG29 A62: John Laing diary.
MG55/24–No299: John Hill fonds.
R11550–0–8–E: Richard D. Robertson fonds.
R3151–0–8–E: William Deal Chinery fonds, 1913.
RG17 Vol. 139, file 14579: Nicholas Bryant of Cornwall re: emigration to Nova Scotia, 1875.
RG76–1–A–1 Vol. 615, file 911684 (m/f C-10435): Young English emigrants sent to Dakeyne Training Farm.

Liverpool City Archives (LCA)
380 BOW: C.T. Bowring papers.
387 MD 35: Journal of brig *Garland* crossing Liverpool to Miramichi (1833).

National Archives of Britain, Kew (NAB)
CO 188: New Brunswick original correspondence.
CO 217: Nova Scotia and Cape Breton original correspondence.
CO 226: Prince Edward Island original correspondence.
CO 384: Colonial Office papers on emigration containing original correspondence concerning North American settlers.
CO 700: Colonial Office maps and plans.
MH 12/11837: (Hoxne Poor Law Union).

T/47/9 and /10: Register of emigrants, 1773–1776.

Nova Scotia Archives and Records Management (NSARM)
Journals of the House of Assembly, 1865 and 1867.
MG 100 Vol. 263, No. 13 (m/f 22,346): Nathaniel Smith to Benjamin Smith, 1774–1807.
MG 1 Vol. 427 (m/f 14920): Harrison family papers.
MG 1 Vol. 1739 (Nos. 7–36): Kennedy B. Wainwright fonds.
MG 1 Vol. 1854 F3: C.B. Fergusson papers.
MG 1 Vol. 1897: Fergusson papers.
MG 1 Vol. 3371: Thomas Neville fonds.
MG 1 Vol. 3196A: Peter Barrett fonds.
MG 100 Vol. 97, No. 27: Home children — list of ships and ports of arrival and departure, 1870–1899.
Nova Scotia Legislative Council, Journal and Proceedings, 1874 and 1875.
RG1: Bound volumes of Nova Scotia Records.
RG1 Vol. 44, doc. 37: An account of the number of passengers from Great Britain 5th April to 5th July, 1774.
RG18 Ser. 1, Vol. 1, No. 1: List of adults and children brought to Nova Scotia by Louisa Birt and Colonel Laurie, 1873–75.
RG18: No. 34 passenger list *Kedar*, Liverpool to Halifax, 1864.
RG18: No. 22 passenger list *Europa*, London to Halifax, 1864.

Oxford University: Rhodes House Library (RHL)
United Society for the Propagation of the Gospel (USPG) Series E: Reports from Missionaries.

Public Archives and Records Office of Prince Edward Island (PAPEI)
AC 2277: Benjamin Chappell fonds.
Acc 2540: Stretch family fonds.
Acc 3067: Port Hill Parish fonds.
Acc 3269: George and Alexander Birnie fonds.
Acc 4362, No. 2: Mark Butcher fonds.
Acc 4561: James Cross fonds.

Provincial Archives of New Brunswick (PANB)
MC 1: Trueman family.
MC 3: No. 340: "Early History of Kent County," by W.C. Milner.
MC 80/319: Report of Mr. Brown's mission in Great Britain and Ireland for the promotion of emigration to New Brunswick (1863).
MC 80/695: History of Stanley Pioneers.
MC 80/701: Historical record of the posterity of William Black.
MC 80/730: "History of Westmorland County — Emmersons and Descendents," by Randall Emmerson.
MC 80/818: "History of Harvey Settlement," by Reverend William Randall.

MC 80/915: *Handbook for Immigrants to the Province of New Brunswick*, 1841.
MC 80/1790: Early families.
MC 80/ 2151: Ancestors and descendents of George Edwin Smith and Alfretta Keith.
MC 80/2472: Yorkshire immigration.
MC 80/2579: *Nathaniel Smith: A Stranger in a Strange Land.*
MC 167 1/1: Dunham and McDougall family collection.
RG 637 26d: Records of the surveyor general.
RS 9: Executive Council, December 9, 1871.
RS 24: Legislative Assembly, *Sessional Records.*
RS 108 (m/f F1035): Land Petitions.

Provincial Archives of Newfoundland and Labrador (PANL)
MHC: Mildred Howard collection (of vital statistics from Newfoundland newspapers).
MG 204: John Thomas Duckworth collection.
MG 252 (R1–K–3): Reverend John Lewis papers.
MG 316: Duder family fonds.
MG 367: Reverend M. Blackmore papers.
MG 504 (1–K-5): Robert Slade papers.

Royal Institution of Cornwall (RIC)
Records of emigrant ships from Cornwall (based on newspaper extracts from C.J. Davies).

Somerset Record Office (SORO)
DD\S\ST/23: Stradling family papers.
DD\SAS\C/795/SW/21: Sweetman collection.

Staffordshire County Record Office (STRO)
D3388: Dyott family papers.
D (W) 1778: Earl of Dartmouth collection.

Suffolk Record Office (Ipswich) (SROI)
Education File 26: Extract from "Gentleman's Magazine," May 1832, 457.
FC 105/G7: Plomesgate Union.
FC 131/G14/1: Benhall Parish records.

Suffolk Record Office (Lowestoft) (SROL)
Acc. No. 868: Papers of John Eustace Grubbe of Southwold (Suffolk).
119: Covehithe Parish records.
124: Halesworth Parish records.
455: Woolnough family correspondence.

University of Hull Archives (UHA)
DBN/27/1: Emigration papers, 1927.

DDSY: Syke family papers.

University of London, School of Oriental and African Studies (SOAS)
LMS: London Missionary Society Papers.
MMS: Methodist Missionary Society Papers.

Warwickshire Record Office (WRO)
CR 114A: Seymour of Ragley papers.

West Yorkshire Archive Service (WYAS)
109: Rockingham letter-books.
219/305/5: Earl of Dartmouth estate papers relating to Yorkshire affairs.
LLD3/719 [197]: Records of all persons aided to emigrate 1906–12.
PL/3/7/1–3: Letters concerning boarding out and emigration 1887–90.
PL3/7/5: Leeds Board of Guardians, Register of emigrant children 1888–95.

PRINTED PRIMARY SOURCES AND CONTEMPORARY PUBLICATIONS

Allison, Leonard A. *The Rev. Oliver Arnold, First Rector of Sussex, N.B.: With Some Account of His Life, His Parish and His Successors, and the Old Indian College.* Saint John, NB: Sun Print Co., 1892.
Anon. *A True Guide to Prince Edward Island, Formerly St. John's in the Gulph of St. Laurence, North America.* Liverpool: Printed by G.F. Harris for Woodward and Alderson, booksellers, 1808.
Anon. *Emigration: Extracts from Various Writers on Emigration, with Authentic Copies of Letters from Emigrants from Norfolk, Suffolk, and Sussex, Now Settled in Upper Canada, Containing Useful Information Respecting That Country.* Norfolk, U.K.: Bacon and Kinnebrook, 1834.
Anon. *Information for Emigrants to British North America.* London: C. Knight, 1842.
Anon. *Information Published by His Majesty's Commissioners for Emigration Respecting the British Colonies in North America.* London: Charles Knight, publisher to the Society for the Diffusion of Useful Knowledge, 1832.
Anon. *Practical Information to Emigrants, Including Details Collected from the Most Authentic Accounts Relating to the Soil, Climate, Natural Productions, Agriculture etc. of the Province of New Brunswick,* London: John Richardson, Royal Exchange, 1832.
Anon. *The Cricketer.* Saint John, NB: George A. Knodell, 1886.
Anon. *The Irish Unitarian Magazine (and Bible Christian).* Belfast: 1846.
Anspach, Reverend Lewis Amadeus (late a magistrate of that island and missionary for the district of Conception Bay). *History of the Island of Newfoundland: Containing a Description of the Island, the Banks, the Fisheries, and Trade of Newfoundland, and the Coast of Labrador.* London: printed for the author, 1819.
Atkinson, Reverend W. Christopher. *An Historical and Statistical Account of New*

Brunswick, British North America, with Advice for Emigrants. Edinburgh: Printed by Anderson & Bryce, 1844.

Baillie, Thomas. *An Account of the Province of New Brunswick, Including a Description of the Settlements, Visitations, Soil and Climate of That Important Province with Advice to Emigrants*. London: J.G. & F. Rivington, 1832.

Bouchette, Joseph, *The British Dominions in North America: A Topographical and Statistical Description of the Provinces of Lower and Upper Canada, New Brunswick, Nova Scotia, the Islands of Newfoundland, Prince Edward Island and Cape Breton*. Vols. 1 and 2. London: Longman, Rees, Orme, Brown, Green and Longman, 1832.

Brown, R. *The Coal Fields and Coal Trade of Cape Breton*. London: Sampson, Low, Marston, Low & Searle, 1869.

Brown, Richard. *A History of the Island of Cape Breton*. London: Sampson Low, Son and Marston, 1869.

Buckingham, J.S. *Canada, Nova Scotia, New Brunswick and Other British Provinces in North America: With a Plan of National Colonization*. London, Paris: Fisher & Sons, 1843.

Calnek, W.A., and A.W. Savery, ed. *History of the County of Annapolis, Including Old Port Royal and Acadia: With Memoirs of Its Representatives in the Provincial Parliament And Biographical and Genealogical Sketches of Its Early English Settlers and Their Families*. Toronto: W. Briggs, 1897.

Cambridge, John. *A Description of the Island of St. John in the Gulf of St. Laurence, North America: With a Map of the Island, and a Few Cursory Observations Respecting the Climate, Natural Productions, and Advantages of Its Situation, In Regard to Agriculture and Commerce; Together with Some Remarks, As Instructions to New Settlers / by a Person Many Years Resident There*. London: Printed and sold by R. Ashby and W. Winchester, 1798.

Campbell, Duncan. *History of Prince Edward Island*. Charlottetown, PE: Bremner Bros., 1875.

Cattermole, William. *Emigration: The Advantages of Emigration to Canada: Being the Substance of Two Lectures Delivered at the Town-Hall, Colchester, and the Mechanics' Institution, Ipswich*. London: Simpkin & Marshall; Woodbridge: J. Loder, 1831.

Census of New Brunswick, 1851, 1871.

Census of Newfoundland, 1857.

Census of Nova Scotia, 1871.

Census of Prince Edward Island, 1881.

Champion, Thomas Edward. *The Anglican Church in Canada*. Toronto: Hunter, Rose, 1898.

Cobbett, William. *The Emigrant's Guide in 10 Letters Addressed to the Taxpayers of England: Containing Information of Every Kind, Necessary for Persons About to Emigrate; Including Several Authentic and Most Interesting Letters from English Emigrants, Now in America, To Their Relations in England*. London: author, 1829.

Cooney, Robert. *A Compendious History of the Northern Part of the Province of New Brunswick and of the District of Gaspé in Lower Canada*. Chatham, NB: D.G. Smith, 1896.

Cormack, W.E. *Narrative of a Journey Across the Island of Newfoundland: The Only One Ever Performed by a European*. St. John's, NL: Morning Chronicle Print, 1873.

Cramp, J.M. "The Centenary of Baptists in Nova Scotia." *General Report of the Nova Scotia Baptist Education Society*. Halifax: Printed at the Christian Message Office, 1860.

Crosskill, W.H. *Prince Edward Island: Garden Province of Canada: Its History Interests and Resources with Information for Tourists etc*. Charlottetown, PE: Murley & Garnhum, 1906.

Dixon, James Dunbar. *History of Charles Dixon*. Sackville, NB, 1891.

Eaton, Arthur Wentworth Hamilton. *The Church of England in Nova Scotia and the Tory Clergy of the Revolution*. London: J. Nisbet & Co., 1892.

Edgar, James. *New Brunswick As a Home for Emigrants: With the Best Means of Promoting Immigration and Developing the Resources of the Province*. Saint John, NB: Barnes & Co., 1860.

Feild, Edward. *Newfoundland: Journal of a Voyage of Visitation in the "Hawk" Church Ship, On the Coast of Labrador, and Round the Whole Island of Newfoundland in the Year 1849*. London: Society for the Propagation of the Gospel in Foreign Parts, 1850.

Gesner, Abraham. *New Brunswick with Notes: For Emigrants, Comprehending the Early History, Settlement, Topography, Statistics, Natural History, etc*. London: 1847.

Haliburton, Thomas Chandler. *An Historical and Statistical Account of Nova Scotia*, 2 Vols. Halifax: J. Howe, 1829.

Harris, John. *The Life of Francis Metherall and the History of the Bible Christians in Prince Edward Island*. Toronto: Bible Christian Bookroom, 1883.

Harvey, Daniel Cobb, ed. *Journeys to the Island of Saint John or Prince Edward Island, 1775–1832*. Toronto: Macmillan Co. of Canada, 1955.

Hill, George W. *Review of the Rise and Progress of the Church of England in Nova Scotia: Being a Sermon Preached Before the Honourable, the Board of Governors and Members of the University of King's College, Windsor, on the 24th June, 1858*. Halifax: the author, 1858.

Hill, S.S. *A Short Account of Prince Edward Island Designed Chiefly for the Information of Agriculturist and Other Emigrants of Small Capital by the Author of the Emigrant's Introduction to an Acquaintance with the British American Colonies*. London: Madden, 1839.

Inglis, John. *Journal of the Visitation of the Dioceses of Nova Scotia in New Brunswick in the Autumn of 1840 by the Right Rev. the Lord Bishop of Nova Scotia: Communicated to the Society for the Propagation of the Gospel in Foreign Parts*. London: R. Clay, 1841.

Johnston, J.F.W. *Notes on North America: Agricultural, Economical and Social*, 2 Vols. Edinburgh: William Blackwood & Sons, 1851.

Johnstone, Walter. *A Series of Letters Descriptive of Prince Edward Island in the Gulph of St. Laurence Addressed to the Rev. John Wightman, Minister of Kirkmahoe, Dumfries-shire*. Dumfries, U.K.: printed for the author by J. Swan, 1822.

Kendall, E.N. *Reports Nos. 1 and 2 on the State and Condition of the Province of N.B. with Some Observations on the Company's Tract Laid Before the Court of Directors of the New Brunswick and Nova Scotia Land Company by E.N. Kendall*. London: W. Day, 1835.

Lawrence, J.W. *Footprints: Or Incidents in the Early History of New Brunswick*. Saint John, NB: J. & A. McMillan, 1883.

Lawson, John. Letters on Prince Edward Island by John Lawson, Esq., barrister at law and Judge Advocate. Charlottetown, PE: G.T. Haszard, 1851.

Lee, Herbert G. *An Historical Sketch of the First Fifty Years of the Church of England in the Province of New Brunswick.* Saint John, NB: Sun Publishing Co., 1880.

Lloyd's Shipping Register 1775–1855.

MacGregor, John. *Historical and Descriptive Sketches of the Maritime Colonies of British America.* London: Longman, Rees, Orme, Brown and Green, 1828.

Marsden, Joshua. *The Narrative of a Mission to Nova Scotia, New Brunswick and the Somers Islands with a Tour to Lake Ontario.* Plymouth-Dock, UK: Printed and sold by J. Johns, 1816.

Martin, R. Montgomery. *History of Nova Scotia, Cape Breton, The Sable Islands, New Brunswick, Prince Edward Island, the Bermudas, Newfoundland.* London: Whittaker & Co, 1837.

Mellish, John T. *Outlines of the History of Methodism in Charlottetown, Prince Edward Island.* Charlottetown, PE: 1888.

Miller, Thomas. *Historical and Genealogical Record of the First Settlers of Colchester County Down to the Present Time.* Halifax: A. & W. Mackinlay, 1873.

Moore, Reverend D.C. (Rector of Christ Church, Albion Mines). *Letters and Facts Concerning the Church of England in the County of Pictou.* Halifax: Baillie and Anderson, 1879.

More, James F. *The History of Queens County, Nova Scotia.* Halifax: Nova Scotia Printing Co., 1873.

New Brunswick and Nova Scotia Land Company. *Practical Information Respecting New Brunswick for the Use of Persons Intending to Settle Upon the Lands of the New Brunswick and Nova Scotia Land Company.* London: Pelham Richardson, 1843.

New Brunswick and Nova Scotia Land Company. *Sketches in New Brunswick: Taken Principally with the Intention of Shewing the Nature and Description of the Land in the Tract Purchased by the New Brunswick & Nova Scotia Land-Company in the Year 1833, and Illustrating the Operations of the Association During the Years 1834 & 1835.* London: Ackerman, 1836.

New Brunswick, Department of Provincial Secretary. *Handbook for Emigrants to the Province of New Brunswick.* Fredericton, NB: Queen's Printed, 1841.

Nova Scotia House of Assembly, Proceedings, 1875.

Nova Scotia Legislative Council, Journal and Proceedings, 1874.

Perley, Moses Henry. *A Handbook of Information for Emigrants to New Brunswick.* Saint John, NB: H. Chubb, 1854.

Potts, Thomas. *Prospectus of the English Agricultural Colony of New Brunswick: With a Statement of Conditions Concerning Free Houses, Free Grants of Land and Assisted Passages.* Bristol: Jeffries, 1874.

Prowse, D.W. *A History of Newfoundland, from the English, Colonial, and Foreign Records.* London: Eyre and Spottiswoode, 1896.

Report of the Wesleyan Methodist Missionary Society, 1838

Robinson, John, and Thomas Rispin. *A Journey Through Nova Scotia: Containing a Particular Account of the Country and Its Inhabitants; With Observations on the*

Management in Husbandry, the Breed of Horses and Other Cattle, and Every Thing Material Relating to Farming; to Which is Added an Account of Several Estates for Sale in Different Townships of Nova-Scotia, with Their Number of Acres and the Price at Which Each Is Set. York, UK: Printed for the authors by C. Etherington, 1774.

Smith, Sidney. *The Settler's New Home, or, Whether to Go, and Wither?: Being a Guide to Emigrants in the Selection of a Settlement, and the Preliminary Details of the Voyage, Embracing the Whole Fields of Emigration, and the Most Recent Information Relating Thereto.* London: John Kendrick, 1850.

Society for the Propagation of the Gospel in Foreign Parts. *An Account of the State of the Schools in the Island of Newfoundland, Established or Assisted by the Society for the Propagation of the Gospel in Foreign Parts.* London: Printed for the Society and sold by C. and J. Rivington, 1827.

Society for the Propagation of the Gospel in Foreign Parts, *Annual Reports.*

Stevenson, Benjamin R. *Report on Immigration to New Brunswick in 1873.* Saint John, NB: Daily Telegraph Printing, 1874.

Stewart, John. *An Account of Prince Edward Island, in the Gulph of St. Lawrence, North America: Containing Its Geography, a Description of Its Different Divisions, Soil, Climate, Seasons, Natural Productions, Cultivation, Discovery, Conquest, Progress and Present State of the Settlement, Government, Constitution, Laws, and Religion.* London: Printed by W. Winchester, 1806.

Watts, Samuel. *Facts for the Information of Intending Emigrants about the Province of New Brunswick.* Saint John, NB: Provincial Government, 1870.

Waylen, James. *A History, Military and Municipal of the Ancient Borough of the Devizes and Subordinately of the Entire Hundred of Potterne and Cannings.* London: Longman, 1859.

Wesleyan Methodist Missionary Society. *Annual Reports.*

PARLIAMENTARY PAPERS

Annual Reports of the Immigration Agent at Quebec (1831–55).

PP 1828 (148) Vol. XXI (Appendix to Colonel Cockburn's Report).

PP 1831–32 (724) XXXII: emigration report, 1831.

PP (1835) XXXV: "First Annual Report of the Commissioners Under the Poor Law Amendment Act."

PP 1836 (567) XVII: "Report of the 1836 Select Committee Appointed to Inquire Into the Causes of Shipwreck."

PP 1844 (181) XXXV: emigration report, 1843.

PP 1852–53 (1647) XV: "Thirteenth Report of the Colonial Land and Emigration Commissioners."

PP 1854 (1833) XXVIII: "Fourteenth Report of the Colonial Land and Emigration Commissioners."

CONTEMPORARY NEWSPAPERS

Acadian Recorder (Halifax)
Berwick Advertiser
Bristol Mercury
Cape Breton News
Colonial Herald (Charlottetown)
Dumfries and Galloway Courier
Eastern Chronicle (Pictou)
Evening Telegram (St. John's)
Hull Advertiser
Hull Packet
Ipswich Journal
Liverpool Daily Post
New Brunswick Courier
New Brunswick Gazette
Newcastle Chronicle or Weekly Advertiser
Newcastle Courant
The Newfoundlander
North Devon Journal
The Nova Scotian
Prince Edward Island Gazette
Prince Edward Island Register
Quebec Mercury
Royal Gazette (New Brunswick)
Royal Gazette (Charlottetown)
Suffolk Chronicle
The Times (London)
Trewman's Exeter Flying Post
York Chronicle and Weekly Advertiser
Yorkshire Courant

CONTEMPORARY MATERIAL OF LATER PRINTING

Cobbett, William. *Rural Rides*, edited by Ian Dyck. London: Penguin Books, 2001 (first published 1830).

Fisher, Peter. *History of New Brunswick*. Saint John, NB: reprinted jointly by the Government of New Brunswick and W.S. Fisher under the auspices of the New Brunswick Historical Society, 1921 (originally published 1825).

Munro, Alexander. *New Brunswick with a Brief Outline of Nova Scotia and Prince Edward Island*. Belleville, ON: Mika Studio, 1972. (First published 1855 by Richard Nugent, Halifax).

Murray, Jean M. ed. *The Newfoundland Journal of Aaron Thomas, Able Seaman in HMS Boston: A Journal Written During a Voyage from England to Newfoundland and from Newfoundland to England in the Years 1794 and 1795, Addressed to a Friend*. London: Longmans, 1968.

Rawlyk, G.A., ed. *Henry Alline: Selected Writings*. New York: Paulist Press, *circa* 1987.

White, Patrick, Cecil Telford., eds., *Lord Selkirk's Diary 1803–04: A Journal of His Travels Through British North America and the Northeastern United States*, Toronto: The Champlain Society, 1958.

Whitelaw, Marjorie, ed. *The Dalhousie Journals*. Ottawa: Oberon, 1978–82.

Wilson, Isaiah W. *A Geography and History of the County of Digby, Nova Scotia*, Belleville: Mika Studio, 1972 (originally published by the author in 1893).

SECONDARY SOURCES

Acheson, T.W. "A Study in the Historical Demography of a Loyalist County." *Social History*, No. 1 (April, 1968), 53–65.

Allen, Robert S. *The Loyal Americans: The Military Role of the Loyalist Provincial Corps and Their Settlement in British North America*. Ottawa: National Museum of Canada, *circa* 1983.

Anon. "Middlemore Home Children in P. E. I." *P. E. I. Genealogical Society Newsletter*, No. 93, Vol. 24, No. 2. (April 2000), 17–19.

Anon. *One Hundred Years of Child Care: The Story of Middlemore Homes 1872–1972*. Birmingham: The Middlemore Homes Committee, 1972.

Archer, John E. *By a Flash and a Scare — Incendiarism, Animal Maiming and Poaching in East Anglia 1815–1870*. Oxford: Clarendon Press, 1990.

Bailyn, Bernard, *Voyagers to the West: Emigration from Britain to America on the Eve of the Revolution*. New York: Alfred A. Knopf, 1986.

Baird, Reverend Frank. *History of the Parish of Stanley and Its Famous Fair*. Fredericton, NB: Printed by McMurray Book & Stationery, 1950.

Barker, H.W. "The Maugerville Church and the American Revolution." *Church History: Studies in Christianity and Culture*. Vol. 7, No. 4 (December 1938), 371–72.

Beamish, Derek, John Dockerill, and John Hillier. *The Pride of Poole, 1688–1851*. Poole, UK: Borough and County of Town of Poole, 1974.

Bean, P., and J. Melville. *Lost Children of the Empire*. London: Unwin Hyman, 1989.

Bird, William R. *A Century at Chignecto: The Key to Old Acadia*. Toronto: The Ryerson Press, *circa* 1928.

Birt, Lilian M. *The Children's Home Finder*. London: J. Nisbit, 1913.

Bitterman, R. *Rural Protest on Prince Edward Island: From British Colonization to the Escheat Movement*. Toronto: University of Toronto Press, 2006.

Blom, Margaret Howard, and Thomas E. Blom, eds. *Canada Home: Juliana Horatio Ewing's Fredericton Letters 1867–69*. Vancouver: University of British Columbia Press, 1983.

Bolger, F.W.P., ed., *Canada's Smallest Province: A History of Prince Edward Island*. Halifax: Nimbus, 1991.

Bouquet, Michael. "Passengers from Torquay: Emigration from North America 1849–1859." In *Ports and Shipping in the South-West*, edited by H.E.S. Fisher, Exeter, UK: University of Exeter, *Exeter Papers in Economic History*, No. 4, 1971, 131–47.

Bowser, Reginald Burton, *A Genealogical Review of the Bowser Family: Researches with Particular Reference to Thomas Bowser of Yorkshire, England and Sackville, New Brunswick, Canada*. Moncton, NB: R.B. Bowser, *circa* 1981.

Bradley, John. *Letter-Books of John and Mary Cambridge of Prince Edward Island, 1792–1812*. Devizes, UK: the author, 1996.

Bradley, John. *Shipshape Cambridge Fashion or John Cambridge of Prince Edward Island, Bristol and Wooton Under Edge: A Transatlantic Voyage into Family History*. Great Britain: Hurst Village Publishing, 1994.

Brayshay, Mark. "The Emigration Trade in Nineteenth Century Devon." In Michael Duffy et al., *The New Maritime History of Devon*, Vol. 2. London: Conway Maritime Press, 1994, 108–18.

Brayshay, Mark. "Government Assisted Emigration from Plymouth in the Nineteenth Century." *Report of the Transactions of the Devon Association for the Advancement of Science*, Vol. 112 (1980), 185–213.

Brebner, John Bartle. *The Neutral Yankees of Nova Scotia: A Marginal Colony During the Revolutionary Years*. New York: Columbia University Press, 1937.

Buckner, Phillip. "Introduction." *British Journal of Canadian Studies*. Vol. 16, No. 1 (2003), 1–5.

Buckner Phillip. *Peoples of the Maritimes: English*. Tantallon, NS: Four East Publications, 2000.

Buckner, Phillip. "The Transformation of the Maritimes: 1815–1860." *The London Journal of Canadian Studies*, Vol. 9 (1993), 13–30.

Buckner, Phillip, and John G. Reid, eds. *The Atlantic Region to Confederation: A History*. Toronto: University of Toronto Press, 1993.

Bumsted, J.M. *Land Settlement and Politics on Eighteenth Century Prince Edward Island*. Kingston, ON: McGill-Queen's University Press, 1987.

Bumsted, J.M. *The Peoples of Canada: A Pre-Confederation History*, Vol. 1. Toronto: Oxford University Press, 1992.

Cadigan, Sean T. *Newfoundland and Labrador: A History*. Toronto: University of Toronto Press, 2009.

Callbeck, Lorne C. *The Cradle of Confederation: A Brief History of Prince Edward Island from Its Discovery in 1534 to the Present Time*. Fredericton, NB: Brunswick Press, 1964.

Cameron, Wendy, Sheila Haines, and Mary McDougall Maude. *English Immigrant Voices: Labourers' Letters from Upper Canada in the 1830s*. Montreal: McGill-Queen's University Press, 2000.

Campbell, Mildred, "English Emigration on the Eve of the American Revolution," *American Historical Review*, Vol. 61 (1955), 1–20.

Campey, Lucille H. *'A Very Fine Class of Immigrants': Prince Edward Island's Scottish Pioneers, 1770–1850.* Toronto: Natural Heritage Books, 2001.

Campey, Lucille H. *After the Hector: The Scottish Pioneers of Nova Scotia and Cape Breton, 1773–1852,* Toronto: Natural Heritage Books, 2004.

Campey, Lucille H. *An Unstoppable Force: The Scottish Exodus to Canada.* Toronto: Natural Heritage Books–Dundurn Press, 2008.

Campey, Lucille H. *Fast Sailing and Copper-Bottomed: Aberdeen Sailing Ships and the Emigrant Scots They Carried to Canada.* Toronto: Natural Heritage Books, 2002.

Campey, Lucille H: *Les Écossais: The Pioneer Scots of Lower Canada, 1763–1855.* Toronto: Natural Heritage Books, 2006.

Campey, Lucille H. *The Scottish Pioneers of Upper Canada, 1784–1855: Glengarry and Beyond.* Toronto: Natural Heritage Books, 2005.

Campey, Lucille H. *The Silver Chief: Lord Selkirk and the Scottish Pioneers of Belfast, Baldoon and Red River.* Toronto: Natural Heritage Books, 2003.

Campey, Lucille H. *With Axe and Bible: The Scottish Pioneers of New Brunswick, 1784–1874.* Toronto: Natural Heritage Books–Dundurn Press, 2007.

Carrier, N.H., and J.R. Jeffrey. *External Migration: A Study of the Available Statistics 1815–1950.* London: HMSO, 1953.

Carrigan, D. Owen. "The Immigrant Experience in Halifax, 1881–1931." *Canadian Ethnic Studies,* Vol. 20, No. 3 (1988), 28–41.

Carrington, Philip. *The Anglican Church in Canada: A History.* Toronto: Collins, 1963.

Chadwick, St. John. *Newfoundland: Island into Province.* Cambridge: Cambridge University Press, 1967.

Charlesworth, Andrew. *An Atlas of Rural Protest in Britain, 1545–1900.* London: Croom Helm, 1983.

Clark, Andrew H. "Old World Origins and Religious Adherence in Nova Scotia." *Geographical Review,* Vol. 1 (1960), 317–44.

Clark, Andrew Hill. *Three Centuries and the Island: A Historical Geography of Settlement and Agriculture in Prince Edward Island, Canada.* Toronto: University of Toronto Press, 1959.

Clark, Samuel Delbert. *Church and Sect in Canada.* Toronto: University of Toronto Press, 1948.

Condon, Ann Gorman. *The Loyalist Dream for New Brunswick: The Envy of the American States,* Fredericton: New Ireland Press, 1984.

Conrad, Margaret, with Alvin Finkel and Cornelius Jaenen. *History of the Canadian Peoples,* Vol. 1. *Beginnings to 1876.* Toronto: Copp Clark Pitman, 1993.

Conrad, Margaret. *Intimate Relations: Family and Community in Planter Nova Scotia.* Fredericton, NB: Acadiensis Press, 1995.

Conrad, Margaret. *They Planted Well: New England Planters in Maritime Canada.* Fredericton: Acadiensis Press, 1988.

Conrad, Margaret, and Barry Moody, eds. *Planter Links: Community and Culture in Colonial Nova Scotia.* Fredericton: Acadiensis Press, 2001.

Constantine, S. "Empire Migration and Social Reform." *Migrants, Emigrants and*

Immigrants: A Social History of Migration, edited by C.G. Pooley and I.D. Whyte. London: Routledge, 1991, 62–83.

Cooney, Michael F. *Emigrants of Yorkshire, 1774–1775.* Kingston-upon-Hull, UK: Abus, *circa* 1994.

Corbin, Harry S. "The Church of England in Nova Scotia 1758–1851." Halifax: Dalhousie University, Department of History, unpublished MA thesis, 1949.

Cowan, Helen. *British Emigration to British North America: The First Hundred Years.* Toronto: University of Toronto Press, 1961.

Craig, Helen C. *The Craigs of Harvey Settlement, Red Rock and the Pontiac.* Fredericton, NB: author, 1999.

Dallison, Robert. *Hope Restored: The American Revolution and Founding of New Brunswick.* Fredericton, NB: Goose Lane Editions and the New Brunswick Military Heritage Project, 2003.

Davis, Ralph. *The Industrial Revolution and British Overseas Trade.* Leicester, UK: Leicester University Press, 1979.

de Jong, Nicholas, and Marven E. Moore. *Shipbuilding on Prince Edward Island: Enterprise in a Maritime Setting, 1787–1920.* Hull, QC: Canadian Museum of Civilization, 1994.

Debenham, Mary H. *Men Who Blazed the Trail: Stories of the Church's Pioneers in Canada, Australia and New Zealand.* London: Society for the Propagation of the Gospel in Foreign Parts, 1926.

Dictionary of Canadian Biography. Toronto: University of Toronto Press, 1979–85.

Dixon, John Thornton. "Aspects of Yorkshire Emigration to North America 1760–1880," Leeds: University of Leeds, School of History, unpublished PhD thesis, 1981.

Duncanson, John V. *Township of Falmouth, Nova Scotia.* Belleville, ON: Mika Publishing Co., 1983.

Eaton, Arthur Wentworth Hamilton. *History of Kings County, Nova Scotia: Heart of the Acadian Land, Giving a Sketch of the French and their Expulsion; and a History of the New England Planters Who Came in their Stead, with Many Genealogies, 1604–1910.* Salem, MA: Salem Press Co., 1910.

Elliott, Bruce. "Emigrant Recruitment by the New Brunswick Land Company: The Pioneer Settlers of Stanley and Harvey." *Generations,* the Journal of the New Brunswick Genealogical Society (Winter 2004), 50–54; (Spring 2005), 34–40; (Summer 2005), 11–17; (Fall 2005), 7–12.

Elliott, Bruce S. "English Immigration to Prince Edward Island." *The Island Magazine* Part One, No. 40 (1996), 3–11; Part Two, No. 41 (1997), 3–9.

Elliott, Bruce. "Regional Patterns of English Immigration and Settlement in Upper Canada." *Canadian Migration Patterns from Britain and North America*, edited by Barbara J. Messamore. Ottawa: University of Ottawa Press, 2004, 51–90.

Elliott, Bruce. "The English." *The Encyclopedia of Canada's Peoples*, edited by Paul Robert Magosci. Toronto: Published for the Multicultural History Society of Ontario by the University of Toronto Press, *circa* 1999, 462–88.

Erickson, Charlotte. *Leaving England: Essays on British Emigration in the Nineteenth Century.* Ithica, NY: Cornell University Press, 1994.

Evans, Eric J. *The Forging of the Modern State: Early Industrial Britain, 1783–1870.* Harlow, UK: Pearson Education, 2001.

Fellows, Robert. "Loyalists and Land Settlement in new Brunswick." *Canadian Archivist,* Vol. 2 (1971), 5–13.

Fingard, Judith. *The Anglican Design in Loyalist Nova Scotia.* London: SPCK, 1972.

Finney, Pat. *Nathaniel Smith: A Stranger in a Strange Land.* Sackville, NB: Tantramar Heritage Trust, 2000.

Fischer, David Hackett. *Albion's Seed: Four British Folkways in America.* Oxford: Oxford University Press, 1989.

Flewwelling, Susan Longley (Morse). "Immigration to and Emigration from Nova Scotia 1839–51." *Nova Scotia Historical Society (Collections),* Vol. 28 (1949), 66–97.

Fothergill, Gerald. *Emigrants from England, 1773–76, Transcribed by Gerald Fothergill: Reprinted from the New England Historical and Genealogical Register,* Vols. 62, 63, 64, 65. Baltimore, MD: Genealogical Publishing Co., 1964.

Fraser, Douglas. "More Elusive Immigrants." *The Island Magazine,* No. 26 (Fall/Winter 1989), 35–40; No. 27 (Spring/Summer 1990), 38–41.

Gallant, D. "Early Settlers in South Western New Brunswick." Mount Allison, NB: unpublished BA Thesis, 1959.

Gallant, Peter, and Nelda Murray. *From England to Prince Edward Island.* Charlottetown, PE: P.E.I. Genealogical Society, 1991.

Ganong, W.F. "Monograph of the Origins of Settlements in the Province of New Brunswick." *Transactions of the Royal Society of Canada,* 2nd series (10), sections 1–2 (1904), 1–185.

Garrad, John Adrian. *The English and Immigration 1880–1910.* London, New York: Published for the Institute of Race Relations, by Oxford University Press, 1971.

Gilroy, Marion. *Loyalists and Land Settlement in Nova Scotia.* Halifax: PANS Publication No. 4, 1937.

Grant, Alison, and Peter Christie. *The Book of Bideford.* Buckingham, UK: Barracuda Books Ltd., 1987.

Greenhilll, Basil, and Anne Giffard. *Westcountrymen in Prince Edward's Isle.* Toronto: University of Toronto Press, 1967.

Guillet, Edwin C. *The Great Migration: The Atlantic Crossing by Sailing Ships Since 1770.* Toronto: University of Toronto Press, 1963.

Hallam, Lilliam Gertrude Best. *When You Are In Halifax: Sketches of Life in the First English Settlement in Canada.* Toronto: Church Book Room, 1937.

Handcock, W.G. "English Migration to Newfoundland." *The Peopling of Newfoundland: Essays in Historical Geography,* edited by John J. Mannion. St. John's, NL: Institute of Social and Economic Research, Memorial University of Newfoundland, 1978, 15–48.

Handcock, W. Gordon. *Merchant Families and Entrepreneurs of Trinity in the 19th Century.* St. John's, NL: Government of Newfoundland and Labrador, 1981.

Handcock, W. Gordon. *So Longe As There Comes Noe Women: Origins of English Settlement in Newfoundland.* St. John's, NL: Breakwater, *circa* 1989.

Handcock, W. Gordon. "Spatial Patterns in a Trans-Atlantic Migration Field: The British Isles and Newfoundland During the Eighteenth and Nineteenth Centuries." *Proceedings of the 1975 British-Canadian Symposium on Historical Geography. The Settlement of Canada: Origins and Transfer*, edited by Brian S. Osborne. Kingston, ON: Queen's University, Department of Geography, 1976.

Handcock, W.G. "The Poole Mercantile Community and the Growth of Trinity, 1700–1839." Paper read before the Newfoundland Historical Society, January 26, 1984.

Hannay, J. *History of New Brunswick: Its Resources and Advantages*. 2 Vols. Saint John, NB: John A. Bowes, 1909.

Harrison, Phyllis, ed. *The Home Children: Their Personal Stories*. Winnipeg: Watson and Dwyer Publishing Ltd., 1979.

Harvey D.C. "Early Settlement in Prince Edward Island." *Dalhousie Review*, Vol. 11, No. 4 (1932), 458–59.

Heath-Stubbs, Mary. *Friendship's Highway: Being the History of the Girls' Friendly Society 1875–1935*. London: Girls' Friendly Society, 1935.

Hebb, Ross N. *The Church of England in Loyalist New Brunswick 1783–1825*. Madison, NJ: Farleigh Dickinson University Press, 2004.

Hewitt, Martin. "The Itinerant Emigration Lecturer: James Brown's Lecture Tour of Britain and Ireland, 1861–2." *The British Journal of Canadian Studies*, Vol. 10, No. 1 (1995), 103–19.

Hobsbawn, E.J., and George Rudé. *Captain Swing*. London: Lawrence & Wishart, 1969.

Holmes, Jane Elizabeth. *The Pre-Loyalist Emigration from New England and Resettlement of Nova Scotia*. Sackville, NB: Mount Allison University Archives, 1973.

Horn, Pamela. "Agricultural Trade Unionism and Emigration." *The Historical Journal*, Vol. 15, No. 1 (March 1972), 87–102.

Hornsby, Stephen J. *Nineteenth Century Cape Breton: A Historical Geography*. Montreal: McGill-Queen's University Press, 1992.

Howell, Colin D. *Blood, Sweat and Cheers: Sport and the Making of Modern Canada, Themes in Canadian Social History*. Toronto: University of Toronto Press, 2001.

Howells, Gary. "Emigration and the New Poor Law: Norfolk Emigration Fever of 1836." *Rural History*, Vol. 11, No. 2 (October 2000), 145–64.

Howells, Gary. "'On Account of Their Disreputable Characters': Parish-Assisted Emigration from Rural England, 1834–1860." *History*, Vol. 88, No. 292 (October 2003), 587–605.

Hyde, Susan Anne, and Michael Bird. *Hallowed Timbers: The Wooden Churches of Cape Breton, Nova Scotia*. Erin, ON: Boston Mills Press, 1995.

James-Korany, Margaret. "Blue Books as Sources for Cornish Emigration History." *Cornish Studies One*, edited by Philip Payton. Exeter, UK: University of Exeter Press, 1993, 31–45.

Jeffrey, Betty M., and Carter W. Jeffrey. *The Jeffery Family of the Island of Wight and P.E.I.* Alberton, PE: Therles Press, 1998.

Johnson, D.W. *History of Methodism in Eastern British America, Including Nova Scotia, New Brunswick, Prince Edward Island*. Sackville, NB: Tribune Printing, 1925.

Johnson, Stanley C. *A History of Emigration from the United Kingdom to North America, 1763–1912.* London: G. Routledge, 1913.

Kimber, Stephen. *Loyalists and Layabouts: The Rapid Rise and Faster Fall of Shelburne, Nova Scotia, 1783–1792.* Toronto: Doubleday Canada, 2008.

Kinsmen, Rev. Barry, *Fragments of Padstow's History.* Padstow (Cornwall), UK: Padstow Parochial Church Council, 2003.

Kohli, Marjorie. *The Golden Bridge: Young Immigrants to Canada, 1838–1939.* Toronto: Natural Heritage Books, 2003.

Latta, Peter. "Eighteenth Century Immigrants to Nova Scotia: The Yorkshire Settlers." *Material History Bulletin,* Vol. 28 (Fall 1988), 46–51.

Lee, Robert C. *The Canada Company and the Huron Tract, 1826–1853: Personalities, Profits and Politics.* Toronto: Natural Heritage Books, 2004.

Leetooze, Sherreall Branton. *A Corner for the Preacher with the Introductory Chapter by Elizabeth Howard, and a Preface by Colin Short.* Bowmanville, ON: L. Michael-John Associates, *circa* 2005.

Leetooze, Sherrell Branton. *Bible Christian Chapels of the Canadian Conference.* Bowmanville, ON: Lynn Michael-John Associates, 2005.

Levy, G.E. *The Baptists of the Maritime Provinces 1753–1946.* Saint John, NB: Barnes-Hopkins, 1946.

Little, John Irvine. *Nationalism, Capitalism and Colonization in Nineteenth Century Quebec, the Upper St. Francis District.* Kingston, ON: McGill-Queen's University Press, 1989.

Lower, Arthur R.M. *Great Britain's Woodyard: British America and the Timber Trade 1763–1867.* Montreal: McGill-Queen's University Press, 1973.

Macdonagh, Oliver. *A Pattern of Government Growth 1800–1860: The Passenger Acts and Their Enforcement.* London: MacGibbon & Kee, 1961.

Macdonald, C. Ochiltree. *The Coal and Iron Industries of Nova Scotia.* Halifax: Chronicle Publishing Co., 1909.

MacDonald, Reverend D. *Cape North and Vicinity, Pioneer Families, History and Chronicles: Including Pleasant Bay, Bay St. Lawrence, Aspy Bay, White Point, New Haven and Nell's Harbour.* Port Hastings, NS: the author, 1933.

MacDonald, Norman. *Canada, Immigration and Settlement 1763–1841.* London: Longmans & Co., 1939.

MacKinnon, Donald A., and A.B. Warburton. *Past and Present of Prince Edward Island.* Charlottetown, PE: B.F. Bowen, 1906.

MacKinnon, Neil. *This Unfriendly Soil: The Loyalist Experience in Nova Scotia 1783–1791.* Montreal: McGill-Queen's University Press, 1986.

MacLaren, George. *The Pictou Book: Stories of our Past.* New Glasgow, NS: Hector Pub. Co., 1954.

MacLean, John. *William Black — The Apostle of Methodism in the Maritime Provinces of Canada.* Halifax: Methodist Book Room, 1907.

MacNutt, W.S. *New Brunswick, A History: 1784–1867.* Toronto: Macmillan of Canada, 1984.

MacNutt, W.S. *The Atlantic Provinces: The Emergence of Colonial Society 1712–1857*. London: McClelland & Stewart, 1965.

Macpherson, Alan G. "A Model Sequence in the Peopling of Central Bonavista Bay, 1676–1857." *The Peopling of Newfoundland: Essays in Historical Geography*, edited by John Mannion. St. John's, NL: Memorial University of Newfoundland, Institute of Social and Economic Research, 1978, 102–35.

Magosci, Paul Robert, ed. *The Encyclopedia of Canada's Peoples*. Toronto: Published for the Multicultural History Society of Ontario by the University of Toronto Press, *circa* 1999.

Martell, J.S. "Early Coal Mining in Nova Scotia." *Dalhousie Review*, Vol. 25, No. 2 (1945), 156–72.

Martell, J.S. *Immigration to and Emigration from Nova Scotia 1815–1838*. Halifax: PANS, 1942.

Martin, Chester. "The Loyalists in New Brunswick." *Ontario Historical Society, Papers and Records*, Vol. 30 (1934), 160–70.

Matthews, F.W. *Poole and Newfoundland*. Poole, UK: Poole & Parkstone Standard, 1936.

Matthews, Keith. "A History of the West of England-Newfoundland Fishery." University of Oxford: unpublished PhD thesis, 1968.

Matthews, Keith. *Lectures on the History of Newfoundland, 1500–1830*. St. John's, NL: Maritime History Group, 1973.

McCormack, Ross. "Cloth Caps and Jobs: The Ethnicity of English Immigrants in Canada." *Ethnicity, Power and Politics in Canada*, edited by Jorgen Dahlie and Tissa Fernando. Toronto: Methuen, 1981, 38–55.

McCreath, Peter L., and John G. Leefe. *A History of Early Nova Scotia*. Tantallon, NS: Four East Pub., 1990.

McDonald, Donna. *Illustrated News: Julian Horatia Ewing's Canadian Pictures, 1867–1869*. Toronto: Dundurn Press, 1985.

McDonald, Terry. "Where Have All the (English) Folk Songs Gone?" *British Journal of Canadian Studies*, Vol. 14, No. 2 (1999), 180–92.

McIntosh, Robert. "'Grotesque Faces and Figures': Child Labourers and Coal Mining Technology in Victorian Nova Scotia." *Scientia Canadensis: Canadian Journal of the History of Science, Technology and Medicine*, Vol. 12, No. 2 (1988), 97–112.

McKim, Eleanor. "Newfoundland Claims First Methodist Preacher." *Newfoundland Quarterly*, Vol. 65, No. 2 (1966), 31–32.

Milner, W.C. *History of Sackville, New Brunswick*. Sackville, NB: Tribune Print Co., 1934.

Milner W.C. "The Records of Chignecto." *Collections of the Nova Scotia Historical Society*, Vol. 15 (1911), 1–86.

Moir, John S. *The Church in the British Era: From the British Conquest to Confederation*. Volume Two of History of the Christian Church in Canada, general editor, John Webster Grant. Toronto: McGraw-Hill Ryerson Ltd., 1972.

Morse, Susan Longley. "Immigration to Nova Scotia 1839–51." Halifax: Dalhousie University, unpublished MA thesis, 1946.

Murray, Nelda, ed. *The Valiant Connection: A History of Little York*. Charlottetown, PE: York History Committee, 1993.

New Brunswick Genealogical Society, Passengers to New Brunswick: Custom House Records — 1833, 34, 37, and 38. Saint John, NB: 1987.

O'Flaherty, P. *Lost Country: The Rise and Fall of Newfoundland.* St. John's, NL: Long Beach Press, 2005.

O'Flaherty, Patrick. *Old Newfoundland: A History to 1843.* St. John's, NL: Long Beach Press, *circa* 1999.

Orlo, J., and D. Fraser. "Those Elusive Immigrants, Parts 1 to 3." *The Island Magazine*, No. 16 (1984), 36–44; No. 17 (1985), 32–37; No. 18 (1985), 29–35.

Padley, Taunya Jean. "The Church of England's Role in Settling the Loyalists in the Town of Digby, 1783–1818." Acadia University, unpublished MA thesis. 1991.

Parker, Roy. *The Shipment of Poor Children to Canada 1867–1917.* Bristol, UK: University of Bristol, The Policy Press, 2008.

Parrott, Kay. "The Apprenticeship of Parish Children from Kirkdale Industrial Schools, Liverpool, 1840–70." *The Local Historian,* Journal of the British Association of Local History, Vol. 30, No. 2 (May 2009), 122–36.

Parr, Joy. *Labouring Children.* London: Croom Helm, 1980.

Payton, Philip. "Cornish Emigration in Response to Changes in the International Copper Market in the 1860s." *Cornish Studies Three*, edited by Philip Payton. Exeter, UK: University of Exeter Press, 1995, 60–82.

Paxman, Jeremy. *The English: The Portrait of a People.* London: Michael Joseph, 1998.

Payton, Philip. "Cousin Jacks and Ancient Britons: Cornish Immigrants and Ethnic Identity." *Journal of Australian Studies*, Vol. 68 (June 2001), 54–64.

Payton, Philip. "Reforming Thirties and Hungry Forties: The Genesis of Cornwall's Emigration Trade." *Cornish Studies Four*, edited by Philip Payton. Exeter, UK: University of Exeter Press, 1996, 107–27.

Payton, Philip. *The Cornish Overseas.* Fowey, UK: Alexander Associates, 1999.

Powell, Karen L. *Shelburne County, Nova Scotia.* Shelburne, NS: Shelburne County Genealogical Society, 2004.

Pratt, T.K., ed. *Dictionary of Prince Edward Island English.* Toronto: University of Toronto Press, 1988.

Punch, Terrence. "Nova Scotia Arrivals by Sea in 1864." *Nova Scotia Genealogist,* Vol. 22/2 (2005), 93–95.

Purdy, Judson Douglas. "The Church of England in New Brunswick During the Colonial Era, 1783–1860." Fredericton: University of New Brunswick, Department of History, unpublished MA thesis, 1954.

Rayburn, Alan. *Geographical Names of Prince Edward Island; Toponymy Study.* Ottawa: Department of Energy, Mines and Resources, 1973.

Robertson, Barbara. *Sawpower: Making Lumber in the Sawmills of Nova Scotia.* Halifax: Nimbus Pub. Ltd. and the Nova Scotia Museum, 1986.

Roberston, Ian Ross. "Highlanders, Irishmen and the Land Question in Nineteenth Century Prince Edward Island." *Interpreting Canada's Past*, Vol.1, edited by J.M. Bumsted. Toronto: Oxford University Press, 1986, 359–73.

Rogers, Inkerman. *Ships and Shipyards of Bideford, Devon 1569 to 1938: A Record of*

Wooden Sailing Ships and Warships Built in the Port of Bideford from 1568 to 1938, with a Brief Account of the Shipbuilding Industry in the Town. Bideford, UK: Gazelle Printing Service, 1947.

Rose, Michael E. *The English Poor Law 1780–1930*. Newton Abbott, UK: David & Charles, 1971.

Ross, Duncan. "Case Studies in Emigration: Cornwall, Gloucestershire and New South Wales, 1877–1886," *Economic History Review*, Series 2, Vol. 16 (1963–64), 272–89.

Ross, Julie Martha. *Jacob Bailey, Loyalist: Anglican Clergyman in New England and Nova Scotia*. Ottawa: National Library of Canada, 1994.

Rowe, John. *Cornish Methodists and Emigrants*. Redruth, UK: Cornish Methodist History, 1967.

Rowse, A.L. *The Cornish in America*. London: Macmillan, 1969.

Sager, Eric, with G.E. Panting. *Maritime Capital: The Shipping Industry in Atlantic Canada 1820–1914*. Montreal: McGill-Queen's University Press, 1990.

Saunders, Ivan. "The New Brunswick and Nova Scotia Land Company and the Settlement of Stanley, N.B." Fredericton: University of New Brunswick, Department of History, unpublished MA thesis, 1969.

Scobie, Charles H.H., and John Webster Grant, eds. *Contribution of Methodism to Atlantic Canada*. Montreal: McGill-Queen's University Press, *circa* 1992.

Semple, Neil. *The Lord's Dominion: The History of Canadian Methodism*. Montreal, Buffalo: McGill-Queen's University Press, *circa* 1996.

Sharpe, Errol. *A People's History of Prince Edward Island*. Toronto: Steel Rail Publishing, 1976.

Shepperson, W.S. *British Emigration to North America: Projects and Opinions in the Early Victorian Period*. Oxford: Blackwell, 1957.

Shortt, A., and A.G. Doughty, eds. *Canada and Its Provinces. A History of the Canadian People and Their Institutions by One Hundred Associates*. Vols. 13 and 14. Toronto: Publishers Association of Canada, 1913–17.

Short, Al. "The 1817 Journey of the Brig *Trafalgar* with its Immigrants." *Generations* (Journal of the New Brunswick Genealogical Society) (Spring 2006), 12–16.

Siebert, Wilbur Henry, "The Loyalists in Prince Edward Island." *Transactions of the Royal Society of Canada*, Series 3, Vol. 4, Section 2 (1910), 109–17.

Smith, H.M. Scott. *Historic Churches of Prince Edward Island*. Halifax: SSP Publications, 2004.

Snell, K.D. *Annals of the Labouring Poor: Social Change and Agrarian England 1660–1900*. Cambridge: Cambridge University Press, 1985.

Snowdon, James. "Footprints in the Marsh Mud: Politics and Land Settlement in the Township of Sackville, 1760–1800." Fredericton: University of New Brunswick, unpublished MA thesis, 1974.

Starkey, David J. "Devonians and the Newfoundland Trade." *The New Maritime History of Devon*, Vol. 1, edited by Michael Duffy et al. London: Conway Maritime Press, in association with University of Exeter, 1992, 163–71.

Stevenson, John. *Popular Disturbances in England, 1700–1832*. London: Longman, 1992.

Storr, Paul. *The Last of the Goldsmiths*. London: Batsford, 1954.

Taylor, Thomas Griffith. *Newfoundland: A Study of Settlement with Maps and Illustrations.* Toronto: Canadian Institute of International Affairs, 1946.

Throop, Louise Walsh. "Early Settlers of Cumberland Township, Nova Scotia." *National Genealogical Society Quarterly,* Vol. 67 (September 1979), 182–92.

Tranter, Neil. *Sport, Economy and Society in Britain, 1750–1914.* Cambridge: Cambridge University Press, 1998.

Trueman, Howard. *The Chignecto Isthmus and Its First Settlers.* Toronto: William Briggs, 1902.

Vernon, C.W., *Bicentenary Sketches and Early Days of the Church in Nova Scotia.* Halifax: Chronicle Printing, 1910.

Wagner, Gillian. *Children of the Empire.* London: Weidenfeld and Nicholson, 1982.

Walsh, Edward, and H.T. Holman. "An Account of Prince Edward Island, 1803." *The Island Magazine,* No. 15 (Spring/Summer 1984), 9–13.

Warburton, A.B. *History of Prince Edward Island.* Saint John, NB: Barnes & Co., 1923.

Wright, Esther Clark. "Cumberland Township: A Focal Point of Early Settlement on the Bay of Fundy." *Canadian Historical Review,* Vol. 27, No. 1 (1946), 27–32.

Wright, Esther Clark. *Planters and Pioneers.* Wolfville, NS: the author, 1982.

Wright, Esther Clark. *The Loyalists of New Brunswick.* Fredericton: 1955.

Wynn, Graeme. "A Region of Scattered Settlements and Bounded Possibilities: North Eastern America, 1775–1800." *Canadian Geographer,* Vol. 31 (1987), 319–38.

Wynn, Graeme. *Timber Colony: An Historical Geography of Early Nineteenth Century New Brunswick.* Toronto: University of Toronto Press, 1981.

Young, Louise Ryder. *The Yorkshire Antecedents and American Descendents of the William H.A. Richardson Family of Sackville, New Brunswick, Canada and Reading, Massachusetts.* Ellicott City, MD: the author, 1984.

INDEX

ABOUT THE AUTHOR

Ottawa-born Dr. Lucille Campey is a professional researcher and historian who began her career in Canada as a scientist and computer expert, having previously obtained a degree in chemistry from Ottawa University. Following her marriage in 1967 to her English husband, Geoff, she moved to England. Lucille gained a master's degree at Leeds University based on a thesis that dealt with medieval settlement patterns. She subsequently gained a doctorate at Aberdeen University on a study that focused on the regional links associated with Scottish emigration to Canada. Having written eight books about Scottish emigration to Canada, all published by Natural Heritage Books, a Member of the Dundurn Group, she has now turned her attention to the English. Lucille and Geoff travel regularly in Canada in connection with Lucille's writing and to keep in touch with family and friends. They live near Salisbury, in Wiltshire.

Lucille Campey has two websites: *www.scotstocanada.com* for her books on Scottish emigration to Canada and *www.englishtocanada.com* for her books on English emigration to Canada.